WONDERS OF SAND AND STONE

WONDERS

of

SAND

and

STONE

A HISTORY *of* UTAH'S
National Parks *and* Monuments

FREDERICK H.
SWANSON

THE UNIVERSITY OF UTAH PRESS
Salt Lake City

The Defiance House Man colophon is a registered trademark of The
University of Utah Press. It is based on a four-foot-tall Ancient Puebloan
pictograph (late PIII) near Glen Canyon, Utah.

Library of Congress Cataloging-in-Publication Data

Names: Swanson, Frederick H. (Frederick Harold), 1952–author.
Title: Wonders of sand and stone : a history of Utah's national parks and
    monuments / Frederick H. Swanson.
Description: Salt Lake City : The University of Utah Press, [2020] |
    Includes bibliographical references and index.
Identifiers: LCCN 2019054512 (print) | LCCN 2019054513 (ebook) | ISBN
    9781607817659 (cloth) | ISBN 9781607817666 (paperback) | ISBN
    9781607817673 (ebook)
Subjects: LCSH: National parks and reserves—Utah—History. | National
    monuments—Utah—History.
Classification: LCC SB482.U8 S93 2020 (print) | LCC SB482.U8 (ebook) |
    DDC 363.6/809792—dc23
LC record available at https://lccn.loc.gov/2019054512
LC ebook record available at https://lccn.loc.gov/2019054513

Maps by Frederick H. Swanson

Errata and further information on this and other titles available
online at UofUpress.com.

Printed and bound in the United States of America

CONTENTS

PREFACE

My first and most enduring memory of Utah's national parks came not in the deep backcountry of Zion or Canyonlands, but in a campground—the kind with paved loop roads and vault toilets. On a gray, chilly evening in late December 1976, my wife and I pulled into Devils Garden Campground in Arches National Park, finding it nearly deserted. After setting up our tent and heating dinner, we walked over to a slickrock outcrop where the land sloped off to the east. Cradling warm mugs in our hands, we watched the full moon rise over the distant Uncompahgre Plateau, lighting up layers of cloud and casting the cliffs and hollows below us into sharp relief. A subtle light burnished the sandstone monuments around us as we stood there, shivering but entranced.

That evening, and during the days that followed as we explored Arches and a bit of Canyonlands as well, the magic of southern Utah's landforms lodged somewhere deep within me. So has it also for a great many other travelers. This remarkable section of the Colorado Plateau Province, which once seemed so remote and empty, now figures in the vacation plans of millions of Americans. Trails we used to share with a handful of other hikers now host throngs of happy visitors. Yet I keep coming back with new family members, joining a stream of pilgrims who seek many of the same challenges and enjoyments that we do. It may be a marked trail to a well-known arch, a certain vista we've seen on social media, or something more—perhaps an encounter with the land's deep stillness. What we find in these places is a matter of concern for all of us who love our national park lands, and indeed the whole of what is known as "canyon country."

As Utah's red-rock landscapes grow ever more popular, it's worth asking why these places were set aside in the first place—and for what purposes. This has much to do, I think, with the sense of awe and wonder that people have felt when confronted with these extraordinary landforms. My experience at Arches was hardly unique, as the accounts of early-day travelers in

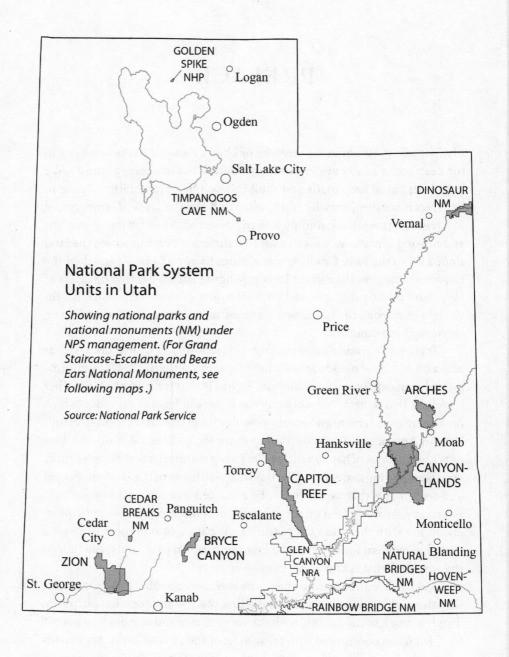

GOLDEN
SPIKE
NHP
Logan

Ogden

Salt Lake City

TIMPANOGOS
CAVE NM

DINOSAUR
NM

Vernal

Provo

National Park System
Units in Utah

*Showing national parks and
national monuments (NM) under
NPS management. (For Grand
Staircase-Escalante and Bears
Ears National Monuments, see
following maps .)*

Source: National Park Service

Price

Green River

ARCHES

Hanksville

Moab

Torrey

CANYON-
LANDS

CAPITOL
REEF

CEDAR
BREAKS
NM

Panguitch

Escalante

Monticello

Cedar
City

BRYCE
CANYON

GLEN
CANYON
NRA

NATURAL
BRIDGES
NM

Blanding

ZION

St. George

HOVEN-
WEEP
NM

Kanab

RAINBOW BRIDGE NM

the Colorado Plateau Province attest. Whether they were explorers and scientists, artists and writers, or businesspeople and railroad publicists, their
amazement led to action in the offices of the Department of the Interior,
the White House, and in Congress—giving us some of the most captivat-
ing national parks and monuments in the nation.

This book is my attempt to tell the story of these far-seeing individuals
and what they accomplished. Many of them had the tourist dollar in mind,
but this did not blind them to the greater purposes embodied in our century-
old system of national parks. Others sought to advance science, preserve history, or promote cultural awareness—goals that are especially evident in
the park units of northern Utah, including Golden Spike National Historical Park and the California, Pony Express, Old Spanish, and Mormon Pioneer National Historic Trails. North or south, in mountains or in desert,
these sites offer an incomparable education as well as a chance to just stand
and stare in wonder, as I did that first evening at Devils Garden.

Today the need to envision a high purpose for our national park lands
is as great as ever, and that requires that we know something of their history. Yet there have been no comprehensive accounts of how Utah's national
parks and monuments were created since Angus Woodbury's 1950 classic,
A History of Southern Utah and Its National Parks. C. Gregory Crampton's
Standing Up Country, first published in 1964, remains the standard work on
canyon country history, but it ends just as Utah's largest national park, Canyonlands, was being established. Crampton's outstanding contribution was
to define and characterize the region: he noted how the Colorado Plateau's
vast scale made it difficult to comprehend as a whole, to see it as an "incomparable wilderness of eroded sandstone."[1] It is exactly this wild quality of
the Utah canyon lands that is in danger of disappearing today.

Utah now boasts five stunning national parks (Arches, Canyonlands,
Capitol Reef, Bryce Canyon, and Zion), as well as eight equally interesting
national monuments, ranging from tiny enclaves at Timpanogos Cave, Hovenweep, and Rainbow Bridge, to larger designations at Natural Bridges, Cedar
Breaks on the Markagunt Plateau, and Dinosaur in the Uinta Basin. These
units are managed by the National Park Service, an agency present in Utah
for more than a century. The NPS also manages the sprawling Glen Canyon National Recreation Area, Utah's second most visited federal park unit.
The much more recent Bears Ears and Grand Staircase–Escalante National

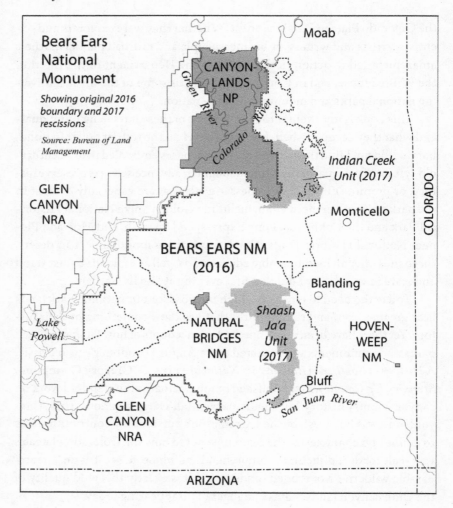

Bears Ears
National
Monument

*Showing original 2016
boundary and 2017
rescissions*

*Source: Bureau of Land
Management*

Moab

CANYON-
LANDS
NP

Green River

Colorado River

Indian Creek
Unit (2017)

COLORADO

GLEN
CANYON
NRA

Monticello

BEARS EARS NM
(2016)

Blanding

*Lake
Powell*

NATURAL
BRIDGES
NM

*Shaash
Ja'a
Unit
(2017)*

HOVEN-
WEEP
NM

Bluff

GLEN
CANYON
NRA

San Juan River

ARIZONA

Monuments are managed by the Bureau of Land Management, with a portion of Bears Ears also managed by the U.S. Forest Service.

This book focuses primarily on the twelve national parks and monuments lying within Utah's section of the Colorado Plateau Province.[2] From Dinosaur in the northeast to Zion in the southwest, these collectively receive the greatest use and have attracted the most controversy. Why has southern Utah provided the source rock for so many protected places? Geologists point to its stunning landforms, most of which have no equal on this planet,

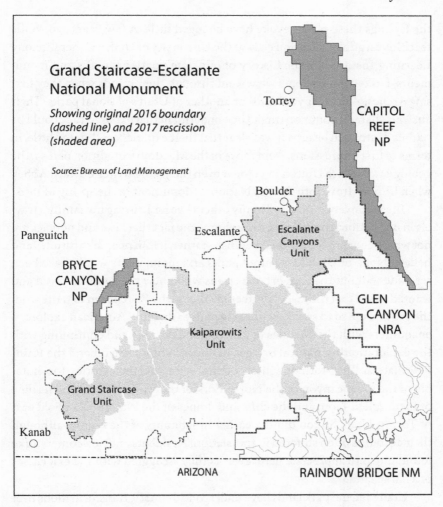

Grand Staircase-Escalante
National Monument

*Showing original 2016 boundary
(dashed line) and 2017 rescission
(shaded area)*

Source: Bureau of Land Management

Torrey

CAPITOL
REEF
NP

Boulder

Panguitch

Escalante

Escalante
Canyons
Unit

BRYCE
CANYON
NP

GLEN
CANYON
NRA

Kaiparowits
Unit

Grand Staircase
Unit

Kanab

ARIZONA

RAINBOW BRIDGE NM

but that alone does not explain the nearly universal response people have to these cliffs and canyons. Utah guidebook author Ward Roylance may have come closest when he labeled this strange quality of canyon country as "ineffable"—something that begs for an artistic and contemplative response.

A century ago, boosters who wanted to publicize some natural feature would label it as a "wonder." Utah was no exception: at one time we had a Wonder Cave (Timpanogos), a New Wonderland (Bryce Canyon), and a Valley of Wonders (Zion Canyon). Our scenic terminology has evolved, but the feelings these places evoke have changed little. A few years ago, while teaching an adult education class at the University of Utah's Osher Lifelong Learning Institute on the history of our state's national parks and monuments, I asked my students what went through their minds when they first saw Arches, Zion, Canyonlands, or another of Utah's national parks. Their answers shared a common thread of wonderment that exposed rock could be sculpted into such beauty. It was clear that their experiences differed little, in terms of first impressions, from those of the Macomb expedition of 1859, the geologist Clarence Dutton in 1880, or even the young writer Edward Abbey when he first drove into Arches National Monument in the spring of 1956.

These conversations, and many others I've had during my family's travels in our national park lands, drove home the fact that laws and policies are not where concern for the land begins—rather, it is in people's attitudes and beliefs. None of Utah's treasured parks and monuments would have been set aside without the support of citizens who knew the lands involved and wanted to see that they were protected. That's why I've chosen to write from the ground up, so to speak, beginning with early Euro-American explorers' encounters with the Needles of Canyonlands in 1859 and continuing with the explorations of natural bridges in upper White Canyon and the Rainbow Plateau. The Mormon settlers of this region told their stories, too, notably of the great canyon of the North Fork of the Virgin River, which some of them called Zion, and the cliffs and domes of the Waterpocket Fold east of Torrey, Utah. So too did the earlier inhabitants of the region, although their accounts often suffered in translation. Residents and newcomers alike found much to appreciate here, even as they struggled with the exigencies of a harsh land.

Utah's federal park lands have undergone dramatic transformations over the past 160 years. In tracing their history, we will see how this mysterious landscape has influenced us—and how we might keep this legacy we have been so generously granted. The future of the entire region known as the Colorado Plateau will depend on the engagement of those of us who have inherited these amazing assemblages of not-so-ordinary stone.

Frederick H. Swanson
November 28, 2019

ACKNOWLEDGMENTS

In today's world of online scholarship, a researcher can borrow from an immense library. In this book I drew freely from the National Park Service's excellent series of administrative histories, to whose authors I am greatly indebted. The NPS has also made available a wealth of e-books covering the history, culture, politics, and science of our national parks and monuments. Still, without the help I received from the Park Service's historians and cultural resource specialists, many hidden gems would have remained just that. I especially owe thanks to Colleen Hyde at Grand Canyon NP, Peekay Briggs and Vicki Webster at Canyonlands NP (Southeast Utah Group), Chris Goetze at Glen Canyon NRA, Lori Rome at Capitol Reef NP, and Miriam Watson at Zion NP. Other NPS staff who provided timely assistance include Jim Dougan, superintendent of Natural Bridges NM, Khaleel Saba of the Western Archeological and Conservation Center in Tucson, and Cami McKinney of Timpanogos Cave NM.

Claudia Jensen of the Denver Public Library's Western History and Genealogy Department, Janet Seegmiller and Paula Mitchell of the Gerald R. Sherratt Library at Southern Utah University, Tammy Gentry of the Special Collections and Archives Department at Dixie State College, and the staff of the Special Collections Department at the J. Willard Marriott Library at the University of Utah provided invaluable assistance. Tom Krause and Pat Hadley of the University of Utah Press patiently guided the work to completion, with Laurel Anderton applying her remarkable editing skills at the finish.

For companionship on the trail, Bessann and Ellie were there almost from the start. May there be many more camps under a starry sky. (As well as for Charlotte, with whom these Utah journeys began.) And for inspiration, I have more to thank than red rocks and rushing rivers. Many years ago, sitting in the living room of Ward and Gloria Roylance's little home in Torrey, I learned what dedication to an ideal meant. To all of you, blessings and gratitude.

ACKNOWLEDGMENTS

INTRODUCTION

The stories of how America's national parks were created are suffused with a kind of mythic grandeur, born of our longing for a deeper connection to the land. In Yellowstone, a band of nineteenth-century explorers was said to have dreamed up the idea of reserving a park for the public's use while warming themselves at a campfire by the Madison River. In Yosemite we see John Muir gazing up at Half Dome and, it would seem, into the universe itself. Grand Canyon has Teddy Roosevelt exhorting a crowd at the South Rim in 1903 to "leave it as it is"—words he backed up five years later by designating much of the canyon as a national monument.

Utah's national parks and monuments possess as much splendor as Old Faithful or El Capitan, and as much sublimity as the view from El Tovar, yet for years they languished in the shadows cast by Yellowstone, Yosemite, and Grand Canyon. Uncertain of how to interpret the strange erosional forms found in this section of the Colorado Plateau Province, writers drew fanciful analogies to European antiquity, seeing ruined castles in Bryce Canyon's spires, Greek temples in the cliffs of Zion. Outside of a few terms borrowed from the Utes, Paiutes, and Navajos who made use of these lands, there seemed to be no native language for this kind of scenery. Tourism promoters struggled to describe the sedimentary geology of southeastern Utah in a way that might lure travelers to vacation there.

The chroniclers of Utah's desert wonders kept at it, though, and by the late twentieth century "canyon country" had become a marketable commodity. Spurred by word of mouth, social media, and sophisticated advertising campaigns, visitation to the state's five national parks has spiraled ever upward. In 2016 Zion National Park edged out Yellowstone in visitors, while Arches National Park, which sixty-five years ago lacked so much as a graveled road, hosted a million and a half tourists eager to see its iconic sandstone spans. Trails and boardwalks are jammed with visitors, and most backcountry campsites require reservations. Traffic congestion lasts virtually the whole year in gateway towns such as Springdale and Moab, while social trails created by visitors to these parks thread in every direction. All this leaves park superintendents with difficult choices as they try to reconcile their legal mandate to protect the natural values of our national parks and monuments while providing for their use and enjoyment.[1] Where it was once assumed that establishing a national park would protect its features from misuse, such is no longer guaranteed. This is the dilemma that the popularization of this once-overlooked corner of the American Southwest has left us.

John Ise, a prominent historian of America's national parks, once observed that our National Park System arose "not as a result of public demand but because a few farsighted, unselfish, and idealistic men and women foresaw the national need."[2] These individuals often were drawn from an elite class of travelers, intellectuals, artists, writers, and businesspeople from both coasts who enjoyed vacationing out West. But many of the best-known figures associated with our first national parks, including John Muir and Theodore Roosevelt, never paid a visit to Zion Canyon or gazed down at the colorful pinnacles of Bryce Canyon. To a great extent, it fell to local citizens to popularize Utah's scenic high points. They included Joseph Hickman, a schoolteacher from the village of Bicknell who propounded the beauty of the remote Waterpocket Fold; Alexander Ringhoffer, an immigrant prospector from Hungary who called attention to the wondrous sandstone towers and natural arches north of Moab; and Henry Culmer, a British-born artist and mining entrepreneur who was captivated by the natural bridges in upper White Canyon in southeastern Utah. They and other Utah citizens realized early on that desert scenes could rival those found in the Rocky Mountains or High Sierra.

The nation's railroads played a major role in the development of Utah's national park system, just as they had in Yellowstone, Yosemite, and other western parks. Officials of the Union Pacific and Denver & Rio Grande Western railways understood that promoting national parks as vacation destinations would encourage well-to-do passengers to ride their lines. Businesspeople in Salt Lake City and southern Utah's "Dixie" region enthusiastically embraced railroad tourism, seeing national parks as a means of preserving the grandest examples of American scenery without interfering with other economic prospects. The result, as historian Alfred Runte argues, was a de facto policy of setting aside certain monumentally scenic places that had little value for timber or minerals.[3] This imperative shaped Utah's first entries in the National Park System, including Zion and Bryce Canyon.

The road that led to Utah gaining a total of thirteen national parks and monuments travels the breadth of the twentieth century. In 1908 Teddy Roosevelt employed the Antiquities Act to protect three massive sandstone spans in upper White Canyon in San Juan County, establishing Natural Bridges, Utah's first national monument. His successors would employ the Antiquities Act twelve more times in the Beehive State, beginning with Mukuntuweap National Monument (the forerunner of Zion National Park) in 1909. Bryce Canyon, Arches, and Capitol Reef would take the same route to national park status, while Rainbow Bridge, Dinosaur, Timpanogos Cave, Hovenweep, and Cedar Breaks, established from 1910 to 1933, would remain (along with Natural Bridges) as national monuments under the supervision of the National Park Service.[4] In 1964 Congress set aside Canyonlands, Utah's largest national park, followed in 1972 by the Glen Canyon National Recreation Area, which takes in the heavily used surface of Lake Powell and large areas of near-wilderness surrounding it.

The Antiquities Act encored in 1996 and 2016 with Grand Staircase–Escalante and Bears Ears National Monuments, which represented the high-water mark, in terms of acreage, for Utah's system of federal parks and monuments. In December 2017 President Donald Trump broke these into five smaller units, omitting lands known to have mineral resources. That decision was challenged in court by monument proponents, but as of this writing the dismemberment of these outstanding reservations still stands.

President Trump's retrograde action was based on the belief that the Antiquities Act set strict limits on the size and scope of national monuments. This was the operating principle with Utah's first national monuments, although as early as 1908 Teddy Roosevelt designated an 808,120-acre national monument at Grand Canyon. In the 1930s, a few visionary Park Service officials—among them the superintendent of Grand Canyon—realized that much more was at stake in southern Utah's canyon lands than a handful of marvelous arches or dramatic cliffs. This led to a wholly different—and highly controversial—approach to land protection in the Colorado Plateau. The gigantic Escalante national monument proposal of the 1930s is often thought to be the brainchild of Harold Ickes, Franklin Roosevelt's activist interior secretary. But it was a Park Service official named Roger Toll, superintendent of Yellowstone at the time, who set the gears in motion for what would have been the grandest of America's national monuments outside Alaska. This was a vision gained out of doors, not in some meeting room: in the fall of 1933 Toll drove up onto the shoulder of the Aquarius Plateau with Ephraim Pectol, the Mormon bishop of Torrey, where he gazed out at a stunning scene of mesas, canyons, mountains, and ridges extending to a distant horizon. Toll understood at once that this was the source material for significant new park-building.

The Escalante proposal forms the pivot point in this account of Utah's national park lands. Before Escalante, there were proposals for mostly small national parks and monuments protecting individual scenic features such as Rainbow Bridge or Zion Canyon. Afterward, and despite its failure, there were mostly big ideas: Canyonlands National Park, a greatly enlarged Capitol Reef National Monument, Grand Staircase–Escalante, and most recently, Bears Ears. All of these grew out of the core vision that Roger Toll had on the Aquarius Plateau. Toll's successors (tragically, he died the year after he helped formulate the Escalante proposal) expanded the scope of national parks and monuments to include much of southeastern Utah. Not all of their proposals were successful, but they introduced the concept of setting aside large sections of the Colorado Plateau as integral landscapes, not just a collection of individual landmarks, however scenic.

This region-wide approach informed efforts to establish Canyonlands, Utah's largest national park. On a fine spring day in 1961, Secretary of the Interior Stewart Udall flew over the Colorado River at the point where it joined the Green River, marveling at a landscape that he recognized as being of park caliber. Udall, along with Arches National Monument superintendent Bates Wilson, are rightly honored for their roles in establishing Canyonlands National Park. These men came late to the party, however. For more than two decades, various Park Service officials had maintained that the stunning landscape surrounding the confluence of the Green and Colorado Rivers deserved national park status. Their ideas lay fallow until political leaders with the courage to implement them—including Utah senator Frank Moss—carried legislation through a bitter, three-year-long fight in Congress.

Under Moss's leadership, Canyonlands was given a modest expansion in 1971, while Arches and Capitol Reef National Monuments were granted park status that same year. Along with the Glen Canyon NRA, these designations completed southern Utah's national park system, while Grand Staircase–Escalante and Bears Ears National Monuments came much later and remained under their original management jurisdictions (the Bureau of Land Management, or BLM, for Grand Staircase and the BLM and Forest Service for Bears Ears). Spanning more than a century of land preservation efforts, these areas have advanced a vision of Utah's canyon lands as more than a collection of isolated scenic attractions that happen to be popular with tourists.

The National Park System holds an honored place in American culture, but it is how these lands are managed that will determine their value in the future—not just for tourism, but as reservoirs of biotic diversity, sites of cultural heritage, and arenas for scientific study and education. Stewart Udall alluded to this in his 1963 book *The Quiet Crisis*, in which he observed that not only were America's most beautiful landscapes in trouble, but the total environment was at risk. Udall noted how our newfound powers of space travel carried the danger of losing respect for the land that sustained us. It seems no coincidence that part of what would become Canyonlands National Park was then being used as a drop zone for rocket boosters fired from a military launch site thirty miles northwest of the park. Some of the uranium that had been mined from Utah's desert canyons during the 1950s—including deposits next to Canyonlands, Arches, and Capitol Reef—found its way into nuclear bombs carried by air force rockets and airplanes. In the mid-1980s, depleted nuclear fuel from commercial power reactors looked to be headed to a repository site adjacent to Canyonlands.

Udall understood the manifold power of new technologies to alter natural landscapes, including some of our greatest national parks. His warning also underscores how Utah's national parks and monuments are influenced by the lands surrounding them. What was once an undiscovered hinterland is undergoing tremendous pressure from industrial and recreational uses, all of which could easily erase what is left of the region's wild character and ecological integrity.

The list of conflicts over how our parks should be managed seems end-less: Will improved roads and parking facilities alleviate traffic congestion in Arches National Park? Should tour aircraft and helicopters be allowed to buzz over Canyonlands as they do in Grand Canyon? Should off-road vehicles cavort in "play areas" next to Lake Powell? What about opening hiking trails in national parks to mountain bikes? Allowing target shooting in national monuments? Or permitting tourists to cluster beneath Rainbow Bridge, a site sacred to Navajo and Paiute people?

Nor is human overuse the only problem besetting our parks, as any ranger or superintendent in the Southwest will attest. Each of the more than fifty national parks and monuments in the region faces challenges from outside its borders. The brilliant starlit sky as seen from Bryce Canyon may soon grow dimmer from floodlight from a nearby coal strip mine. Oil and gas wells with their associated roads, pipelines, and emissions creep closer to Arches and Canyonlands each year. Uranium prospects are staked out in the desert adjoining Capitol Reef. Helicopters drop off canyoneering parties on state lands bordering Canyonlands, their noise carrying for miles. Looting of prehistoric artifacts and vandalism of rock art sites continues across virtually all of the Colorado Plateau. And beyond these issues rises the looming face of the Anthropocene, in which changes to the Earth's climate are certain to alter natural conditions in the desert lands of the Southwest in ways that are hard to predict. There is a critical need for a regional perspective on these problems; with all our multiplying technologies, park boundaries cannot guarantee the ecological integrity of the lands they enclose.

Today, millions of visitors seek their own rendezvous with the landscapes of the Colorado Plateau. Whether we step out of a tour bus at Bryce Canyon's Inspiration Point or rappel into the Maze in Canyonlands, what matters is how we treat the lands within our view—and beyond. The challenge that Stewart Udall identified in the 1960s—to turn our love for national parks into concrete action to protect them—remains as relevant today as it was in his time. Will we treasure Utah's national park lands in all their variety, as places of wonder, solitude, beauty, and uncommon adventure? Or will we allow these lands to devolve into something much less valuable? What follows is an argument for treating Utah's national parks and monuments as integral parts of one of our planet's most extraordinary natural and cultural regions.

1

EXPLORATION

In the eyes of Charles Dimmock, a young civil engineer attached to Captain John N. Macomb's San Juan Exploring Expedition of 1859, the sage plains of southeastern Utah Territory offered little to stimulate the mind. Riding through the heat and dust of late summer, Dimmock was growing tired of the prickly brush and muddy water holes. "Nothing to the right of us, nothing to the left of us, but deep mouthed cañons," he wrote in his journal, parodying a line from Tennyson. At least there were intermittent clouds to lessen the force of the sun, and sometimes a rain shower in the evening.[1]

Macomb's party had turned west from the Old Spanish Trail that led up from Santa Fe and Durango in order to search for the confluence of the Grand and Green Rivers, located somewhere beyond the northern flank of the Abajo Mountains. To venture so far off of the known route carried "no small degree of danger," Dimmock observed in his journal for August 21. That morning an advance party had returned with news that the terrain ahead was too difficult for pack animals. It was decided that the following morning Macomb, Dimmock, expedition geologist J. S. Newberry, and army lieutenant Milton Cogswell would set off to find another route to the confluence. "We are to bed early in view of the fatigues ahead," Dimmock wrote.[2]

The following morning, the four men, accompanied by five support personnel, left camp to explore farther west. Soon they entered a canyon that led northwest, toward the presumed meeting of rivers. Its sheer walls rose a thousand feet above them and were carved (as Dimmock noted) into "all imaginable curves, shapes & fancies."[3] After hours of riding, they reached a point where the cliffs drew apart to reveal a huge amphitheater extending for miles around them. In a report he prepared after the expedition, Dimmock described the scene as "a wild of fantastic mesas & isolated buttes," each of which dwarfed the pyramids of Giza. Their goal lay still farther west,

Head of Cañon Colorado, lithograph by J. J. Young from a field sketch by geologist J. S. Newberry. Young's depiction of the Sixshooter Peaks in the present-day Needles section of Canyonlands National Park shows the influence of European Romanticism, in which the human presence is dwarfed by immense earth forms. Plate 8 in Captain John N. Macomb's *Report of the Exploring Expedition from Santa Fe, New Mexico, to the Junction of the Grand and Green Rivers, 1859. Biodiversity Heritage Library.*

through yet another maze of canyons. Disappointed, the men made an early camp at a water pocket on the treeless slickrock surface.[4]

The following day the party explored farther down a red-walled gorge—today's Indian Creek Canyon—but were turned back at an impassable pouroff.[5] Miles from the confluence of the two rivers, they would have to abandon their quest, but first Dimmock, Newberry, and Cogswell looked for a route up one of the canyon walls. Stripping off most of their clothes in the heat, they climbed to the top of an exposed butte and gazed over a wholly unfamiliar topography. "Few, if any other whites, were ever the beholders of so magical a variety of towering, sierra-like mesas," Dimmock noted. Off to the south they could see "isolated pinnacles and clustered, castled summits" that "gave the effect of a grander city than dream land contains."[6] Newberry, too, resorted to architectural metaphors, describing a "forest of Gothic spires" that reminded him of Manhattan's Trinity Church, then the tallest building in America.[7] These three men were among the first Euro-Americans to

view the strangely eroded sandstone pinnacles we know today as the Needles within Canyonlands National Park.

Captain Macomb was forced to accept failure in the primary purpose
of his expedition, which was to locate a more direct supply route from Santa
Fe to the recent Mormon settlements along the Virgin River—important in
case hostilities broke out with Brigham Young's followers.[8] The War Department also wanted to know why the historic Spanish Trail swung so far to
the north, crossing the Green River almost at the Book Cliffs. Its planners
had not reckoned with the contorted topography of southeastern Utah's
canyon country, a region that had long defied explorers and mapmakers.

Nor did Macomb see much hope of colonizing the barren lands surrounding the Green and Colorado. To him it was a "worthless and impracticable
region," unsuitable for agriculture and admitting no passage for wagons.[9]
These Utah canyon lands were where Manifest Destiny ran aground, thwarted
by angular topography and irredeemable soils. Even the Mormon coloniz-
ers who managed to establish villages around its rim considered the region
a wasteland, a place that did nothing more than stitch the world together.

Their dismissal bore the mark of a deep cultural myopia. Although
the land on either side of the Colorado River appeared uninhabitable to
Macomb, humans had been making use of it for ages, as could be seen from
the granaries, dwellings, and rock art that Puebloan peoples had left behind.
Above the canyon walls lay broad, forested plateaus that were a rich source
of foodstuffs, firewood, and medicinal plants for contemporary Ute, Paiute, and Navajo Indians. Another half century would pass before the last of
these free peoples were forced to relinquish the lands they regarded as home.

This was a time of great turmoil among the native inhabitants of the
region. Their ancestral hunting and foraging territories were being relent-
lessly rolled back under the influx of gold miners, sheepherders, and cattlemen streaming into southwestern Colorado. Pressured also by the expanding
Mormon presence in Utah and Arizona, they would find that their future lay
on reservations, which were mostly delineated by 1900. Even those boundaries, however, would remain in flux because of ever-changing federal policies toward Native tribes.

The topographic surveys sponsored by the federal government were
essential to this westward expansion. These were the latest in a long string
of attempts dating to the Spanish *entradas* to "shape the landscape to pre-
existing expectations," as historian Paul T. Nelson put it, imposing straight

lines on topography that was anything but.[10] The architectural metaphors Dimmock and Newberry employed when confronted with the strange rock forms surrounding the Colorado River fit the same mold. Faced with a nearly incomprehensible geology, they reduced cliff and monolith to forms that were understandable and familiar. Their use of such images indicated that Utah's canyon lands would not yield easily to interpretation.

Neither would its Native inhabitants; Newberry, for instance, seemed uninterested in how the Utes and Paiutes made use of the land, studying instead the stone dwellings, storage cisterns, and irrigation ditches of the long-vanished Puebloans. But these crumbling structures also fit the image of decay and ruin that seemed to characterize this broken-down landscape.

Yet if the Utah canyon country proved difficult to comprehend for minds used to well-watered landscapes, it captivated them as well. Paul Nelson writes that observers such as J. S. Newberry displayed "a clear movement from outright disgust, to uneasy intrigue, to unbridled fascination" with what they saw.[11] Not all came away convinced that the Utah canyon lands held anything of value, but a seed was planted for later travelers and writers to nurture. By recasting the canyon landscape in terms of wonderment instead of ruin and desolation, they hung the intellectual backdrop needed to create Utah's network of national parks and monuments.

After failing to reach the confluence of the Green and Grand Rivers, the Macomb party continued south along Recapture Creek to the San Juan River, where they turned east toward Santa Fe and the end of their expedition. Along the way Newberry took note of the "island-like mountains" to their west, which the Spanish had named the Sierra Abajo. "South of these," he wrote, "is the little double-peaked mountain, called by the Mexicans Las Orejas del Oso—the bear's ears."[12] He was not aware that this twin prominence marked an ancestral home for Navajos and Utes, who knew it as a place of fertility and shelter. Five years later, some Navajo families would take refuge in the canyons, heading beneath the Bears Ears in order to avoid the forced exodus of the Diné to New Mexico.[13]

Nor could Newberry have realized that a century and a half later, the country that he and his fellow explorers were attempting to penetrate would become the locus of a bitter political struggle involving descendants of these indigenous tribes and the Mormon pioneers who arrived two decades later. The Bears Ears would come to symbolize divergent claims to the land and its resources, whether it was minerals and livestock forage for the Anglo settlers, wild game, firewood, and plant foods for the native residents, or recreational opportunities for Americans eager to witness the leavings of an ancient culture.

As repellent as Captain Macomb and his men found the Colorado River canyon lands, they also saw something unusual in these arid wastes—a stirring prospect that would come to define the region in the minds of later generations. The Macomb expedition established the pattern for subsequent explorations of southern Utah's canyon country: toil and hardship in the unrelenting heat, poor forage for the animals, rough or nonexistent trails across a savagely broken landscape. But all of this led, in the prepared at least, to experiences of awe and wonderment. It was this transformation of a seemingly worthless region into a source of beauty and exaltation that set the stage for the first efforts to establish national monuments, and eventually national parks, in the Utah canyon lands.

Ten years after the Macomb expedition came to a halt in the depths of a Colorado River side canyon, a one-armed Civil War veteran led nine men in four overloaded wooden boats down the Green River to the confluence that Macomb had sought. Major John Wesley Powell's pioneering voyage of 1869 was even more beset by mishap, suffering near disaster through the loss of a boat in the rapids of Lodore Canyon before reaching the calmer waters of Labyrinth and Stillwater Canyons. Despite their running low on provisions, Powell found time to climb up to a vantage point in what he later named Cataract Canyon. Surveying the scene, he found "a wilderness of rocks . . . where the rivers are lost beneath cliffs and towers and pinnacles." All around them stood "ten thousand strangely carved forms in every direction; and beyond them, mountains blending with the clouds."[14] Such was the view that today's visitor to Canyonlands National Park can approximate with a seven-mile drive on a jeep road leading west from Squaw Flat in the Needles section of the park.

Powell repeated his journey down the Green and Colorado in 1871 with a mostly different crew who took photographs, surveyed the river's bends, and explored more of its tributaries. His voyages launched two decades' worth of government-sponsored exploration, mapmaking, and geological and ethnographic investigations under his command. The Powell Survey,

Land of the Standing Rocks, a woodcut made in about 1877 from a photograph by W. H. Holmes of the Powell Survey. It depicts the landscape west of the confluence of the Green and Colorado (Grand) Rivers, which Powell and his men saw during their river voyages of 1869 and 1871. Plate 11 in C. E. Dutton, *Tertiary History of the Grand Cañon District. U.S. Geological Survey, Denver Library Photographic Collection.*

along with the competing federal surveys of the southwestern territories under Hayden, Ives, and Wheeler, were intended to locate railroad routes, find habitable valleys for agriculture, determine possibilities for irrigation, and establish land lines for eventual disposal of the public domain. Time after time, however, the geographers, geologists, and artists working in Utah Territory returned with accounts of a weird and wondrous topography within the heart of what Powell named the Plateau Province.

More than any group of miners, cattlemen, or land barons, Powell and his fellow geologists and geographers had the most lasting influence on our understanding of the Utah canyon lands. Erudite and trained in the latest sciences, they published superbly written records of their reconnaissances into southern Utah and northern Arizona. Army captain Clarence E. Dutton, geologist G. K. Gilbert, topographer Almon H. Thompson, and Powell himself delineated the region's lofty mesas, isolated buttes, slickrock expanses, and endless winding canyons, establishing boundary lines needed for early settlement. But they did more than advance science: these explorers of strata and outcrops, whom Wallace Stegner called "probably the most brilliant geological team in the business," looked at scenes such as those that baffled Captain Macomb's men and endowed them with meaning.[15] They gave names to Glen Canyon, the Dirty Devil River, Waterpocket Fold, Henry Mountains, Navajo Mountain, Escalante River, and Kaiparowits Plateau, among many others. Along with the Grand Canyon, Mesa Verde, and a deep sandstone chasm in southwestern Utah that Powell called the Mukuntuweap, these striking landforms are now enshrined in some of our most magnificent national parks, monuments, and recreation areas.

Whereas G. K. Gilbert focused intensely on research, making groundbreaking discoveries such as the igneous structure of the Henry Mountains, his colleague Clarence Dutton, who also joined the Powell Survey in 1875, carried a broader perspective into the field. Dutton's cultured prose, full of classical allusions and the apt metaphor, lets readers relive his amazing topographic forays into the Plateau Province. His masterwork, the *Tertiary History of the Grand Cañon District*, is best known for its vivid portrayal of its namesake canyon, but it leads off with one of the finest depictions of the landscape bordering today's Zion National Park. Dutton correctly predicted that the panorama of cliffs and towers along the Virgin River would one day come to rank among the world's greatest.[16]

Historian Stephen Pyne observed in *How the Canyon Became Grand*, his sweeping intellectual history of the Grand Canyon, that scientists such as Newberry, Gilbert, and Dutton placed the Colorado Plateau Province at the center of American geology. These wide-ranging and broadly trained scientists not only "discovered lost earth empires, like ancient mountains worn to oblivion in the Triassic"; they "gave the New World natural wonders to compete with decaying castles and lofty cathedrals . . . of the Old World."[17] In doing so, they laid the foundation for later proponents of national parks, who would make the protection of the region's geologic features into an act of overt patriotism. If the Colorado Plateau's strange landforms could be made familiar through the use of architectural metaphor, nonscientists could learn to appreciate them—and that, as much as topographic maps or stratigraphic columns, became these scientists' lasting legacy.

Although the Powell and Wheeler Surveys conducted a great deal of work north of the Colorado River, it took nearly a century for the Utah canyon country to achieve the same intellectual or cultural prominence as the

Grand Canyon. Nor did Powell or Dutton issue a call to set aside these landscapes as national parks or monuments. The Grand Canyon captured the bulk of their attention and the outside world's as well. Dutton applied his most inspiring names to Grand Canyon features—Brahma Temple, Hindu Amphitheater, the Esplanade, Cape Final. In contrast, the Paiute names Powell favored in Utah—Mukuntuweap, Parunuweap, Paunsaugunt, Markagunt—seemed more appropriate, if less evocative. They commemorated a people who once occupied the land and derived sustenance from it through intimate knowledge and long experience.[18]

Utah's portion of the Plateau Province held a great patrimony of scenic wealth, but it would take more than a century to set aside most of the key geologic and cultural features of this region, starting with Natural Bridges National Monument in 1908 and ending with Grand Staircase–Escalante and Bears Ears National Monuments in 1996 and 2016. It would take nearly as long to build the roads and infrastructure that would permit the average tourist to see these great canyons and rivers in comfort. None of this could have taken place so long as Utah's canyons and plateaus held only rough trails and incomprehensible topography.

When Charles Dimmock and J. S. Newberry raised their sweat-stained faces to behold the sandstone spires of the Needles, when Major Powell scrambled to precarious viewpoints a thousand feet above the Colorado, when Clarence Dutton paused to record the shifting cloud shadows upon the Vermilion Cliffs, they elevated a whole landscape as well. People have been lifting their gaze to these scenes ever since, perhaps to gain the same exaltation from this wind-blasted, contorted, and endlessly fascinating land. In this weird, wondrous terrain of red rock and deep canyons, the urge to exploit ran into the human need for awe and wonder—a clash we have yet to resolve today.

2

THE BRIDGES OF WHITE CANYON

At the dawn of the twentieth century, the interior of the Plateau Province (John Wesley Powell's name for the physiographic region between the Rockies and the Great Basin) remained sparsely populated and inadequately mapped. Cattlemen ranged their stock across most of its windblown expanse and gold seekers probed its canyons, while Mormon settlers clung to homesteads along the flood-prone Fremont, Paria, and San Juan Rivers. To those who came from well-watered eastern states, something about this land seemed to defeat human effort, and its fierce and unforgiving aspect repelled the imagination as well. The names they gave many of its features— Carcass Canyon, Death Hollow, Poison Spring—highlighted its desiccation and inaccessibility. From the phantasmagorical forms on the horizon to the cussed ground beneath one's feet, this was a land that refused to blossom, that defied human will.

Yet it was often these same cattlemen and prospectors, not government men, who came across some of the Plateau Province's most interesting geological marvels during the late nineteenth century. Canyons that could hide a missing cow also concealed strange erosional oddities, freaks of nature that appealed to the human sense of wonder. Cowboys working the meager rangelands north of the San Juan River in the 1870s probably noticed the three giant sandstone spans hidden within upper White Canyon, a tributary of the Colorado River, but it remained for an itinerant prospector to bring outside attention to these impressive features. Cass Hite, a Civil War veteran from Missouri, had roamed the West in search of pay dirt before coming to southern Utah in 1880 to investigate rumors of a Navajo silver mine between Monument Valley and Navajo Mountain. Several years of prospecting south of the San Juan River made him no richer, so in September 1883 he headed north to the Colorado River, possibly at the suggestion of the Navajo leader Hashkéniinii (or Hoskaninni), whom he had befriended during his visits to Dinétah, the Navajo homeland.[1] By following the relatively level benches flanking White Canyon's western rim, Hite and a party of eight other miners reached the Colorado at a place he named Dandy Crossing, since it was the only place within many miles where horses could ford the river.

By shoveling the Colorado's placer sands into makeshift sluice boxes, Hite found he could amass enough of the fine gold to turn a slim profit, although he seems to have made most of his money brokering claims for other hopeful miners. He would spend much of the rest of his life at his little homestead at the mouth of Trachyte Creek, joined from time to time by his two brothers and other family members. The improbable little village of Hite would have a long history in Glen Canyon, attracting miners, river runners, and adventurers until Lake Powell swallowed it in 1964.

It may have been on a return trip up White Canyon that Cass Hite chanced on the great natural bridges in its upper reaches. He gave them the unimaginative names of President, Senator, and Congressman, and his discovery aroused little attention. In 1895 J. A. "Al" Scorup of Bluff, who with his brother James had been running cattle on the surrounding plateaus, heard about the bridges from a fellow rancher named Emery Knowles. Later that year Al and two of his cowboys went to have a look, but their visit likewise did not result in any publicity.[2]

Gold commanded more attention than scenery. Hite's placer discovery induced hundreds of men from Utah and neighboring states to leave their farms and towns for the Colorado's sandbars. Few earned much for their efforts, nor did the mechanized sluicing operations run by out-of-state promoters fare any better. One of the more bizarre attempts at making the Colorado yield its fine gold was undertaken by the Hoskaninni Company, organized by railroad promoter Robert Brewster Stanton in 1898.[3] In 1900, Stanton's men hauled the disassembled pieces of a hundred-foot-long dredge over the Henry Mountains and launched it into the muddy stream. The rig was unable to concentrate the Colorado's "flour" gold, and the company soon went bankrupt. New owners attempted to revive it, and in March 1903 one of the partners who was visiting the site, an engineer named Horace J. Long, heard about the bridges in White Canyon. He asked James Scorup to take him there.[4]

Scorup met Long at Dandy Crossing with pack stock and provisions for a week's journey. He was apprehensive that the three bridges might not live up to their billing, but his client was not disappointed. Exercising explorers' rights, the men gave the bridges new names, calling the larger of the two spans within White Canyon the Augusta, after Long's wife. A natural bridge at the junction of White and Armstrong Canyons became the Caroline, after Scorup's mother. A third span, located four miles up Armstrong Canyon, became the Little Bridge.

Long made rough estimates of the bridges' size and sent his notes and photographs to his boss, W. W. Dyar, who wrote up the "discovery" for *Century* and *National Geographic* magazines. Dyar lavished praise on the bridges, particularly the Augusta. It was "doubtless the most wonderful natural bridge in the world," he exulted, "a structure so lofty and magnificent, so symmetrical and beautiful, that an army could march over it in columns of companies."[5] A drawing showed how the Capitol Dome could fit underneath its huge opening. Once again, architecture provided the yardstick for measuring the magnificence of these canyon wonders.

Dyar's articles attracted the notice of Colonel Edwin F. Holmes, a mining and lumber magnate from Salt Lake City who was past president of the city's Commercial Club. Sensing an opportunity to publicize Utah's scenery, he asked H. L. A. Culmer, an artist and fellow club member, to mount an expedition to the White Canyon bridges. Henry Culmer, a native of Kent, England, held interests in various Utah mining properties but was best known for his striking paintings of western landscapes. He accepted Holmes's challenge and recruited S. T. Whitaker, an Ogden architect and photographer, to join the expedition. Carlton Holmes, Edwin's son, completed the party.

The Commercial Club expedition of 1905 was undertaken in the style of the great geographic discovery expeditions that were then probing the polar regions and the Himalayas. Besides charting new geologic wonders and rendering them artistically, Culmer sought to find something of economic value in the southeastern Utah canyon lands. He told a reporter that he was attracted to the "weird beauty of the desert" and hoped to sketch the "strange forms and shifting beauty of the wilderness," but he and his friends also had practical goals. "Three thousand square miles of unknown land is too large for the people of this State to leave unexplored," Culmer said, and its potential for mining, agriculture, and other forms of economic development needed to be assessed.[6]

Before departing from Salt Lake City on April 1, Culmer and his friends shipped their camp outfit by rail to the desert outpost of Thompson Springs, where it would be loaded onto wagons for the journey south. Included were surveying instruments, rope ladders equipped with grappling hooks, rifles and revolvers, and a "telescopic or long distance camera" for Whitaker's use that cost $1500.[7] They intended to locate, measure, and sketch the three natural bridges in the upper reaches of White Canyon, thereby adding these geologic wonders to the West's pantheon of worthy destinations. Along the way they would explore for minerals, search for fossils and prehistoric ruins, and marvel at scenery that Culmer expected to be "unique in its character and extraordinary in its majestic proportions."

The journey south from Thompson Springs involved more than a hundred miles of difficult travel, their wagons "jolting over rocky wastes or dragging slowly through deep sands," Culmer wrote in a 1908 article recalling the trip.[8] Al Scorup, whom they engaged to guide them to the bridges, met them at his ranch south of Monticello and accompanied them to Bluff, where they were forced to wait several days for the spring rains to clear. On April 12 the party set out on horseback with two wranglers, a camp cook, and a dozen mules to carry provisions.

Their route followed Butler Wash, which led north along the dramatic sandstone hogback known as Comb Ridge. Culmer called it "one of the dizziest things on earth—narrow, steep and rocky."[9] They passed by without investigating the numerous slickrock drainages that flowed down from this ridge, in which were hidden cliff dwellings of the Puebloan people who had lived there centuries earlier. Farther north, on the shoulder of Elk Ridge, the party spent a night in a large cave that contained evidence of early habitation, but Culmer noted that the site had already been worked over by artifact hunters.

Once atop Elk Ridge they turned west, traversing miles of pinyon- and juniper-covered uplands dominated by the twin buttes known as the Bears Ears. On April 13, they reached the edge of Armstrong Canyon, directly across from the Little Bridge, which towered over a small ravine in the slickrock. "Wonderfully lofty, graceful in style and very symmetrical," Culmer noted in his journal that evening.

Culmer rose at sunrise to sketch the bridge. Whitaker and Holmes found a route onto its flat top and dropped a measuring tape 111 feet to its base. Not satisfied with its diminutive name, they decided to call it the Edwin after Carlton's father, the expedition's sponsor. They climbed the canyon wall to investigate "the remnants of some so called cave dwellers" but found that "it had already been looted."

Continuing down Armstrong Canyon to its juncture with White Canyon, they found the Caroline bridge arcing over the sandy stream course. At its base were "hieroglyphics or picture paintings or scratchings" in the soft sandstone, Culmer noted, along with the names of Charles McLoyd and C. C. Graham, two artifact collectors who had investigated the bridges during the winter of 1892–93. Culmer assessed the Caroline as "heavy and clumsy," whereas the Augusta, a few miles farther up the main canyon, was "one of the most magnificent and shapely structures ever achieved by Nature." Unpacking their rope ladders, Carlton Holmes and two of Scorup's cowboys carefully climbed onto its summit, measuring its height as a vertiginous 265 feet. The opening spanned 320 feet in width and 230 feet in height, making it the largest natural bridge yet documented in the United States. As sheer spectacle it ranked with Niagara Falls, Yellowstone, and the Grand Canyon, according to Culmer. The bridge had the feel of the ages about it, a timeless presence that was enhanced by the cliff dwellings they observed on nearby ledges.

Culmer made sketches of the Augusta bridge for later use and with his friends spent several days exploring the nearby cliffs and caves, using their climbing gear to reach undisturbed habitation sites. Despite the "looting" they noted at other sites, they could not resist collecting "trophies" such as clay pots, sandals, and a digging stick. This was one year before Congress passed the Antiquities Act in an attempt to curb the widespread plundering of the Southwest's prehistoric sites, but these men would certainly have been aware of scientific concerns about unauthorized and poorly documented collecting of artifacts. As their use of the word "trophies" suggests, they wanted to bring back evidence of their difficult journey as well as call attention to the mysterious qualities of the land they had visited.

Culmer's party concluded its journey with an exploration of lower Grand Gulch, fifteen miles southwest of White Canyon. Entering the gulch via a cowboy trail down Collins Canyon, they found picturesque sandstone cliffs lined with "splendid old cottonwoods . . . twisted and bent in dragon writhings." They explored the canyon's serpentine loops for miles downstream without reaching its confluence with the San Juan River. McLoyd and Graham had collected extensively in upper Grand Gulch, but Culmer and his friends mostly engaged in sightseeing within its pleasant confines. These canyons and the entire surrounding region were "a rich field for the geologist,

Henry Culmer's 1905 studio painting of the Caroline Natural Bridge, which hangs in the Utah State Capitol. Now called the Kachina Bridge, it is one of three major spans within Natural Bridges National Monument. *Used by permission, Utah State Historical Society.*

naturalist, botanist, and archaeologist," according to S. T. Whitaker, who gave an interview to the *Ogden Standard* upon their return.[10]

Returning to Bluff, where they hoped to cross the San Juan River and visit Monument Valley, Culmer's party met two men who had just arrived from a trek across the Colorado River at Hole-in-the-Rock. Worn out, they had lost the track and had gone without food for nearly five days before running across James Scorup's camp in Grand Gulch. In an account of the expedition that appeared in the January 1907 issue of *National Geographic*, Edwin Holmes emphasized the difficulty of travel in this remote section of the Southwest. No one should make such a trip without studying the local conditions, he wrote; even the local guides had limited knowledge of the country.

Holmes called for designating the area around the bridges as a national park "so that roads may be opened and these greatest of the world's natural bridges can be made accessible." He envisioned a connection between the Denver & Rio Grande Western rail line in southwestern Colorado and the Santa Fe in northern Arizona, which would permit tourists to travel from Mesa Verde, newly designated as a national park, to the White Canyon bridges and on to the Grand Canyon. It would be, Holmes predicted, "a scenic route comparable to nothing else in the world."[11] This was an early conception of what later boosters would advertise as a grand circle of railroad-served parks in the Southwest, most of which, including Zion and the Grand Canyon, had yet to come into existence.

Edwin Holmes's brief account in *National Geographic* was enhanced by reproductions of Henry Culmer's studio paintings of the three bridges. Based on careful on-site sketches and measurements, his huge canvases were rendered in the lavish, romantic style of the nineteenth century. In company with other artists who portrayed the natural landmarks of the West as if they had encountered them in upstate New York or perhaps England's Lake District, Culmer bathed the White Canyon bridges in a warm, pleasing light, lining the canyon bottom with mature broadleaf trees. Like the lithographs that artist J. J. Young prepared from J. S. Newberry's sketches of the Utah canyon lands in 1859, Culmer's paintings suggested mountain majesty more than aridity and desolation.[12] Realistic or not, Culmer's paintings fit then-current ideas of wild scenery and helped gain recognition for an outstanding cluster of natural bridges that the party believed to be the largest in the world. Historian C. Gregory Crampton credited Culmer with helping to fashion the public's conception of the Utah canyon country and called his paintings of southeastern Utah scenes "his best work."[13]

The Culmer party's widely publicized expedition suggested that in southern Utah's canyon country, it was still possible to test oneself against raw nature in a primitive, awe-inspiring setting—a type of experience that many Americans feared was fast disappearing in a modernizing nation. Yet the expedition also exemplified the divided and contradictory motives for exploring such country. Explorers such as Culmer saw themselves as being in the forefront of economic progress. A stated goal of their expedition was to locate new mineral prospects and fertile ground for agriculture; that they failed to find any mattered little, for the way was now open for others to follow under the banner of American progress.

Four years later, in fact, Culmer would investigate the little-known San Rafael Swell in Utah's Emery County, bringing back glowing descriptions of colorful rock formations as well as a vision of progress that included a proposed reclamation project on the San Rafael River at Mexican Bend, which would irrigate lands to the east of the Swell. A dam and reservoir would only make the place more attractive, he believed. "It is quite within reason to believe that before many years have passed, this new wonderland will be a popular resort for tourists." New national parks and monuments fit neatly beneath the flag of Progress, on which also appeared the symbols of agriculture and industry.

Despite his practical intentions, Henry Culmer discovered something else during his 1905 sojourn among the bridges of White Canyon. More evanescent than adventure, more intriguing than awe, it was a feeling that perhaps came most easily to an artist. After returning to camp near the Caroline bridge, Culmer took a stroll after dark along the sandy streambed. "The moon rose late," he wrote, "and in the starlight I wandered among the spacious caverns that surround the bridge, making my way alone in the silence through deep and dismal passages among the desolated abiding places of a long-forgotten people. As the night grew, a faint warm glow lit the distant spires and domes and touched upon nearby crags. Soon fingers of silver light stole beneath the arch, playing with the mystery of those dusky galleries; and slowly the white moon rose over one of the great abutments of the bridge."

Anyone who has witnessed a moonrise in canyon country will understand how such a scene would have stirred Henry Culmer's soul. The grand and picturesque aspect of the White Canyon bridges—their "massive and towering cliffs, the sweeping lines" that he described in 1908—made good copy and aided efforts to protect these wonders as a national monument. But there were personal illuminations to be found in the intimate spaces amid all this grandeur. The quest for beauty and inspiration encompassed more than the awesome and the sublime. For travelers open to such experiences, the canyons and plateaus of southern Utah offered a window into a wilder nature, where humans were insignificant observers within an enormous landscape.

3

THE OBJECTS TO BE PROTECTED

In the summer of 1907, two years after Henry Culmer's expedition to White Canyon, the residents of Bluff were surprised to find a stranger of somewhat advanced years approaching their town on foot. A German, he was following the San Juan River as it flowed west out of Colorado and New Mexico, hoping to come upon some new mineral prospect. He carried with him a small map of the Four Corners region, but its hachures petered out where the San Juan made its way past Bluff toward the Colorado River. This gentleman was heading into the proverbial blank spot on the map, a region in which even experienced travelers could easily lose their bearings. A reporter in town at the time noted that "had all that country been surveyed and mapped, the old German would have seen endless winding canyons, ranges of hills, broken country which no horse can cross." He noted that as they spoke, "the sun beat down on the rocks with relentless heat."[1]

Whether the lone prospector made it to the Colorado and joined the handful of placer miners still working its sandbars is not recorded. The citizens of Bluff doubted he could survive such a journey, for there were many who still remembered making the arduous trek across this desert during the winter of 1879–80. Now, having lived a quarter century in Bluff, they watched helplessly as the San Juan's frequent floods gradually claimed the arable land along the river. Some residents were preparing to head for the prosperous new settlement of Grayson (now Blanding), twenty miles to the north.

That same summer, Professor Byron Cummings of the University of Utah and several of his students were taking measurements of the natural bridges in White Canyon and looking into the caves in which the Commercial Club party had found so many ancient artifacts. The heat was more bearable than on the San Juan and there was shade and water in the cottonwood-lined canyon. Writing of their experience later that summer, Cummings asked rhetorically, "Have you ever spread your blanket on the soft, shifting sand of one of the many lofty mesas of southern Utah and gazed into the star-decked canopy of the sky? . . . No atmosphere was ever clearer, no sky ever revealed more of its secrets and more of the beauty and glory of its design-ing than this."[2] Well supplied for a lengthy stay, Cummings and his students could afford to savor their surroundings.

Later that summer, Cummings moved his excavations to Alkali Ridge, a site farther east above Montezuma Creek. Although he held a professorship in classics, he was becoming increasingly fascinated with geology and pre-history. In 1906 he had visited Nine Mile Canyon northeast of Price, Utah, where dozens of prehistoric rock art panels lined the canyon walls. Thereaf-ter he devoted much of his free time, and eventually his career, to the study of southwestern prehistory.

Like Edwin Holmes and Henry Culmer, Cummings viewed the stone monuments in White Canyon as objects of pride for his state. He called for the bridges' designation as a national monument under the 1906 Antiqui-ties Act, which gave the president the power to withdraw important fea-tures of geologic, scientific, and archaeological interest from appropriation under nineteenth-century land disposal laws. Cummings had been among those who pressed Congress for such a law in order to stem the tide of com-mercial pothunting and vandalism that threatened to destroy southeastern Utah's irreplaceable prehistoric remains.[3]

Fortunately the White House at the time was occupied by a conserva-tionist who was eager to use his new authority. On April 16, 1908, Theodore Roosevelt signed a proclamation establishing Natural Bridges National Mon-ument, Utah's first entry in what would become a miniempire of national parks and monuments. Consisting of a scant forty-acre parcel around each of the three bridges, it was intended mainly to prevent their falling into pri-vate hands; another fifteen years would pass before the Interior Department would appoint a uniformed officer to guard them.

In the interim, the department sent William B. Douglass, an exam-iner of surveys for the General Land Office, to investigate and record the new monument. He drew a sketch map of the bridges' locations and tried to determine what names the region's Ute and Paiute Indians used for them. Finding none, he proposed three Hopi words that appeared to be descriptive of the bridges.[4] The Augusta became Sipapu, meaning "place

A mounted party atop the Edwin, or Owachomo Natural Bridge in White Canyon in 1907. *Charles Goodwin/Herbert E. Gregory Collection, Special Collections, J. Willard Marriott Library, University of Utah.*

of emergence"; the Caroline was changed to Kachina, referring to rock art figures found at the base of the bridge; and the Edwin became Owachomo, or "rock mound," referring to a protrusion above the span. All this was in keeping with the country's romantic attachment to the original inhabitants of the Desert Southwest. That fall President William Howard Taft issued a new proclamation, based on Douglass's survey, which enlarged the protected zone around the three bridges to 2,860 acres and added an unrelated archaeological site near Cigarette Spring, farther south on Cedar Mesa in the Fish Creek drainage. The government also adopted Douglass's proposed names, although the older appellations remained in use among locals for years.

Byron Cummings urged the state's business leaders to heavily advertise the new monument as a tourist attraction, much as Colorado was doing with Pikes Peak and the Royal Gorge. In 1909 the Salt Lake City Chamber of Commerce featured a reproduction of the Sipapu bridge (still calling it the Augusta) at a local industrial fair promoting Utah's economic potential. The exhibit spanned the entire length of the meeting hall and was said to be "exact in its details."[5] Like Henry Culmer, Cummings envisioned that a railroad would one day bring tourists from Mesa Verde National Park to view these wonders. No rail line was in the offing, however, and it would be decades before so much as a crude road linked Natural Bridges to the outside world.

Americans' interest in the pre-Columbian history of the Southwest grew steadily throughout the nineteenth century as explorers came across the stone villages of vanished peoples. During the 1880s Adolph Bandelier investigated sites at Pecos and in Frijoles Canyon in New Mexico under the auspices of the Archaeological Institute of America. In Arizona, the prehistoric O'odham structures known as Casa Grande drew nationwide interest, leading to their protection in 1892 under an executive order of President Benjamin Harrison.[6]

Popularly supposed to have been of Aztec origin or even (in some Utahns' supposition) built by wandering Hebrews, these ruins and the intricate and colorful designs left on nearby sandstone walls stoked a fascination with antiquity. With wealthy individuals seeking to possess the artifacts of lost civilizations, a new market for collectibles was born. Farmers and their families excavated sites for pottery and other collectibles that could supplement their meager incomes.

Richard Wetherill, a rancher from Mancos, Colorado, was one of those hardscrabble settlers who took to collecting artifacts, including some he found in small ruins near his ranch. His Ute Indian ranch hands told him of much larger abandoned villages up on the mesa to the south, but initially he discounted the stories. In December 1888 a Ute named Acowitz accompanied Wetherill and fellow rancher Charlie Mason up on the plateau to look for stray cattle, showing the two men what he called the "big city" in Cliff Canyon. Impressed, the two ranchers let themselves down the cliff using rope ladders. With little time left in the day, they grabbed a few artifacts and returned home.[7]

Wetherill shared his discovery with two other Anglo collectors, Charles McLoyd and J. H. Graham, who were working their way along the Mancos River.[8] It was the beginning of a period of intensive exploration and artifact collection that quickly spread into southeastern Utah, homeland of many of the ancestral Puebloans. The great stone city that Wetherill and Mason called Cliff Palace, along with nearby pueblo sites known as Spruce Tree

House and Square Tower House, became the centerpieces of Mesa Verde National Park.

Mesa Verde was the seventh national park to be designated by Congress and the first in the Southwest. It owed its creation in large part to two Colorado women, Virginia McClurg and Lucy Peabody, who led a nationwide campaign to preserve the sites. McClurg first visited Mesa Verde in 1882 and returned four years later. Concerned over the steady loss of antiquities and damage to the pueblo sites, she launched what was likely the first grassroots campaign to protect a specific landscape in the West, giving a series of lectures in Denver and circulating a petition asking Congress to protect the area. "The Cliff palace is the prey of the spoiler," she wrote, "soon it will be too late to guard these monuments."[9]

Mesa Verde would become the first national park created for the purpose of safeguarding prehistoric sites. Its creation required a series of land exchanges with the Weeminuche, or Ute Mountain Utes, whose leaders stated afterward that they had been strong-armed into accepting unfavorable terms. Added to this was their dislike of white people entering the cliff dwellings and removing artifacts, which they believed was disrespectful and dangerous spiritually. But the new park established a federal precedent for control of antiquities that was reinforced by passage the same year of the Antiquities Act—a law that had significant ramifications for setting aside public lands elsewhere in the Colorado Plateau.

During the 1890s, Richard Wetherill joined Charles McLoyd and C. C. Graham, Howard Graham's older brother, to excavate numerous sites on Mesa Verde and later in southeastern Utah's Grand Gulch, Butler Wash, and Comb Ridge. Many of the artifacts they found made their way through intermediaries to New York's American Museum of Natural History, while some were exhibited at the 1893 World's Columbian Exposition in Chicago. University-affiliated anthropologists such as Byron Cummings labeled these men as pothunters, believing them incapable of properly recording and preserving the artifacts they found. Cummings, who did not hold an appointment in anthropology, pointed to his own work in Montezuma Canyon and Alkali Ridge (which he continued in 1908) as the "first scientific digging in San Juan County." He bemoaned the "great destruction" brought about by relic hunters, who "have kept no records and often have failed to see that there was a scientific value in the things they were ruthlessly destroying."[10]

Museums and institutions nonetheless depended on the Wetherills and their cooperators to build their collections. Richard, to his credit, kept detailed records of his finds, and his discovery in 1893 of "a people still older than the cliff dwellers who occupied the same caves" was a milestone in American archaeology. He called them the "Basket People" for the woven baskets they found, while his partner B. T. B. Hyde termed them "Basketmakers."[11]

Calls for legislative action to protect American antiquities arose as early as 1880, after Adolph Bandelier of the newly formed Archaeological Institute of America documented losses at the Pecos site in northern New Mexico. Edgar Lee Hewett, an anthropologist from Colorado who had spent time in New Mexico with Bandelier, cultivated the support of Iowa congressman John Lacey, a noted conservationist and chair of the House Public Lands Committee.[12] In 1900 Lacey's committee took up various bills designed to preserve prehistoric sites, which led six years later to passage of "an Act for the preservation of American antiquities," commonly known as the Antiquities Act. The law delegated to the president the authority to establish national monuments to protect "historic landmarks, historic and prehistoric structures, and other objects of historic or scientific interest." The act specified that national monuments were to be "confined to the smallest area compatible with proper care and management of the objects to be protected." It made provision for scientific collecting of antiquities within the monuments and regulated collecting at other sites not designated under the law.[13]

Theodore Roosevelt used his authority to set aside eighteen national monuments in the West, including spectacular geological formations such as Wyoming's Devils Tower and California's Mount Lassen as well as archaeological sites such as New Mexico's Chaco Canyon and Arizona's Montezuma Castle.[14] The Antiquities Act enabled Roosevelt and subsequent presidents to protect such sites without the need to maneuver national park legislation through Congress (Mesa Verde being a notable exception).

Many of the early national monuments, like the initial 120 acres at Natural Bridges, were tiny indeed. Roosevelt, however, saw no reason to be confined to small enclosures when expansive, magnificent landscapes were at stake. In 1908 he liberally expanded the scope of the Antiquities Act by setting aside 808,120 acres of national forest land in northern Arizona as Grand Canyon National Monument. Terming the canyon an "object" worthy of protection, his principled redefinition of Congress's intent would have important ramifications for later monument designations in Utah and the western states.

Henry Culmer, Byron Cummings, and their colleagues came to southern Utah in the service of science, art, grand adventure, and sometimes personal gain, but they also took pride in the western landscape, seeking ways to protect rather than to exploit it. By calling for designation of the White Canyon bridges and other outstanding geologic and cultural features as national parks or monuments, they helped set a course that would lead, more than a half century later, to Utah's becoming home to five of America's best-loved national parks. Their coming affirmed the vision of the early twentieth-century artists, scientists, and promoters who saw something in these canyons and mesas that spoke of the ineffable.

4

RAINBOW IN STONE

In a region known for its remoteness, the northern flank of Navajo Mountain represents the wildest reach of the Colorado Plateau Province. A dozen incised canyons flow down from the mountain through tilted layers of Mesozoic sandstone, joining the Colorado and San Juan Rivers in a labyrinth of naked rock. Major Powell passed by the mouths of these canyons on his voyages of 1869 and 1871, his crew short on supplies and unwilling to explore further. Even by the turn of the century no roads came within fifty miles of the mountain, and its resident Navajo and Paiute Indians lived lives isolated from modern America. That would change little even after word of the great sandstone span in Bridge Canyon reached outside ears early in the twentieth century.

Formed by stream erosion cutting through a narrow sandstone fin, Rainbow Bridge would have entranced the first Paleo-Indians who ventured into Bridge Canyon's recesses. They may have marked their passage with offerings of seeds or sacred objects, a visitation that persisted well into the Christian era.[1] Paiute Indians made use of these convoluted canyons after the exodus of Puebloan people in the thirteenth century, adopting agricultural practices that were in evidence in nearby areas when the Domínguez-Escalante expedition encountered them in the late autumn of 1776. By then the Navajos (or Diné) had also become established around Navajo Mountain, an area they, too, utilized for its springs, streams, and available food plants. Conflict arose as the Navajos expanded into what was the homeland of the San Juan band of the Southern Paiutes. In 1908, the San Juan Paiutes were accorded their own reservation south of the Colorado and San Juan Rivers, but it was rescinded fourteen years later.[2]

Rainbow Bridge has strong spiritual significance for the Diné, whose names for it mean "rock span" or "bridge."[3] In one creation account, Bridge

Canyon was the childhood home of the Hero Twins, Monster Slayer and Born for Water, who were protected under a magic rainbow that had been turned to stone. They, in turn, gave protection to those who were fleeing Kit Carson's soldiers during the time of the Long Walk to New Mexico. The bridge is inseparable from Navajo Mountain, known as "Head of the Earth Woman." Water from a spring at the base of Rainbow Bridge "is used in the prayers and to wash the sacred bundles of the medicine man," according to Nakai Ditloi, a Navajo singer whom anthropologist Kevin Luckert interviewed in 1974 as part of a court case involving tourism at the bridge. "Ground turquoise and shells are given to the spring to aid in the prayers from rain," he said. "Prayers are renewed and knowledge of the earth and the ways of the Diné is increased when the medicine men come to the cave."[4]

The veneration of Navajo Mountain and Rainbow Bridge by Navajo people is by no means unique in the Colorado Plateau Province; to many Native Americans, "landscape" is a living entity with particular spiritual properties, which manifest more clearly in certain places.[5] Euro-American "discoverers" of Rainbow Bridge would apply their own interpretations to this striking rock formation, based largely on aesthetic values developed under European Neoclassicism and Romanticism. Elsewhere in the Plateau Province, sites such as Zion Canyon would be given meanings based on Mormon texts, or, more often, be thought to have no sacred value whatever. Only these soaring rocks would remain immovable and largely unchanged, a blank slate upon which awestruck and reverential visitors could register their own impressions.

Until 1909 none of the Paiutes, Navajos, or Anglos who ventured north of Navajo Mountain recorded their travels, so it is not known how often people came across the great span in Bridge Canyon. A Navajo named Jayi Begay, or Blind Salt Clansman, told others that he had seen it while tracking a lost horse during the time of refuge in the 1860s.[6] Some historians believe that nineteenth-century fur trappers, including the enigmatic French American Denis Julien, may have seen it. The arrival of Anglo prospectors at Navajo Mountain in 1882, in a party that included Cass Hite, signaled the encroachment of outside interests into the Rainbow Bridge area.[7] Placer miners working the Colorado's sandbars in the 1880s and 1890s could easily have walked the six miles up Aztec Creek and its tributary, Bridge Canyon. Even the most gold-hungry prospector would have stood and stared in wonder.[8]

The recorded history of Rainbow Bridge began with the first "discovery" expedition in 1909, which came about after Louisa Wetherill, who with her husband, John, had established a trading post beneath Oljeto Mesa in 1906, was told by Blind Salt Clansman of a great stone arch forty miles to the west. Louisa passed the news to her husband and his business partner, Clyde Colville, who separately may have tried to find the bridge during the early summer of 1908. The first part of the journey would have taken them across the mesas and wide canyon bottoms of the western Navajo Reservation, but as they circled around the north side of Navajo Mountain they were confronted with a strange territory of bare sandstone domes and windblown hollows that baffled even their Navajo guides.[9]

John Wetherill got another chance the following year, when two individuals with an interest in the area's prehistory arrived at his isolated trading post. Byron Cummings and William Douglass, men with very different loyalties, would draw Rainbow Bridge out of its shadowed past and into the modern era. Their quest for "discovery" rights, and the fame that came with it, would contrast with the purposes of the Navajos and other Indians who visited the bridge for protection and spiritual renewal.

Following his investigations at Alkali Ridge in 1908, Byron Cummings headed for Tsegi Canyon in northern Arizona, where he hoped to excavate a group of spectacular cliff dwellings he had seen the year before. Reaching Oljeto in early August, he found John Wetherill occupied and unable to guide him, so the expedition was postponed until the following summer. During their visit, though, the Wetherills told him of the great natural bridge north of Navajo Mountain, which added a further element of discovery to their 1909 undertaking. Billed as the "Utah Archaeological Expedition," Cummings's party consisted of relative neophytes, including Cummings's youngest son, Malcolm; his nephew Neil Judd, who had accompanied him on previous expeditions and would go on to do significant work in the field of archaeology; and Stuart Young, a grandson of Brigham Young and the expedition photographer.

With the passage of the Antiquities Act—which Cummings supported— the federal government was taking a new interest in the disposition of prehistoric artifacts from the public domain. A permit was required to dig in

Rainbow Bridge, as photographed by William B. Douglass on the 1909 Cummings-Douglass-Wetherill "discovery" expedition. *Herbert E. Gregory Collection, Special Collections, J. Willard Marriott Library, University of Utah.*

ruins or even to remove the odd flint point. The days of free and easy col-
lecting were over, at least officially, but the Interior Department had few
agents to patrol the Southwest or even to monitor protected sites such as
Natural Bridges. William B. Douglass, who had surveyed Natural Bridges
National Monument in 1908, stepped into this role. Following his work in
White Canyon that fall, he headed south to investigate pueblo ruins on
the Navajo Reservation, but like Cummings he was unable to secure John
Wetherill as a guide. He learned from a Paiute in Bluff, Utah, named Mike's
Boy that there were cliff dwellings in Tsegi Canyon, and on March 9, 1909,
without having visited the site, Douglass recommended to the commissioner of the General Land Office that it be designated as a national monument. Three weeks later the required papers were prepared for President
Taft, who signed the proclamation setting aside six hundred acres of public land as Navajo National Monument.[10] Douglass recommended John
Wetherill as its custodian, a logical choice since most visitors to the monument would pass through Oljeto. Wetherill, like other early-day monument
custodians, served at essentially no pay, instead earning money by guiding
scientists and tourists to the monument.

Mike's Boy also told Douglass that he had been to a great natural bridge
north of Navajo Mountain, so Douglass hired him to guide an exploration
party in the summer of 1909. Cummings, hearing that Douglass was headed
for the bridge, delayed his departure from Oljeto for two days to confer with
him.[11] They decided to combine their expeditions, but Douglass, who dis-
puted Cummings's right to dig at Navajo National Monument, made a difficult partner. Most accounts tell how he jockeyed for position during the
final ride down Bridge Canyon in order to gain the first glimpse of the enormous span that became known as Rainbow Bridge. Later he belittled the
contribution of Cummings, Wetherill, and Wetherill's hired guide, Nasja
Begay, a Paiute, and instead promoted Mike's Boy, who seems to have been
of less help in finding the bridge.[12]

John Wetherill actually spied the bridge before either Cummings or
Douglass, but he wisely kept himself in the background. Byron Cummings
described the journey in an article for *National Geographic* magazine the
following year, giving the General Land Office equal credit for the discovery without mentioning Douglass or their dispute. Cummings called the
bridge Nonnezoshi, after a Navajo word meaning "span" or "bridge," and
described it as "more properly an enormous flying buttress that has been

chiseled out by the ages and left as a specimen of the handiwork of the Master Builder." He noted that the Native Paiutes "look upon it with awe," and that when Clyde Colville visited the bridge later that fall, his Paiute guide "would not pass beneath the arch because he had forgotten the prayer that must be said before doing so."[13]

Douglass took measurements of the bridge and drew a plan sketch, which became the basis for a 160-acre withdrawal under the Antiquities Act. On May 30, 1910, President Taft made Rainbow Bridge Utah's third national monument, following Natural Bridges in 1908 and Mukuntuweap in 1909.[14] The lingering controversy between Douglass and Cummings, however, cast an unpleasant air over the expedition, which was significant for publicizing the continent's largest and most spectacular natural bridge. Properly termed a rediscovery, the expedition received wide publicity from Cummings's *National Geographic* article, which featured Stuart Young's photographs of the bridge. In contrast, the designation of Rainbow Bridge National Monument in 1910 drew scant attention from Utah newspapers, although the *Salt Lake Herald* took pains to credit Byron Cummings with the discovery.[15]

John Wetherill continued to guide clients to the bridge after he and Louisa relocated their trading post to Kayenta, Arizona, in 1911. Among the adventurers who were drawn to this remote locality were Theodore Roosevelt and Zane Grey, each of whom visited Rainbow Bridge on separate trips with Wetherill in 1913. The former president, who was fifty-five years old at the time, brought his sons Archie and Quentin along, wanting to show them something of the strenuous adventures he had known as a younger man. His cousin Nicholas made arrangements for the trip, which began at the South Rim of the Grand Canyon in mid-July. After crossing to the North Rim to hunt cougars on the Kaibab Plateau, they descended into the "grim desolation" of the House Rock Desert, where they found "little save the sand and the harsh, scanty vegetation," Roosevelt wrote in his 1916 book *A Book Lover's Holiday in the Open*. After crossing the Colorado River at Lees Ferry, the party rode south to Tuba City and thence northeast to Kayenta, where they engaged John Wetherill for the journey to Rainbow Bridge. Roosevelt called it "one of the wonders of the world . . . a triumphal arch rather than a bridge."[16] He and his sons spent a night underneath the bridge, building a fire against one of its buttresses and, like Henry Culmer at Natural Bridges, enjoying the scene by moonlight. The ashes and soot they left behind presumably carried no sacred meanings to these adventurers.

It was Zane Grey, though, who placed Rainbow Bridge into the western canon through his novel *The Rainbow Trail*. Published in 1915, two years after his visit to the bridge, the book makes liberal use of the landscape and people he encountered, including a Navajo he calls "Nas Ta Bega" and the trader Withers—stand-ins for the guides Nasja Begay and John Wetherill. His description of the bridge and its environs, like Roosevelt's, evokes the wonder that many first-time visitors experience in such landscapes. John Shefford, the book's protagonist, found that "this thing [Rainbow Bridge] was glorious. It silenced him, yet did not awe or stun." As it was approached, the canyon "did not widen, though the walls grew higher. They began to lean and bulge, and the narrow strip of sky above resembled a flowing blue river. Huge caverns had been hollowed out by some work of nature, what, he could not tell, though he was sure it could not have been wind."[17]

In the early 1920s Charles Bernheimer, a New York textile manufacturer and inveterate explorer, employed Wetherill and Utah guide Ezekiel Johnson on a series of expeditions to the bridge and its surrounding country. These included a pioneering trip in 1921 around the western side of Navajo Mountain through a narrow slot they named Redbud Pass, which became the favored route to Rainbow Bridge.[18] Two years later, the brothers Hubert and S. I. Richardson, who operated a trading post at Kaibito Spring, opened a new tourist lodge south of Navajo Mountain and began using this shorter route to guide visitors to the bridge. Rainbow Bridge was now on the tourist map, a fascinating emblem of the wonders to be found within the Plateau Province, and a new kind of sacred place for a culture that was lamenting the loss of its own past.

5

THE GREAT AMERICAN PLATEAU

For all his novels' purple prose and stilted romance, Zane Grey made rea-
sonably accurate observations of the landforms of the Colorado Plateau
Province. His books give a sense of the region's vast scale, an immense
openness in which worn-out easterners could seek a new life. This, in
Grey's mind, was the source of the region's transformative power. The
notion that there were still remnants of the Old West appealed to many
Americans well into the twentieth century, and their consumption of novels and motion pictures on this theme reinforced efforts to protect such
landscapes. Grey's foreword to his 1915 book *The Rainbow Trail* makes this
clear when he invokes "the strange wild life of the last American wilderness—wild still, almost, as it ever was."

Historian Thomas J. Harvey places Grey and his fellow exponents of
the rugged outdoor life in the context of a rapidly modernizing America.
"In the Old West," he writes, "at the moment of industrialization and its
changing of the physical landscape and economic and social roles, Anglo-
Americans found a past in which human beings were close to nature, to their
economy, and to their social roles." Like the late Romantic-era author James
Fenimore Cooper and the landscape artist Albert Bierstadt, Grey and his
fellow popularizers of the West "attempted to 'fix' the changing landscape
in a moment of preindustrial time, to preserve the primitive before it dis-
appeared."[1] This was not entirely a work of the literary imagination; in the
tortuous canyons and wind-whipped plateaus along the Utah-Arizona border, it was still possible to find places where modernity had scarcely touched
the land and its inhabitants. This desire to witness a premodern landscape
enticed a handful of adventurous travelers during the late nineteenth and

early twentieth centuries to venture north from the Santa Fe rail line and into the little-known canyons and mesas of southernmost Utah.

One of the first independent travelers to explore and publicize this section of the Plateau Province was a New York pathologist and amateur anthropologist named T. Mitchell Prudden. Beginning in 1892 he made eight trips to the Four Corners region to study its prehistory and ethnology, guided by one or more of the Wetherill brothers. His 1897 article for *Harper's Magazine*, titled "An Elder Brother to the Cliff-Dwellers," helped publicize Richard Wetherill's discovery of the Basketmaker culture in Grand Gulch.

Prudden's 1906 book *On the Great American Plateau*, which drew from his magazine writings, called attention to a 130,000-square-mile region stretching from northern Arizona and New Mexico into Wyoming and Colorado. This was the domain of "mighty wind-swept uplands and bewildering gorges, of forest and desert and plain," which "lies to-day almost as the Spaniards found it more than three hundred years ago."[2] Historian Samuel Schmieding credits Prudden as the first amateur explorer to call attention to the canyon lands section of the Colorado Plateau as a worthy destination for travelers—a remote, challenging wilderness in contrast to the packaged experience available along the Santa Fe line.[3]

Prudden invited his readers to leave the comfort of the Pullman car and the Fred Harvey dining room and explore what lay beyond. "Out of sight of the settlements and out of hearing of the locomotives," he wrote, "you are face to face with the naked earth as the great sculptors, flood, wind, and sand, have left it."[4] Most of *On the Great American Plateau* is devoted to the pueblos of northern Arizona and New Mexico, but Prudden also gives an account of a long horseback journey he made in July 1897 into the heart of the Glen Canyon country, crossing the Colorado River at Hite and climbing up onto the Paunsaugunt Plateau before descending to Kanab and points east. Much of this country appeared to be divorced from the modern age. Prudden described the impoverished and news-starved men and women they met along the way, including cattlemen who were "glad to leave their lonesome cabins among the pines and ride for miles beside us to hear our story and to tell their own." Sometimes he came across "forlorn hovels, whose Mormon inmates had memories clear enough of better times in other lands."[5]

For these residents of hardscrabble farms and ranches on the Mormon frontier, scenery was little more than an obstacle to their practical needs, whether it was to build a water supply for their town, obtain forage for their herds, or simply gain greater contact with the outside world. Viewing canyon country not as a picturesque wilderness but as unredeemed land, they awaited the infrastructure—principally better roads—that would tie them to their Mormon brethren farther west in Utah and to a better life. Even primitive wagon tracks represented what historian Jedediah Rogers called "physical evidence of the Mormons' unquestioning faith in divinely inspired human ingenuity to subdue the land and make it useful to human beings."[6] This led them to give much different meanings to the landscape of southern Utah than the picturesque or sublime interpretations of travelers such as Prudden. The difference would persist throughout the twentieth century and would lead to a great deal of conflict over how the land should be treated.

While the geological and archaeological features of the Desert Southwest drew much interest from amateur and professional scientists, relatively few paid attention to the region's flora and fauna.[7] An exception was Ellen Powell Thompson, sister of John Wesley Powell, who served as the Powell Survey's botanist while based at Kanab in 1872 along with her husband, Almon H. Thompson. She collected numerous plants, some of which now carry her name, while accompanying her colleagues on their various peregrinations throughout the Plateau Province. Her discoveries remained subordinate to the expedition's topographic work, however, and were not well known until her diaries came to light in 1994.[8]

Another pioneering botanist who made important contributions in this field was Alice Eastwood, a largely self-taught scientist-explorer best known for her work in Colorado and California. On a series of trips to the Four Corners area from 1889 to 1895, she made the first systematic observations of the flora of the lower San Juan region, discovering nineteen new plant species and making observations on the ecology and ethnobotany of desert plants—long before either of those fields was well established.[9] In late May 1892, Eastwood journeyed south from the rail station at Thompson Springs, Utah, to the Montezuma Creek area on a trip outfitted by Al Wetherill of Mancos, Colorado. South of Moab, a village that Eastwood described as an oasis of "green fields, lovely orchards, and extensive vineyards," she discovered a new species of gilia that was "worth thirty-five miles [traveling] through the dust and heat. It is one of the most beautiful of the genus, and well deserves the name *superba*, which was bestowed upon it."[10]

Eastwood was seeing the southeastern Utah desert at full bloom, when virtually every forb and shrub was in fragrant flower. Dwarf lupine (*Lupinus pusillus*) "was so abundant over large areas that the earth seemed to mirror the sky," she observed.[11] Although the trip was a reconnaissance, she speculated about how desert conditions affected plant growth, morphology, and seed distribution. Later researchers would uncover the almost unbelievable diversity of plant and animal forms in the Colorado Plateau's seemingly barren landscapes, but they would have a difficult time dispelling the common belief that desert environs were biologically impoverished. Subsequent investigations by biologists such as Walter Cottam, Angus Woodbury, Elzada Clover, and Lois Jotter in the 1930s would add to this storehouse of knowledge about the high desert environment, helping to create a baseline for later studies of changing ecological conditions in the national parks.[12]

By the turn of the twentieth century, the Utah canyon country had been mapped at a general scale, but knowledge of its geologic structure remained incomplete. In 1915, the U.S. Geological Survey assigned Herbert Gregory, who had recently completed a geologic and hydrographic reconnaissance of the Navajo Indian Reservation, to continue his studies farther north in Utah. An erudite and knowledgeable traveler as well as an accomplished scientist, Gregory held a professorship in geology at Yale University. Following his Navajo Reservation work, he undertook six overland traverses through the canyon country of the Colorado Plateau, intending to fill the gaps in knowledge left by the Powell and Wheeler Surveys. As well as delineating geologic faults and formations, he and his colleague Raymond Moore examined prospects for agriculture, mining, and petroleum development in the remote hinterland surrounding Glen Canyon.

Gregory's 1915 reconnaissance began at Lees Ferry on the Colorado River, traversed the benches and canyons on the north side of Glen Canyon to Dandy Crossing, and then headed southeast up White Canyon past Natural Bridges National Monument. He continued his work in 1918 out of Green River, Utah, examining the San Rafael Swell, the Waterpocket

[handwritten margin note: AT HITE]

Fold, the Escalante River canyons, and the vast Kaiparowits Plateau, parts of which (as he wrote in a 1931 monograph coauthored with Moore) had been seen by white people only within the last ten years. Moore joined him in 1921 to examine possible oil fields in the Circle Cliffs, an isolated part of the Escalante River drainage where the Ohio Oil Company was drilling an unsuccessful well. In 1922 he and Moore examined the coal deposits of the Kaiparowits Plateau, and in 1925 and 1927 he extended his research eastward through the Glen Canyon and San Juan River regions.[13]

Though there was little romance in Gregory's writing, he was clearly as fascinated with this country as his predecessor, Clarence Dutton. Describing the "terraced plateaus, cliff-bound mesas, monoclinal ridges, and straight-sided canyons" of the Kaiparowits Plateau, he noted that "features in the landscape unnoticed here would be prominent and picturesque landmarks in other surroundings."[14] Besides mapping geology, Gregory took an interest in the region's inhabitants, hoping that scientific knowledge could be used to improve water supplies and perhaps open new mines and oil fields. The lack of decent roads was the paramount difficulty; the few routes that connected the region's villages to the outside world "are in reality trails with alternating stretches of sand, bare rock, and steep inclines over which a skillful driver may conduct a strongly built, lightly loaded wagon."[15]

Gregory could offer little encouragement for further settlement of this region, owing chiefly to its unpredictable rainfall. "In exceptionally dry years the only water received by the Colorado between the Escalante River and the Paria River is probably contained in the liquid mud supplied by the San Juan," he wrote.[16] The villages of Paria and Adairville along the Paria River east of Kanab subsisted and even grew during the 1870s, but flooding in 1883 and 1884 washed away most of the farmers' land. By 1920 the entire region had reached its maximum population—2,164 souls divided among the villages of Escalante, Boulder, Tropic, Henrieville, and Cannonville, with perhaps 8 more hanging on in Paria.[17]

Despite the region's sparse population, its human inhabitants were leaving their mark. Gregory noted that by 1922, cattle and sheep ranges that had generally been in good condition during his earlier traverses of the Kaiparowits region were now heavily grazed, and that by 1924, "no grass or browse of any kind was found in unfenced areas of the Butler Valley and about Canaan Peak."[18] He believed that the heavy use of the range was responsible for the rampaging creeks and rivers that bedeviled homesteaders in the region.

Gregory called for government regulation of rangelands, which would not come until 1934 with the passage of the Taylor Grazing Act. This law set up individual grazing allotments on the public domain, which amounted to permanent leaseholds for area ranchers. During the 1930s, efforts to create new national parks and monuments in southern Utah would run afoul of these interests.

Economic geology was a key focus of Gregory and Moore's work. They outlined extensive coal outcrops in the Straight Cliffs and on the Kaiparowits Plateau but noted that they were too inaccessible to represent a significant economic resource. This would remain the case until the 1960s, when utility companies in the Southwest would eye the plateau as the site of a major coal-fired power plant. Nor did anything in the way of petroleum materialize for another half century, when a small oil field was located west of Escalante. The gold excitement in Glen Canyon had played out by the time Gregory visited, leaving little prospect of boom times in Utah's canyon country.

Utah's canyon country was as hard and unyielding as a cliff of Wingate Sandstone, as Gregory's field studies made clear. In describing his arduous days in the field, the lack of water, the poor roads, and the heavy hand of humanity that was already in evidence, he broke with the Romanticism displayed by scientists such as J. S. Newberry and Clarence Dutton a generation or two earlier. Their pioneering surveys of the Colorado Plateau spun newly developed understandings of geologic time and Darwinian biology into what Stephen Pyne calls "a vista of cultural, spiritual, and moral evolution by humans and their institutions."[19] Gregory's approach was more in the spirit of John Wesley Powell's cold-eyed assessment of the Plateau Province in his *Report on the Lands of the Arid Region of the United States*, published in 1878. These lands were, and would remain, difficult to make bloom. The limiting conditions of water, soil, topography, and minerals that T. Mitchell Prudden, Alice Eastwood, and Herbert Gregory observed formed an unyielding bedrock that even the most enterprising Mormon settlers could not overcome.

Given such conditions, it was to be expected that the residents of towns and villages at the edge of southern Utah's canyon lands would evaluate proposed national parks for what they might contribute to their own lives—especially as a means of improving roads and bringing in tourist dollars. This orientation would take shape first in Utah's Dixie region, where farmers and other small-scale entrepreneurs realized that they could supplement their meager incomes by accommodating travelers on their way to the North Rim of the Grand Canyon and the gorge of the North Fork of the Virgin River. Soon the call went out for better roads into this wonderful canyon, which Powell had named Mukuntuweap. In this great valley, aesthetics would merge with economic imperatives to give Utah its first and most famous national park.

6

DESERT YOSEMITE

More than a century ago, the great canyon of the North Fork of the Virgin River spoke wonders to scientists, travelers, and local inhabitants alike. If their reasons for coming to this canyon differed, each found a unique splendor in its towering sandstone cliffs and fern-lined grottoes. Named Mukuntuweap by John Wesley Powell, and called Little Zion by its Latter-day Saint settlers, the canyon's walls enclosed scenes of intimate beauty. Graceful cottonwoods lined the river bottom, keeping the summer heat at bay, while delicate vegetation ringed dripping springs and plunge pools. Zion Canyon was said to surpass Yosemite in sheer scenic magnificence, and it was easy to see why. One wanted to linger in this sheltering desert Eden, a place that seemed set apart from the outside world.

An early resident of Springdale named Isaac Behunin found the verdant canyon bottom both useful and beautiful. In 1863, he built a one-room cabin of cottonwood logs near the site of the present-day Zion Lodge, which he and his family used as a summer farm. Several other families joined them, forming a tiny settlement that Behunin called Zion. To him, the canyon suggested a place of refuge, a sanctuary where one might turn one's thoughts toward higher things. Old-timers recalled that sometimes he would just sit outside his cabin and admire the scenery. Referring to the Mormon temple that was under construction in Salt Lake City, he was reported to have said, "Here we have natural temples. We can worship as we please."[1]

Behunin appears to have taken seriously the idea of a spiritual refuge in the desert, calling the canyon "Little Zion" in deference to the greater Zion of Salt Lake City. The name displeased Brigham Young, the Latter-day Saints' leader, who visited the canyon in the spring of 1870. Observing Behunin's tobacco plants behind his cabin, he supposedly remarked, "No, no, not

Zion, Zion is the pure in heart."[2] Nonetheless, "Little Zion" remained in use within Utah well into the twentieth century.

By the early 1900s, Zion Canyon was attracting travelers from afar who found in it a refuge from the noise and industry of the modern world. Zion National Park, established in 1919, became a secular version of the religious pilgrimage sites that were common in Europe. Writers and publicists frequently referred to its towering walls as temples or shrines.[3] The present-day national park abounds with names with religious or spiritual significance—Western Temple, Towers of the Virgin, Cathedral Mountain, and Court of the Patriarchs, among others.

Investing spectacular natural features with numinous or spiritual qualities, even if in name only, placed them apart from more utilitarian landscapes and made it possible to reserve them as national parks—an effort that a number of businesspeople in Utah's "Dixie" region would earnestly support. In doing so they essentially ratified the federal government's displacement of the Mormon pastoralists who had used the canyon for decades—to say nothing of the indigenous Paiute Indians who had made use of it for centuries.[4] For all the religious imagery found in Zion Canyon, pecuniary interests—chiefly the desire to stimulate tourism and upgrade the regional road system—lay behind the establishment of Utah's first national park. The spiritual qualities of Zion's stunning rock forms could be marshaled to serve practical interests. This modern vision would take decades to develop and would depend heavily on the financial backing of the Union Pacific Railroad. Through its advertisements and the rapturous accounts of dozens of awestruck travelers, Utah would gain a natural wonder of world renown.

Humans have inhabited the land along the Virgin River more or less continuously for thousands of years. Members of the Southern Paiute Tribe believe it to be part of their homeland since they were created as a people; most anthropological accounts hold that they moved into the area around 1100–1200 AD, perhaps intermingling with the Puebloan people then in residence.[5] Although little has been recorded showing how Paiute people used Zion Canyon itself, it is clear from recent interviews of living tribal members that their ancestors made frequent use of the canyon and surrounding lands for hunting deer and other mammals, gathering edible and medicinal plants, and probably farming as well. They were not afraid of the canyon, as depicted in stories circulated by some of the early Mormon settlers.[6] Certainly they would have witnessed rockfalls and landslides, which are common in the canyon; a respect for these forces, as embodied in the coyote-like trickster spirit they called Kinesava, would have come naturally to these dwellers in the land.

By the late 1860s, the Paiutes were experiencing great hardship throughout the Virgin River region owing to the fencing of rangelands and introduction of cattle by the new settlers, as well as the removal of pinyon pine, a key Paiute food source, for the settlers' firewood.[7] Their numbers had already been reduced significantly from conflicts with other, horse-mounted Indian tribes, as well as by the diseases that swept through Native populations as a result of Euro-American entry into North America. When Latter-day Saint settlers began to expand into Utah's "Dixie" region in the 1850s and 1860s, they encountered a people already living under great stress.[8]

In the early 1860s, after establishing towns at Virgin City and Grafton, settlers continued to work their way upriver, founding Rockville, Springdale, and several other villages such as Northrup and Shunesburg that did not last into the modern era. All of the Mormon villages along the upper Virgin except Rockville were abandoned around 1866 during the conflict with Ute, Navajo, and other Native American tribes known as the Black Hawk War. Settlement of the upper canyon resumed in 1879 when Rockville resident William R. Crawford purchased land at the mouth of Oak Creek, building a homestead where he and his family would live until the 1930s. Other parts of the canyon were used for pasturage and raising crops until shortly after the establishment of Zion National Park in 1919. This long history of human use defined the canyon as something other than a wilderness, which may partly account for the benign, welcoming imagery so many writers have used in describing it.

Unlike in the interior of Utah's canyon country, the settlement of Zion Canyon mostly preceded official government exploration and mapping. Early explorers of the West, from the Domínguez-Escalante party of 1776 to John C. Frémont in 1844, passed through southern Utah without investigating the canyons of the upper Virgin. John Wesley Powell explored the headwaters of the Virgin River in 1872 with a few of his men, making a descent of the river's East Fork through the deep defile he named Parunuweap. Powell must have heard of the local name for Zion Canyon, but he generally favored Native terms and settled on "Mu-Koon-Tu-weap" (later simplified to

Mukuntuweap), a conjoined word that was perhaps an unfortunate choice.[9] "Tuweap" refers to a valley or place in the Paiute language, while "Mukun" may have referred to the canyon's straightness, its roaring waters, a yucca plant found within it, or even the name of a Paiute headman.[10] The name never was popular, although it did recognize the long Paiute presence in and around the canyon.

Unlike the reports and photographs from F. V. Hayden's 1871 visit to the Yellowstone, which aided its designation as a national park the following year, the published work of the Powell Survey did not immediately lead to calls for setting aside Zion Canyon or its surroundings. This was not for want of vivid depictions of the landscape. In 1873, Powell invited landscape painter Thomas Moran, whose stunning canvas of the Grand Canyon of the Yellowstone significantly bolstered efforts to pass park legislation, to make a visit to the Grand Canyon of the Colorado River. Along the way Moran, accompanied by *New York Times* correspondent Justin Colburn, made a brief foray into the sheer-walled canyons draining the Kolob Terrace east of Kanarraville, as well as a longer excursion into the Mukuntuweap. Moran's sketches became the basis for several large paintings, including *The Cliffs of the Rio Virgin*, which depicted the Western Temple above Rockville, and *Valley of Babbling Waters*, a watercolor that was displayed in a portfolio of his western paintings in 1876. An idealized view of the huge monoliths of the main canyon of the Mukuntuweap, it reveals why Moran felt that "for glory of scenery and stupendous scenic effects [Zion] cannot be surpassed."[11]

Colburn, too, was dazzled by the valley's crags and temples, which he described as "vast arches, cathedrals, columned temples, monuments and gates so perfect that the forms are recognizable without any aid from fancy."[12] To him the valley compared favorably with Yosemite, then the standard for scenery in the West. Colburn's *New York Times* article was likely the first description of the Mukuntuweap to appear in a major newspaper. Woodcut engravings from Moran's field sketches appeared in *The Aldine*, a New York art magazine, in April 1875.

Moran was not the first artist to visit the stunning gorge of the North Fork. Around 1870 or 1871, a self-taught Salt Lake City painter named Alfred Lambourne explored and sketched in the canyon, possibly as part

Thomas Moran, *Valley of Babbling Waters, Southern Utah*. Chromolithograph by L. Prang Company, ca. 1876. *Library of Congress Prints and Photographs Division, Washington, D.C.*

of Brigham Young's party; he may have suggested the trip to Moran. Lambourne returned in 1875 with his friend Charles R. Savage, a Salt Lake City photographer, and later that year completed *Mu-Kun-Tu-Weap Valley, Rio Virgin, Utah*, the first painting of the canyon by a Utah artist.[13] Lambourne's *Temples of the Rio Virgin, Southern Utah* was exhibited the following year at the American centennial exhibition in Philadelphia.

Savage had visited Zion Canyon in 1870 in company with Brigham Young and took what are apparently the first photographs of the canyon. Two years later Jack Hillers, a photographer with the Powell Survey, brought back some well-composed images as well.[14] None of these visual depictions managed to stir the kind of national interest that greeted William Henry Jackson's photos of Yellowstone or Charles Weed's and Carleton Watkins's photographs of Yosemite. Zion Canyon lay too far off the usual western routes of travel, a destination for knowledgeable travelers willing to go to some lengths for new scenery.

Words could depict the landscape of the upper Virgin as brilliantly as oils, and in 1880 Clarence Dutton brought his gifts of geological expression to the stair-stepped topography that lay north of the Mukuntuweap. Standing on the southwestern edge of the Markagunt Plateau at nearly eleven thousand feet above sea level, Dutton gazed out over "numberless rock-forms of nameless shapes, but often grotesque and ludicrous, starting up from the earth as isolated freaks of carving or standing in clusters and rows along the white walls of sandstone."[15] His perspective was from above, whereas Colburn and Moran had gazed up from beneath the massive sandstone cliffs of the Kolob Terrace, which remained the usual tourist's view.

One of the deepest clefts in the entire Zion plateau was the Narrows of the North Fork of the Virgin River, so named by the geologist G. K. Gilbert, who made the first recorded descent in 1872 during his explorations with the Wheeler Survey. He found that "many times our upward view was completely cut off by the interlocking of the walls, which, remaining nearly parallel to each other, warped in and out as they ascended." Gilbert called the Narrows "the most wonderful defile it has been my fortune to behold."[16]

Despite these glowing descriptions, Zion Canyon was largely overshadowed by the attention given to the Grand Canyon, where hostelries were already serving tourists at the South Rim. In 1901 the Atchison, Topeka and Santa Fe Railway completed a spur line from Williams to the rim, where several hotels were already operating. Four years later it opened the elegant El Tovar hotel at the very edge of the canyon, stealing a march on Utah boosters who hoped to popularize the canyon's North Rim as a destination for tourists arriving by rail from Ogden or Salt Lake City.

With no prospects for a direct rail connection to Zion Canyon, civic promoters in Cedar City, St. George, and Kanab turned their attention to road improvements. It would take years, however, before the unsurfaced, rutted, and often abysmally muddy road leading up the Virgin River was made ready for normal automobile travel. Isolated in its rockbound glory, Zion Canyon remained out of reach to most tourists until 1917, when a graded dirt road was extended as far as Weeping Rock and the Wylie Way company opened a tent camp near the present-day Zion Lodge.

Zion Canyon first received significant national attention in 1904, when Frederick Dellenbaugh, who had joined Major Powell's second Colorado River expedition at the age of seventeen as an artist and assistant topographer, published an article titled "A New Valley of Wonders" in *Scribner's Magazine*.

Dellenbaugh had visited the Mukuntuweap with the Powell Survey in 1876 but did not return until 1903. That spring he and two companions drove a covered wagon up the Virgin River past the villages of Virgin City, Grafton, and Rockville, savoring the grand procession of cliffs and towers rising around them. Mount Kinesava, which he called the "Great Temple of the Virgin," stood "unique, sublime, adamantine" above the river valley.[17]

Dellenbaugh had spent considerable time in the Mormon outposts of southern Utah, and on this trip he paid close attention to the living conditions of the local inhabitants. He admired their irrigated fields and orchards of "grapes, peaches, almonds, figs, pomegranates, melons, etc., of choicest flavor." The verdant farms contrasted with the spiny desert vegetation, which seemed ready to retake any untended land. Presciently, Dellenbaugh observed how "the world here still seems in the making, and humanity scarcely sheltered from the blows of Nature's sledge." The residents of Rockville would experience dangerous landslides and rockfalls throughout the next century; the cliffs that induced rapture in visitors sometimes shed a deadly burden.

By 1903, human settlement and pasturage had worked into every corner of the Virgin River drainage. At Oak Creek, near the site of the present-day Zion Human History Museum, Dellenbaugh found plowed fields belonging to the Crawford family extending nearly from cliff to cliff. He would depict these fields in lush greenery in a painting he made later that year.[18] Farther up the canyon they came across the spectacular cable works that a young Springdale resident named David Flanigan had erected on the east rim to lower lumber to the valley floor. This was not the remote wastes of the San Juan River or the otherworldly Rainbow Plateau, although like Alfred Lambourne thirty years earlier, Dellenbaugh and his friends had the upper canyon to themselves. Cattle had heavily grazed most of its pastures, and with their horses wanting for feed, they returned reluctantly to Springdale.

Dellenbaugh's panorama of Zion Canyon was displayed at the 1904 World's Fair in St. Louis, where it attracted considerable attention. Historian Angus Woodbury related how Rockville resident David Hirschi visited the fair and was surprised to hear onlookers question whether such a gorgeous scene actually existed. Hirschi drew a crowd when he pointed to a hillside in Dellenbaugh's painting where he had shot a deer and showed the amazed onlookers his buckskin shoelaces as proof.[19]

Even with the growing interest in Zion Canyon, its first recognition as a federal reserve came by happenstance, after a group of ranchers living near the canyon asked the General Land Office to conduct a survey to identify parcels of public land for disposal. Undertaken in 1908, the survey was led by Leo Snow, a deputy GLO surveyor from St. George, and included Angus Woodbury, who was then working as a ranger on the Dixie National Forest (he would go on to become Zion National Park's first naturalist and historian). Climbing to the high platform now known as Observation Point, they enjoyed views that, in Snow's opinion, were surpassed only by those of the Grand Canyon. Snow recommended to his superiors in the Interior Department that the main canyon be designated as a national park, but Secretary Richard Ballinger opted for a national monument, which required no action by Congress. On July 31, 1909, President William Howard Taft signed a proclamation under the Antiquities Act establishing Mukuntuweap National Monument, Utah's second such designation.[20]

The 15,200-acre monument took in little of the plateau lands surrounding the canyon, and it was dwarfed by the 808,120-acre national monument that Taft's predecessor, Teddy Roosevelt, had established at Grand Canyon only nine months before. Roosevelt wanted to secure Arizona's great wonder against further proliferation of commercial enterprises such as mining claims, new hotels, and dubious homesteads. Fitful settlement had been going on in Zion Canyon since the 1860s, and ranchers from Cedar City and elsewhere grazed sheep, horses, and cattle throughout the surrounding plateaus, but despite the heavily used range and the watershed damage that was occurring, there seemed to be less urgency to create a large, landscape-level federal reservation. Unlike in the Grand Canyon or Yellowstone, Zion's scenic allure was concentrated within a single, compact gorge, so reserving it from commercial development would inconvenience only a few settlers, who in any event would be allowed to graze their livestock in the canyon bottom for another decade.

No federal appropriations were made for the new monument in Zion Canyon, nor was a custodian appointed to watch over it. Agents of the General Land Office who came to inspect the monument had to lodge with local families and hire wagons to get there.[21] Lacking a decent access road, Mukuntuweap languished out of the public's view, awaiting the publicity and funding that only designation as a national park could bring. Still, its designation represented a change from a landscape of utility to one of wonder and enchantment—a bargain that most civic leaders in Utah were happy to make.

7

SEE AMERICA—AND
ESPECIALLY UTAH—FIRST

In contrast to the remote national monuments at Natural Bridges and Rainbow Bridge, the Mukuntuweap lay at the edge of Mormon settlement in Utah's Dixie region. Its future as a tourism magnet was still years away, however. No rail line reached closer than ninety miles to Springdale, and the wagon road that threaded up the Virgin River valley was in no shape to receive automobile traffic. The first auto to reach the monument, driven in 1912 by Rockville native Elmer Stout, had to take a circuitous route over a mountain pass to the southwest in order to avoid the multiple river crossings along the usual road.[1]

It would take the combined efforts of tourism promoters in southwestern Utah and in Salt Lake City, backed by the financial muscle of the Union Pacific (UP) Railroad, before Zion Canyon—still called "Little Zion" by most Utahns—welcomed significant numbers of tourists. This was a story of cooperation between Utah tourism boosters, state officials, the UP and its subsidiaries, and the National Park Service, including its first two directors, Stephen Mather and Horace Albright. Their success demonstrated that tourism had a strong future in southern Utah's scenic lands.

Up until this time, Utah's major tourist draw was not a geologic feature in its southern canyon lands, but Salt Lake City itself. Henry T. Williams's popular guidebook *The Pacific Tourist*, first published in 1876, listed Utah's capital city as an important stop for travelers on the Union Pacific's Overland Route. Disembarking at Ogden for the short ride south on the Utah Central Railroad, visitors could take in the much-advertised Mormon Temple, the Assembly Hall, and the Great Salt Lake west of town. When Williams extolled "the sublimities of Colorado, the Rocky Mountains, canons of Utah [sic], and the Sierra Nevada," he was not suggesting a visit to the red-rock wonders of southeastern

Utah; he was referring to Weber and Ogden Canyons along the UP line, which set the standard for local scenery.[2] It would be several decades before significant numbers of tourists made their way south to see Utah's *other* canyons.

Tourists arriving on the Union Pacific's trains could also head north to Yellowstone National Park via the Oregon Short Line, which eventually linked Ogden to West Yellowstone, Montana. A southern rail connection to California was completed in 1905 when the UP opened the San Pedro, Los Angeles and Salt Lake Railroad, known as the Salt Lake Route, which ran through Utah's westernmost desert. Passengers wishing to visit Zion Canyon had to arrange for a wagon team to meet them at the rail stop in Lund, a forlorn desert outpost thirty miles northwest of Cedar City.[3] With no regularly scheduled transportation available to either Zion Canyon or the North Rim of the Grand Canyon, these scenic destinations lay beyond the reach of all but the most enterprising travelers.

Tourism promoters in southern Utah worked to improve access to these natural wonders, sometimes taking up subscriptions from fellow business owners and other townspeople to pay for needed roadwork. Much of the impetus for better roads, however, came from Salt Lake City's Commercial Club, the forerunner of its chamber of commerce. The club led efforts to improve the state's transportation infrastructure as well as to awaken interest in the state's scenic resources, sponsoring ventures such as Henry Culmer's 1905 expedition to the natural bridges of White Canyon. That same year, the Commercial Club's secretary, a former hotel manager named Fisher S. Harris, developed an ambitious vision of how the western states could work together to attract tourists to what was eventually known as the "grand circle" of southwestern parks and monuments.

The key was scenery—*American* scenery. In 1905, Harris circulated a letter to railroad officials and business leaders across the nation, asking whether some part of the $150 million Americans were spending on trips to Europe could be kept at home. "As conditions now stand," he wrote, "many of our people are heard raving over the beauty of the Trossachs, the glory of the Rhine, the magnificence of the Alps, who have never seen and have but small conception of the grandeur of the Rocky Mountains or the splendor of the Columbia River." Harris coined a slogan for his new campaign: "See Europe If You Must, But See America First."[4]

The Commercial Club adopted Harris's idea and announced a national convention, to be held in Salt Lake City the following January, to promote a program of domestic incentives to tourism. Invitations went to the governors of each state, various business organizations, and four thousand newspapers. The response was enthusiastic, and on January 25, 1906, amid a blanket of chilly fog, 125 individuals representing thirteen states convened in Salt Lake's National Guard armory to call on Americans to get to know more of their own country—and to spend their dollars here.

Harris was elected to lead the new See America First League and that summer embarked on a nationwide speaking tour. Meeting with railroad executives at a national convention in Chicago that July, he urged a coordinated campaign to direct Americans' attention to its homegrown attractions. He also helped found the *Western Monthly*, a Salt Lake City periodical that served as the league's official organ and featured his monthly column titled "Scenic America."[5] Harris's death in 1909 interrupted the league's work, but chambers of commerce, railroad passenger agents, excursion companies, and civic organizations throughout the West continued to tout the advantages of their local scenery. The outbreak of war in Europe in 1914 fortuitously redirected many Americans to explore domestic attractions, and as the nation prepared to enter the conflict in 1917, some observers pointed out that citizens who traveled the country's length and breadth and took in its magnificent sights would patriotically choose to fight for it as well.[6]

A journey along southern Utah's back roads promised not only stunning scenery but considerable adventure, as the Commercial Club's Wesley King discovered on a visit to Mukuntuweap National Monument with his wife in the summer of 1911. Traveling by wagon and accompanied by Kanab guide Dave Rust, the Kings came under the spell of Zion's sheer walls and verdant glades. But as King wrote in an article for the *Salt Lake Tribune*, poor roads made it difficult to see this magnificent place. Washington and Iron Counties possessed "great natural resources and wonderful possibilities which will blossom into realities only when the transportation problem has been solved. Each county can do little by itself in road building."[7]

As late as 1912 the entire state of Utah had just sixty-eight miles of paved macadam or concrete roads.[8] Rural roadwork, as King noted, was largely up to each county, resulting in a patchwork of unsurfaced roads, passable in some places but exceedingly rough or muddy in others, with nary a gas station or repair shop for miles. The autos themselves were prone to break-downs, and stranded tourists were often forced to call for help at nearby ranches and farms.

The need to bring America's roads out of the wagon-rut days had been evident since the 1880s, when farmers and mail carriers joined enthusiasts of the new sport of bicycling in what was termed the "Good Roads" movement. Initially centered in the populous northeastern states, where farmers needed better means of taking produce to market, the movement spread west after the first autos began making inroads into places traditionally served by horse and wagon. In 1905 the Utah legislature petitioned Congress, unsuccessfully, for a $250,000 appropriation to improve the state's roadways. A Good Roads convention held in Salt Lake City in 1909 brought forth a proposal for a $3 million state bond to fund road construction, but this ran into opposition from budget conservatives and, ironically, from farmers who did not want the new "motors" traveling on roadways they used for hauling crops and driving livestock.[9]

To help smooth the tourists' path, the *Salt Lake Tribune* and *Deseret News* published detailed road logs for tourists wishing to visit Yellowstone, Zion Canyon, or other scenic destinations on their own. W. D. "Bill" Rishel, a former bicycle racer from Salt Lake City, logged numerous "Pathfinder" trips for the *Tribune*, including a trek to the North Rim of the Grand Canyon in 1913. In 1916, he added Zion Canyon to his itinerary, although his car broke down thirty miles from Hurricane and had to be towed by horse team into town. During the two-week wait for parts, Rishel and his party took in the sights of Little Zion by horse and wagon.[10]

The need for improved road access became clear to a group of Union Pacific passenger agents who visited Zion Canyon in October 1913 to scope out a commercial touring operation based from the rail stop at Lund. Utah governor William Spry joined the party, as did representatives of the Wylie Permanent Camping Company, which operated tent camps in Yellowstone. Excited residents along the Virgin River rode with the party into the canyon they were still calling Little Zion, where horse and wagon were the only conveyance. At Weeping Rock, Spry watched from a safe spot as a man rode the lumber cable to the rim and back; afterward the party rode horses into the Narrows of the Virgin River.

Governor Spry gave speeches extolling the beauty of the canyon and predicted it would become a great tourist attraction. But Howard Hays of the Wylie Company injected a note of realism in an article for the *Salt Lake Tribune*, cautioning that while the Mukuntuweap might be more beautiful than Yosemite, "only modern highways will earn for it such recognition. This is an age that demands comfortable and rapid travel."[11] Spry returned in the summer of 1916 with another party of UP agents and a representative of Raymond and Whitcomb, a Boston tour company that catered to the eastern elite. Sixteen eager youths, most of whom had never seen an auto, crammed into their ten-passenger touring car to ride as far as Springdale. One railroad official ventured that with further improvements, as many as twenty to twenty-five Salt Lake tourists might visit Little Zion every day.[12]

Zion Canyon would not get its hoped-for road until 1917, after Utah senator Reed Smoot obtained a $15,000 federal appropriation for road improvements within Mukuntuweap National Monument. Construction began in November 1916, and by the start of the 1917 season crews had finished a graded dirt road as far as Cable Mountain.[13] It was the largest such appropriation for any Utah park unit to that date, exceeding the entire budget for the Park Service's national monuments in the Southwest. According to historian Hal Rothman, this largesse was possible only because Stephen Mather envisioned the Mukuntuweap soon becoming a national park. Zion was a key part of his plan for a circuit of southwestern national parks, each connected by a good road.[14] Smoot's appropriation was a harbinger of the dominant role Washington would play in developing roads to the nation's parks.

Two enterprising brothers from Cedar City were the first to take advantage of the opportunity the new road presented. Twenty-eight-year-old Gronway Parry was a former county agricultural agent who sold cars and managed a hotel on the side; his younger brother Chauncey helped at the hotel and ran an auto shuttle from the hotel to St. George. Chauncey served as guide for a road survey crew working in Zion Canyon during the fall and winter of 1915–16, where he observed the crew's enthusiasm for Zion's scenery. Realizing that the canyon could support a tour business, he and Gronway applied for a concession to transport visitors from the rail stop at Lund to the monument.[15]

J. H. Manderfield, a UP passenger agent who had accompanied Governor Spry on his two visits to Zion, put the brothers in touch with William W. Wylie, the originator of the "Wylie Way" tent camps in Yellowstone. Now retired and living in Pasadena, Wylie was interested in a new venture and, with a $13,000 advance from the Union Pacific, agreed to open a camp in the Mukuntuweap. He joined with the Parry brothers to form the National Park Transportation and Camping Company, which offered the first regular auto service and overnight facilities in Zion Canyon. The Parrys ferried tourists from Lund to the camp in a seven-passenger Hudson and a Model T Ford, taking an entire day for the ninety-mile journey. The cost was $26.50 for the round trip, including lunches in Cedar City and two nights at the Wylie camp, meals provided.

Located halfway up the canyon in a shady grotto just south of the present-day Zion Lodge, the Wylie camp was patterned after Yellowstone's, with colorfully striped tent cabins arranged in a semicircle, and offering lodging and meals at six dollars a night. Fresh fruit and vegetables from local families graced tables in the central dining hall, with entertainment provided at the camp lodge. Cabins were equipped with wooden floors, a small stove, and rudimentary furniture. The operation catered to those who "appreciate a 'homey' atmosphere, not too familiar and not too distant," according to a publicist for the Salt Lake Route.[16]

Both Wylie and the Parrys received substantial financial aid from the railroad to buy needed equipment and vehicles, but without a closer rail connection to deliver tourists to the monument, it was a financially risky venture.[17] For the next eight years tourists to Little Zion would be served by these small-scale entrepreneurs, who relinquished their operations only after the Park Service decreed that national park concessions would be in the hands of larger corporate entities that offered a higher standard of service.

The Colorado Plateau's geologic wonders were not limited to cliffs, canyons, and natural bridges; its Mesozoic and Tertiary strata concealed significant paleontological treasures as well. Federally sponsored surveys beginning with John C. Frémont in 1845 had found fossil remains throughout southeastern and northeastern Utah. In 1859, J. S. Newberry of the Macomb expedition had collected fossil bones from a partially exposed sauropod skeleton in a canyon east of the Colorado River. It was the first such discovery from the now-famous Morrison Formation.

The Uinta Basin became a well-known fossil-collecting locality following the pioneering work of Othniel C. Marsh of Yale University in the 1870s. Local residents and scientists representing natural history museums

Workers remove a fossil bone from the Carnegie dinosaur quarry east of Vernal, Utah. In 1915 President Wilson designated the quarry area as Utah's fourth national monument. *Used by permission, Utah State Historical Society.*

in Chicago and New York found dinosaur fossils in the Morrison Formation, but the most significant find came in the summer of 1909, when Earl Douglass, a forty-four-year-old geologist working for the Carnegie Museum of Pittsburgh, discovered a rich locality east of Vernal, Utah. Searching the dry washes and hillslopes near the Green River below Split Mountain, he came across "eight of the tail bones of a Brontosaurus in exact position. It was a beautiful sight."[18] Further excavations uncovered an astonishing trove of Jurassic fossil dinosaur bones that would yield beautiful specimens for the next fifteen years. The *Vernal Express* described the partially exposed skeleton, which turned out to be seventy-one feet long, as "the most immense creature that ever roamed the tropical forests. It was there in its entirety except for part of its tail, and Mr. Douglas [*sic*] found that a few feet away."[19]

Douglass soon found additional sauropod specimens at the site, leading the Carnegie Museum to fund his ongoing work at the quarry. The find drew hundreds of curious onlookers from Vernal and the surrounding area, including tours of schoolchildren. Before long, visitors from as far as California were braving poor roads to witness this extraordinary sight. To secure the museum's discovery, Douglass filed mining claims on and around the site, terming the fossils "stone for quarry purposes."[20] After four years of deliberations and equivocations, the Interior Department rejected the claims and instead drew up a proclamation establishing the quarry site as a national monument. This was accomplished on October 4, 1915, with the signature of President Woodrow Wilson.

Dinosaur National Monument, at eighty acres in size, became Utah's fourth and smallest national monument. At the recommendation of the Interior Department's General Land Office, the monument proclamation gave the Carnegie Museum exclusive rights to continue excavation at the quarry as a scientific endeavor under the Antiquities Act. Fossil shipments to Pittsburgh continued until 1924, when excavations ended and Douglass resigned his position with the museum.[21] Douglass's original find, now termed *Apatosaurus*, was mounted in the Carnegie Museum's Hall of Vertebrate Paleontology, complete with a head that was later determined to belong to a different species of dinosaur.

A temporary shelter was erected over the site in the 1950s, anticipating the construction of a visitor center to give tourists an up-close look at the exposed quarry. The strikingly modern Quarry Visitor Center, built under the Park Service's Mission 66 program of park improvements, opened in June 1958 and would remain a popular attraction.[22] By this time Dinosaur National Monument had been vastly expanded, reflecting the broader purposes of the Antiquities Act as a tool of landscape preservation. Paleontology would surface again in 1996 as one of the justifications for designating Grand Staircase–Escalante National Monument.

8

A GREAT AND BEAUTIFUL
PLAYGROUND

For more than four decades after the creation of Yellowstone National Park in 1872, the Interior Department administered the national parks with little guidance from Congress as to which uses would be allowed in them. National monuments received even less attention; many of them, including the four in Utah, initially lacked on-site caretakers or any budget for improvements. Conflicts inevitably arose with resource users who assumed they held prior rights to park lands. Livestock grazing was ongoing in Mesa Verde, Yosemite, and Sequoia, dams and reservoirs were proposed within Yellowstone and other parks, and in many parks tour operators worked virtually without restriction, often erecting substandard facilities and competing with each other for the tourist's dollar.[1]

Attempts to put the system to rights came as early as 1900, when Iowa congressman John Lacey introduced legislation to create a bureau of national parks within the Interior Department. In 1911 Utah senator Reed Smoot, a Republican who had supported President Roosevelt's establishment of national forests, introduced a similar bill.[2] The legislation attracted support from many of the key players in the nation's Progressive conservation movement, including J. Horace McFarland of the American Civic Association, who worked closely with Congress and the Interior Department to promote such a bureau. Mary Belle King Sherman spearheaded grassroots efforts on behalf of the 2.5-million-member General Federation of Women's Clubs, which had been active in promoting better forest practices and other Progressive causes such as federally funded irrigation. Women's clubs were broadly represented throughout America, and although most women lacked the right to vote, the federation's publicity efforts proved crucial to getting the legislation passed.[3]

Stephen T. Mather and Horace M. Albright; the first two directors of the National Park Service. Both men visited Utah often and took particular interest in Zion and Bryce Canyon National Parks. *National Park Service.*

The nation's rail lines, too, lent their considerable influence to the cause. In 1916 the Union Pacific, Great Northern, Santa Fe, and fourteen other rail lines underwrote publication of the *National Parks Portfolio,* a handsomely bound edition of photographs of the national parks created by Robert Sterling Yard, a New York newspaperman and friend of Stephen Mather who joined his staff in 1915. The book was an important lobbying tool in the battle to pass the Park Service bill, with Mather arranging for copies to be given to every member of Congress. Ultimately 350,000 copies were printed and distributed; Mary Sherman provided Mather with a mailing list of 275,000 names from her organization.[4]

These efforts proved sufficient to overcome budget concerns and opposition from western livestock interests, which had held up the needed organic legislation. On July 1, 1916, the House of Representatives passed a Park Service bill sponsored by William Kent of California. It permitted livestock grazing within the national parks, which Reed Smoot opposed. Smoot was able to amend the bill in committee to restrict grazing in most of the national parks, which he considered necessary to avoid the denudation of mountain slopes that was creating havoc with watersheds throughout the West. This provision was removed in the conference committee that was called to reconcile the differing House and Senate versions of the bill.[5] Livestock use would remain a contentious issue in adopting new park proposals throughout the twentieth century.

The Act of August 25, 1916, known as the National Park Service Organic Act, established the National Park Service and placed it in charge of the more than forty national parks and monuments then in existence. Stephen T. Mather, a Californian who had grown wealthy in the borax mining business, was named as its director. Mather joined the Interior Department in 1915 at the invitation of Interior Secretary Franklin Lane, who wanted a man with considerable energy and charisma to organize the new bureau. An avid mountaineer, Mather had taken a keen interest in the fledgling national parks of the West and drew Secretary Lane's attention when he ventured criticism of how they were being managed. Supposedly Lane wrote back and said, "If you don't like the way things are run, come to Washington and run them yourself."[6]

Mather's workaholism and zeal for his mission may have contributed to an incapacitating mental breakdown in 1917, which left his deputy, Horace Albright, effectively in charge of the new agency. Albright had joined the Interior Department in 1913 as Franklin Lane's secretary and had been a capable congressional liaison during the effort to enact the Park Service organic legislation. Determined not to be a Washington bureaucrat, Albright took a hands-on approach to management, making an extensive tour of the western parks that summer. At the urging of Douglas White of the Union Pacific's Salt Lake Route, he scheduled a visit to Mukuntuweap National Monument in 1917—the first by any Park Service official.

Albright and White arrived in Cedar City in early September, meeting Chauncey Parry for the auto ride to the monument. David Hirschi, a farmer and rancher from Rockville who held the position of bishop in the local LDS church, joined the party, along with a state senator from Cedar City and another rancher. In high spirits, the men sang Mormon hymns en route to the monument, bouncing over some of the worst roads Albright had experienced. He later recalled the trip as "a real test of physical endurance." After spending several days exploring the canyon, including climbing to its rim and wading far into the Narrows of the Virgin River, Albright told reporters in Salt Lake City that the Mukuntuweap had given him "one of the surprises of my career." Designating the canyon and additional surrounding lands as

a national park would "guarantee Utah a place among the wonder-possess-
ing states of the Union," he proclaimed.[7]

Albright telegrammed his boss with a glowing account of the monument, leading Mather to reply that he "must have been taken in by the local
chamber of commerce."[8] Albright, however, would return many times to
make certain the monument was properly advertised, cared for, and made
accessible to visitors. Stephen Mather, too, would come under the spell of
Zion's cliffs, grottoes, and pine-clad rims, promoting it in his 1918 report to
Congress as a possible "all year round resort." According to historian Hal
Rothman, Mather looked to the American Southwest as a fertile field for
new parks, since the region offered stunning scenery without a dense population that would make park acquisition difficult. "The Grand Canyon was
Mather's pinnacle," Rothman noted, "but as more Americans began to own
automobiles, he also wanted to have national parks within driving distance
along the dusty western roads."[9] Regional road improvements would soon
put the Grand Canyon's North Rim within a day's drive of the Mukuntuweap, and there were enticing possibilities for additional national parks farther to the north and east, at the edge of Utah's High Plateaus and on into
its vast canyon lands.

One of the vexing questions Mather and Albright would deal with as their
new bureau began its work was the extent to which national parks would
become "pleasuring grounds," to use the term found in the 1872 law that
established Yellowstone. The agency's organic act directed it to balance
public use and enjoyment of the national parks with the need to "conserve
the scenery and the natural and historic objects and the wildlife therein."
This so-called dual mandate has both guided and perplexed park managers
ever since. But Mather and Albright did not inherit a national park system
as a blank slate; many of the parks then in existence, including Yellowstone
and Yosemite, already had extensive visitor facilities, including hotels of a
high standard. Park Service historian Richard Sellars has pointed out that
these facilities sprang up in an era when fancy resorts, especially those featuring thermal springs, were immensely popular among the traveling public. (The nation's first federal reserve, at Hot Springs, Arkansas, had been
set aside in 1832.) To some, Yellowstone seemed as if it, too, might become a

kind of high-elevation spa, its mineral springs potentially offering curative powers. Mark Daniels, the Park Service's first landscape architect, spoke of "the inevitableness of creating villages in the parks," pointing to the heavily developed floor of Yosemite Valley as a model.[10]

The question of park development was especially important in Utah, where the three national monuments in southern Utah were nearly a blank slate. Only Zion Canyon had ongoing human uses, and the Wylie tent camp hardly constituted a permanent facility. The valley floor was large enough (and certainly scenic enough) to support a grand hotel along the lines of El Tovar or Old Faithful Inn. Such a future seemed entirely possible with the backing of a major railroad; this, in fact, would be the future of parks such as Glacier and Mount Rainier.

During the various national park conferences held from 1911 to 1917, railroad representatives outlined their vision for attracting an elegant class of tourists to the parks. At the second conference, held in Yosemite in 1912, a Northern Pacific spokesperson stated that "the majority of the people who can afford a trip to the national parks are of a class who are in their daily life used to a reasonable degree of comfort, and no matter how ardent their love of nature may be they will not make the park trip unless it can be done with a reasonable degree of comfort and safety."[11]

This was the clientele that the western railroads' advertising departments aimed to attract through heavily funded print campaigns. By 1930, the Union Pacific was spending more than half a million dollars annually on newspaper and magazine ads, with Zion, Grand Canyon, and Rocky Mountain National Parks as its primary destinations.[12] Accommodating leisure travelers in grand style helped to fulfill Stephen Mather's dream of an enduring constituency for the National Park Service. These were not vacationers who would be satisfied with a flea-ridden, crowded tourist camp such as had sprung up in Yellowstone's early years.

In contrast to the railroads' conception of what the national parks should provide, Progressive-era activists such as Mary Sherman and Horace McFarland held a somewhat different notion of the worth of such parks, believing they should be more than vacation spots for the wealthy. In their view, working Americans undergoing the pressures of a rapidly industrializing society also needed places of rest and resort. This represented a remarkable shift in attitudes toward both nature and the city. By the end of the nineteenth century, historian Roderick Nash writes, "cities were regarded with a hostility once reserved for wild forests."[13] Photographers and reformers depicted urban slums in which wage workers toiled long days in clanking factories, only to return to equally stifling conditions at home. Their children had little recourse to fresh air, clean water, or greenery-filled playgrounds. Mary Sherman, in a talk given to the fourth National Parks Conference in 1916, said that the women's clubs she represented "were fully awake to the human need for more places for play and recreation." Children in New York City were being arrested for playing in the street, she observed, and for their parents "the stress and strain of life grows more exacting every year."[14] Not only urban parks were needed (as Horace McFarland advocated through his "City Beautiful" movement), but also national parks that preserved the grand scenery that was every American's birthright.

As for the privileged Americans who up until that time had constituted the National Park System's main clients and beneficiaries, John Muir had some choice words. In his 1901 book *Our National Parks*, Muir observed that these individuals—many of whom were his travel and business associates—were "awakening from the stupefying effects of the vice of over-industry and the deadly apathy of luxury" and were "washing off their sins and cobweb cares of the devil's spinning in all-day storms on mountains, sauntering in rosiny pinewoods or in gentian meadows . . . getting in touch with the nerves of Mother Earth."[15]

Muir never visited Zion Canyon, although if he had, he certainly would have extolled it as a place where one could get in touch with the Earth. He would have recognized a kindred spirit in Frederick Vining Fisher, an Ogden, Utah, minister who invested the great cliffs and towers of the Mukuntuweap with religious and classical symbology. Traveling up the canyon with two young men from Rockville in the fall of 1916, Fisher took note of the names they gave to various features, including three monoliths representing the biblical patriarchs Abraham, Isaac, and Jacob. Fisher bestowed some fanciful names of his own, calling the giant embayments in the canyon walls Court of the Wind, Court of the Sun, Court of the Patriarchs, and so on. Farther on, his young companions pointed out the Great Organ, a fluted sandstone tower opposite Flanigan's cable works. A huge monolith that bore the Spanish name "El Gobernador" on government maps impressed Fisher as the Great White Throne. The name stuck, but most of Fisher's terminology did not, including a "Court of Poets" that included towers representing Homer, Milton, and Shakespeare, and a "Cave of Everlasting Rain"—today's Weeping Rock.[16]

Little Zion was "the Canyon Sublime," Fisher announced in an article for the *Washington County News*, a St. George newspaper. It was "no place for a tourist resort but a place of pilgrimage for poets, patriots, artists, dreamers and worshipers." Reverend Fisher may have wanted the canyon to remain as it was in Isaac Behunin's time—a sacred space that offered refuge from the crowds and banality of modern civilization—but Utah's business leaders, particularly the agents of the Salt Lake Route, had other ideas. They realized that once Zion Canyon overcame its bad roads and lack of visitor facilities, it would join Yellowstone and Grand Canyon as a major travel destination. With no rail line directly reaching this Yosemite in the desert, the key to getting tourists to come lay with a new form of transportation: the automobile. Railroad men would put Zion on the map, but the family traveling in a Ford, Essex, or Maxwell would turn this colorful canyon into one of America's favorite destinations.

As America became embroiled in the European conflict in 1917, prospects for western travel suddenly dimmed. Only three hundred individuals visited the Mukuntuweap that summer, owing partly to a wartime ban on rail travel for pleasure. Following the war, the nationwide influenza epidemic further limited travel. Losing money on his Zion and North Rim camps, W. W. Wylie unceremoniously removed the Parry brothers, who were serving with the army in Europe, from the National Park Transportation and Camping Company's board of directors. This started a dispute over the company's ownership that would be resolved only when the UP acquired the entire venture in 1921.[17]

Following the war, the Parrys continued their operations independently of Wylie and the Union Pacific, running their own tours to Zion Canyon and the North Rim of the Grand Canyon. The UP also began taking tourists to the North Rim, hosting them at Bright Angel Point, where the Wylies' daughter Elizabeth had opened another tent camp.[18] With far greater financial resources, the railroad was poised to become the dominant player in regional tourism. Many in Utah were already referring to Zion as a national park, dispensing with the cumbersome name of Mukuntuweap and anticipating its imminent change in status.

In March 1917, the Utah state legislature passed a resolution calling for the establishment of Zion Canyon as a national park. In 1918, Reed Smoot introduced the first such bill in Congress. It would pass the following year, but already state officials as well as businesspeople in Utah's "Dixie" were confident that their long-awaited parity with neighboring states in the tourist field was at hand. C. C. Goodwin, editor of an influential Salt Lake City weekly, observed that the time would come when the Great Salt Lake and the salt desert to its west "will be known as the least interesting of all Utah's scenic attractions." Greater wonders lay in the state's eastern and southern sections, he insisted, including the fossil quarry then being excavated by Earl Douglass near Vernal, the cliff dwellings and natural bridges west of Blanding, and "the new national park, Little Zion Valley."[19] Thanks to better roads and new forms of transportation, tourists who wished to "See America First" would have world-class wonders aplenty to occupy their patriotic travels.

During his 1917 visit to the Mukuntuweap, Horace Albright appointed Walter Ruesch, a Springdale resident who had been taking care of some government road equipment, as the monument's custodian. His first assignment was to remove the cattle and horses that for years had freely grazed within the monument, reducing parts of the valley floor to what later park naturalist Angus Woodbury called "dust beds" filled with "unpalatable weeds."[20] Ruesch was able to accomplish this with the support of David Hirschi, president of southwestern Utah's Grand Canyon Highway Association and a strong promoter of tourism. Hirschi met with local farmers and persuaded them of the need to beautify the canyon.[21] Fencing out livestock symbolically completed Zion's transition from a Mormon back pasture to a true public reservation—one that would soon become a key stopover on the "grand circle" of national parks in the Southwest.

On March 18, 1918, with the support of Albright and Smoot, President Woodrow Wilson signed a proclamation expanding Mukuntuweap National Monument to 76,800 acres and changing its name to Zion. Smoot continued to take a close interest in the monument, both as chair of the Senate Public Lands Committee and as director of the Salt Lake Route, which stood to gain from rail traffic to the new park.[22] In November 1918, he introduced a bill, drafted by Albright, designating it as Zion National Park. Reintroduced the following year, the measure quickly cleared Smoot's committee and was attached to a civil appropriations bill, which passed the Senate that summer. After some negotiation over the disposition of private inholdings in the park, the House of Representatives passed the bill on November 15, 1919, and sent it to the president. Four days later Woodrow Wilson's signature gave Utah its first national park.[23] It would become a "great and beautiful playground," the *Salt Lake Telegram* editorialized, but only if it were sufficiently publicized. "We must advertise," the newspaper insisted. "Zion Canyon should and can rank with Yellowstone, Yosemite and the Grand Canyon. It is in their class."[24] In the years ahead, the Union Pacific Railroad would supply the advertising to make Zion National Park one of the nation's top travel destinations.

9

NEW WONDERLAND

The strikingly colored cliffs that define the eastern edge of the Paunsaugunt Plateau stand out from fifty miles away, but one must draw closer to notice the strange rock spires tucked within eroded ravines and amphitheaters below the rim. These curiously shaped remnants have evoked wonder for many centuries. To the Paiute Indians who made extensive use of the plateau and surrounding region, these were "legend people" whose bodies, complete with painted faces, had been turned to stone by the trickster Coyote for their ill deeds. Buried under red mud, their remains formed an entire city that only recently had been exposed to view.[1]

Mormon scouting parties, which passed through the upper Paria Valley in 1866 during the ongoing Anglo-Indian conflict known as the Black Hawk War, made no mention of the colorful Paunsaugunt cliffs. An 1870 expedition that explored the upper Sevier and Paria Rivers for possible settlement reported "canyonlike vales of red and white sandrock" as well as "isolated rocks or cliffs of singular castle- and fortification-shaped resemblances."[2] In 1871 Almon H. Thompson, a geographer for the Powell Survey, traversed the benchlands and canyons of the upper Paria River, taking note of cliffs below the rim of the "Pauns-á-gunt" Plateau that "show in the distance a beautiful pink color." That same year G. K. Gilbert, a member of the competing Wheeler Survey, looked down upon "a perfect wilderness of red pinnacles" beneath the plateau. He called it "the stunningest thing out of a picture."[3]

In 1875, J. W. Powell detailed Clarence Dutton to make a more thorough reconnaissance of the sprawling High Plateaus of south-central Utah. In his 1880 report, Dutton portrayed the upper Paria amphitheater in his inimitable style, proposing that "a race of genii" with "giant hands" had built the remarkable towers along its high escarpment. He took note of the "rare color, intensely rich and beautiful," which illuminated the Tertiary

Bryce Canyon National Park, as photographed by Maurice Cope, the park's first permanent ranger. *National Park Service, Bryce Canyon National Park, BRCA 532/001-206.*

rocks of the Pink Cliffs at sunrise and sunset.[4] In 1876 a government surveyor named T. C. Bailey likened the fluted columns in the Bryce amphitheater to "sentinels on the walls of castles; monks and priests with their robes; attendants, cathedrals, and congregations."[5] Something in these pinnacles cried out for personification, satisfying a human need to make sense of such strange rock forms.

Mormon settlers staked out homesteads in the upper Paria beginning in 1874, calling their village Clifton after the cliffs that rose precipitously to the west. Among them was Ebenezer Bryce, a carpenter from Scotland who had helped found the remote community of Pine Valley in southwestern Utah. He and his family soon moved to a farmstead a few miles farther north of Clifton, on the east side of the Paria River. Bryce obtained timber and firewood from a canyon that headed under the Paunsaugunt cliffs; investigating its headwaters one day, he was impressed by the unusual rock formations below the rim. According to some family members, he predicted that the area would one day be a national park.[6] By 1881 Bryce and his family had left for Arizona, leaving the remaining settlers to continue their struggle to make a living in the upper forks of the silt-slick and frequently flooding Paria River. "Bryce's Canyon," as the amphitheater at the head of Bryce's creek was known, would remain for a later generation to rediscover.

In 1905, President Theodore Roosevelt established the Sevier Forest Reserve on the lofty Markagunt Plateau to the west of Panguitch, Utah. The neighboring Paunsaugunt Plateau was added the following year and the entire expanse renamed the Sevier National Forest. Bryce Canyon appeared on an early map of the forest, but nothing further in the way of publicity came until a new forest supervisor, J. W. Humphrey, arrived in the summer of 1915. At the urging of one of his district rangers, he drove out to the Paunsaugunt's dramatic eastern edge, where he found a scene of "indescribable beauty." Humphrey resolved to publicize the place and make it accessible to the public. He arranged for George Goshen, a photographer from the Forest Service's regional office in Ogden, to take scenes from the rim, and for Arthur Stevens, a staff cartographer, to write descriptive articles for the travel magazines of the Union Pacific and Denver & Rio Grande Western (D&RG) Railways. At the time, the Forest Service was competing with the newly formed National Park Service as a conservator of the nation's scenery. Bryce Canyon was a splendid sight, but in spite of supervisor Humphrey's efforts, his agency would eventually be forced to relinquish it to its rival.[7]

A visit in the summer of 1917 by Le Roy Jeffers, a world traveler and mountain climber, led to more publicity for this hidden wonderland. Jeffers had been exploring the Kaibab Plateau and the Grand Canyon with guide Dave Rust, but on their return trip to the D&RG rail stop at Marysvale, Utah, Rust suggested they take in the view from the eastern Paunsaugunt. Jeffers was bowled over by the myriad spires and hoodoos under the plateau rim. In an article titled "The Temple of the Gods in Utah" that appeared in *Scientific American* the following year, Jeffers described "fantastic towers 25 to 400 feet in height, some of them isolated and others linked together in companies. So symmetrical are these linked and fluted pillars that they seem almost to have been turned by a lathe." Like Dutton and others before him, he let his imagination run riot, seeing in the stony assemblage "a vast city of prehistoric ruins" or a "stage setting for a fairy opera."[8]

William Seegmiller, a state senator from Kanab, also took an interest in Bryce Canyon and helped arrange for the *Salt Lake Tribune* to send its photographer, Oliver Grimes, to document it. Grimes's front-page photographs ran under the title "Utah's New Wonderland," and his accompanying article did much to arouse interest within Utah.[9] In 1919 Grimes, having joined the staff of Governor Simon Bamberger as a press agent, persuaded him to seek a resolution from the state legislature asking Congress to designate the area as the "Temple of the Gods National Monument."[10] Establishing national monuments was the president's prerogative, not Congress's, and it would take four more years and resolution of a land dispute before Utah's new scenic attraction would join its growing roster of national monuments.

In November 1919 Stephen Mather was meeting with his park superintendents in Denver when the president signed Reed Smoot's bill creating Zion National Park, so afterward he sped off in his personal chauffeured automobile to see it. He was accompanied by Lafayette Hanchett, a Salt Lake City banker who represented the city's Commercial Club, and Herbert W. Gleason, a photographer from Boston who had been inspecting new park proposals for the Interior Department. Zion was closed for the season, but Howard Hays and William Wylie met them for a brief tour. Afterward the group headed north to Salt Lake City, where the Commercial Club was holding a gala banquet in honor of the new park. At Hanchett's suggestion they detoured onto the Paunsaugunt to take in the views at Bryce Canyon. Mather was delighted and told the Commercial Club attendees that Bryce, too, should become a national park.[11]

Reed Smoot, acting on the strength of Gleason's letter, had just introduced a bill to create a "Utah National Park" at Bryce Canyon, but the area was managed by the Forest Service, which had its own interest in promoting it. Still, Mather foresaw that his agency would ultimately take control of this second Utah wonderland. At the Commercial Club banquet, he noted that "a great task lies ahead" for promoters of both Zion and Bryce Canyon and urged the club to press for good hotels and tourist camps throughout the scenic reaches of southern Utah. If visitors continued to experience primitive conditions within the parks, they would bad-mouth them and do them "a great deal of harm."[12]

Mather probably underestimated the hardy folks who were attracted to the western parks, many of whom did not mind pitching a tent beneath the trees or cliffs. His conception of the parks' clientele was formed in an age when travel was a pastime for the wealthy. Well-dressed vacationers arrived at grand lodges in Glacier, Yellowstone, or Grand Canyon, where a waiting hospitality staff saw to their comfort and entertainment. Spectacular viewpoints lay a few steps away along a constructed trail or boardwalk, with tea taken afterward on the hotel veranda and dinner in a log-beamed dining room. But as the twentieth century shed Victorian sensibilities and class distinctions, an increasing number of visitors would pull up to the park gate in their automobiles, looking to pitch a tent under a cottonwood tree or somewhere out in the sagebrush. By 1923, more than half of all visitors to the national parks got there by motorcar, a trend that was not lost on Park Service officials, including Mather.[13] As early as 1916 he observed that motorists were "contributing by way of automobile fees large sums of money toward park improvement and administration. They have the right, then, to expect that the Federal Government will pursue a broad policy in the extension of road systems in the several parks."[14]

Significant road construction funds became available for park purposes in 1921, when Congress amended the Federal Aid Road Act of 1916 to set up a cost-sharing system with the states. Still, with hundreds of miles of roads to build, maintain, and improve within Utah, the money could go only so far. Governor Bamberger famously told Horace Albright that "I build no more roads to rocks," a statement that supposedly showed his disdain for national parks, but it more likely reflected the higher priority of building a workable transportation network along the Wasatch Front.[15] Albright, for his part, promised Bamberger that if the state would bring a good highway to the gates of Zion, he would see to construction of an equally good road within the park.[16] This became the model for making national parks accessible to the public, cementing an alliance between the National Park Service, the road construction lobby, and the western states, all of which stood to gain from making these increasingly popular destinations accessible to auto travelers.

Albright made good on his promise. In 1924 construction crews completed a $70,000 gravel-surfaced road from the park's south entrance to the Temple of Sinawava, a mile below the mouth of the Zion Narrows. State highway engineers were overseeing improvements to the highway leading south from Cedar City to Toquerville, including the long, dangerous downhill run beneath Black Ridge. Work was also scheduled on the road leading from Rockville to the south entrance of Zion. These improvements came in time for the yearly opening of the park, on May 15, 1925, at which Governor

George Dern opened an oversize symbolic padlock with a golden key. A lunch of trout and fried chicken followed at the newly opened Zion Lodge, with a dance held that evening. Joining the party were three members of the Paiute Tribe, who conducted a ceremony lifting the "veil of fear" that had supposedly dissuaded their ancestors from entering the canyon. The way was now open for thousands to visit this new wonderland in the desert.[17]

The 1920s saw the western national parks emerging as top vacation destinations, thanks to the automobile as well as general national prosperity. The National Park Service would increasingly orient its thinking to these travelers, aware that congressional budget committees kept close track of park visitation numbers. Turning autos loose in the parks led to what historian Dietmar Schneider-Hector termed the "coevolution of both the parks and vehicles in American cultural experience as the demand escalated for the development of more and better roads in the parks."[18] But the influx of so-called sagebrushers—campers in autos who set up their tents in meadows or anywhere they could—threatened the railroads' near monopoly over western tourism. During the first years of the century they had been able to keep the national parks off limits to automobiles, concerned about competition with their own touring services, which in places such as Yellowstone employed horse-drawn carriages. Louis Hill of the Great Northern Railway, which enjoyed a similar monopoly at Glacier National Park, stated flatly that it would be "absurd" to open Yellowstone to autos, since it would "make it possible to see the park in one short day" instead of the leisurely tours the railroad's subsidiary offered.[19]

The ban did not stand for long, however, as Good Roads advocates, backed by concessionaires not linked to the railroads, pressed for opening the parks to autos. Yellowstone as well as all other national parks were opened to motorcars for the 1915 summer season, leading one delighted auto adventurer to call the park "the happy touring ground for the motorist of America."[20]

The railroads' response to the new trend was to heavily advertise their tour services, promising visitors to the national parks a thrilling adventure without leaving behind the comforts of a hotel bed and good meal at the end of the day. The Union Pacific's print advertisements touted Zion Canyon as a "Colorful Kingdom of Scenic Splendor," its desert landforms "glowing red and shining white." Tourists on horseback were depicted gazing up in wonder at the mighty precipice of the Great White Throne.[21] Many of its ads were based on photos taken by Cedar City photographer and park booster Randall Jones, who showed his hand-colored images of the park on the lecture circuit back East.

Zion, unlike Yellowstone, Glacier, and Rocky Mountain National Parks, had no rail line to its doorstep, so the UP depended on the Parry-Wylie concern to deliver guests to the park. In 1925 the railroad would open a new lodge inside Zion, giving it a spectacular, accessible destination to compete with the Great Northern at Glacier, the Northern Pacific at Yellowstone, and the Santa Fe at the Grand Canyon.

10

GRAND CIRCLE

In 1916, the same year the Park Service released the railroad-sponsored *National Parks Portfolio*, Stephen Mather proposed to connect the national parks of the West by a great circular automobile route, to be known as the National Park-to-Park Highway. It would tie together Yellowstone, Glacier, Mount Rainier, Crater Lake, Lassen, Yosemite, Sequoia, Mesa Verde, and Rocky Mountain National Parks, as well as Grand Canyon, soon to become a national park, and Petrified Forest National Monument, giving Arizona important links on the 4,700-mile route.[1] The projected route looped clear around Utah, however, leaving the soon-to-be-designated Zion National Park at the end of a long detour on the Arrowhead Highway leading north from Needles, California.

W. D. "Bill" Rishel, a former bicycle racer who promoted auto touring for the *Salt Lake Tribune*, saw Utah's central position as an advantage. "Our national parks and national monuments were carefully deposited in a grand circle, each equidistant from Salt Lake, a natural starting point for all those millions who were later to come and see." With Yellowstone and Glacier to the north, Rocky Mountain to the east, Yosemite to the west, and Zion, Bryce Canyon, and Grand Canyon to the south, all that was needed was good highways to make Salt Lake City a hub for the national parks of the Intermountain West.[2]

J. E. Broaddus, a Salt Lake City optometrist and amateur photographer, joined Rishel as a tireless publicist for what he called the "great circle trip" through the park lands of southern Utah and northern Arizona. In a 1921 publication of the Denver & Rio Grande Western Railway (D&RG), the Union Pacific's rival for Utah tourist traffic, Broaddus touted the new wonderland at Bryce Canyon as a scenic stop en route to the North Rim of the Grand Canyon. Travelers could return to Salt Lake City via Zion National

Park, making a quick side visit to the colorful cliffs above Cedar City, known locally as the Cedar Breaks. Broaddus claimed that the trip was "one of the grandest tours in the world and will be so recognized."[3]

Considerable work would be needed, however, before Zion, Bryce Canyon, and the North Rim were linked by all-weather roads. Tales abounded of vehicles stuck or stranded en route to these destinations, leaving motorists to deal with breakdowns far from help. As if to illustrate the need for federal road funds, in 1922 floods washed out all the bridges in Zion National Park.[4] It would not be the last time that work crews had to rush in to reopen the park.

The trying aspects of travel in southern Utah did not stop some enterprising motorists from venturing into the mysterious outback of the Colorado Plateau—and sometimes off the roads altogether. In 1917, W. H. Hopkins, a Salt Lake City dentist, met up with Dolph Andrus, a high school principal in the town of Bluff, for a 420-mile journey through the Navajo Reservation, following what they optimistically called the "Monumental Highway." Traveling in a Maxwell auto, they found the route tremendously scenic, but their log of the trip made it clear that getting stuck in the sand and fixing blown tires was part of the adventure. This did not dissuade tourism boosters from envisioning a bright future for motor tours to remote destinations such as Monument Valley.[5]

Although Hopkins's "Monumental Highway" was decades from becoming a reality, improvements were sooner to come for the more popular, railroad-served routes to Zion and Bryce Canyon National Parks. By 1922 the Parry brothers, once again working for the renamed "Utah-Arizona Parks Transportation Company," purchased (with the railroad's help) seven- and twelve-passenger touring cars to take visitors across the arid, windswept Arizona Strip to the North Rim, with a rest stop at the new national monument at Pipe Spring. As knowledge of Bryce Canyon filtered into the touring community, Chauncey Parry offered to take his more adventurous clients there as well, which involved a lengthy trip north of Cedar City to Parowan, thence east through Panguitch. After taking in the views at Bryce, clients returned to Cedar City via a newly built road across the Markagunt Plateau, finishing with more views of colored cliffs and spires at Cedar Breaks. The entire tour, which included meals and lodging, took eight days and cost $125, a not inconsequential sum, but it was within the means of upper-middle-class Americans who wanted a memorable vacation in one of the country's least-visited regions.[6]

Broaddus's Grand Circle tour, as it would become known, proved to be a durable concept. A shorter, regional version of the National Park-to-Park Highway, it would eventually take in the new parks and monuments of southeastern Utah such as Arches and Capitol Reef. The route appealed to motorists who wanted the freedom to wander far from railway stations, camp where they pleased, and follow their own schedules. Circle tours became a mainstay of the state's tourism advertising, drawing support from residents of southern Utah's isolated communities who looked forward to better highways linking them to the outside world.

Despite increasing interest in auto vacations, the railroads continued to invest heavily in their park operations. In 1922 Union Pacific president Carl Gray visited Utah to examine the possibilities for an integrated tourist operation at Zion Canyon, Bryce Canyon, and the North Rim of the Grand Canyon. This led in 1923 to the UP setting up the Utah Parks Company as a touring subsidiary of the San Pedro, Los Angeles and Salt Lake Railroad. Far better capitalized than the Wylie-Parry concern, it acquired forty eleven-passenger cars, some with retractable tops, to shuttle visitors between Zion, the North Rim, Bryce Canyon, and Cedar Breaks. The Utah Parks Company initially engaged the Parry brothers as salaried employees to run the operation, but as it solidified its hold on the southern Utah parks, it displaced the Parrys from their former monopoly on traffic to Zion.[7]

The Union Pacific had high ambitions for its Utah parks venture, initially investing some $1.7 million for rail improvements, lodging, and vehicles. These included a rail spur from Lund to Cedar City, which allowed tourists to avoid the dusty, tiresome auto ride across the western Utah desert, and the completion of a hotel in Cedar City to accommodate tourists on their way to the parks. Located next to the railway station, the El Escalante hotel became the base for Utah Parks Company tours to Zion National Park, Bryce Canyon, Cedar Breaks, and the North Rim.[8]

President Warren Harding inaugurated the El Escalante in the summer of 1923 during a tour of the western states that included visits to a number of national parks. Crowds lined the roads en route to Zion and bands feted the president with music at several stops. Reaching the end of the road at the Wylie camp in Zion Canyon, the party of twenty-four men transferred to horses and rode as far as the cable works.[9] Harding's exhausting itinerary continued with a visit to Yellowstone and on to Alaska, where he evidently suffered a heart attack. He died on August 2 in San Francisco, his journey uncompleted. The tragedy cast a pall on what was otherwise a grand series of celebrations of America's scenic high points.

Before embarking on his ill-fated western trip, President Harding took a series of noteworthy actions that helped bolster his conservation legacy, which had been badly tainted by the Teapot Dome scandal. In October 1922 he established Timpanogos Cave National Monument in Utah's Wasatch Range, protecting an important group of limestone caverns on national forest land in American Fork Canyon. The first of these caverns had been discovered by Martin Hansen, a logger from the local area, in 1887. Hansen cut a crude trail to his discovery and for the next four years guided visitors to it for a small fee. Mining claims were subsequently filed on Hansen's cave, with calcite minerals, believed at the time to be onyx, removed for decorative stonework.[10]

In 1913 or thereabouts, two local youths discovered an opening to a second, larger cave nearby that contained stalactites and other beautiful flowstone formations. As interest in the cave grew, it became clear than an active agency presence would be needed to prevent visitors from pocketing specimens and causing other damage. This, along with a threat of further mining raised by yet another group of claimants, led the Forest Service in 1921 to seek the caves' designation as a national monument. By this time a third cave between the two known caves had been discovered, and a committee consisting of local citizens was formed to develop them for visitors' enjoyment. The names Fairy Cave or Wonder Cave were suggested for the second, larger cave, following the popular terms of the day, but forest supervisor Dana Parkinson suggested Timpanogos, after the mountain on whose north flank the caverns were located. The name originally referred to the lower Provo River, where Numic-speaking Utes historically gathered fish.[11]

President Harding signed the proclamation establishing the 250-acre Timpanogos Cave National Monument on October 14, 1922. It was the sixth underground cavern to be so designated, joining Lehman Caves National Monument, another limestone cavern located in the Snake Range of eastern Nevada, which Harding established in January of that year. In an unusual move, the Forest Service delegated day-to-day management of the new monument to the Timpanogos Outdoor Committee, an offshoot of the

Commercial Club of American Fork. Timpanogos Cave and Lehman Caves National Monuments preserved not only spectacular speleothems but a considerable history of use by cowboys, prospectors, and Native Americans. The two monuments would remain under Forest Service control until 1934, when they were transferred to the National Park Service as part of an executive reorganization.

In March 1923, Harding signed a proclamation establishing Hovenweep National Monument in far southeastern Utah, protecting a cluster of striking rock towers erected during the thirteenth century, shortly before the general disappearance of Puebloan people from lands north of the San Juan River. The monument also included numerous older sites dating to the Archaic era, reflecting the more or less continuous habitation of this high mesa for ten thousand years—nearly as long as the known human occupation of the Americas.[12]

The smallest of the national monuments that Harding proclaimed during this period was a forty-acre parcel at Pipe Spring on the desolate Arizona Strip, designated in May 1923. Once the headquarters of a cattle ranch owned by the LDS Church, it had since fallen into disrepair. Pipe Spring nonetheless offered a shady stop for travelers undertaking the long, hot ride from Zion to the North Rim of the Grand Canyon. Its designation came at the request of Stephen Mather, who had spent two nights there as the guest of its owner, Jonathan Heaton, when Mather's car broke down during a tour of the region in August 1922.[13] Mather, according to historian Hal Rothman, wanted a series of waypoints along the roads between the western national parks, and national monuments served this need admirably. When Heaton suggested the government acquire his property as a historic monument to the Mormon presence in northern Arizona, Mather was immediately interested. An accident of geography thus helped to elevate Pipe Spring to national monument status.[14]

Rothman noted that the advent of auto-based tourism changed the concept of national parks as well. No longer did they represent the vast, mysterious frontier of a Bierstadt canvas, in which cliff and mountain dwarfed all human presence; by the 1920s, autos had given Americans "the sense of power that came from navigating the roads, trails, and paths of the American West. This broadening of national park holdings and the new means to reach them were instrumental in the emergence of recreational tourism," he observed.[15] But if the automobile shrank what was once a frontier, this came as a disappointment to those who still hoped to find some remnants of it in the Desert Southwest. Their narratives during the 1920s and 1930s would help change both public perceptions of Utah's canyon country and, eventually, the Park Service's auto-friendly mind-set.

Stephen Mather and Horace Albright were often willing to use national monument designations as a way station toward eventual national park status. This was the case with the colorful, intricately carved hoodoos of Bryce Canyon, which President Harding designated as the Utah National Monument in June 1923, shortly before leaving for the West. The Forest Service had been promoting Bryce Canyon as a tourist destination since 1916 and had built a campground, walking trails, and a landing strip nearby.[16] Reed Smoot's measure to designate Bryce Canyon as a national park awaited resolution of a land ownership issue involving a square-mile section owned by the state of Utah. Its location, next to the most spectacular part of the rim between Sunrise and Sunset Points, meant that whoever controlled it would have a prime tourist property. In 1919 Reuben and Minnie Syrett, a Panguitch couple who had homesteaded land a few miles to the north, began hosting friends and other visitors at a primitive tent camp they had established on this land. Before long the Syretts were serving meals from a cookstove they brought from home, as well as supplying mattresses and bedding for overnight stays. Their visitors included W. H. Hopkins, the Monumental Highway pioneer, who persuaded the Syretts to build a cabin and make a business of their hospitality. Hopkins also wrote to the Utah State Land Board asking it to grant a lease to the Syretts for their accommodations, but the board appears to have given no more than verbal permission—an oversight the Syretts would regret.[17]

"Tourists' Rest," as Reuben and Minnie named their small lodge, was built in 1920. The central building was a homey, informal place, thirty feet by seventy feet, with a porch built around a pine tree and a bathtub in a hollowed-out log. Guests were encouraged to carve their names on the swinging front doors. A cluster of nearby cabins provided sleeping quarters. The Syretts' operation lasted only a few years; lacking a formal lease to the property, they were forced to make way for the Union Pacific railroad, which coveted this prime property for its own tourist operations at the rim.

Tourists' Rest, a homey cabin built by Reuben and Minnie Syrett in the early 1920s, was the first lodging at Bryce Canyon. *Used by permission, Utah State Historical Society.*

In 1923 the railroad, having obtained the proper lease, offered $10,000 for the Syretts' interest in their land, buildings, and a valuable water right they held. This opened the way for the Utah Parks Company to erect the Bryce Canyon Lodge, designed by Los Angeles architect Gilbert Stanley Underwood. The lodge opened in 1925, and when finally completed in 1928, it featured seventy-five upstairs sleeping rooms, with sixty-seven cabins clustered about it. Separate dining and recreation halls could each seat two hundred guests. The Syretts decamped for their own land outside the national monument, where they built another lodge, named Ruby's Inn, which still serves visitors today.[18]

Smoot's bill to establish a national park at Bryce Canyon passed Congress on June 7, 1924, transferring to the National Park Service 14,480 acres of national forest land next to and below the rim. The area remained a national monument until the Utah state section, now leased to the Union Pacific Railroad, could be transferred to the federal government. The railroad assented to this only after wrangling an unusual proviso from the federal government—one that involved Zion National Park, not Bryce Canyon.

The UP wanted to intensively promote its "Grand Tour" of Zion, Bryce Canyon, Cedar Breaks, and the North Rim, but this still involved a lengthy and unpleasant ride across the Arizona Strip. Why not shorten this route, its officials reasoned, by constructing a new road leading east from Zion to Mount Carmel on the East Fork of the Virgin River? This would offer a much shorter route to both Bryce Canyon and the North Rim, the latter by way of Kanab. The only engineering obstacle lay in the sheer cliffs of Zion Canyon itself, which could be surmounted by means of a tunnel at the head of Pine Creek.

Under an agreement that Horace Albright reached with UP officials at an unpublicized meeting in Yellowstone in 1927, the railroad would transfer its property interest at Bryce Canyon to the National Park Service, retaining an exclusive contract to operate its lodge and other concessions. The Zion Tunnel, in turn, would be constructed and mostly paid for by the federal government. Albright agreed to this unprecedented arrangement, clearing the way for Utah to gain its second national park.[19]

In 1925, the Union Pacific completed work on its new lodge in Zion National Park, located just north of the Wylie family's tent camp. Stephen Mather had originally opposed a lodge in favor of smaller camps similar to the Wylie establishment, but railroad officials insisted that hotel-type accommodations were needed for the class of travelers they expected. As it had at Bryce Canyon, the railroad engaged Gilbert Stanley Underwood to design the lodge. His first design was for a grandiose, sprawling structure with three long bedroom wings and an equally long loading platform. The Park Service rejected it and asked Underwood to come up with something that fit the intimate canyon environment. The design as adopted featured a central dining and reception hall of rustic wood-and-stone construction, with forty-six outlying cabins for sleeping quarters.[20] Guided horseback rides, ranger-led hikes, and evening entertainment completed the package.

The rustic, scaled-down Zion Lodge nonetheless fit Stephen Mather's and Horace Albright's vision for park lodging of a high standard. It replaced the Wylies' tent camp, which was retained as employees' quarters until housing facilities were built a few years later. With funding from the Union Pacific, the Utah Parks Company also opened Underwood-designed lodges at Cedar Breaks in 1924 and the North Rim in 1928. These also incorporated local timbers and stone and were intended to harmonize with their forested surroundings.

In 1927, Chauncey and Gronway Parry sold the remainder of their interest to the Utah Parks Company. Touring the parks was now in the hands of a major corporation that was prepared to dramatically expand service—so long as the federal government would build the roads needed to bring in more tourists. From 1925 into the 1950s, the tourist experience at Zion and Bryce centered on the UP's elegant lodges. Motorcars would pull up to the portico to be formally welcomed by hotel staff. After taking in the views and being dined and entertained, guests would assemble outside the lodge the next morning for departure to the next park. Hotel employees would gather on the steps for a "sing-away"—a sentimental bon voyage that cemented the tourists' fond memories of their vacation.

Tourist facilities in Utah's national parks never attained the luxurious heights of Yosemite's Ahwahnee Hotel (which was Underwood's next assignment after designing the Zion Lodge), or the studied, elegant rusticity of Grand Canyon's El Tovar. By 1928, however, Zion Lodge boasted a swimming pool and bathhouse for guests to cool off in after a day on the trails. The Utah Parks Company advertised its three Utah park destinations, along with the North Rim, as a complete vacation package—a commodity worth millions. The Utah Parks Company tour enabled the railroad to compete with the Northern Pacific at Yellowstone and the Santa Fe at Grand Canyon for the western travel business.[21]

Viewing national parks as efficient generators of tourism revenue clashed with an emerging vision of the Colorado Plateau as a place to celebrate wild nature. The first suggestion that there might be more to protect in southern Utah than a handful of isolated scenic wonders came from Robert Sterling Yard, who left Stephen Mather's employ in 1919 to establish the National Parks Association, a nonprofit organization intended to increase public support for the parks. In 1920, the organization published a slim volume, written by Yard, titled *The New Zion National Park: Rainbow in the Desert*. Besides publicizing Utah's first national park, Yard also drew attention to Bryce Canyon, which was attracting notice outside the state. He proposed that it become the centerpiece of a much larger "High Plateau National Park," which, he wrote, would take in "enough of the Paria Amphitheater to show the greatness and sublimity of Utah's stupendous exhibit" and would "place Utah squarely in the front rank of national park states."[22]

Nothing came of Yard's proposal, and he made it clear in his booklet that the concept needed to be fleshed out by scientists familiar with the High Plateaus. It was hardly a radical idea; there were other large, landscape-level national parks and monuments in the West, including Grand Canyon, Yellowstone, Glacier, and Olympic, that took in considerable land surrounding their main geologic features. Yard's suggestion that the National Park Service take a more encompassing look at the Colorado Plateau Province would lie fallow for another fifteen years, until new personnel in the agency would arrive with a broader conception of what national parks could represent in the region.

DESERT REEFS AND STONE ARCHES

On the first day of June in 1925, some two thousand residents of Paiute, Wayne, and Garfield Counties gathered in the town of Panguitch for a gala celebration opening Bryce Canyon to summer traffic. Governor George Dern and Congressman Don Colton headlined the party, which left town in a procession of some four hundred automobiles. In keeping with Bryce's fairyland theme, the entrances to two tunnels on the road up Red Canyon were hung with vines and flowers, with twenty schoolchildren dressed as elves, sprites, and fairies waiting to welcome the entourage. A lunch banquet was held at the newly opened Utah Parks Company lodge, at which Dern, Colton, and officials of the Union Pacific and Denver & Rio Grande Western Railroads praised the tremendous scenery on tap in southern Utah. Both Dern and Colton urged the communities of southern Utah to offer good accommodations and hospitality to visitors.[1]

The event was remarkable for having been organized in just two weeks, yet it attracted a sizable crowd. It had taken less than a decade for Bryce Canyon to rise from obscurity to an object of pride and interest for local citizens. It would take another three years, however, before the legislation that created Utah National Park (Bryce Canyon's official name) would take effect, once the section of state land leased by the Union Pacific Railroad was formally transferred to the federal government. The park would be renamed Bryce Canyon at that time. For most Utahns, however, the deed was as good as done.

The Panguitch celebration also impressed certain individuals in nearby Wayne County who wanted to spotlight their local scenery. Joseph Hickman, a high school principal from Bicknell, was seeking greater recognition for what he and his brother-in-law, Ephraim Pectol, were calling the "Wayne

Wonderland"—a series of sandstone cliffs and beehive domes that formed part of the nearly one-hundred-mile-long monocline known as the Water-pocket Fold. These and other nearby geologic features such as Velvet Ridge, a dramatic outcrop of dark red Moenkopi shale north of Torrey, appeared to Hickman and Pectol to be as worthy of recognition as Zion or Bryce Canyon.[2] Hoping to hitch a ride on the growing popularity of these parks, Hickman and Pectol looked to the Denver & Rio Grande's Marysvale spur as a means to draw tourists to these relatively unknown scenic spots, including the for-ested environs of Fish Lake, where Hickman hoped to build a fancy resort.

At the very center of the Wayne Wonderland was the tiny village of Fruita, where in the 1880s a few families had established farms and orchards underneath the tall cliffs of Wingate Sandstone. By 1904, four families held nearly all of the arable land beneath the cliffs.[3] Both Hickman and Pectol came from ranching families that had settled in Caineville, farther east along the Fremont River, during the 1890s. Repeated floods early in the twenti-eth century persuaded most of its residents to leave, including Hickman, who went on to college and a career as an educator. Pectol, too, departed Caineville, settling in Torrey, where he opened a grocery store that doubled as a minimuseum of the prehistoric artifacts he collected throughout the Waterpocket Fold and Escalante River canyons. In the early 1920s he orga-nized a Boosters Club, later called the Wayne Wonderland Association, to promote the area.[4]

In 1924, Joseph Hickman won election to the Utah state legislature, where he worked to create a state parks commission, hoping to designate the Fruita cliffs and their surroundings as Utah's first state park. He also intro-duced a resolution calling for establishing a national monument in the area. Nothing immediately came of these measures, but Hickman continued to publicize the area, printing five thousand copies of a booklet titled *Wayne Wonderland, Fish Lake, and the Proposed Capitol Reef State Park.*[5]

After viewing Bryce's grand opening in June 1925, Pectol and Hickman decided to put together an event of their own to call attention to Wayne County's spectacular cliffs and gorges. Held in mid-July, the event featured a rodeo, a gala ball, and a ceremony the following morning at a rim view-point east of Torrey, complete with "daintily clad children" perched about an entrance gate. Governor George Dern was again the featured speaker, and he quickly got to the heart of the matter. "I can't blame you for wanting some tourist business, and wanting it this year," he told the audience. He

Hickman Natural Bridge in the Waterpocket Fold, 1937. Known originally as Fremont Bridge or Broad Arch, it was renamed in honor of Joseph S. Hickman, promoter of the "Wayne Wonderland." *Charles Kelly/Used by permission, Utah State Historical Society.*

supported Hickman's plan to designate a state park in the cliffs of the Fold but cautioned that it would take time to arrange a transfer of land from the federal government.[6]

Following remarks by other officials, including Harry Cushing, a passenger agent for the D&RG railroad, the crowd of several hundred took to their cars and drove through a flag-draped portal into the Wayne Wonderland. The road was hardly more than a wagon track, but it took visitors through geologic layers representing more than a hundred million years of Earth's history. In an interview with a Salt Lake City newspaper earlier that year, Cushing noted that along the Fremont River were outstanding examples of "hieroglyphics" left by the ancient "cliff dwellers" and, hidden in a small watercourse above the river, "one of the most perfect natural bridges yet known by man." Called by locals the Fremont Bridge, or sometimes the Broad Arch, it would later be renamed in honor of Joseph Hickman.[7]

Hickman did not live to see his dreams for a park in the Waterpocket Fold fulfilled. With the Wayne Wonderland celebration behind him, he retired to the cool shores of Fish Lake, no doubt satisfied with the progress he and Pectol were making in publicizing the Fold's attractions. On July 24, Utah's Pioneer Day, Hickman and three companions were boating in rough water when they noticed another boat in difficulty. Turning around to offer help, a wave struck their boat, which filled with water and sank. The others were rescued, but Hickman could not swim and was drowned. The loss came as a "severe shock" to local residents, according to the *Richfield Reaper,* which by odd coincidence ran an accompanying story claiming that the Interior Department had just set aside 480 acres in the Fruita area for a possible new park.[8] The report proved false, and despite Pectol's efforts, it would be six years before the first Park Service employee took a good look at the Wayne Wonderland. Another six years would pass before the federal government officially recognized this hidden landscape as a national monument.

Part of the delay lay with the Park Service's insistence that new parks possess the scenic magnificence of Yellowstone, Yosemite, or Grand Canyon. Its initial investigations into the Wayne Wonderland, while positive, fell short of that high but admittedly unquantifiable standard. The sheer isolation of eastern Wayne County also delayed the creation of a national monument in the Waterpocket Fold. Towns such as Torrey saw few travelers passing through to explore the nearby reefs and canyons. Nor was Harry Cushing able to capitalize on the proximity of the D&RG's Marysvale line to Bryce Canyon; beset by financial difficulties, the railroad ceded tourist services to the Union Pacific and its Utah Parks Company subsidiary. Bryce Canyon, soon to become a national park and possessing a new lodge, was in some respects an easier place to visit, with spectacular views arrayed conveniently along an accessible rim. Like Zion Canyon, it was a focal landscape, in contrast to the long, open spine of the Waterpocket Fold, which took days or weeks to fully appreciate. And without the tourist infrastructure that a major railroad could provide, the Wayne Wonderland was decades away from becoming the major travel destination its local admirers desired.

In the early 1920s, an unusual collection of eroded sandstone fins far to the east of the Wayne Wonderland was also attracting notice. Travelers on the old wagon road leading south from the Denver & Rio Grande rail stop at Thompson could see a long, rocky ridge to the east that featured several "windows" punctuating a skyline of bare rock. Henry Culmer had observed these on his 1905 journey to the White Canyon bridges, noting in his diary that they would be "worth taking [in] if we had time."[9] The few who did venture into this maze came across great amphitheaters of bare sandstone, massive stone-framed windows, and miniature canyons concealing improbable spans of the thinnest rock. No roads led through this confusing terrain and a visitor could easily become disoriented in it. Yet there was an undeniable beauty to these odd lithic remnants.

Photographs of the largest of these windows appeared in Moab's *Grand Valley Times* as early as 1913, and not long after, they attracted the attention of University of Michigan geologist L. M. Gould, who was investigating the La Sal Mountains east of Moab. During the early 1920s he enlisted J. Marvin Turnbow, who owned a hardscrabble ranch on Salt Creek, to guide him into this hidden wilderness.[10] Gould made additional trips into the area with J. W. Williams, Moab's sole doctor, who made rounds throughout Grand County with horse and buggy. Entranced with these geologic curiosities, both men undertook to publicize them over the next few years.

Meanwhile, a different assemblage of slickrock fins and cliffs at the western edge of Salt Valley had drawn the attention of a prospector named Alexander Ringhoffer, a Hungarian immigrant who had arrived in Moab around 1917. Hidden within this rocky, jumbled area, which he called "Devils

Garden," was a large sandstone arch. The place had a certain appeal, and in 1923 he called it to the attention of Frank Wadleigh, a D&RG agent in Denver. Sensing a potential tourist attraction, Wadleigh and a photographer named George Beam met Ringhoffer at the Thompson station that September and headed south in Ringhoffer's Model T Ford, taking to foot when they could drive no farther.[11]

Wadleigh was impressed with the area and advised Stephen Mather, whom he knew through his railroad work, of this potential new park acquisition. It contained "stupendous sandstone formations of very remarkable shapes unlike anything I have seen in the Rocky Mountains," he wrote. Intrigued, Mather arranged for a General Land Office surveyor to investigate the area the following summer. Uncertain where to look, the surveyor explored a different cluster of fins and arches closer to Moab. Ringhoffer called this area the "Window Castles" and informed Wadleigh that they were a good ten miles southeast of *his* Devils Garden. What's more, the surrounding area contained "probably 10,000 or more acres of various kinds of natural wonders besides the Castles."[12]

A second survey, conducted in June 1925, examined still another part of this intriguing landscape on the high ridge north of the Windows section, and it was here that Ringhoffer's "Devils Garden" finally stuck.[13] As many early visitors would discover, it could be difficult to orient oneself in this convoluted country.

Professor Gould, who spent the summer of 1924 in the Moab vicinity, wrote to Senator Reed Smoot to suggest national monument status for the Devils Garden and Windows areas. Smoot passed the idea along to Stephen Mather, who arranged for an independent investigation by Dr. Frank R. Oastler, a professor of surgery at Columbia University and a member of the Park Service's citizen advisory board. An active conservationist and lover of wildlife, Oastler advocated a strong education program within the Park Service and supported the acquisition of wildlife-rich areas such as Michigan's Isle Royale. In the spring of 1925, he and his wife, Maude, made an extensive tour of southern Utah's backcountry in the company of guides Zeke Johnson and Dave Rust.[14] During his travels, which included a boating trip down Glen Canyon, Oastler took note of several areas of high geologic interest, including Arch Canyon in southeastern Utah's Cedar Mesa.

During his Utah visit, Oastler arranged to meet Alexander Ringhoffer and an Interior Department inspector named F. J. Safley for a tour of the new discoveries north of Moab. Ringhoffer drove them to the cliffs he was still calling Devils Garden, where they climbed up to what Oastler described as "an immense amphitheater of striking grandeur." Working through a narrow break in the cliff, they came to a "graceful arch with a span of 200 feet—almost a perfect oval in shape." Above it stood a huge column of rock, which suggested the name Tower Arch.[15] Today it is the centerpiece of the Klondike Bluffs area in Arches National Park.

Ringhoffer then took his guests by car farther up Salt Valley Wash to investigate the Castle Windows section. Oastler described it as "a maze of courtyards and arenas surrounded by vertical walls carved in many curious forms." Continuing on, they came across "eight natural arches of enormous size" and two nearly circular openings that formed a neat double window. Oastler termed this feature "the most wonderful in existence." It is known today as Double Arch, a stunning culmination to the Windows section of Arches National Park.

The Oastlers described these erosional features to a reporter from the *New York Times*, who in a 1926 article predicted speedy designation of the area as a national monument. Meanwhile Frank Pinkley, the Park Service's regional supervisor, came to see the area and added his recommendation for monument designation. He suggested that it be called Arches to distinguish it from Natural Bridges National Monument, whose spans lay over watercourses.[16]

Opposition from the Coolidge administration delayed action until April 12, 1929, when President Hoover signed the proclamation creating Arches National Monument. It consisted of two sections totaling 4,520 acres, one in the Windows area and the other in the newly named Devils Garden with its sandstone fins and hidden arches. Ringhoffer's cliffs—today's Klondike Bluffs—were not included in the new monument, nor was the graceful, solitary span now known as Delicate Arch.[17]

Monument designation for Arches brought no real change on the ground; Frank Pinkley, its titular superintendent, was stationed five hundred miles away in Coolidge, Arizona. Not until November 1933 would Arches gain its first on-site custodian: Marvin Turnbow, who received a dollar a month to keep an eye on the monument's windows and arches.[18] Still, it was a step toward recognition for these unusual geologic features. Loren Taylor, editor and publisher of the *Moab Times-Independent*, termed the new designation "pleasing news to the people of Moab and Grand County" and predicted that once a road was built to the isolated monument, it would "gain fame as one of the most scenic regions of the west."[19]

Although Arches National Monument lay far off the main tourist track, its potential was obvious to those who visited it. In mid-December 1933 the Park Service fielded a fifteen-person crew to survey its boundaries, working through the winter and into the following spring. Part of their job was to catalog the monument's arches and other scenic features. Zion superintendent Preston Patraw, whose duties extended to all of Utah's national park units, joined the group at times, as did two Park Service landscape architects who were charged with finding the best road access into the Devils Garden area. Frank Beckwith, a photographer and newspaper editor from Delta, Utah, assisted with the investigation and filed reports with the *Moab Times-Independent*. He observed that the existing access via Willow Spring "cannot be called a road under any flattery; it ends four miles from the arches, and for the first mile and a half it is so repellent that it will 'damn' the rest of the trip." To Beckwith, "the only way to 'sell' the Arches monument to the tourist is to make it easily accessible by auto. In no other way can the tourist trade be brought about."[20]

Beckwith encouraged Grand County officials to press for national park designation for Arches, substantially expanding its boundaries to include Courthouse Wash and the Klondike Bluffs area, which Alex Ringhoffer had initially wanted to include. He also urged an eastward expansion to take in a lovely rock span above Winter Camp Wash, which he called Delicate Arch. It was "one of the most beautiful in the region," Beckwith wrote, and "it would be a shame not to include it."[21] His proposal found support among the Moab Lions Club, whose president, J. W. "Doc" Williams, had pressed for Arches' designation as a national monument a decade earlier. Loren Taylor added his newspaper's blessing, noting it would confer on Arches "the dignity attaching to a national park"—and would bring an improvement over the benign neglect with which the National Park Service treated the region's existing monuments.

Better access to Arches National Monument would remain a priority for both Taylor and the Park Service. Help arrived in the fall of 1935 when a Civilian Conservation Corps camp was opened at Dalton Wells near Willow

Springs, a former stage stop on the Moab-Thompson road. Crews of youths set to work constructing trails in the Windows section and began clearing an entrance road toward Balanced Rock at the edge of the Windows section. Storms frequently put the road out of commission, but their work made it possible for the first automobile to make the trip to the Windows. In June 1936 Harry Goulding, owner of a well-known trading post at Monument Valley, Arizona, steered a V-8 Ford equipped with oversized tires along the sandy track leading east from Willow Spring. He returned to the monument on the following two days with other interested passengers, including Jesse Nusbaum, superintendent of Mesa Verde National Park, who would go on to take a strong interest in southeastern Utah's wonders.[22] For the time being, though, the difficulty of reaching the monument's arches and obelisks meant it would remain a destination for hardy tourists in search of something unusual to write home about. As with the Wayne Wonderland, national park designation awaited the development of better roads and a supporting infrastructure that would lend itself to serious tourism.

SCENIC DRIVES
AND ROCKY TRAILS

The land-for-a-highway deal that Horace Albright brokered with the Union Pacific Railroad in 1927 removed the last obstacle to Bryce Canyon becoming Utah's second national park. The following year, Senator Reed Smoot introduced legislation to acquire the UP's interest in the square-mile section of Utah state land within the park. On September 15, 1928, President Herbert Hoover signed the law creating Bryce Canyon National Park, encompassing 14,480 acres along the eastern edge of the lofty Paunsaugunt Plateau. While Smoot's bill resolved the immediate land ownership issues, the Park Service foresaw the need to extend the park south along the plateau to its terminus at Rainbow and Yovimpa Points. At its request, Smoot introduced legislation that authorized the president to expand the park boundaries to take in the desired parcels. In 1931, President Hoover issued two proclamations that expanded Bryce Canyon to the south and north, including lands on the northeast at Shakespeare Point, an area of scenic cliffs named for a local ranching family. These proclamations brought the park to 35,980 acres, essentially its current size.[1]

The remainder of Albright's agreement with the Union Pacific would be written in stone, as workers in 1927 began blasting through more than a mile of sheer cliff above Pine Creek at Zion National Park's eastern edge. The Zion–Mount Carmel Highway, with its spectacular mile-long tunnel, was an engineering achievement of the first order, greatly shortening the distance between Zion and Bryce Canyon National Parks. On the Fourth of July in 1930, Albright (now the Park Service's director following Stephen Mather's death the year before) formally accepted the new highway from the Bureau of Public Roads, which had overseen the $1.4 million project. Utah's share of the cost came to $98,000, while park administrators siphoned funds from other western parks to complete the project.[2] At a celebration held in the park, Utah governor George Dern and Union Pacific Railroad president Carl Gray gave congratulatory speeches, praising the close cooperation of the state of Utah, the railroad, and the federal government in completing the tunnel and highway.

The Zion–Mount Carmel Highway was an extraordinary accommodation of private interests by the federal government and helped launch an era of intensive (some would say too intensive) road building in the national parks. This relationship—it would be called a "partnership" today—extended to park concessionaires as well, with the Utah Parks Company granted exclusive rights to provide tourist services within Zion and Bryce Canyon. Its contract with the National Park Service permitted a 6 percent annual return on its investment—not exactly robber-baron profits, but a boon for its parent company, the Union Pacific, which also benefited from passenger traffic to the parks. By the mid-1920s the UP had tied together Bryce, Zion, the North Rim of the Grand Canyon, and Cedar Breaks (then under Forest Service control) into a complete tour package, including overland transportation from the railhead in Cedar City and comfortable lodging, meals, and entertainment within the parks.

The response, however, was perhaps not what Carl Gray and his associates had anticipated. Visitation to Zion National Park doubled in 1925, the year Zion Lodge was opened, but much of the increase came from independent automobile travelers, not Utah Parks Company tours. In 1929, the Park Service recorded 33,383 visitors to Zion, but only 5,151 of these took the stage tour. In 1930, with the Zion–Mount Carmel Highway open, tour participants actually decreased to 4,056, while visitors arriving by auto jumped to 51,202. Bryce Canyon recorded 35,962 visitors in 1930 despite its short summer season, 32,047 of which arrived in their own cars.[3] The Zion Tunnel opened both parks to much greater traffic, and while many of those visitors presumably stopped at one of the Utah Parks Company lodges, the railroad was at first reluctant to reorient its services toward the independent traveler.[4]

The Union Pacific and other western rail lines continued to offer escorted vacations to the parks well into the 1950s, although their share of traffic to the national parks continued to dwindle as more Americans took to their cars for a summer vacation. The democratization of travel brought about by the automobile and the Interstate Highway System not only transformed cities and countryside but irrevocably changed what national parks could offer the public.

From the time he took the helm of the National Park Service, Stephen Mather made it clear that tourism would play a major role in the national parks. His publicist, Robert Sterling Yard, reinforced this message in a 1916 article titled "Making a Business of Scenery." Yard emphasized that the new bureau was not about to lock people out: "We want our national parks developed," he wrote. "We want roads and trails like Switzerland's. We want hotels of all prices from lowest to highest. We want comfortable public camps in sufficient abundance to meet all demands. We want lodges and chalets at convenient intervals commanding the scenic possibilities of all our parks."[5] This business-friendly model for the national parks received enthusiastic support from the nation's nascent travel industry and led local politicians—including many within Utah—to call for new parks that might bring in the tourist dollar.

At the same time, Mather was mindful of the growing interest among some Americans in more primitive forms of travel. Tourist development would not be allowed to run rampant in the parks, he insisted in his annual report for 1924. Large sections of the western parks would remain accessible only by trails, and any roads that were needed would lie lightly on the land.[6] Mather, in fact, had to restrain his protégé, Horace Albright, from approving several unusual proposals to increase tourist access, including a mammoth aerial tram system in the Grand Canyon that would have scooted tourists from the South Rim to the top of a butte deep within the inner gorge.[7]

Even some individuals who were prominent in the Good Roads movement argued for keeping the parks as temples of contemplation, not mass entertainment. Fisher Harris of the Salt Lake Commercial Club, who helped originate the See America First movement, believed that those who partook of the West's grand scenery and natural environments should come away with something more than souvenirs and photographs. Echoing John Muir, Harris wrote that "jaded overworked men and women of the crowded cities" needed to immerse themselves in the "fields and streams, the mountains, lakes and canyons of the West" as part of their "working out of their physical and mental salvation." Simply breathing in the West's pure air "brings life to the lifeless, hope to the hopeless, and happiness to the miserable."[8]

Harris, like Muir and other prophets of the outdoor life, viewed the grand manifestations of nature in the western states as a soul-enriching tonic for those who knew only the crowded cities and polluted air of the

East. But the Park Service now had a mandate from Congress to not only preserve the magnificent scenery of the American West, but to exploit it as a tourist attraction. Stephen Mather and Horace Albright's shared vision was that with proper planning and management, preservation could exist alongside tourism. The national parks would offer rustic but well-designed lodges, good roads to scenic overlooks, and trained rangers to interpret the views. The parks would avoid the worst manifestations of commercial tourism, of which Niagara Falls was a frequently cited example. There would be no boardwalks lined with shops hawking curios and tours, no substandard accommodations, no noisy amusements beyond a dance band to enliven evenings in a lodge. The cruder aspects of mass tourism (and Mather and Albright may not have anticipated this) would instead become a feature of many so-called gateway towns outside the national parks.

Historian Stephen Pyne makes a case for a kind of intellectual devolution taking place on the Colorado Plateau in the early twentieth century, simultaneous with its rise as a tourist destination. Rail transport had brought "ease of geographic access" to the Grand Canyon, Pyne writes, and with it "an equal ease of intellectual access." Whereas John Wesley Powell was willing to engage in the "patience and toil" needed to penetrate the canyon's depths, and Clarence Dutton undertook the "strenuous cultivation, the hard labor of thinking" that gave heft to his writing, this did not suit the new age of rail and auto travel. As a result, Pyne writes, "the visitor replaced the explorer, the Kodak snapshot the grand canvas."[9]

While it is undoubtedly true that most visitors to the national parks in the first decades of the twentieth century did not care to replicate the physical and intellectual heavy lifting that characterized Powell and Dutton, this is not to say they were unappreciative of what they saw. Many visitors availed themselves of the Park Service's interpretive programs, in which rangers made the stratigraphy and denudation of Colorado Plateau landscapes comprehensible, as well as deepening their understanding of historic and cultural values. Ranger-naturalist Angus Woodbury began interpretive work in Zion National Park in 1925, followed by geologist Edwin McKee at Grand Canyon in 1929. At Mesa Verde, rangers had been giving guided tours of the park's cliff dwellings since 1908, two years after it was established. As Stephen Mather stated in his first report as director of the National Park Service, "one of the chief functions of the national parks and monuments is to serve educational purposes."[10]

Interpretation extended beyond the ranger corps; the Wylie camps as well as the Utah Parks Company offered evening lectures to their guests, while in the late 1920s University of Utah geology professor Frederick J. Pack set up "Intelligence Tours," taking passengers on six- and nine-day auto expeditions to Zion, Bryce Canyon, the North Rim, and Cedar Breaks. Pack advertised these trips as "especially designed to provide the tourist with an understanding of what he sees." Accompanied by a "skilled geologist" (often Pack himself), these tours appealed to a clientele desiring more than a snapshot of the parks. Pack's tour brochure from 1927 stated that "within recent years he has never visited any of the playgrounds of Western America without being confronted by groups of people who wanted to know the meaning of the wonders before them."[11]

There were also those for whom a package tour could not substitute for direct, personal experience. To these dedicated wanderers, the Colorado Plateau of the 1920s and 1930s offered horizons far broader than the national parks and monuments themselves. Some, like T. Mitchell Prudden or Charles Bernheimer, were well off, while others, like Alice Eastwood and Herbert Gregory, had the backing of educational or government institutions. There were also those who had neither source of support yet made some of the most intriguing forays into the region. Their exemplar was Clyde Kluckhohn, a young man who during the 1920s made some of the most intriguing forays into the Navajo Reservation and the Kaiparowits Plateau.

At the age of seventeen, after a bout with rheumatic fever forced him to leave his studies at Princeton University, Kluckhohn retired to a family-owned ranch in Ramah, New Mexico. There he developed an interest in Navajo Indian culture that, combined with a certain wanderlust, led him in 1923 to set out on horseback with a sole companion across the Navajo Reservation to Rainbow Bridge. He chronicled the journey in his 1927 book *To the Foot of the Rainbow*—one of two books he wrote of his southwestern travels in a region that was still largely devoid of automobile tracks. His accounts testify to the unique value of landscapes that lay beyond the comfortable confines of ordinary tourism.

Rainbow Bridge was the high point of Kluckhohn's 1923 trip, yet even this celebrated destination did not satisfy his wanderlust. During a visit to

John and Louisa Wetherill's trading post at Kayenta, a comment by one of John's cowboy guides caught Kluckhohn's interest. As they approached the bridge, the guide said, they would see "a big high mesa stretchin' back a hundred miles into Utah." [12] Supposedly no white man had been on top of it. At once Kluckhohn had a destination to exceed even the fabled Nonnezoshi. Their provisions were too low to explore the mesa that summer, but the seed was planted for another expedition that would explore the forbidding territory north of the San Juan and Colorado Rivers.

Kluckhohn became obsessed with reaching "Wild Horse Mesa," the fictional name that Zane Grey had given the broad upland of southern Utah's Kaiparowits Plateau. Returning to college at the University of Wisconsin, he devoured the limited printed material on the region, including Herbert Gregory's 1917 report on the Navajo Reservation and Neil Judd's 1924 *National Geographic* article "Beyond the Clay Hills," which described the southeastern Utah canyon lands as "still practically unknown and unexplored . . . unmapped mesas stretch away mile after barren mile."[13] This was all Kluckhohn needed to know—here was a frontier that had somehow persisted well into the twentieth century.

From 1926 to 1929, Kluckhohn and various of his college friends undertook three horseback expeditions to seek out the fabulous destination.[14] His first attempt, in 1926, ended deep in Navajo country when one of their horses threw its rider. The following year Kluckhohn, two of his friends from the previous year, and two new recruits made it as far as Rainbow Bridge but were unable to cross the flooding Colorado. In 1928, the now-experienced band of desert wanderers (they called themselves the "Filthy Five"), accompanied by Dogi, a young Navajo, forded the San Juan River and made their way to the Colorado at Hole-in-the-Rock. An old boat left there by earlier river runners allowed them to ferry 1,200 pounds of supplies across the river. They exited the canyon via an improbable route located a mile upstream from the one pioneered by the Mormon emigrants of 1879–80.

Emerging from the depths of Glen Canyon, they beheld the steep eastern rampart of the Kaiparowits, known today as Fiftymile Mountain. A break in the cliff gave access to its summit, where they set up a base camp and spent several leisurely weeks exploring. They hoped to find great Mesa Verde–style pueblos tucked under the plateau's convoluted rim but were content to discover smaller shelters and storage sites left by prehistoric people in hidden caves and overhangs. The Kaiparowits was not unknown to

On the Escalante bench near the head of Davis Gulch, with the Straight Cliffs of the Kaiparowits Plateau in the background. Clyde Kluckhohn and his friends climbed to the rim near here during their 1928 excursion to "Wild Horse Mesa." Photo by Herbert E. Gregory, 1944. *Herbert E. Gregory Collection, Special Collections, J. Willard Marriott Library, University of Utah.*

modern humans; there were cattle atop the mesa and, scratched in the rock alongside ancient pictographs, the names of cowboys from Mormon ranches to the north. Still, they were entranced to find a place where they had only themselves for company.

In *Beyond the Rainbow*, his 1933 book on the Wild Horse Mesa expedition, Kluckhohn took note of a proposal advanced by Charles Bernheimer and John Wetherill to substantially enlarge Rainbow Bridge National Monument and designate it a national park.[15] Kluckhohn believed the Kaiparowits would be a spectacular addition to such a proposal, but he also issued a caution: "I wonder if we want to make Wild Horse Mesa into a National Park, after all. . . . It suggests too much carefully built roads and elaborate regulations." He contrasted the tourist who viewed the Grand Canyon from a boardwalk along the South Rim with their own sweat-stained efforts to reach the top of the Kaiparowits Plateau. To him, "the view from the rims of Wild Horse Mesa is purchased at high price, and perhaps is therefore understood and appreciated the more."[16] This was Kluckhohn's clearest indication of how he privileged adventure over mere "tourism," seeking to ground his many attempts to reach Wild Horse Mesa in the mythos of the Old West and the great explorers of the nineteenth century.

Kluckhohn suggested an alternative to a national park: the government could "simply turn the Mesa into a national preserve denied to settlement. That is not a fantastic suggestion. The area involved is large, but is economically not of great value." The key to such a preserve, he believed, was to build no roads. "The last thing wanted is an appropriation for 'developing' the area and for upkeep.... The one regulation that would be necessary would be: NO ROADS, NO BUILT TRAILS."

Clyde Kluckhohn and his friends may have been seeking a nineteenth-century encounter with the landscape of the Colorado Plateau, but his concern about what might happen to those lands was a modern one. At a time when Stephen Mather and Horace Albright were hiring engineers and landscape architects to transform the national parks into national pleasuring grounds (albeit carefully planned and tightly regulated ones), a small number of Americans saw a need to preserve a different kind of recreational experience in the West—one that was closely hitched to the mythic West of the cowboy, the wild Indian, the horse and pack string. Historian Thomas J. Harvey observes that Kluckhohn's deep interest in the primitive landscapes of the American Southwest (as well as his later professional interest in its Native peoples) was a reaction to the process of modernization, which "unleashed deep changes in American culture that forged new ways of living in, looking at, depicting, and experiencing the world." Kluckhohn's Southwest became "a storehouse of the past and therefore, primitive and authentic."[17]

During his travels across northern New Mexico and Arizona, Kluckhohn came into contact with all of these western emblems, but north of the San Juan and Colorado Rivers the human presence, to his delight, was virtually absent. As he wrote in *Beyond the Rainbow*, "We rejoiced that there were yet regions uncrossed by trail where one would be able to travel days or weeks without meeting a wandering Indian."[18] But this empty landscape was a result of significant depopulation. The San Juan band of the Southern Paiutes had lived in this area for perhaps six hundred years, but their numbers had recently been decimated by influenza, an epidemic spread by contact with Euro-Americans. Kluckhohn and his friends were enjoying a sojourn in country once crossed by many trails, which had only recently been emptied out. As Thomas Harvey notes, "The notion that the celebration of an Anglo-American landscape was of an imperial nature did not influence the direction of young Kluckhohn's books."[19]

Clyde Kluckhohn would go on to become a respected ethnographer, fluent in Navajo and a keen student of their lifeways, so it is perhaps unfair to lay the burdens of Euro-American conquest (and the mythos that grew up in its aftermath) on his shoulders. He and his friends were far more attentive to their surroundings than the average tourist. They took note of the plateau's diverse flora and fauna, prehistoric ruins and inscriptions, and outstanding geological formations. These attributes, along with others such as the yet-to-be discovered paleontological resources of the Kaiparowits, would be cited sixty-three years later in a presidential proclamation that established a vast new national monument on the plateau and in much of the surrounding canyon lands. By then the call for a new form of landscape preservation to protect the wild and the primitive had grown into a national movement. The southern Utah canyon lands would emerge as one of its key battlegrounds.

Zeke Johnson, the first custodian of Natural Bridges National Monument, at the Goblet of Venus, September 11, 1935. This striking monument, located west of Blanding, was toppled by vandals in 1948. *George A. Grant/National Park Service.*

ZEKE'S BRIDGES

In the convoluted canyon landscape stretching from Moab to Lees Ferry, the field personnel of the National Park Service consisted of exactly one person: the indomitable Zeke Johnson, custodian of Natural Bridges National Monument, who patrolled his tiny domain from spring to fall. He had ranged extensively throughout southeastern Utah during his long and varied career as a cattleman and backcountry guide, but his heart was centered on his three bridges, which he guarded with a storekeeper's concern. Johnson's efforts to win recognition for his tiny domain at Natural Bridges, chronicled in amusing typewritten reports he filed with his boss, Frank Pinkley, stand in counterpoint to the growing popularity of the region's larger and more popular park units.[1] An example of what historian Hal Rothman termed a "second class site," Natural Bridges was among the monuments that represented "cultures and landscapes that were lost to twentieth-century America."[2]

Ezekiel "Zeke" Johnson, like Arches custodian Marvin Turnbow, had grown up in southern Utah, working as a cowhand, rancher, farmer, and prospector with varying degrees of success. Well acquainted with the vast backcountry between his home in Blanding and his birthplace in Bellevue, Utah, south of Cedar City, he supplemented his income by leading adventuresome horse packing trips with clients such as Charles Bernheimer and Frank Oastler. Appointed as custodian at Natural Bridges in 1923, he received a dollar a month for his labors, along with the exclusive right to guide visitors within the monument. It hardly amounted to an income, but as he told Frank Pinkley, "I love my little job." More than anything, Johnson wanted to share his monument with those who, as he put it, "have a little pioneer blood in their veins and can see beauty in every crack and ledge."[3]

Johnson took a proprietary interest in the White Canyon bridges, arriving as soon as the snow cleared and remaining until it returned, working out of a tent perched on the rim above Armstrong Canyon. There he awaited the few tourists who arrived at this remote destination. An inveterate optimist, he noted in his July 1933 report that there were "quite a lot of cars coming out to see me . . . two yesterday and three today."

During the 1930s it took a determined tourist to brave the fifty miles of rock-studded, tire-popping road that led west from Blanding and ended next to Johnson's makeshift headquarters. He tried to greet each visitor himself and would offer directions and encouragement to those willing to hike to the three bridges. Johnson had constructed a short trail leading down into Armstrong Canyon and the Edwin (Owachomo) Bridge, but it was a much longer hike down canyon to the Caroline (Kachina) Bridge, and still farther up White Canyon to the Augusta (Sipapu) Bridge, the most impressive of the lot.

An affable, outgoing character, Johnson expressed a contagious enthusiasm for the geologic wonders contained in "his" monument. One thing reliably set him off, though: anyone who didn't come prepared to respect and appreciate this canyon domain. "Tourists," he claimed, "are people with money and no brains to use it, people just rushing around who can't appreciate beauty when they find it, littering up lovely places they get into with discarded papers and tin cans. They are always going somewhere and are always disappointed when they get there."[4] He was especially disdainful of those who felt compelled to inscribe their names on the cliffs, and he would often seek out the offenders and make them remove their inscriptions.

Despite his dim regard for tourists, Johnson hoped to make Natural Bridges into a much greater attraction. A decent road was the key to this endeavor; in the 1930s he helped volunteers from Blanding hew out the beginnings of a route, and by August 1934 he could boast two hundred visitors to the monument in one month. With further improvements to the road the following year, Natural Bridges saw gradual increases in visitation, reaching just over one thousand by 1939.

Frank Pinkley rationalized the low levels of use within the region's national monuments as appropriate to their educational and preservation purposes, in contrast to the primarily recreational uses of the national parks. He believed that those who took the trouble to seek out the diverse monuments of the Desert Southwest displayed greater curiosity and interest than the typical visitor to a national park—"he knows there is a story behind what his eyes can see at the monument and he wants that story," Pinkley observed in a 1938 Park Service report.[5] When no more than a half dozen inquiring travelers would show up on a typical day, which was often the case at Natural Bridges or Hovenweep, that story was not too difficult to provide. With easier access came a different class of visitor, but to most field personnel, including Johnson, this seemed both inevitable and desirable.

Zeke Johnson continued his own educational outreach work without pay during the winters he spent in Salt Lake City, giving talks to various civic and educational groups. In 1933 he received a federal service appointment with a summertime salary of $140 a month. By the time he retired in 1941, a visit to Natural Bridges no longer required a horseback expedition such as Henry Culmer undertook in 1905. For another decade, though, the monument would remain a hidden enclave within the greater canyon lands region, offering a respite from an increasingly mechanized and noisy human world.

Travelers continued to flock to Utah's two national parks as the Great Depression took hold across the nation. In 1931, more than forty-one thousand tourists took in the views from Sunset Point and other vantages at Bryce Canyon, despite the park's brief June–September season. Zion, which was open all year, attracted more than fifty-nine thousand visitors that year. These numbers dropped somewhat as the Depression worsened, but for a dollar entrance fee tourists could drive into Zion Canyon, gaze up at the Great White Throne, hike the trails to the Emerald Pools and Angels Landing, and motor on to Bryce via the newly opened Zion Tunnel.[6]

Virtually all of Zion's visitors—98 percent by the Park Service's estimate—arrived by private auto during the 1931 season. This far exceeded the thousand or so who paid for the Utah Parks Company's package tour, which included the North Rim of the Grand Canyon, Bryce Canyon, and Cedar Breaks. Rail travel was down nationwide, and faced with competition from motorists, the Union Pacific subsidiary reduced its rates for the 1933 season to just under sixty dollars for the five-day tour. At the Park Service's urging, it also made its facilities in Zion and Bryce Canyon available to independent travelers. A two-person cabin cost $4.50 per night, and the new cafeteria at Zion Lodge, which was open mid-May through mid-October, provided quick meals for auto tourists eager to be on their way.[7]

The railroads had helped to create and publicize the national parks, but the comfortable, escorted trips they offered were giving way to the independent auto tourist. By the mid-1930s all aspects of national park operations, from concessioners' guest services to the Park Service's construction budgets, were oriented toward the needs of tens of thousands of newly mobile Americans who wanted to experience scenic America at lower cost and on their own schedule. At Bryce Canyon, crews extended the main entrance road south along the Paunsaugunt Plateau toward Rainbow Point, carving out additional viewpoints over the Paria River amphitheater and at a natural bridge spanning a small canyon on the plateau top.[8] By 1935 nearly sixty-five thousand visitors were taking in the sights from these and nearby viewpoints. Zion saw improvements to the East Rim tunnel, already a landmark attraction, as well as to the main canyon road, helping the park to draw nearly one hundred thousand visitors that year.

No longer limited to travelers willing to brave muddy wagon tracks and sleep in the sagebrush, Zion and Bryce Canyon supplied the hoped-for foundation of a tourism economy in southern Utah. These parks also served as a conduit for federal largesse under the New Deal. By the fall of 1933, more than five hundred workers were building roads and completing other projects within Zion and Bryce Canyon. Many came from outside the state, but administrators also hired Utah workers (known as "local experienced men") to help oversee these projects.[9] Federal payrolls, along with the stream of visitors seeking meals, lodging, and gasoline in the parks, helped to ameliorate the economic hardships facing southern Utah's isolated towns and villages.

Many residents of Springdale, Rockville, Panguitch, and Tropic took justifiable pride in their nearby national parks, which were among the scenic highlights of the Intermountain West. The management of Zion and Bryce Canyon generated remarkably little controversy, partly because early-day rangers and custodians (such as Zion's Walter Ruesch) often came from the local area. J. L. Crawford, who grew up underneath Zion's cliffs on a farm homesteaded by his grandfather, recalled that other than some discontent when livestock grazing was halted in the park, most local people looked on the Park Service with favor, realizing the benefits that came with better roads and employment in tourism and in the park itself.[10]

Proposals to expand existing parks and monuments were another matter, however. The enlargement of Bryce Canyon in 1931 met with concern from Tropic Valley ranchers who held grazing permits on the Paunsaugunt

Plateau. Although much of this range was in poor condition, Park Service administrators agreed to allow continued grazing with the proviso that the rights could not be sold or transferred without approval from Washington. It took another thirty-three years to eliminate cattle from the park.[11]

Further conflict arose when Horace Albright aggressively sought to acquire Cedar Breaks, the colorfully eroded bluffs and canyons at the western edge of the Markagunt Plateau, from the Forest Service. Sheep and cattle ranchers in the area strongly objected to the transfer of management, fearing that the Park Service would eventually obtain all of the plateau south to Zion National Park. Nor were Forest Service officers enthusiastic about losing control of a prime scenic destination. Even Roger Toll, Albright's point man for new park acquisitions, was lukewarm about Cedar Breaks when he visited it in 1932, terming it inferior to the grand displays at Bryce.

Albright persisted, receiving support from the Cedar City Chamber of Commerce, which foresaw increased tourism possibilities, and from Zion superintendent Thomas Allen, who saw the acquisition as a way to better regulate the Utah Parks Company, which already operated a lodge at Cedar Breaks.[12] Franklin Roosevelt established the 5,700-acre national monument in August 1933, shortly before Albright retired as head of the Park Service. Along with Pipe Spring National Monument on the Arizona Strip, travelers could now take in a wide variety of scenic and historic sites on the much-touted circle tour of Zion, the North Rim, and Bryce Canyon, which traversed geologic and climatic environments spanning nine thousand feet in elevation. These parks and monuments helped advance Albright's goal of a strong Park Service presence in the Southwest and fulfilled Stephen Mather's mandate to make an "all year-round resort" of the various properties the agency controlled on the Colorado Plateau. According to historian Hal Rothman, southern Utah "was being groomed as a new American outdoor vacationland" under the Park Service's watchful care.[13]

Later that fall, the Park Service acquired a second Forest Service property in Utah, this one already carrying the designation of a national monument. Timpanogos Cave, comprising three limestone caverns high on a hillside in American Fork Canyon in the Wasatch Range, had been designated by President Warren Harding in October 1922. For eleven years it was managed by the Forest Service by delegation to the Timpanogos Cave Committee—an indication of how this agency maintained close ties to the local communities served by national forests. Horace Albright believed that all such monuments, as well as national historic sites, should be administered by a single federal agency—namely, his. He persuaded Franklin Roosevelt to sign an executive order in June 1933 transferring all Forest Service monuments to the National Park Service. At Timpanogos Cave, the actual transfer did not take place until the following July, and the Park Service chose to let the Timpanogos Cave Committee continue to guide tours and patrol the caverns. Like the other small national monuments in southern Utah, it continued to operate on virtually no budget, with tour fees paying for the services of a custodian-ranger.[14]

Visitation to Timpanogos Cave climbed steadily for several years following its transfer to the Park Service. The Civilian Conservation Corps worked on a new zigzag trail to the entrance of Hansen Cave, and by 1939 tunnels had been built linking the caves, allowing visitors to make a one-way tour of the three caverns. Further improvements were made using federal emergency relief funds, and by the outbreak of World War II Timpanogos Cave had outgrown its days as a merely local attraction.[15]

Federal relief programs played an important role in mitigating unemployment in Utah during the Depression, but county officials in southern Utah also looked to new parks as a way to tap the federal treasury for needed road projects. In May 1933 state representative Emil Gammeter introduced a memorial in the Utah legislature asking the Park Service to designate a national monument in the "Monumental Valley" south of the San Juan River, which since 1925 had been featured in spectacular western movies. Gammeter supported this proposal as a means of getting new roads and highways built, helping to alleviate the long isolation under which the residents of southern Utah labored. He noted that agriculture and mining in Utah were limited by water supply and international demand, but "our scenery will always be here." If places such as Monument Valley and the Goosenecks of the San Juan River were made accessible by road, Gammeter said, "we will have capitalized on one of our biggest assets."[16]

The idea of designating a new national park south of the Colorado and San Juan Rivers was first broached by Charles Bernheimer, the New York adventurer who traveled widely across the region in the 1920s with John Wetherill and Zeke Johnson. In 1928 Bernheimer had written to Reed Smoot and Stephen Mather to propose changing the status of Rainbow Bridge from a national monument to a national park. The Park Service demurred, citing the difficulty of managing and developing a new park in such a remote locality. There was also the problem of the Paiute Strip, formerly a reservation for the San Juan band of Southern Paiute Indians, which was in the process of being folded into the Navajo Reservation.[17]

Bernheimer persisted, however, and by early 1929 he had broadened his proposal to include most of the northern Navajo Reservation, taking in Monument Valley as well as Rainbow Bridge and Navajo Mountain. It included the ancient cliff dwellings at Betatakin, Keet Seel, and Inscription House, which were part of Navajo National Monument, and the wild country south of the Colorado River and west of Navajo Mountain. Bernheimer used his connections in the business and public spheres to lobby for such a park, even traveling to Washington, D.C., in early 1929 to meet with Park Service officials.[18]

Horace Albright, who replaced Mather in January 1929, grew interested in the proposal and detailed Roger Toll, his principal investigator for new parks, and M. R. Tillotson, superintendent of Grand Canyon National Park, to make a field examination. Their report, in the form of a letter Toll sent to Albright in April 1931, enthusiastically endorsed the idea of a new park on the Navajo Reservation. The area was "of such outstanding quality that it would be an important addition to the national park system," he wrote. "The scenery is varied, full of interest and is of impressive magnitude. There were also, he added, almost as an afterthought, "unusual features of ethnology and archaeology."[19]

Toll suggested that the park consist of four detached units, taking in Monument Valley, the Rainbow Bridge–Navajo Mountain area, and Tsegi Canyon, as well as five possible smaller units in areas such as the Goosenecks of the San Juan River and various dinosaur track localities. He pointed out that the Paiute Strip was no longer a reservation and had been "opened to entry because of oil possibilities." As for the Navajo Reservation itself, Toll advised Albright that the area was "government land, reserved for the use of the Navajo and Hopi Indians"—indicating that neither he nor the federal government recognized Indian sovereignty over it.

Toll's letter prompted Albright to make his own trip to northern Arizona in the summer of 1932, in a party that included M. R. Tillotson and Albright's son, Bob. John Wetherill took them on the overland trip to Rainbow Bridge, using the western trail that led from Rainbow Lodge over Redbud Pass. The party also climbed to the top of Navajo Mountain, the view from which astounded Albright. "I have seen all the other glories of this great country just south of the San Juan," he wrote afterward to Neil Judd, a prominent archaeologist who as a young man had taken part in the 1909 Cummings-Douglass expedition. "What a country it is!"[20]

Navajo tribal leaders, though, were far from enthusiastic about a national park on what they considered their lands, fearing curtailment of grazing use and the possible removal of Diné from their homes. Albright promised that such a designation would not interfere with traditional Navajo uses, but neither he nor Commissioner of Indian Affairs John Collier was able to persuade tribal leaders to back the idea. Collier's Bureau of Indian Affairs was at the time embarking on what would become a highly unpopular livestock reduction program on the Navajo Reservation, which only added to the level of mistrust.[21]

In 1933 the Paiute Strip was placed under control of the Navajo Tribal Council. With the council wary of the federal government, and with Congress turning its attention to the nation's economic crisis, nothing more came of Bernheimer's park proposal. Despite the growing interest in the park among Utah civic leaders such as Emil Gammeter, there would be no expansion of Park Service control on the Navajo Reservation.

The Navajo national park proposal was nonetheless significant in that it raised the possibility of a landscape-wide park in the Four Corners region, supplanting the scattered and isolated national monuments then in existence. Such a park, its promoters believed, would attract many more tourists than a handful of tiny national monuments, and it would serve as a basis for needed road improvements. The Bernheimer proposal also appears to have sensitized certain Park Service personnel to other values found in this region, including its long history of occupation by Native Americans going back to Archaic times.

Standing on top of Navajo Mountain certainly seems to have awakened Horace Albright to the magnificence of the canyon lands along the San Juan and Colorado Rivers. Roger Toll and M. R. Tillotson likewise became intrigued with these intricately carved canyons and far-reaching vistas. In a little over a year, Toll would gain his own long-distance outlook from a mountaintop farther north, leading him to initiate what was arguably the most astonishing park proposal in the agency's history.

14

THE VIEW FROM THE
AQUARIUS PLATEAU

The economic cataclysm of the Great Depression brought a temporary drop in the number of visitors to Utah's two national parks, although by 1935 visitation to both Zion and Bryce Canyon had rebounded to new highs. The Depression actually increased the National Park Service's funding and prestige as it took on important parts of the New Deal's recovery efforts, including projects under the Works Progress Administration and Civilian Conservation Corps. These programs left a legacy of many historic buildings, roads, and trails throughout the National Park System. Utah gained three new national monuments during the 1930s—Capitol Reef, Cedar Breaks, and the Kolob section of Zion National Park—as well as substantial expansions to Bryce Canyon National Park and Arches and Dinosaur National Monuments. All of these reflected Interior Secretary Harold Ickes's strong support for expanding the national parks. But the largest potential park acquisition of them all—the enigmatic Escalante national monument proposal of the mid-1930s—failed to gain a foothold in Utah during this turbulent period.

One of the most visible manifestations of New Deal conservation efforts was the Civilian Conservation Corps. Starting in 1933, CCC camps sprang up at Zion, Bryce Canyon, Cedar Breaks, and Arches, providing workers to build trails, improve roads and campgrounds, plant trees, and stabilize eroded stream banks. In Arches, young men from the Dalton Wells camp built a primitive track from Willow Spring to the Balanced Rock–Windows area, giving autos their first, albeit difficult, access into the national monument. Farther west, a crew under the direction of the Forest Service worked on a road leading from Torrey up onto the eastern flank of the Aquarius Plateau, known locally as Boulder Mountain. This route eventually reached the isolated village of Boulder, where it joined the tortuous track coming from Escalante over the sandstone hogback known as Hell's Backbone.

Better roads were welcome in southern Utah, but the New Deal also brought greater federal oversight of public lands through the Taylor Grazing Act, which organized the open ranges of the West into managed grazing allotments. To assuage concerns about the increased federal presence in the West, the Interior Department set up various planning boards to coordinate relief work with the states and to review possible new park designations. For the first time the Park Service hired staff specifically to evaluate new park proposals, led by Roger Toll, the superintendent of Yellowstone National Park, who maintained an office in Denver during the winter. In October 1932, Toll visited five potential park sites in Utah, including the Kolob Canyons west of Zion, Cedar Breaks on the Markagunt Plateau, a pictograph site in Johnson Canyon east of Kanab, Arches National Monument, and the Wayne Wonderland.

After spending three days on horseback among the sheer cliffs and narrow canyons of the Kolob area, Toll was sufficiently impressed to recommend that it be designated a national monument. This could be expedited through administrative channels rather than undertaking the lengthy legislative process to add it to Zion National Park, and it was thought that it might also reduce opposition from grazing interests.[1] Toll felt that Cedar Breaks and the Johnson Canyon pictographs, while significant, did not merit acquisition by the Park Service. (Horace Albright felt otherwise about Cedar Breaks.)

Toll's visit to the Wayne Wonderland came at the request of Thomas Allen, the superintendent of Zion National Park, who had viewed the area in July 1931 with Ephraim Pectol following a meeting in Loa of the Associated Civic Clubs of Southern Utah. The civic clubs had offered a vague proposal for a new park in the Fruita area, taking in the scenic canyon of the Fremont River but little of the nearby Waterpocket Fold. Pectol wanted to include more of the cliffs south of Fruita and to extend the park to the eastern slopes of Boulder Mountain, but local ranchers objected to a large withdrawal that could mean the loss of their grazing privileges.[2]

Toll, like Allen, spent only one day in the Wayne Wonderland, driving from Torrey down the rough road to Fruita, then on through Capitol Wash toward Hanksville. He felt that the Wayne Wonderland was "scenic, highly colored, and remarkable in several respects," although it "lacked any one distinctive feature that is superlative." He told Horace Albright that "it impresses one as being only a little below the standard of existing national parks. If a number of new parks were to be created, this might easily be one of them."[3]

Those parks, Toll stated in his report to Albright, might also include the San Rafael Swell, a broad uplift north of the Waterpocket Fold, and Barrier Canyon, a long defile farther east across miles of sandy, windswept desert, which sheltered a spectacular collection of ancient pictographs. In fact, as Toll wrote, "the entire region flanking the Colorado River from Moab to Lees Ferry "was likely to contain some places of spectacular scenery."[4] This was a considerable understatement, but it showed how little the Park Service knew about the Utah canyon country more than thirty years into the twentieth century.

Despite its uncertain beginnings, the Wayne Wonderland proposal enjoyed a degree of local support, thanks to Ephraim Pectol's unflagging efforts. Shortly after Joseph Hickman's death in 1925, Pectol enlisted J. E. Broaddus, a Salt Lake City optometrist and tourism promoter, to photograph the area around Fruita. Broaddus developed a slide lecture on the Wayne Wonderland and gave glowing accounts for Utah's newspapers, describing the "fantastic erosions at the foot of towering cliffs and pinnacles" along the drive from Torrey to Fruita. Broaddus took visitors through Capitol Gorge and Pleasant Creek, as well as to the Fremont or Broad Arch, which would later be renamed Hickman Bridge in honor of the Wayne Wonderland's first advocate. A bit optimistically, local papers termed the bridge's 130-foot span the "world's largest."[5]

Like Joseph Hickman before him, Ephraim Pectol won election to the state legislature in 1932 and the following March secured passage of a resolution calling on the federal government to establish a national park or monument in eastern Wayne County. It identified three areas for further study by "competent authorities": the banded cliffs northwest of Torrey known as Velvet Ridge, the Fremont River gorge immediately southwest of town, and a larger area of cliffs and canyons centering on Fruita but excluding the settlement itself. The resolution stated that "such a national park or monument would be a logical unit in a chain of natural wonders" stretching from Mesa Verde in Colorado through Natural Bridges, Bryce Canyon, Zion, and Cedar Breaks.[6] The intent was to link these scenic destinations by a new road reaching from Blanding to Hanksville and on to Torrey, placing Wayne County on an equal footing with its southern neighbors in catering to tourists.

With local civic groups and the state legislature all boosting the Wayne Wonderland, Roger Toll returned to Torrey on the last day of October 1933 for another look. This time Pectol spent four days with the Park Service official, traveling on foot, on horseback, and by car. To gain an overview of the Waterpocket Fold, Pectol took Toll over the new CCC road high up on Boulder Mountain. Leaving their auto at the Wildcat forest ranger station, they climbed up to Chokecherry Point, a nearly eleven-thousand-foot-high vantage point looking out over the Henry Mountains and beyond.

The scene that unfolded seems to have had a pronounced effect on Toll. In his subsequent report to Park Service director Arno Cammerer, who had replaced Horace Albright that August, Toll described "a vast area, almost uninhabited, with many spectacular canyons and scenic areas, seldom visited and little known." Off to the north lay the San Rafael Swell, while far below them the Caineville Mesas rose out of a bare desert. The long ridge of Mount Ellen dominated the eastern skyline, with the Kaiparowits Plateau bulking to the south. Navajo Mountain, another laccolithic extrusion, stood in the southern distance. The foreground slopes of Boulder Mountain were "a tumble of multi-colored sandstones, dotted with grass lands."[7]

The view from the Aquarius was magnificent, but Toll's immediate task was to evaluate the Wayne Wonderland proposal. In his April 1934 report to Cammerer, he recommended enlarging it to include Grand Wash, the Hickman natural bridge, and more of the Fremont River, while omitting Velvet Ridge, which was mostly Forest Service land. He proposed that the area be designated a national monument, knowing that park legislation would be much more difficult to enact, especially after ranchers in eastern Wayne County circulated a petition opposing any Park Service designation. Cammerer agreed with Toll's analysis, which disappointed the Wayne Wonderland's boosters in Utah, who had hoped a new national park would bring generous federal appropriations for roads and tourist facilities.[8]

Nonetheless, Ephraim Pectol did all he could to smooth the path toward monument designation, obtaining endorsements from Governor Henry Blood and Utah's congressional delegation. He also tried to placate local ranchers by assuring them that their grazing rights would be protected. Several issues remained contentious, though, such as whether to include the

Capitol Gorge, as seen in this 1935 photo by NPS photographer George A. Grant, was the only passage for automobiles through the Waterpocket Fold until 1962. *National Park Service, Harpers Ferry Center, VA, HPC-000196.*

village of Fruita and the Fremont River gorge farther upstream. In March 1935, Zion National Park superintendent Preston Patraw visited the area and recommended that the entire village be included in the new park or monument, realizing that its attractive fields and orchards would inevitably be developed with tourist lodges and other facilities if left in private hands. These private lands could be acquired as funds became available, he noted.[9]

By the summer of 1935, the government appeared to have a monument proposal that almost everyone could agree on. It would take in the scenic cliffs, domes, and canyons in the Fruita–Capitol Gorge area, most of which were unsuitable for livestock grazing, and include a section of the Fremont River gorge upstream of Fruita. An area of striking sandstone pinnacles at the base of Boulder Mountain called Fish Creek Cove, which contained fine examples of prehistoric rock art, was omitted owing to objections from state legislators.[10] Surveyors were dispatched to ascertain boundaries, and Park Service photographer George Grant made a tour of the area in a specially outfitted panel truck that served as his field darkroom. It seemed likely that Utah would soon acquire a new federal designation that would boost Wayne County as a new vacationland.

Thus far, discussions over land designations in southern Utah had been mostly a courteous back-and-forth between Park Service officials and local business and railroad interests, but that was about to change. Ironically, Ephraim Pectol may have been responsible: when he took Roger Toll up onto the crest of the Aquarius Plateau, he opened the bureaucrat's eyes to a vast new landscape. The field of view extended far beyond the Waterpocket Fold, lending itself to a vision that exceeded the dreams of local business-people and civic boosters. Roger Toll had been to the mountain and seen larger possibilities, and he and his Park Service colleagues would soon unveil a grand concept that would upstage the long-awaited Wayne Wonderland proposal. It would also embroil Utah in a debate that, eighty years later, still has not ended.

Harold Ickes, Franklin Roosevelt's irascible interior secretary, is often thought to have launched what would have been the greatest Park Service acquisition in history: the seven-thousand-square-mile Escalante national monument in southern Utah's canyon country. This gigantic proposal seemed to come out of nowhere when it was announced in 1936, hence the assumption that a distant bureaucracy in Washington had cooked it up. Yet the Escalante proposal was a direct result of Roger Toll's and M. R. Tillotson's investigations into new park proposals in the early 1930s. Their recommendations introduced the idea of including a much larger share of southern Utah's canyons and mesas within the National Park System rather than simply designating a few thousand acres around an isolated natural bridge or scenic canyon. Although the Escalante proposal ran into heavy opposition within Utah and was later withdrawn, it transformed how the Park Service would think about the canyon lands region for the remainder of the century. The Toll-Tillotson proposal was the direct ancestor of Canyonlands National Park, an expanded Capitol Reef National Park, the Glen Canyon National Recreation Area, and (in a lineage dating back sixty years) President Clinton's 1996 proclamation establishing the Grand Staircase–Escalante National Monument.

Although Harold Ickes advanced a number of major new park proposals in the 1930s, including Olympic in Washington State and Kings Canyon in California, it is unlikely that he came up with the idea of an all-encompassing national monument in southern Utah. Few people in the Park Service knew the Utah canyon lands well, as Roger Toll's visits had made clear. Dr. Frank Oastler, the New York physician and national park advocate who in 1926 had urged Horace Albright to designate Arches National Monument, also suggested a number of other possible monuments in southeastern Utah, but at that time the Park Service had no formal procedure for evaluating such proposals.

Roger Toll's visit to the Aquarius Plateau in the fall of 1933 alerted him to the possibilities for new park and monument designations in the region north of the San Juan. Additional impetus came from a Texas oil geologist named Harry Aurand, who had been prospecting the Four Corners region for the Midwest Oil Company during the 1920s. Aurand was impressed with the canyons and rims of southeastern Utah, and in a 1934 letter to Toll he suggested that several sites be considered for national monuments, including Dark Canyon, the Goosenecks of the San Juan River, and Monument Valley. He even proposed that the remote Kaiparowits Plateau be considered as a national park. "The scenic value, the geology involved, and the educational and recreational possibilities of many of the areas which I visited in Southeastern Utah and Northwestern Arizona appear almost limitless," he wrote.[11]

Toll was receptive to Aurand's ideas and forwarded his letter to Arno Cammerer, along with the comment that "the area of southeastern Utah, including the Colorado River from [the confluence with the] Green River to the state line and the territory on both sides of the river, comprises one of the most scenic areas in the United States that is not now contained within a national park." The whole region was "difficult of access and is now practically unavailable to the traveling public," he observed. He suggested that the Park Service take immediate steps to acquire a large part of this area with the intention of developing roads and tourist facilities later on.[12]

Toll probably had in mind designating a number of smaller national monuments, not creating a vast wilderness park such as Clyde Kluckhohn had proposed in 1933. But his memo led Arthur Demaray, the acting Park Service director, to ask Secretary Ickes to defer issuing livestock grazing leases in those parts of Utah that were under consideration for park status. These included the relatively small Kolob Canyons and Wayne Wonderland areas that Toll had been investigating, as well as a portion of the Yampa River drainage on the Utah-Colorado border. Dwarfing these, however, was a thirty- to forty-mile-wide grazing exclusion along the Colorado and Green Rivers, extending from near the town of Green River clear to Lees Ferry in northern Arizona. Ickes approved the request on January 23, 1935, setting in motion the field studies that would emerge as a full-blown monument proposal.[13]

M. R. Tillotson, the superintendent of Grand Canyon National Park who had recently investigated the proposed Navajo national park, personally directed the study of the "Lower Colorado River Exclusion" during the spring and summer of 1935. Joining him were Toll, Mesa Verde superintendent Jesse Nusbaum, park planner Thomas Vint, and Emery Kolb, the renowned Grand Canyon photographer. Traveling by horse, auto, and airplane, they surveyed the vast terrain stretching from the Orange Cliffs near Moab to beyond the Escalante River. Tillotson solicited advice from other Park Service personnel who were familiar with the Southwest.[14] Each apparently suggested additional lands to include, and by the end of 1935 their collective thinking had solidified into a truly grand idea: Rather than designate a series of smaller parks and monuments within the Utah canyon lands, why not protect the region in its entirety? Virtually every scenic feature along the canyons of the Green and Colorado Rivers appeared worthy of inclusion, along with a good deal of land to either side—the Henry Mountains,

the Dirty Devil River, Cedar Mesa with its spectacular prehistoric ruins,
the incised canyons of the lower Escalante River drainage, all the way to the
southern edge of the Kaiparowits Plateau.

As superintendents of three of national parks, Toll,
Tillotson, and Nusbaum must hav
nic and geologic features called fo
this in a memo to Arno Cammere
completed their field investigatio
posed Wayne Wonderland nation
Reef, but he also called attention
to the Colorado River, an area la
a handful of inhabitants." Toll fo
ument around Fruita "will not l
than a brief time, except as coup
boring national forests."[15]

In 1872, Congress had seen
in Yellowstone, not just a few se
geysers. Designating a large ar
similar purpose in southeastern Utan, forming
features as Dark Canyon and the Goosenecks of the San Juan that Harry
Aurand had mentioned, and extending west to the Waterpocket Fold in the
Fremont River country.

Back at Grand Canyon, Tillotson prepared a report on their monumental proposal. His office was mere steps from one of the most fabulous pan-
oramas on Earth, but nothing in his estimation exceeded the Utah canyon
country for "a greater variety or a more interesting array of spectacularly
scenic effects," he wrote. The area encompassed "deep canyons, narrow
gorges, terraced plateaus, cliff-bound mesas, tortuous entrenched stream
meanderings, huge buttes and temples, weirdly-eroded formations, wind-
swept desert-like slopes, standing rocks, high escarpments, natural bridges
and colorings so gorgeous as at times to seem almost gaudy and on a scale
as to be difficult of comprehension."[16]

Tillotson completed his report on August 20, 1935, and circulated it to
interested Park Service officials for comment. Additional lands were added
until it took in 6,968 square miles, or 4,459,520 acres—an area twice the size
of Yellowstone. That September, Roger Toll passed the report on to Director Cammerer with his approval.[17] Breathtaking in scope, the proposed

monument reached from a few miles east of the village of Boulder nearly to Blanding, and from a point about twelve miles south of the town of Green River to the San Juan River. Toll admitted it was large but believed it was not excessive. He recommended that the entire area be established as a national monument, subject to future hydropower development, and that existing livestock grazing be allowed to continue "with a view to the gradual reduction and ultimate elimination of domestic grazing."

Toll proposed that the area be named in honor of the "first explorer of the region, Padre Escalante, or possibly for John Wesley Powell." Thus was born the Escalante national monument proposal, on which the Park Service would labor without success for the next decade. Had it succeeded, the monument would have joined Yellowstone, Yosemite, Glacier, and Grand Canyon as one of the nation's premier park designations.

M. R. Tillotson's own views on the Escalante proposal are less clear, since only fragments of his 1935 report have survived. An engineer by training, he favored tourist road development in order to "make the wilderness easy to enjoy," as he put it in his 1929 book *Grand Canyon Country*.[18] He even boasted that given enough money, he could design and build a road to the bottom of the Grand Canyon—a notion that thankfully never came to pass. His view, which was shared by many in the Park Service, was that well-designed park roads brought visitors closer to nature without necessarily spoiling it. Given the right combination of scenic pulloffs and perhaps a few rustic lodges and campgrounds, tourists in large numbers could experience the Utah canyons without marring them. Parks could be a source of jobs and development, combining scenery and economic progress in a package that appealed to rural constituencies.

This was what the National Park Service hoped to offer the state of Utah with its bold proposal for the Colorado–Green River canyon lands. It remained to be seen whether local and state officials would accept the Escalante proposal as a basis for public works and unemployment relief, or oppose it as a federal land grab. As with many New Deal programs, the Park Service was venturing into new territory in the Utah canyon lands, seeking a major expansion of its authority over a hinterland that local people and state officials assumed was theirs to control and use.

THE MONUMENT THAT
ALMOST WAS

For a brief moment in the mid-1930s, it appeared that Utah might gain the largest single unit of the entire National Park System—the 4.5-million-acre Escalante national monument, first proposed in 1936. Like a meteor that flares brightly, astonishes onlookers, and then fades from view, this unprecedented Park Service initiative burned out under the unrelenting resistance of Utah's political leaders and ranching interests. Even in failure, however, its impact was lasting, helping to point the way for numerous other federal designations that now cover much of southern Utah's canyon lands.

Perhaps the more startling aspect of the Escalante proposal was how it emerged from an agency whose largest acquisition in Utah up to that time was 35,800 acres of Forest Service land at Bryce Canyon. Stephen Mather and Horace Albright insisted that new park proposals meet high standards of beauty, scientific significance, and naturalness, which tended to favor smaller acquisitions that took in readily recognized natural features such as the deep gorge of the Mukuntuweap or the cliffs and spires at Bryce.

The Escalante proposal lay in a different category altogether. While it contained numerous scenic attractions—many of which would come to light much later—its distinction was its enormous scale. With the exception of some small private inholdings and mining claims, the lands within the proposed monument belonged to the vast western public domain that came out of the nineteenth century. These remote plateaus and canyons were loosely overseen by the General Land Office, which by 1930 was mostly conducting boundary surveys and disposing of the rare parcel of commercially valuable land, and by the U.S. Grazing Service, which was established in 1935 to bring order to the haphazard (or wholly absent) system of allotting livestock forage in the West. These two agencies would be combined in 1946 to form the Bureau of Land Management.

On January 25, 1936, Interior Secretary Harold Ickes signed off on the 6,969-square-mile Escalante national monument proposal that M. R. Tillotson and Roger Toll had prepared the previous summer and fall. There was no formal unveiling of the proposal, which was likely a strategic blunder on the part of the Park Service. In Utah, park proposals were typically developed in response to calls from local civic or business organizations, but in this case the initiative was entirely its own. Utah state officials were not consulted and had to ferret out the details themselves. Governor Henry Blood learned of the mammoth proposal when it was mentioned in a Department of the Interior report on the recreational possibilities of the Colorado River basin. This little-publicized study was part of the federal government's assessment of the hydropower potential of the Southwest's greatest river, and it gave only a sketchy description of the new monument.[1] But it was enough to alarm Blood, who asked his state's congressional delegation to investigate. Senator William King placed a phone call to Harold Ickes, asking him to delay public release of the proposal until state officials could study it. Congressman Abe Murdock voiced similar concerns in a meeting with Park Service officials in February. All three Utah officials belonged to Franklin Roosevelt's party, but they were opposed to limiting economic development in so large an area.[2]

The only state official to look favorably on the Escalante proposal was Ray West, director of the State Planning Board, which had been set up in 1935 within Governor Blood's office to coordinate Depression-era relief efforts. The board had taken considerable interest in national parks as engines of economic development, and at one point it floated a proposal for a 360-square-mile national park in the Wayne Wonderland. Far exceeding Ephraim Pectol's limited vision for the park, it would have included more of the Waterpocket Fold and the striking desert terrain to the north and east.[3] Little interest in this idea was shown among state officials, so West turned his attention to the larger Escalante proposal. In a report he submitted to Governor Blood on May 1, 1936, he noted that the monument had the potential to accelerate important road-building projects, including the proposed Hanksville-Blanding highway, a pet project of tourism and economic development boosters in southern Utah. State officials hoped the federal government would finance the project as a "park approach road," but

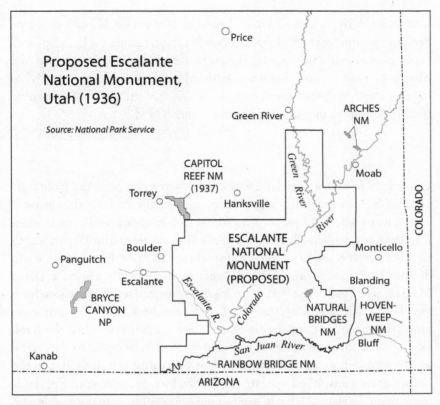

Proposed Escalante National Monument, Utah (1936)

Source: National Park Service

The Escalante national monument, as proposed by the National Park Service in 1936.

regional Park Service staff were cool to the idea, not wanting to become the state's highway builder.[4]

West noted that only about fifty people lived within the proposed monument area, divided between the cliff-bound villages of Fruita and Hite. Little mineral production had occurred within the monument area, leading him to conclude that "the proceeds due directly or indirectly to tourist business will mean more to Southern Utah than those from any other use to which this barren and almost unproductive land may be put." Most of the area served as grazing land, and as he noted, "463 families were dependent upon this area for year round grazing of their livestock." That alone ought to have indicated the opposition the proposal would arouse.[5]

Governor Blood, who chaired the planning board, must have been startled by the map accompanying West's report. Prepared by the Park Service in April 1936, it showed the proposed monument blanketing much of southeastern Utah, amounting to 8 percent of the state. Blood's concerns centered on mining and hydropower development, despite the Park Service's assurances of maintaining prior rights. He forwarded West's report to Abe Murdock, assuring him that it was nothing more than a "factual study" of the lands within the proposed monument and that the rest of the planning board felt that the monument took in too much land.[6]

Objections to such a large land withdrawal were to be expected from state officials, but as word of the proposed monument circulated in the spring of 1936, it was a federal employee who set about organizing public opposition: J. Q. Peterson, who headed the regional office of the Interior Department's Grazing Service, called a meeting of stockmen in Price, Utah, on June 9 to discuss the Escalante proposal. It did not go well for the Park Service. David Madsen, who headed the Park Service's newly formed wildlife division from an office in Salt Lake City, tried to allay the ranchers' fears of an immense lockup of resources, pointing out that the new roads that would be built following monument designation would increase tourist traffic in the region to a tremendous extent. "Here would be the greatest primitive area in the United States, unspoiled by man, untouched by man, or anything pertaining to man," he stated. "That in itself would speak volumes to the people who wish to see it."[7] He advised the skeptical stockmen that grazing and mining had reached their maximum development in the area, and that "millions of dollars of new revenue" could be raised through tourist development.

Several of the ranchers at the Price meeting acknowledged the need to protect scenic areas and increase tourism, but they objected to such a vast set-aside. J. M. MacFarland, a Farm Bureau spokesman, said, "We can't afford to set aside this land for a few bobcats and wildcats. . . . If you turned the tourist loose in that big area you would have to turn out the National Guard to find them." Escalante rancher Milton Twitchell observed that "you might as well go out and take the [cattlemen's] property as to take their grazing rights. You can make it legal, but you can never make it moral."[8] Charles Redd, a prominent citizen of Blanding who represented three grazing district advisory boards in southeastern Utah, told the group that "the record of the Park Service is not very promising to the livestock industry because they are not satisfied as long as there is a sheep or cow left." He said that tourism could be promoted without casting out the livestock industry. "We can achieve all the things that Mr. Madsen points out without the withdrawal of these 4,500,000 acres and destruction of this industry," he said. "We want to achieve these things, but we don't want to destroy the people who have been here for the last fifty or sixty years. This is just a little harder rap than we can take without putting up a battle."

A more conciliatory note was struck by Wilford Clark of Cannonville, Utah, who said that "we are very much in favor of some portions of our country being improved for scientific purposes and also scenic purposes. We have some very good scenic attractions which have never been developed . . . we should give this proposal due consideration." Frank Martinez, president of the Associated Civic Clubs of Southern Utah, said that livestock grazing could work hand in hand with tourism, offering an authentic Old West experience for visitors. "There is room in that vast magnificent country for both industries," he said.[9] Still, he refused to endorse so large a monument, preferring one that could be made easily accessible to tourists.

Stung by the adverse showing in Price, Park Service officials looked for a way to make the monument palatable to ranchers and power development interests. M. R. Tillotson, who had written the 1935 report on the Escalante proposal, put together an informal working group that included David Madsen, Mesa Verde superintendent Jesse Nusbaum, Preston Patraw of Zion National Park, and Merel Sager, a landscape architect in the Park Service's Santa Fe regional office. In October 1936, the five men set off from Mesa Verde on a whirlwind tour of the southern Utah canyon lands by auto and airplane, accompanied by park planner Thomas Vint and photographer George Grant. Among their stops were Comb Ridge and the Goosenecks of the San Juan River, the country bordering Natural Bridges National Monument, which they saw with Zeke Johnson, and Dead Horse Point and nearby viewpoints over the Green and Colorado Rivers. Along the way they spoke with Charles Redd and other San Juan County ranchers opposed to the monument.

Merel Sager filed a report of their investigations the following February.[10] In an attempt to defuse opposition to the original Escalante proposal, he suggested a smaller designation encompassing about two thousand square miles, extending no more than ten or fifteen miles on either side of the Green and Colorado Rivers. This would take in the region's chief scenic features, Sager wrote, and could be protected without significant objections from the livestock industry. The revised proposal left out many areas that later generations of recreationists would treasure, such as most of the Escalante and

Dirty Devil River canyons, yet it still took in rank upon rank of spectacular cliffs and side canyons, most of which remained inaccessible to vehicles.

Sager believed that livestock grazing should be phased out in the remaining monument area, in keeping with usual park policy. He recognized, however, that hydropower interests had a stake in preserving their access to the
Colorado River. Investigations by the U.S. Geological Survey had identified two prime dam sites within the proposed Escalante national monument: one at the lower end of Glen Canyon above Lees Ferry, which would
create a reservoir reaching nearly two hundred miles into Cataract Canyon, and another immediately upstream of this reservoir near the mouth of
Dark Canyon, which would inundate the Colorado to a point above Moab.
Utah state officials strongly supported these projects, and Sager noted that
"it is folly not to recognize the fact that the Colorado River ultimately will
be developed, offering as it does the second largest concentration of water
power in the United States."[11]

The Park Service was not keen to have a power reservoir within a major
park unit, but a precedent existed at Lake Mead farther downstream on the
Colorado, where the Park Service jointly managed the Boulder Dam Recreation Area with the Bureau of Reclamation. Sager believed that a similar
recreation area could be designated in the Utah reaches of the Colorado and
Green Rivers and would offer "natural beauty far superior to Lake Mead."
Other than allowing for one or more reservoirs, Sager recommended that
whether it was designated a national monument or recreation area, most
of the Escalante area should be left undeveloped. "One gets the impression
that because of its sheer ruggedness it will preserve itself," he noted, yet "our
past experience should teach us that man's inherent, constitutional deter-
mination to vanquish primeval landscape[s] is a force which has thus far
never been shackled."[12]

The ranchers who each spring turned their cattle loose within this region
felt otherwise. To them, the scenic landscapes of southern Utah consisted
of little more than "red ledges," a country as old as time and impossible to
ruin. They insisted that the Park Service develop the existing national monuments rather than embark on a vast experiment in land preservation. The
Park Service had crossed a line with the Escalante proposal, violating the
tacit understanding that new parks and monuments would not interfere
with existing uses of the land. Southern Utah was now contested ground,
and neither its stunning beauty nor its seemingly limitless horizons would

overcome the antipathy of local residents to what they saw as the federal bureaucracy's overreach.

16

NEGOTIATIONS

On a fine October day in 1935, a few months before news of the Escalante national monument proposal became public, Zeke Johnson buttoned up his new sixteen-by-sixteen-foot army tent that formed the headquarters of Natural Bridges National Monument, saddled his horse, and headed down White Canyon toward the Colorado River. The cottonwood trees lining the wash were turning golden, making it a perfect time for a sightseeing trip. His companion was M. R. Tillotson, the superintendent of Grand Canyon National Park, who was there to examine a route for a proposed road linking Blanding to Hanksville. Johnson led the way along the benches above White Canyon, following an old cattleman's trail that crossed the Colorado River at Hite. He knew the route well from his days as a backcountry guide, and for years he had been trying to interest Park Service officials in turning the old trail into a tourist highway.

The trip proved to both men that a road could easily be extended to the river and on to the towns and villages along the Fremont River. A dream of San Juan and Wayne County businesspeople for years, the Hanksville-Blanding road would open the way for greater tourist traffic between Mesa Verde, Zion, and Bryce Canyon National Parks, as well as the soon-to-be-designated Capitol Reef National Monument. Once it was built, it was expected to become the main travel corridor within the proposed Escalante national monument, which Tillotson had investigated earlier that year. Zeke Johnson was enthusiastic about the prospect of opening the route, but his boss, Frank Pinkley, was less sanguine about the prospect of a highway slicing through the heart of Utah's canyon country. "I look on it with fear and trambling [sic]," he jotted under Johnson's report of the trip with Tillotson. One concern was vandalism of priceless prehistoric sites; even small monuments such as Natural Bridges could not be constantly patrolled, and opening the wider landscape to vehicle traffic would give pothunters access to many more sites. Tillotson's inspection trip hinted at the complicated relationship between the National Park Service and county officials who viewed roads as a way to ease life in remote areas and bring tourist dollars to local communities. But the federal government was becoming much more involved in the economy of the rural West, with local and state governments seeking any help they could get to ease Depression-era hardships.

A case in point was Arches National Monument, which in the mid-1930s was still far off the tourist track leading from Mesa Verde through Monument Valley and on to the Grand Canyon. Few motorists were willing to brave the sandy, frequently washed-out road leading east from Willow Spring to the Windows section of the monument. The Moab Lions Club wanted to see a new entrance road built closer to town, and to this end it proposed an expansion of the tiny monument to the south and east of the Windows. The local grazing advisory board approved the expansion, with the understanding that what little livestock use was being made of the area would be phased out over a ten-year period. Nearly two years later, on November 25, 1938, President Franklin Roosevelt signed a proclamation that enlarged the monument to 33,680 acres, taking in Delicate Arch and greatly expanding the protected area around Devils Garden and the Windows sections.[1]

Frank Pinkley obtained funds the following year for a Bureau of Public Roads survey of a new entrance road to Arches. It would begin at the entrance to Moab Canyon north of town, surmount the cliffs west of Courthouse Wash, curve past the Courthouse Towers, and continue on to the Windows. Construction did not get underway until October 1940, utilizing workers from a second Civilian Conservation Corps camp that opened north of town that May. Its young workers were able to construct less than a mile of road before World War II intervened and the camp was closed. They also completed a headquarters building and began work on a storehouse and residence, with their work overseen by Henry Schmidt, the new monument custodian.[2]

The expansion of Arches National Monument came on the heels of three other important land designations in Utah's canyon country. These were much more limited in scope than the huge Escalante proposal, and they illustrated the advantage of federal officials working closely with local community leaders. In January 1937, President Roosevelt designated a 49,150-acre national monument in the Kolob Canyons east of Kanarraville. Like the national park that it adjoined, the new monument bore the name Zion, but it retained its separate status for nineteen years before it was formally added to the park. The Cedar City Chamber of Commerce had been promoting the designation for several years for its touristic value, and Park Service officials took the precaution of meeting first with local livestock operators to secure their consent.[3]

The Kolob section of Zion National Park, as it would later be known, encompassed a half-dozen "finger canyons" walled by enormous Navajo Sandstone cliffs that stood out to travelers heading south from Cedar City. Also included was an upland area known as Hop Valley and a series of labyrinthine canyons that fed into La Verkin Creek. Few people ventured into these recesses, which hid the massive span of Kolob Arch, one of the world's largest. Renowned geologist Herbert Gregory called the view of the Kolob cliffs from the Kanarra Valley one of the best examples of erosion, faulting, and volcanism in the Plateau Province.[4]

That August, Franklin Roosevelt put his signature to a proclamation establishing Capitol Reef National Monument, comprising thirty-seven thousand acres in the Waterpocket Fold east of Torrey. Its name harked back to Joseph Hickman's proposed state park, replacing the less felicitous "Wayne Wonderland." The product of more than a decade of efforts by Hickman, Ephraim Pectol, and other Wayne County citizens, the new monument included the dramatic cliffs enclosing Fruita and a ten-mile extension to the south, as well as a narrow neck of land north of the Torrey-Fruita road. The Fremont River gorge was not included, nor was the rock art site in Fish Creek Cove. Private lands in and around Fruita were to remain in their owners' hands until the Park Service was able to negotiate buyouts. Livestock grazing was banned, subject to continued use of historical stock driveways through the Fold. Lands that had existing leases for oil and gas, covering 4,160 acres, were also excluded in order to minimize opposition from the state of Utah.[5] It was an artful compromise that pleased its supporters in Wayne County without raising too many hackles among the ranching community. Still, it left out a huge swath of equally scenic reefs, canyons, and badlands to the north, south, and east. These lands might have become part of the much larger Escalante proposal had it advanced beyond the talking stage.

Dinosaur National Monument, an eighty-acre enclave surrounding the extraordinary Jurassic fossil quarry northeast of Vernal, also came under Park Service scrutiny during the 1930s. Much as with Arches, Cedar Breaks, and

The enormous expansion of Dinosaur National Monument in 1938 took in the vast uplands surrounding the Green and Yampa Rivers. As seen from the Harpers Corner overlook, the Yampa approaches from the east to join the Green River below Steamboat Rock, which emerges on the right. *National Park Service.*

the Wayne Wonderland, local business and civic leaders in Vernal sought to expand the monument as a means of increasing tourism. A well-publicized voyage down the Yampa River in 1928 by a staff writer from the *Denver Post* brought attention to the scenic allure of the upper canyons of the Green and Yampa Rivers, which merged beneath the long cliff of Steamboat Rock at a place John Wesley Powell named Echo Park.[6] In 1933 Park Service director Arno Cammerer dispatched Roger Toll to investigate the area. His report detailed the many attractions of both river canyons, from their colorful human history to the wildlife found along their banks.

Additional support for an expanded monument came in a report prepared by Park Service landscape architect Herbert Evison, who took note of the "extraordinary feature" of Split Mountain, where the Green River plowed through dramatic cliffs before emerging near the dinosaur quarry. The local Lions Club favored a modest expansion of the monument in the hope of sparking a tourism boom, provided that livestock grazing, mineral prospecting, and hydropower development be allowed in it.[7] Interior Secretary Harold Ickes instead opted for a much larger expansion of the monument. In 1938, following his recommendation, Franklin Roosevelt signed a proclamation adding to the monument some two hundred thousand acres surrounding the canyons of the Green and Yampa Rivers in Utah and Colorado. It became the largest Park Service holding in the Colorado River system between Grand Canyon and Rocky Mountain National Parks. The monument proclamation left it unclear whether dams could be built within it, but the Bureau of Reclamation believed that hydropower development within the monument was a foregone conclusion. Twelve years later, the Park Service would come out against plans to site two major dams in the heart of these scenic waterways, leading to much resentment among those in Vernal who hoped an economic boom would come to their isolated locale.[8]

Cedar Breaks, Capitol Reef, and the expanded Arches National Monuments met with general approval in Utah, but this was far from the case with the much larger Escalante proposal. Ray West, the only state official who even tepidly supported the monument concept, had fallen ill shortly before the May 1936 meeting in Price and died that June.[9] His replacement, Sumner Margetts, prepared a lengthy report on the proposal for the State Planning Board, which, in contrast to West's earlier report, pointed to a high potential for resource development in the region around the Colorado and Green Rivers. The area was little explored for minerals, Margetts observed, and was slated for comprehensive river development under the Boulder Canyon Project Act. Opposition to the Escalante monument was as strong as ever, he noted, and there was "no need for action to preserve the canyons of the Colorado."[10]

Faced with unanimous opposition from state officials, Park Service personnel searched for a compromise solution that might win them over. The previous November, park superintendents Jesse Nusbaum and Preston Patraw had met with representatives of stock grower groups in Salt Lake City to propose a nine-hundred-thousand-acre monument that would be limited to a fifteen-mile-wide swath along the Colorado River. The stockmen countered with a proposal for a still smaller monument that would take in little more than the main canyons of the Green and Colorado Rivers. Even within this limited area, they wanted no restrictions on resource production and hydropower development. Margetts characterized the offer as something the Park Service "could not accept and would not accept." Patraw and Nusbaum rejected this abbreviated proposal, pointing out that a larger area was needed for proper administration, including provision of access roads.[11] Given the overtly hostile political situation in Utah, Nusbaum and Patraw probably understood better than their superiors in Washington that the Escalante national monument, at least in its original form, was a dead letter.

Unlike Yellowstone National Park in 1872, no powerful economic interest such as the Northern Pacific Railroad was promoting the Escalante proposal. Moreover, Utah state officials had definite designs on these "barren" lands, particularly the Colorado River, which represented a huge and mostly untapped resource for hydropower and irrigation. The upper basin states' shares of the river's water were then being allotted under the terms of the 1922 Colorado River Compact, with Utah jealously guarding its share against the interests of downstream states. It had also recently won a court case against the federal government over the ownership of the Colorado's riverbed.[12] Governor Blood urged Utah's congressional delegation to resist any erosion of Utah's rights to this precious water, even though there were no immediate plans for its use. "I feel strongly that the state has vast potential rights in this area which much be protected," he wrote."[13]

By this time, however, both the Park Service and the Interior Department had invested a great deal of effort in obtaining some kind of landscape-wide designation in southeastern Utah's canyon lands. In March 1938 Park Service director Arno Cammerer assured Utah state officials and Senator King that any such designation would come only after they had been consulted and "all interests are properly adjusted." He noted that his agency's field studies had disclosed no likelihood of mineral development or even much livestock grazing within the smaller monument area, which now spanned approximately six miles on either side of the Colorado River. This was, the director said, "an amazing wilderness labyrinth, its particular quality of scenic beauty unequalled anywhere."[14]

Cammerer's assurances could hardly have set Governor Blood at ease. At a meeting of the National Reclamation Association in Las Vegas that fall, Blood obtained a resolution opposing the establishment of any new national monument or other federal land reservations without consultations with all parties involved. Even these, the resolution read, should be "limited to cover the specific items intended to be protected." Yet while attending the meeting, Blood learned that the Interior Department was going ahead with establishment of the Escalante monument. His inquiries with Washington produced a telegram from E. K. Burlew, an assistant secretary of the interior, assuring him that the proclamation that had been drafted would be subject to existing rights, including for hydropower withdrawals. "This will settle all controversy," Burlew stated flatly, and in the long run would be "most equitable to state and federal government[s]."[15]

Blood was anything but reassured. It appeared that a presidential proclamation establishing an Escalante national monument comprising about two thousand square miles, or 1,280,000 acres, was imminent. Still, the Park Service's acting director, Arthur Demaray, was hesitant to proceed without Blood's approval. Demaray sent details of the proposal to Burlew that same day, reminding him of the government's assurances that state officials would be consulted and warning that there would be serious repercussions for other park proposals if he went ahead. This included Kings Canyon in California, a favorite of Harold Ickes. "If we antagonize powerful western interests," he told Burlew, "we may have to pay a stiff price."[16]

Ickes, however, was not one to back down from a fight. Within days, he sent the draft Escalante proclamation to President Roosevelt, along with maps, supporting documentation, and illustrative photographs. Advancing a new line of argument, he said the monument area was of "outstanding scientific importance" and was "particularly adapted for use in public education in earth history." The area was "lacking in the common economic resources" and offered little in the way of livestock grazing. Existing rights, including power withdrawals, would be respected.[17]

Governor Blood and his staff kept up their protests after returning to Salt Lake City, spurred by newspaper headlines announcing the monument's imminent creation.[18] Finally, in December 1938, acting Interior Secretary Oscar Chapman threw in the towel, telling Blood that after careful consideration, no proclamation would be issued. He left the door open for a monument in some form if further studies of the Colorado's hydropower potential did not turn up a workable reservoir project.[19] The Escalante proposal had stalled out—for the time being.

Historians tend to agree that the Escalante national monument, as originally proposed, was too large and too poorly prepared to have a chance of becoming reality. Elmo Richardson, writing in 1965, observed that "federal officials let their enthusiasm for the general national park program overreach considerations of real need."[20] Fifty years later Paul T. Nelson, in his book *Wrecks of Human Ambition*, pointed out that "the idea of creating a national monument with the stroke of a president's pen . . . angered residents of an area that had long been marginalized as a territory by the rest of the nation."[21] Those animosities would resurface in full force in 1996 with the designation of Grand Staircase–Escalante National Monument.

The Park Service had not prepared the ground for the Escalante proposal as it had with its smaller proposals for Arches, Dinosaur, Capitol Reef, and Kolob (Zion) National Monuments. Yet even in its failure, the Escalante proposal was significant as the opening move in efforts to create a region-wide network of protective designations in Utah's red-rock landscape. It was the direct ancestor of various later parks, including Canyonlands, that would take shape following the war as the next arena for visionary thinking in the Colorado Plateau canyon lands.

17

WILDERNESS

On an early summer day in 1935, eighteen months after Roger Toll looked out over the Utah canyon lands from the eastern edge of the Aquarius Plateau, another federal official stood at an overlook some 150 miles to the northeast, equally spellbound by what he saw. Bob Marshall was already a legend within the Forest Service owing to his marathon mountain hikes of forty or more miles in a single day. A native of New York State, he found the West congenial to his energy and ambition, and in the 1920s he drew a posting to the Forest Service's research branch in Missoula, Montana. Recruited by Harold Ickes in 1933 to head the Interior Department's Indian Forestry Service, Marshall continued his explorations in the Desert Southwest, making long pack trips into the Navajo Reservation, the Escalante River drainage, and the little-known region north of the Book Cliffs.

Behind those cliffs lay the eight- to nine-thousand-foot-high expanse of the Tavaputs Plateau, part of the Uintah and Ouray Indian Reservation. While inspecting livestock grazing allotments on the reservation, Marshall and a companion visited a sloping upland called Wild Horse Basin. Marshall could not pass up a view, so while his companion rested in a cowboy cabin, he wandered west through the junipers. "All at once the mesa broke away below me," he recalled in an article he wrote two years later. Three thousand feet below him "a strong, gray river tore down the canyon.... Beyond it were myriad side canyons winding tortuously down to the main river, each one a huge slit in the earth's crust." Entranced with the scene, he lingered to let the wind, sunlight, and space flow into him.[1]

Marshall was looking down at the Green River in Desolation Canyon, the same trackless defile through which Major Powell and his men had floated in 1869 and 1871. More than sixty years later, there were no dams or irrigation works to be seen on this stretch of river, and only a single farmstead,

located at the mouth of Rock Creek. Marshall knew that could change, however. He noted that "someday I will read about a road being projected down
the gorge of the Green River. . . . The article will state how many miles the
distance between Vernal and Moab will be shortened, how many men will
get to work, how many tourists will leave their money along the route."

Building roads into the great wild spaces of the West reduced the extraordinary to the commonplace, Marshall believed, vanquishing the isolation and vastness that stirred the visitor at places like Wild Horse Basin.
His words found a ready audience among those who had spent time in the
nation's least developed lands, including such conservation luminaries as
Aldo Leopold and Robert Sterling Yard, who along with Marshall and six
other outdoor devotees formed the Wilderness Society in 1935. The group
took immediate aim at the National Park Service's program of building scenic drives through many of the nation's national parks, notably Shenandoah
and Great Smoky Mountains.[2]

The Park Service, flush with some $220 million in New Deal funds, was
making good on Stephen Mather's promise to make the national parks accessible to the American public. Many of the new roads were engineering marvels, including the Going-to-the-Sun Road in Glacier, the Trail Ridge Road
in Rocky Mountain, and the Tioga Road in Yosemite. Mount Rainier saw
new roads built into the Paradise and Sunrise areas, while Yellowstone's east
entrance road was completed over Sylvan Pass and Grand Canyon's North
Rim gained a scenic drive to Cape Royal.[3]

Southeastern Utah had no national parks as yet, but M. R. Tillotson and
other park officials were aware of the local interest in building a road from
Blanding to Hanksville, which would link Natural Bridges National Monument with the Wayne Wonderland and Bryce Canyon. To Tillotson, building
a highway through the wildest section of the Utah canyon lands was little
more than an engineering problem—a field in which he was trained. The
concerns of those like Frank Pinkley, who understood how the road would
slice a great wilderness region in two, were largely ignored.

Most NPS officials in Utah stood with Tillotson and the road engineers. Zion superintendent Preston Patraw observed in a 1938 magazine article that "we want to make our major inspirational features accessible, so we
plan a road into them if feasible." The Zion–Mount Carmel Highway, with
its amazing tunnel, was one response to this mandate. Henry Schmidt and
Zeke Johnson, custodians of the national monuments at Arches and Natural

Bridges, hoped that funds would soon be granted to construct decent access roads into their domains. Nonetheless, plenty of wild country would remain undeveloped, agency leaders believed. "Beyond these [roads and other trails] lies wilderness," Patraw wrote, "in which the visitor may venture only by his own physical effort and possible discomfort."[4]

To Bob Marshall and his preservationist allies, scenic drives and the fancy tourist facilities that accompanied them dominated the landscape in too many places. "The Park Service seems to have forgotten the primitive," Marshall complained to Harold Ickes in 1937, and it was "wrecking the wilderness environment of those extraordinary scenic areas which were set aside for special protection."[5] No part of any national park was safe from the road builders, he believed, unless the agency adopted an affirmative program to protect such areas. Just as he had urged a primitive area program on the Forest Service, Marshall asked Ickes to identify and protect park regions that would remain wild.

Robert Sterling Yard, who had left Stephen Mather's employ in 1919 to found the National Parks Association, proposed a system of "National Primeval Parks" that would be managed without roads or tourist infrastructure.[6] Ickes did not implement Yard's proposal, although he generally favored minimal development of the larger national parks in the West and expressed distaste for scenic roads in particular. "If I had my way about national parks," he told the *New York Times* in 1933, "I would create one without a road in it. I would have it impenetrable forever to automobiles."[7]

At the time, Ickes was engaged in a turf war with the Agriculture Department over which agency was better suited to manage America's scenic patrimony. Beginning in 1924 with the establishment of the Gila Wilderness Reserve in New Mexico, the Forest Service under Ferdinand Silcox had set aside large areas of the national forests to remain in a more or less primitive condition. Under the urging of Aldo Leopold and Bob Marshall, this policy was codified in 1928, allowing regional foresters to establish so-called primitive areas, which would be reserved from most forms of timber harvesting and road construction. No comparable policy existed within the Interior Department, however, for either national parks or the unappropriated public lands that made up much of the southwestern deserts and canyons.

Bob Marshall shuttled between both departments throughout the 1930s, skillfully playing Silcox and Park Service director Arno Cammerer against each other for leadership in setting aside roadless tracts for their wilderness values.[8] Cammerer defended his agency as best suited to protect the natural conditions of federal lands in the West. "We have been able to conserve the vast bulk of the parks free from roads and buildings, and other artificialities," he assured Harold Ickes in May 1934. The Forest Service could not be trusted to protect wild areas because of its mandate to provide timber, water, and livestock forage, he maintained.[9] But to Marshall, only a bold program of wildland preservation would allow the spacious roadless expanses of the West's mountains and deserts to survive the modern recreational age and its burgeoning mechanization. "The universe of the wilderness, all over the United States, is vanishing with appalling rapidity," he wrote in the same article describing his encounter at Wild Horse Basin. "It is melting away like the last snowbank on some south-facing mountainside during a hot afternoon in June."

Bob Marshall's pack trips in Utah in 1935 gave him a better sense of the mostly undeveloped public domain in southeastern Utah. The following year he depicted this nearly nine-million-acre roadless landscape in an article for *The Living Wilderness*, the magazine of the Wilderness Society.[10] Marshall himself apparently made no formal proposal for a wilderness area in the Utah canyon country, and by 1936 the Park Service's Escalante national monument proposal had taken center stage. But in 1939, Hugh Calkins of the Soil Conservation Service circulated a proposal for an "Escalante Wilderness Area" that closely resembled Marshall's immense roadless area. Calkins was a former Forest Service district supervisor who had worked closely with Aldo Leopold to establish the Gila reserve in New Mexico. He sent his Escalante proposal—of which only a sketch map appears to have survived—to Aldo Leopold, Robert Sterling Yard, and Chester Olsen, the Forest Service's regional forester in Ogden, Utah. All three enthusiastically endorsed the idea, although Olsen cautioned that Utah state officials would need to be consulted lest there occur a repeat of the Escalante monument fiasco.[11]

Chet Olsen had worked closely with Marshall during his visits to Utah in the 1930s and knew the political situation in that state. In a letter to Robert Sterling Yard, he noted that the expansion of Dinosaur National Monument in 1938 had met with disapproval in Salt Lake and Vernal, while state officials continued to battle the Park Service over the Escalante proposal. An even

Gregory Natural Bridge, located in a side canyon of the Escalante River, as photographed by Herbert E. Gregory in 1944. Now under the waters of Lake Powell, this enormous span was one of many stunning geological features that would have been part of the Escalante national monument. *Herbert E. Gregory Collection, Special Collections, J. Willard Marriott Library, University of Utah.*

more restrictive wilderness withdrawal would face tough sailing. Calkins's idea went no further, and the dreams of Marshall, Clyde Kluckhohn, and a few other individuals of a Plateau-wide wilderness would not be fulfilled. More than three decades would pass before a new generation of conservationists would again raise the possibility of protecting substantial parts of Utah's canyon country. By then hundreds of miles of new roads, highways, and uranium-seeking bulldozer tracks sliced through this wild region, rendering the huge roadless area of the 1930s into fragments. America's largest undeveloped landscape outside Alaska would be no more.

Most of Marshall's fellow wilderness advocates tended to associate wilderness with the unbroken forests and glorious mountainscapes of the Rockies, High Sierra, and Cascade Range. Theirs was largely a recreational perspective, born of the desire to experience a primitive West somewhat as George Catlin or Lewis and Clark had encountered it. Aldo Leopold explicitly defined wilderness in terms of its recreational value in a 1925 article in *American Forests*, contending that "wild places are the rock-bottom foundation of a good many different kinds of outdoor play, including pack and canoe trips in which hunting, fishing, or just exploring may furnish the flavoring matter. By 'wild places' I mean wild regions big enough to absorb the average man's two weeks' vacation without getting him tangled up in his own back track."[12]

As the science of ecology gained stature during the 1930s, however, the biotic values of primitive landscapes were becoming clearer. Biologists within the National Park Service such as Adolph Murie and George Melendez Wright raised concerns about illegal hunting and predator extermination, which had been allowed to continue in many national parks, including Yellowstone, where Murie had studied coyote populations during the 1930s. There, Murie concluded that populations of big game animals such as elk, deer, and mountain sheep fluctuated in response more to environmental conditions, especially winter snows, than to predation. He argued that in keeping with the high purposes for which the park had been established, its "flora and fauna should be subjected to a minimum of disturbance. The natural interactions of the members of the fauna and flora and the environment have a place in such a scheme and serve to furnish significance and greater interest in the animal life."[13]

George Wright, an assistant naturalist in Yosemite National Park, had an outsized influence on Park Service wildlife policies through a self-funded study he led, which was published in 1933. Known as "Fauna No. 1," the study called for a complete shift away from the agency's de facto policy of managing wildlife for its touristic value, proposing to end such activities as public feeding of bears, culling unwanted animals, and artificially maintaining high numbers of desirable species such as Yellowstone's elk. Wright and his coauthors maintained that "our national heritage is richer than just scenic features; the realization is coming that perhaps our greatest national heritage is nature itself, with all its complexity and its abundance of life."[14]

Utah's relatively small national parks presented special problems, according to the report, including overgrazing of adjacent rangelands and overenthusiastic shooting and trapping of predators such as mountain lions. At Bryce Canyon, the park's western boundary was "an artificial line following the section lines zigzag fashion up through the timber just above [the East Fork of the Sevier River] valley. Obviously there is nothing to prevent domestic stock from entering the park." The authors urged that the park boundary be expanded to take in the East Fork valley, but this never took place.[15]

To permit certain parks to begin to recover their ecological values, Wright and his fellow biologists proposed a program of "research reserves" in which predator control and habitat alteration would not be allowed. Among the southwestern parks, only Zion and Grand Canyon had designated research reserves within them, and the program, which was never fully accepted by higher-ups in the agency, was eventually abandoned.[16] In 1940, the Park Service's ecology program was transferred to the Bureau of Biological Survey in the Interior Department, leaving the Park Service without any staff dedicated primarily to such work. Not until the 1960s, and the publication of another influential report prepared by a committee chaired by A. Starker Leopold, son of Aldo Leopold, would serious discussion resume in the agency about how national parks and monuments could protect biological diversity as well as magnificent scenery and recreational opportunities.

The desert lands Bob Marshall identified in his 1936 roadless area inventory were far from pristine; livestock grazing had altered range conditions throughout most of the Colorado Plateau. With it came changes to much of the flora and fauna best adapted to withstand the region's harsh desert winds, sparse soils, and climate extremes. Only on remote, inaccessible mesas and canyons was there anything like an original native flora. In 1938, a University of Michigan biologist named Elzada Clover observed such conditions in some of the side canyons of the Green and Colorado Rivers during a float trip with pioneer river runner Norman Nevills down Glen Canyon and Grand Canyon. Clover found four new species of cacti during the trip, which she and graduate student Lois Jotter, who accompanied her, described in two subsequent articles.[17] From their limited survey of the canyons, Clover and Jotter described the ecological relationships of this complex terrain, where elevation differences and the seed transport made possible by the rivers produced a highly varied flora. They made special note of the lush vegetation found in seeps and along ephemeral watercourses leading into the two rivers, where narrow canyons and overhangs gave protection from the wind and sun.[18] These were exactly the biotic features that river basin planners overlooked when they assigned the whole of the Colorado River basin to hydropower development.

Additional botanical and biological studies were pursued in the 1920s and 1930s by Walter Cottam and Angus Woodbury, who were both involved in conservation work in the 1940s and 1950s. Woodbury served as a ranger-naturalist at Zion National Park from 1925 to 1933, while Cottam taught at the University of Utah. Cottam's 1947 monograph *Is Utah Sahara Bound?*, which predicted disaster for the state's rangelands unless cattle and sheep numbers were reduced, became a classic in the field of conservation ecology. Woodbury took note of the deleterious effects of heavy livestock use of Zion Canyon in the years before 1916, when such use was ended.[19]

None of these researches, however, led the Park Service to adopt a lasting scheme of ecologically based management during the 1930s, or indeed until much later. Nor did it embrace Bob Marshall's vision of a vast wilderness area encompassing the Utah canyon lands. The agency's leaders remained wedded to public recreation as a chief use of the parks, with roads to take people to where they wanted to recreate. In the eyes of Park Service leaders such as Arno Cammerer, national parks were not a wilderness; instead they were, as historian David Louter observes, "places for humans in nature, and to simply erect a barrier around them to protect their primitive qualities" would not meet the agency's mandate, as its leaders saw it.[20] It would take decades for the Park Service to wholly embrace both wilderness and ecological concepts in its management of the parks.

18

INSPIRATION
AT DEAD HORSE POINT

Jesse Nusbaum's broad-brimmed Park Service hat shaded a man with a wide range of duties. As the agency's senior archaeologist during the 1930s and 1940s, he was responsible for protecting dozens of important prehistoric sites in the Desert Southwest and elsewhere in the National Park System. He had twice served as superintendent of Mesa Verde National Park, returning to this post a third time during World War II after his replacement was called into service. The tall, youthful-looking superintendent was known as an effective administrator who fought off attempts to loot, log, mine, or overgraze the park.[1] In the midst of these responsibilities he found time to make trips to Moab and Salt Lake City, where he tried to build a case for setting aside a significant portion of the southeastern Utah canyon lands as a national monument or recreation area.

Nusbaum's favorite method was to take reporters and civic leaders to Dead Horse Point west of Moab, where the stupendous views over the canyon of the Colorado River could not fail to impress. This grand overlook would later be ceded to the state of Utah for a state park, but in the 1930s it was still part of the federal domain. Its vertiginous cliffs gave a raven's-eye view of the great river as it flowed in graceful loops two thousand feet below, disappearing into a canyon fastness that had turned back the Macomb expedition nearly a century earlier. By the late 1930s the overlook was accessible via a graded dirt road that led up from the Moab-Thompson highway, and it was drawing a growing number of appreciative visitors.

Writing in the *Moab Times-Independent*, Nusbaum extolled the view from Dead Horse Point: "In no other area in America, to my knowledge, can one see so vast an exposure of highly eroded red-bed formations," he wrote. Visitors should plan to arrive at the point by three o'clock in the afternoon,

The view from Dead Horse Point in the 1940s. *Al Watkins Morton/Used by permission, Utah State Historical Society.*

he said, and stay for sunset. The experience has "convinced even the most skeptical of the scenic merit of this national park service proposal."[2]

Scenery alone would not carry the Escalante monument proposal, although the desire to boost tourism led several civic organizations to support some form of protection for the canyons of the Colorado and Green Rivers. The Moab Lions Club noted that a national monument or recreation area along these river corridors "would immediately bring southeastern Utah to the front as a tourist playground." The group chided Governor Henry Blood for opposing the monument, saying he was holding up the recreational development of their region in return for some "vague hope that at some very distant date something may be done to develop the river resources."[3]

In April 1938, the Moab Lions hosted a meeting of the Associated Civic Clubs of Southern Utah, whose president, Frank Martinez, advocated monument designation as a means of boosting tourism. (He had also been an early supporter of the Wayne Wonderland.) Jesse Nusbaum spoke to the group at its banquet in Moab and accompanied a large party to Dead Horse

Point the following day. He assured them that the Park Service no longer intended to set aside the Escalante area as a national monument or park, although this statement proved premature after Interior Secretary Harold Ickes revived the monument proposal and sent a draft proclamation to Franklin Roosevelt that October.[4]

In the spring of 1939, the Moab Lions invited Ickes to visit Dead Horse Point as part of a tour of the Southwest to be held by the American Planning and Civic Association that October. He never made it to Utah, but the Lions went on to hold an elk steak barbeque at the viewpoint with forty-five of the association's members. Again Nusbaum was there, speaking to the need for better tourist access to the scenic lands within the monument area. Harlean James, the association's executive secretary, hoped that the area could be made a national park.[5] But the group's support could not overcome the entrenched opposition of nearly every public official in Utah, including Governor Blood and all of the state's congressional representatives.

In 1940, in a last attempt to revive some kind of large designation for the Colorado–Green River canyon lands, the Park Service advanced the notion of establishing a national recreation area, which would permit hydropower dams and some other resource uses. Taking in 2,450 square miles on either side of the two rivers, the designation was patterned on the Boulder Dam Recreation Area, created in 1936 under an agreement between the Bureau of Reclamation and the Park Service to manage Lake Mead and its shoreline areas. The Boulder Dam agreement was emblematic of a new direction for the Park Service as overseer of the nation's top recreational and tourism attractions. It also gave the agency a leg up on the Forest Service, which was busy building campgrounds and trails throughout the largely undeveloped national forests of the West.

Park Service director Arno Cammerer believed the recreation area concept could be transplanted to Utah's section of the Colorado River, which appeared destined to be flooded by one or more major power reservoirs. It also would permit livestock grazing to continue, which might remove the ranching community's long-standing objections to a national monument. Loren Taylor, the influential editor of the *Moab Times-Independent*, favored the recreation area concept in order to "make the region accessible, through building of roads, camping, and other facilities, just as they have done at Boulder dam, with the understanding that the resources of the area would be open to development just as they are on the public domain."[6]

The Green River Civic Club added its support to the recreation area proposal, hoping it would boost tourism in this isolated part of Utah. But a recreation area still did not sit well with Utah's political leaders, who remained
wary of any aggregation of federal authority in their state. State engineer T.
H. Humphreys warned that such designation would hinder the construction
of dams on the Colorado River, and Congressman J. W. Robinson believed
that the Park Service would eventually restrict grazing, mining, and other
potential uses.[7]

The opposition of these officials to a less restrictive national recreation
area exasperated Harold Ickes, who threatened to resurrect the former
proposal. To do nothing, Ickes told Governor Blood, would mean "abandoning the area entirely, and thus abandoning [the] high recreational and
scenic values which should be preserved for future generations."[8] Blood,
however, made it clear that he would acquiesce to new federal designations
only if they permitted "the full utilization of land and water for irrigation
and power and flood and silt control and for all agricultural, grazing, mineral, industrial, and sociological purposes." To these he added "unrestricted
road construction and use."[9]

The state's position was unequivocal: national parks and monuments
must be limited to a handful of small, isolated scenic enclaves that would
serve as billboards to draw tourists to gateway communities. Outside these
reserves, full-scale industrial and agricultural development would eventually
fill the map with mines, oil wells, power plants, and dams, all served by a network of roads and highways, to be built with federal dollars. This approach
had little in common with the sweeping national monument that Roger Toll
and M. R. Tillotson had envisioned in 1935, and still less with Clyde Kluckhohn's and Bob Marshall's vision of a breathtaking, landscape-wide wilderness preserve in which rivers ran free, roads were few and far between, and
humans were visitors who experienced the land on its own terms.

Jesse Nusbaum strove to bridge this chasm between park advocates
and Utahns who remained suspicious of NPS intentions. A few of his Utah
contacts, including river runner Norm Nevills and San Juan County stockmen Charles Redd and J. A. Scorup, said they would not have serious objections to a recreation area if grazing were allowed to continue. Advising his
superiors of the divided sentiment in Utah, Nusbaum said that "the accom-
plishment of the great things in life generally requires the united effort of
a number of people who have the vision and the fortitude to complacently

face and solve the problems as they are presented by the more selfish interests."[10] But with livestock and hydropower interests firmly represented
among Utah's political leadership, that vision would remain for a new generation of activists to attempt to fulfill.

The contretemps over the ever-changing Escalante proposal also reflected
conflicting purposes within the Department of the Interior. Harold Ickes
wanted to place restrictions on road development in the National Park System, while many Park Service officials still hoped to court tourists with better roads and visitor facilities. But there were others in the Park Service who
saw values in the Utah canyon lands beyond postcard-worthy scenery. Ronald Lee, supervisor of historic sites for the Park Service, noted in a memo
to Arno Cammerer in early 1940 that little emphasis had been given to the
rich historical and archaeological resources within the Escalante monument area. As examples he cited the Crossing of the Fathers in Glen Canyon
(where the Domínguez-Escalante party found its way across the Colorado
River during the winter of 1776–77) as well as the largely undocumented
and unprotected prehistoric sites that were known to exist throughout the
region. "Even if the undoubtedly imposing scenic features [of the Escalante
monument] should be emphasized, the historical and archaeological factors
should not be minimized," Lee told Cammerer. The conservation of these
resources alone might justify setting aside the entire area, he believed.[11]

Jesse Nusbaum got a chance to educate top Park Service officials about
these values during another visit to Dead Horse Point, in May 1941. His
guests included Newton Drury, who had replaced Arno Cammerer as chief
of the Park Service the previous year, and Frederick Law Olmsted Jr., a private citizen with important ties to the agency. Olmsted was known for his
work in urban planning and landscape architecture—a field his father had
pioneered—and had contributed language to the Park Service's Organic Act
of 1916 establishing its so-called dual mandate.[12] Standing at this encompassing vantage point, Olmsted, Drury, and Nusbaum must have sensed that
here lay new possibilities for the Park Service.

Drury had brought Olmsted to the Southwest to consult on a Park
Service study of the recreational resources of the entire Colorado River
basin. Authorized under the 1928 Boulder Canyon Project Act, the study

was intended to identify new parks and recreation areas that might be created in conjunction with the massive water projects the Bureau of Reclamation was planning throughout the basin. Olmsted's involvement in this study indicated that the Park Service wanted to do more than locate a few sites for marinas and campgrounds. Initially released in June 1946, *A Survey of the Recreational Resources of the Colorado River Basin* drew on a decade's worth of field studies on a wide variety of scientific and cultural topics. But its greatest impact may have been on the agency itself, for the report gave particular attention to the forgotten lands of the Southwest, and especially on what it called the "Canyon Lands" section of the Colorado Plateau.

Ten Park Service staff joined Olmsted in preparing the recreation survey, including Conrad Wirth, an assistant director in charge of land planning who would go on to succeed Drury as head of the Park Service. George Olcott, a park planner from the agency's regional office in Santa Fe, wrote major sections, while M. R. Tillotson brought his experience in conducting field studies for the Escalante proposal. The study team singled out southeastern Utah's canyon country for special mention, observing that "nowhere else in the United States do the curious and fascinating land forms, evidences of the building up and wearing down of the earth's surface, stimulate more interest in geology. Nowhere else are the evidences of prehistoric peoples so obvious and numerous. Nowhere else is there scenery so colorful."[13]

Olmsted's study came too late to revive the Escalante national monument proposal, and a national recreation area designation would require new enabling legislation. By 1940 Congress and the federal government were turning their attention to the crisis in Europe. The recreation area concept, like Olmsted's report, would be deferred until after the war. The November election saw Democrat Herbert Maw replacing Henry Blood as governor, but Maw was an equally ardent supporter of dams and industry.

Jesse Nusbaum must have been frustrated by the continued delays and contention over the various iterations of the Escalante national monument proposal. Witnessing Newton Drury and Frederick Olmsted taking in the view from Dead Horse Point may have given him hope for progress toward a protective designation in the Colorado–Green River canyon lands. It would take many years and several false starts, but the studies then underway would eventually yield Utah's next national park.

The Escalante national monument proposal ran into trouble because relatively few people in Utah, or anywhere else for that matter, knew much about the lands it would have protected. The Colorado River and its canyons remained obscure and seldom trod well into the 1940s. This was still tough territory to get around in: the few roads were rugged and poorly maintained, while the long-sought Hanksville-Blanding "highway" was not completed until 1946. Even then the route remained mostly dirt for nearly two decades, with the North Wash section subject to periodic flash floods. The river itself was only beginning to draw interest from boaters; in 1938 Norman Nevills inaugurated the modern river guiding business in the Grand Canyon and on the San Juan River, but interest in these excursions grew slowly until well after the war was over. Dave Rust had been taking clients down Glen Canyon since 1922, but not in numbers that would attract notice.

Nor was the Park Service able to fully assess the recreational, scientific, historical, or other resources within the Escalante monument area, as specialists such as Ronald Lee had hoped. As late as 1940 the agency could field only a handful of staff other than at Zion and Bryce, and the existing national monuments at Arches, Natural Bridges, and Capitol Reef were woefully understaffed. (Capitol Reef did not have any staff until 1943, when Charles Kelly, a Salt Lake City author and desert rat, was appointed custodian. He served at no pay until 1951, when he was appointed superintendent.) Elden Beck, a zoology professor from Brigham Young University, called this situation to the attention of Governor Blood in 1939, urging him to support an increased Park Service presence in southern Utah. While working in the Waterpocket Fold area, Beck observed widespread destruction of irreplaceable prehistoric sites, with "truckload after truckload" of petrified wood being removed from the Circle Cliffs. "The only way they can be protected is by Federal Supervision," he maintained.[14] But Park Service planners and administrators remained fixated on scenery and recreation as the chief reason for designating new areas, overlooking the significant cultural and scientific values of places such as Cedar Mesa, where the agency in the 1930s briefly considered establishing a national monument in Arch Canyon. It was an oversight that would cost posterity, as artifact collecting and outright looting and vandalism continued almost unchecked, at least outside the agency's few protected holdings in the region.

By the end of 1940, the Escalante national monument, which first saw light in 1936 as a seven-thousand-square-mile proposal, had been pared down and compromised until it had almost no substance. During the coming war, the Park Service would revisit the idea of a smaller national park within this land of superlative scenery. It would take nearly two decades to enact, but the result would be a park unhampered by power reservoirs, oil wells, and politicians who saw only dollars in the red-rock landscape.

19

NEW DISCOVERIES IN AN OLD LANDSCAPE

The Second World War brought a deep hiatus to the national parks of the Southwest as visitation plunged to levels not seen since the 1920s. A mere 7,690 people showed up at Bryce Canyon during the 1943 season, while fewer than a thousand visitors braved the primitive roads into Arches and Capitol Reef National Monuments. New road construction and other improvements were deferred as Civilian Conservation Corps camps closed and young men headed for induction centers. Many Park Service personnel were called up for military service or went to work in wartime industries.[1] Remaining park rangers and monument custodians found their funding cut to minimum levels, but gas rationing meant there were few tourists venturing into remote park areas.

Three technological innovations originating during the war would change much of the southwestern landscape. Two of these, the army jeep and the ten-man rubber assault raft, would be pressed into service by recreationists eager to explore the canyon country following the war. The third innovation had far more significant consequences for world affairs, but it, too, left an unmistakable imprint on the cliffs and washes of southern Utah. The atomic bomb, and the enormous industrial-military complex that grew up around it, precipitated the first real economic boom in a part of the state that for decades had been hoping for one.

The Colorado Plateau's extensive uranium deposits first attracted attention in the early 1900s, when demand for radium led to the development of numerous small bodies of carnotite (a soft, bright yellow mineral that contains trace amounts of radium) in western Colorado and southeastern Utah. Renewed interest came in the 1930s as vanadium, another constituent of carnotite, came into use as an alloy in steel production, particularly for aircraft.

During World War II the federal government offered loans to spur vanadium production, and the Interior Department's Grazing Service built roads into southern Utah's remote regions to aid prospectors. At the same time, workers for the Manhattan Project were quietly sifting through the tailings from vanadium mills to separate out uranium for the first atomic bombs.

A uranium boom did not get underway until 1948, when President Truman lifted a freeze on domestic production and the newly formed Atomic Energy Commission (AEC) set a firm purchase price for uranium oxide ore. Further price increases, plus a $10,000 bonus for locating new sources, brought thousands of prospectors to southern Utah during the early 1950s. Most of the deposits they found were small and yielded little ore, but major producing mines were located in the White Canyon area, the San Rafael Swell, and south of Moab in the Lisbon area. The latter saw the discovery of Charlie Steen's Mi Vida mine, the largest deposit of high-grade uranium ore in the country. Processing mills opened in Monticello and Marysvale, Utah, while in 1949 a smaller mill and ore-buying station opened on the Colorado River at the mouth of White Canyon. A larger processing mill opened at Moab in 1957, adding to the town's already mushrooming population. Ore trucks rumbled down streets, motels hung "No Vacancy" signs, and eleven trailer parks housed more than a thousand boomers and their families.[2]

Restrictions on prospecting on public lands were nonexistent; anyone with a bulldozer could scrape a new road along an outcrop of the Chinle or Morrison Formations, where uranium deposits were most likely. In Capitol Reef National Monument, superintendent Charles Kelly fought an ongoing battle with prospectors who hoped to strike it rich somewhere within the monument. Kelly recalled that at one point he had a stack of prospecting applications five inches thick on his desk. Forced by the AEC (at the behest of Utah representative Reba Bosone) to open the monument to prospecting in 1952, adits, shafts, and bulldozed roads soon appeared in Chinle outcrops along the monument's scenic drive. Little of value was found, however.[3] Further prospecting took place south of the monument in the Circle Cliffs area, as well as around Temple Mountain and Muddy Creek in the San Rafael Swell. Connecting this spiderweb of primitive roads and tracks were hundreds of miles of haul roads built with subsidies from the AEC.

On September 17, 1946, the long-hoped-for dream of a highway connecting Blanding and Hanksville came a step closer to reality when the state of Utah opened a ferry service at Hite on the Colorado River. Some 350 people attended the dedication ceremony, with Governor Herbert Maw and Natural Bridges custodian Zeke Johnson among the featured speakers. Twenty cars crossed the river on the new ferry, which was powered by a Model A Ford engine. Arthur Chaffin and his wife, Della, the only residents of Hite, operated the ferry and dispensed cans of gasoline to motorists from an emergency supply they kept.[4] The road was no highway, and Chaffin's skills with a road grader were often called on to keep the washout-prone route open, but it was now possible for passenger cars to travel between Capitol Reef and Natural Bridges National Monuments in relative safety. But as Frank Pinkley foresaw in 1935, it bisected the immense wilderness along the middle stretch of the Colorado, introducing vehicles to places that had known only boot prints and horses' hooves.

The postwar years were a golden age for amateur desert explorers. Prehistoric ruins and inscriptions, natural bridges and arches, old cowboy camps, hidden canyons with verdant springs—all these awaited backcountry travelers outfitted with war-surplus jeeps. The Willys-Overland Company, which had developed these unique vehicles for the war effort, expanded into the civilian market with a station wagon that featured an innovative fold-down tailgate. Company representatives said it could "climb grades that balk a tank and negotiate rough terrain at 40 miles an hour."[5] Kent Frost, a part-time miner and river guide from Monticello, Utah, took advantage of this new means of transport to offer the first jeep tours in the canyon lands region, taking adventurers into the Needles and other remote attractions surrounding the confluence of the Green and Colorado Rivers. His guests included Randall Henderson, the publisher of *Desert Magazine*, a homegrown periodical that focused on California's Mojave Desert.[6] Henderson began running stories on the fascinating rock spires, deep grabens, and other formations surrounding the Confluence, helping to publicize the area as a future national park.

Often these adventurers didn't realize they were retracing the paths of earlier explorers, such as when A. L. Inglesby of Fruita, a retired dentist and avid rockhound who enjoyed exploring the Waterpocket Fold and its environs, reported seeing a cluster of intriguing sandstone towers in the Middle Desert north of Capitol Reef National Monument. Inglesby first saw these obelisks from a distance in 1945, while traveling with army personnel

Upper Cathedral Valley, part of the land added to Capitol Reef National Monument in 1969. *Travis Lovell/National Park Service.*

who were searching for the wreckage of an airplane that had gone missing the year before. He alerted Charles Kelly, who visited the area in September 1945 with newspaperman Frank Beckwith. They photographed the features and named the area Cathedral Valley, unaware that outfitter Dave Rust had traversed the same area in 1915 with George Fraser, who had also taken photographs of the strange monoliths. An even earlier depiction of two of Cathedral Valley's towers came to light only in 1995, when a photographer realized that an engraving taken from a daguerreotype made by Solomon Carvalho, a photographer attached to John C. Frémont's exploring expedition of 1853–54, represented a cluster of spires in that area. Frémont's expedition was presumed to have traveled farther north, closer to the historic Spanish Trail. Instead it had become mired in snows while climbing over the shoulder of Thousand Lake Mountain, where one of the party died.[7]

Charles Kelly wrote up the "discovery" of Cathedral Valley in Henderson's *Desert Magazine*, and over the next few years he lobbied his superiors to add these features to Capitol Reef National Monument.[8] It would take another twenty years to expand the monument northward, but the fact that these cliffs hid unpublicized geologic wonders for so long—let alone concealed an airplane wreck for nearly a year—gives a sense of their remoteness.

This is what contemporary adventurers yearned for: the chance to stumble across some amazing geologic feature that few others had yet seen. Cathedral Valley would remain far off the tourist track until the Park Service opened a loop road north of the Fremont River. Even then, visitors could revel in the absolute stillness of a desert that, Ozymandias-like, dwarfed humankind's works.

One Utah explorer who availed himself of postwar jeep technology was Ward Roylance, a Salt Lake City guidebook author and educator who devoted much of his life to promoting the Colorado Plateau. Roylance first encountered the Utah canyon lands in 1941, when he and his brother Bill visited Dead Horse Point after reading a description in the Federal Writers' Project's guidebook to Utah (Roylance would later edit a reissue of this work called *Utah: A Guide to the State*). In his memoir *The Enchanted Wilderness*, Roylance described their cliffside moment as an awakening that would change the course of his life. "I sat on the edge of the Orange Cliffs precipice," he wrote, "trying to comprehend and emotionally digest the tumultuous sea of bare rock that began 2,000 vertical feet below the eyrie on which I perched. . . . Never before had I experienced such a visual phantasmagoria, or such silence. . . . Time had stopped and I was suspended beneath earth and sky."[9]

Roylance went on to work as a publicist for the Tourist and Publicity Council (later the Utah Travel Council), and Dead Horse Point was one of the scenic wonders he most liked to extol. He was not alone in calling attention to the awe-inspiring views from the many-pronged plateau that rose above the Green and Colorado Rivers. In July 1943 Paul Brown, a regional Park Service director from the Midwest, described the equally amazing view from Junction Butte, which rose above the White Rim north of the rivers' confluence. Recording his impressions for George Olcott, who was compiling notes for the Park Service's recreational survey of the Colorado River basin, Brown wrote that "the experience of that hour on the great rock where the two walled rivers meet will be with us always. We pledged ourselves to come back again as we left, and so we shall. . . . We have an obligation, it seems to me, to recommend to our superiors that this area be accepted into the National Park System, if and when offered for the permanent enjoyment of the people."[10]

Despite Brown's report, Olcott's study team failed to come up with a comprehensive park proposal for what came to be known as the Canyonlands Basin. It identified a number of outstanding features such as the Needles, the Lands End area west of the Colorado River, and the triangular wedge of land between the Green and Colorado Rivers that included Junction Butte. The latter area appealed to Ben Thompson, chief of the Park Service's lands branch in Washington, who joined Olcott for a further reconnaissance of the area in July 1944. He suggested that they approach Utah representative Will Robinson to sponsor legislation for a "Grand View National Park," which would include smaller, detached units in the Needles, the Lands End–Doll House area west of the two rivers, and the lower Dirty Devil River where it joined the Colorado above Hite. Named for the high promontory that overlooked what was formerly the Grand River, the new park "would make accessible some of the greatest scenery in the United States," Thompson wrote. It would also take in "areas of unusual scientific value and historic interest."[11]

Thompson's proposal apparently did not include the two river canyons themselves, which were set to be flooded by hydropower dams. This skirted the difficulty that had helped sink the Escalante ship a few years earlier. Thompson did not address the contradiction of having a major power reservoir, with all its attendant human use and development, embedded within a national park. It was a timid proposal that seemed not to spark much interest from Utah's congressional representatives or the Park Service itself. Yet it took the agency a step closer to what would ultimately be Utah's fifth national park, and the only one that did not begin as a national monument.

There was also the question of what to do with Dead Horse Point, the overlook that sparked such rapturous wonder. By the mid-1950s word of its fabulous views had spread, thanks to promotional efforts of the Utah state travel council. An estimated fifteen to twenty thousand visitors were coming to the point annually, where the only facilities were a few picnic tables and a couple of toilets. In July 1956 Bates Wilson, superintendent of Arches National Monument, visited the point with members of the Moab Lions Club and Moab Chamber of Commerce. Their members favored making it a state park, but Wilson believed his agency could better manage and promote these areas.[12] Clearly the site had potential, and Wilson thought it ought to become a detached unit of Arches.

In contrast, M. R. Tillotson, the coarchitect of the Escalante monument proposal, urged that the viewpoint become the anchor for a new national park. "There is no question but that Dead Horse Point is in the center of a country second to none from the standpoint of scenic wonders."[13] Park Service director Conrad Wirth concurred, noting that "the scenic qualities of this section of the Colorado River are so important that they deserve some kind of protective status." He pointed to "the scenic and recreational importance of larger, choice areas within which Dead Horse Point is only a dot." With uranium prospecting in full swing, however, he believed that such action remained for the future.[14]

Throughout the 1950s, the Park Service sought to set up either a national park or national recreation area for Dead Horse Point and the adjoining mesas around Grays Pasture and Grand View Point. The newly formed Bureau of Land Management, which controlled the land in question, resisted these moves, pointing out that the area was covered by oil and gas leases and uranium mining claims. After much discussion, the two bureaus signed a memorandum of understanding in January 1956 under which the BLM would retain these lands, including Dead Horse Point, and with technical assistance from the Park Service would develop basic recreation facilities including roads, picnic areas, and trails. Mineral development, meanwhile, would be steered away from the most scenic parts of the area.

The "Dead Horse Point–Junction Butte Recreation Area," to be jointly managed by the BLM and National Park Service, would feature day-use facilities at Dead Horse Point, Junction Butte, and Upheaval Dome, but the plan had no more than been released when Chester Olsen, director of Utah's recently created state parks department, announced that he wanted to acquire Dead Horse Point for a state park. The BLM was amenable to the transfer, and in September 1958 it called off negotiations with the Park Service over the planned recreation area. In December 1959 Dead Horse Point became Utah's first state park, taking in 4,521 acres.[15] It would go on to become one of the most popular scenic attractions in the state.

Utah's acquisition of this superb overlook left open the question of what would become of the entire stretch of land surrounding the Colorado River, down to the Confluence and beyond. Was it enough to set aside a small piece of land for public recreation while leaving the larger landscape open to industrial development—in effect, to protect the viewpoint without protecting the view? For Ward Roylance, who had helped bring Dead Horse Point to the attention of Chet Olsen, the answer became clear in the decades ahead. In 1962 construction began on an underground potash mining operation beside the Colorado River a dozen miles downstream from Moab. It was converted to a solution mining process in 1970, complete with brilliant blue evaporation ponds that lay in full view of Dead Horse Point. The contrast with the surrounding red rocks was extreme, as was the juxtaposition of human handiwork with nature's. For Roylance, the rim overlook that had so captivated him became a place of tears, a reminder of how easily such sublimity could be lost.

20

WATER AND POWER

The canyons and uplands surrounding the Green and Yampa Rivers in Dinosaur National Monument had been in protected status for less than six months when a survey crew from the Bureau of Reclamation arrived in January 1939 to take measurements for the next big dam in the Colorado River basin. The monument did not yet have a full-time superintendent, so the staffer on duty had to write to the bureau's regional office in Denver to find out what was going on.[1] It turned out that there were two ideal dam sites in Dinosaur: one where the Green River emerged from the ramparts of Split Mountain a few miles east of Dinosaur's famous fossil quarry, and another farther upstream at Echo Park, a broad, idyllic opening in the cliffs where the Yampa merged with the Green. Few outside Utah knew of this place, but following the war Echo Park would become a rallying cry for a newly energized conservation movement in America. At stake was the integrity of the National Park System—or so the nation's conservation leaders insisted.

The hydropower potential flowing through Dinosaur's deep canyons was no secret; in 1935 the Utah Power and Light Company filed an application for a dam at Echo Park, but agreed to withdraw it in order to facilitate President Roosevelt's 1938 proclamation, which vastly expanded Dinosaur National Monument. The Bureau of Reclamation managed to insert a provision into the proclamation allowing one or more dams to be built within the monument, and it induced Park Service director Newton Drury to sign a memorandum of understanding in 1941 that would demote Dinosaur to a national recreation area if a dam project went ahead.[2] Drury hoped to keep dams and power reservoirs out of Dinosaur, but if this could not be done, he was prepared to accept a lesser status for the area. Under pressure from conservationists, however, the leaders of the Park Service would decide that the scenery and recreational opportunities in this little-visited national

Pats Hole and Steamboat Rock at the junction of the Green and Yampa Rivers in Dinosaur National Monument. The proposed Echo Park Dam would have flooded this stretch of both rivers. Photographed in 1935 by George A. Grant. *National Park Service, Harpers Ferry Center, VA.*

monument were worth fighting for. This time, unlike in the Escalante conflict, the agency would have powerful friends on its side.

The Bureau of Reclamation's star was in ascendancy in the postwar era as the nation turned its prodigious wartime industrial capacity to domestic economic development. "BuRec," as it was sometimes called, intended to build a series of dams and reservoirs along virtually the entire length of the Colorado River in Utah and Arizona, harnessing what its publicists described as a "natural menace"—the river's unruly and mostly unexploited flow. As soon as the war was over, the bureau began a publicity offensive that promised to remake the Desert Southwest into a prosperous and populous region through hydropower development. Carl Vetter, chief of the bureau's Office of River Control, observed in 1946 that "maximum development of the Colorado River is necessary not only for the economic stabilization and growth of the Colorado River Basin, but also for the benefit of the entire Nation. True national prosperity can be achieved only by prosperity of all component parts of the integrated economic system."[3]

Vetter had a large picture of Boulder Dam hanging in his Washington, D.C., office, but that had been just the first installment in achieving complete control of the Colorado–Green River system. The plan was laid out in a document BuRec issued that year, titled *The Colorado River: "A Natural Menace Becomes a National Resource."* It identified a staggering total of 134 potential water projects within the basin, ranging from small headwater reservoirs and diversions to ten massive main-stem dams on the Green, Colorado, and San Juan Rivers. These included dams on the Green River at Fontanelle in Wyoming, Flaming Gorge, Echo Park and Split Mountain within Dinosaur National Monument, and Desolation and Gray Canyons farther downstream. The San Juan River was slated for impoundment throughout most of its length, including the scenic Goosenecks below Mexican Hat.

The Colorado would be the workhorse of the system, impounded almost from its origins at Grand Lake, Colorado, downstream through Bridge Canyon in Arizona. The latter project especially upset officials in the National Park Service, who noted that the reservoir would back water into Grand Canyon National Monument and eighteen miles into Grand Canyon National Park itself. "In place of a thundering, silt-laden river, it would be harnessed by dams into a series of quiet mill-ponds," according to the agency's recreation report on the Colorado River Basin. A reservoir in the lower Grand Canyon would be a "conspicuous, insistent intrusion into the broader part of the canyon visible from the rim."[4]

The same could have been said for any of the proposed dams on the main stem of the Colorado, from Marble Canyon in Arizona to Glen Canyon, Dark Canyon, and Dewey Bridge in Utah. The Dark Canyon dam, deep within Cataract Canyon in one of the wildest reaches of the Colorado, would also have flooded Meander Canyon, a serene stretch of cliff-bound river reaching from the Spanish Valley at Moab downstream to the Colorado's confluence with the Green. The reservoir would bury the town of Moab under thirty to forty feet of water, yet for a time BuRec considered the Dark Canyon dam superior to upstream sites, despite its virtually inaccessible location. Utah senator Abe Murdock lauded the proposal, saying it could lead to construction of an aluminum mill that would take advantage of southeastern Utah's alunite resources.[5]

The Park Service's field personnel in the Southwest, which included men with long experience in the region such as Jesse Nusbaum and M. R. Tillotson, realized that scenic and cultural resource protection would necessarily take a back seat to economic development. They believed they stood little chance of stopping dams within Glen Canyon or Cataract Canyon, and they assured Utah politicians that any new parks, monuments, or recreation areas in the Utah canyon lands—even one taking in the Confluence, as staffer Ben Thompson proposed in 1944—would not interfere with the proposed dams.

The Park Service's 1946 survey of recreation resources in the Colorado River system took a less negative view of the Glen Canyon and Dark Canyon reservoirs than the one in Bridge Canyon, asserting that while they "would eliminate for the few the thrills of boating down the untamed river and reduce the apparent depths of the river canyons . . . they would provide a means of access for many to see the wonders of the canyons." The dams themselves, the report stated, "would be lost in the canyons and have little or no effect on the surrounding scenery."[6]

These contrasting Park Service evaluations may simply have reflected the political realities of the day. Even in Dinosaur, the Park Service initially wavered over whether to oppose BuRec's dams, knowing their popularity in Utah and among western congressional representatives. In the end, though, it came out firmly against them and helped conservationists win a major (if ultimately flawed) victory.

Townspeople in nearby Vernal enthusiastically embraced the dam projects in Dinosaur. After BuRec's dam studies were announced in 1941, the local Lions Club formed a special committee to build support for the Echo Park dam, which BuRec had moved to the top of its list. Touted as a means to supply irrigation water to Uinta Basin farmland as well as develop the basin's phosphate deposits, the Echo Park project was seen as economic salvation for those living in this isolated region.[7]

Dam site and access road studies continued after the war, accompanied by a constant drumbeat of publicity for the project from Vernal's newspaper and its civic clubs. The project was included in legislation introduced by Utah's congressional delegation for the $300 million Central Utah Project, a projected network of reservoirs, pipelines, and tunnels intended to divert Uinta Mountain water to the growing Wasatch Front. Interior Secretary Julius Krug appeared alongside Reclamation commissioner Michael Straus at a meeting of local and state officials in Salt Lake City in 1946, pledging

"100 percent" cooperation on the two projects. Yet three years later Krug, speaking in Glenwood Springs, Colorado, announced that he would not support the Dinosaur dams because they would conflict with the purposes of the National Park System.[8]

Krug's change of heart sparked outrage in Vernal, but he was getting pressure from Newton Drury to abandon the Dinosaur dams. Some Republicans in Congress also criticized BuRec's ambitious program as fiscally irresponsible (federal river basin development was a mainstay of the Democratic Party's platform). But after Krug resigned unexpectedly in late 1949, Oscar Chapman, his replacement, announced his support for the Colorado River Storage Project (CRSP), which authorized dams at Echo Park, Split Mountain, Flaming Gorge, and Glen Canyon. Citing the "demonstrated need for water," Chapman directed the Bureau of Reclamation to proceed with studies leading to congressional authorization.[9] Political leaders and opinion makers in Utah applauded the decision. The *Salt Lake Telegram* editorialized that "we can easily have both" reservoirs and a tourist attraction at Dinosaur.[10]

Relatively few Utahns openly opposed these dams, although Vernal river guide Bus Hatch and his son Don quietly worked to raise awareness of Dinosaur's beautiful canyons. It took a former Utahn with a sharp pen to bring the issue to national attention. Bernard DeVoto had left the Beehive State in 1915 to study at Harvard and went on to a distinguished career as a writer, historian, and social critic. He raised hackles in Utah by penning barbed commentaries on its religious and cultural conformity, while his seminal 1947 essay "The West against Itself" challenged the hostile-yet-dependent attitude of many westerners toward the federal government. "It shakes down to a platform—get out and give us more money," he wrote.[11]

The same theme informed his 1950 article in the *Saturday Evening Post* titled "Shall We Let Them Ruin Our National Parks?" Aiming for a wide audience, DeVoto stated the issue in the plainest terms. "Right where the scenery is, that's where they want to build dams," he opened his essay.[12] "They," in this case, were the sponsors of big, expensive water projects that benefited an astoundingly small number of ranchers, farmers, and businesspeople. To boosters who contended that a dam or two would improve Dinosaur National Monument by bringing in thousands of tourists to boat, fish, and water ski, DeVoto countered that the reservoir behind Echo Park dam would be "a mere millpond" that would engulf the Yampa's magnificent scenery. It was the same term the Park Service had used against the proposed Bridge Canyon dam in the Grand Canyon. DeVoto believed that the principle applied to the entire National Park System, including little-known places such as Dinosaur.

Newspapers in Salt Lake City and Vernal denounced DeVoto's stance, some claiming that the Park Service had written the *Saturday Evening Post* piece.[13] One Salt Lake Chamber of Commerce official called the conservationists "screwballs . . . eastern bird-lovers and mountain climbers, who have never been to Utah or Colorado and who know nothing of our economic problems."[14] E. O. Larson, regional director of the Bureau of Reclamation in Salt Lake City, pointed out that the dams would not affect Dinosaur's emblematic fossil beds—a red herring, since the eighty-acre site was downstream from the proposed dams.

Newton Drury resigned not long after DeVoto's article appeared, under pressure from Oscar Chapman to mute his opposition to the dams. His successor, Conrad Wirth, was more politic in his statements, but he nevertheless continued the Park Service's resistance. He received crucial help from the nation's top conservation groups, which, thanks in part to DeVoto's articles, were growing increasingly concerned about the Interior Department's designs on southwestern rivers. Their interest in Dinosaur, a long-neglected outlier of the National Park System, was spurred by Stephen Bradley, an avid kayaker from Berkeley, California, who floated the Yampa with Bus Hatch in the early 1950s. Bradley enlisted his father, Harold, who was active in the Sierra Club, in the campaign to preserve the river canyon. On a subsequent family trip down the Yampa in 1952, the elder Bradley made a home movie that helped to personalize the Dinosaur issue for conservationists. David Brower, the club's executive director, knew little about river running, but after floating through Dinosaur with fellow Sierra Club members in 1953 (also on a trip outfitted by Bus Hatch), he, too, fell under the spell of the soaring cliffs of the Green and Yampa's canyons and organized a campaign to preserve them.

Brower saw no compatibility between dams and the National Park System. Working through an ad hoc coalition of conservation groups called the Emergency Committee on Natural Resources, he introduced many of the tactics that would be used in subsequent conservationist campaigns, including prolific press coverage and multimedia publicity. He commissioned noted author and historian Wallace Stegner, like DeVoto a former Utahn, to edit a book called *This Is Dinosaur*, which was financed by publisher Alfred

Knopf. He also engaged New York filmmaker Charles Eggert to make *Wilderness River Trail*, which depicted families of all ages enjoying the rapids of the Yampa. It was shown widely across the nation and inaugurated a series of Sierra Club films about threatened wild places.

Brower consulted with sympathetic engineers and hydrologists who found gaps in the Bureau of Reclamation's justification for impounding water in the national monument. At a congressional hearing on the Echo Park dam, he pointed out what appeared to be a simple arithmetic error that had skewed their engineers' evaporation-loss calculations in favor of the Echo Park dam site.[15] It was an embarrassing mistake that damaged BuRec's credibility with Congress.

Later in the campaign Brower took out a full-page newspaper advertisement against the dams—a tactic he would repeat later in fighting proposed dams in the Grand Canyon. Still, he and other conservationists made it clear from the outset that they did not oppose the entire CRSP; in fact, much of their testimony contended that reclamation needs could easily be met by the dams planned for Flaming Gorge and Glen Canyon. The Wilderness Society pointed out in its journal *The Living Wilderness* that "substitutes may be found which will not only furnish more water storage and more hydroelectric power, but will cost far less for the results obtained."[16] These included sites that BuRec had placed on the back burner, including Desolation-Gray Canyon on the Green River and Dewey Bridge and Dark Canyon on the Colorado River. The conservationists' willingness to accept these dams—as well as a taller dam in Glen Canyon—seems surprising today, but no one in a leadership position among the conservation groups was aware at that time of the full extent of the wonders within the Colorado-Green River canyon lands.

The combined opposition of conservationists, California irrigation interests, and fiscal watchdogs in Congress led Congress to adopt a revised CRSP bill that did not include the Echo Park and Split Mountain dams.[17] The final bill, signed into law in April 1956, was a compromise that saved Echo Park from inundation but ensured that equally beautiful stretches of the Green and Colorado Rivers in Flaming Gorge and Glen Canyon would be flooded. At the time, neither canyon was well known among conservationists, although a handful of river rats had been exploring Glen for decades. As construction crews began to tip concrete buckets into the framework for a new dam hundreds of miles downstream from Echo Park, word got out of an exquisite river canyon that was soon to go under—too late for conservationists to act in its defense.

MISSION 66

The adventuresome tourists who visited southeastern Utah's national monuments in the years leading up to World War II were well advised to bring along several spare tires, a tow chain, a shovel, and plenty of water and gasoline. It took serious effort—and no small risk to one's vehicle—to visit Natural Bridges, Hovenweep, and Arches National Monuments, which remained remote destinations with poor road access. Henry Schmidt, the custodian at Arches from 1939 to 1942, noted in his report for October 1941 that 234 visitors "bumped, sloshed, cussed and skidded their way" over the Willow Springs entrance road on their way to see the sandstone spans in this tiny protected enclave. Many turned back before they reached Balanced Rock, unwilling to punish their vehicles any further. Those who pressed onward often registered their displeasure in the visitor log Schmidt placed in a kiosk at the end of the road near this improbable monolith.[1]

Schmidt said he looked forward to the day "when visitors can make this trip over a good highway, in comfort, and will then confine their remarks to the grandeur of the Arches instead of the impassibility of the road." Faced with fighting the same erosive forces that had exposed the monument's Entrada Sandstone fins, he noted that "when the car of a visitor is stuck in the sand, we lend a hand, show them the particular features of the monument they wish to see, and suggest that, perhaps, sand isn't quite as annoying as mud when one's car is stalled."[2]

Schmidt's task grew even harder after the war began and most of the Civilian Conservation Corps workers at the nearby Dalton Wells and Moab camps left for military service. Schmidt moved on at the end of 1941, but complaints about the entrance road continued to fill the visitor register. One tourist wished that "God had spent a little more time on the road and not on the rocks," while another observed that "I started out with a new car and now I'll get another as soon as I get back in civilization."[3]

In 1948 crews from Grand County graded the Willow Springs road and extended it to Devils Garden, Delicate Arch, and the Windows. The new road segments, funded largely by the state of Utah, were feted that May with a barbecue at Devils Garden hosted by the Moab Lions Club.[4] Dr. J. W. Williams, Moab's pioneer doctor and an early booster of the monument, was among the four hundred guests. Scarcely a week later, Park Service director Newton Drury announced plans for a permanent, paved entrance road costing $700,000, which would lead from the monument headquarters west of Moab to Devils Garden.[5] Funding for this project was not forthcoming, however, and new monument custodian Russell Mahan faced ongoing repairs to the washout-prone road.

Bates Wilson, the first superintendent of Arches, took over from Mahan in April 1949. He, too, found himself assisting stuck motorists, some of whom he invited to dinner. Not all were so lucky; he noted in October of that year that one motorist who challenged Courthouse Wash when it was running "sank deep in the quicksand and abandoned his car when the water started running in the window."[6]

Lack of road access was not a problem at Zion, Bryce Canyon, and the other great national parks of the West; rather, it was the condition of the facilities once people got there. Neglected during the war and designed to accommodate 1930s levels of use, most park infrastructure was showing severe strain by the 1950s. The number of visitors entering Yellowstone topped one million for the first time in 1948, and by 1952 Grand Canyon had doubled its prewar visitation. More than two hundred thousand tourists were arriving at Bryce Canyon each year, with half again as many taking in the sights along Zion Canyon. Lodges, roads, and campgrounds were crowded and showing wear, while interpretive programs remained understaffed. Bernard DeVoto, the *Harper's Magazine* columnist who had appointed himself watchdog over the western public lands, laid out the situation in a provocative essay titled "Let's Close the National Parks." After visiting fifteen national parks and monuments in 1952, he cataloged the complaints of irate tourists who had to stand in line at restrooms, couldn't find suitable accommodations, or had to repair pothole-damaged tires.[7]

Congress had starved Park Service budgets for too long, DeVoto wrote, leaving the parks understaffed and in disrepair. Overworked rangers were forced to "drop their specialties to join a garbage disposal crew or a rescue party, to sweep up tourist litter, to clean a defouled spring, to do anything else that has to be done but can't be paid for." When they did get some sleep, it was in substandard housing. The workload was taking a toll on morale and diverted staff from interpretation work.

DeVoto's "solution" was meant to raise eyebrows: "Let us, as a beginning, close Yellowstone, Yosemite, Rocky Mountain, and Grand Canyon National Parks—close and seal them, assign the Army to patrol them, and so hold them secure till they can be reopened." This extreme expedient would get the public to badger their congressional representatives until they properly funded park operations and personnel. Just as citizens had stood firm with Director Drury against building dams in Dinosaur National Monument, DeVoto hoped that people would come to the agency's aid in the less glamorous arena of Washington budget politics.

Americans loved their national parks, and DeVoto's facetious call to close them brought a deluge of constituent mail to Congress. It responded with what one historian called "the largest single appropriations increase ever awarded the National Park Service before or since."[8] Newton Drury's replacement, Conrad Wirth, was only too happy for the help. A Washington insider who had never held a park superintendency, he saw the crisis as an opportunity to increase the agency's funding over the long term, as well as to implement his own vision for the national parks, which was focused more on automobile-based recreation than on preserving wild spaces.

Wirth and his chief assistant, park planner Thomas Vint, envisioned a ten-year program for modernizing the national parks with better access roads and proper visitor facilities. "Mission 66," a billion-dollar overhaul of the entire park system, would be completed by 1966, the Park Service's fiftieth anniversary. In an internal memo announcing the program in February 1955, Wirth called on his field staff to use "imagination and vision" in proposing specific projects for funding. He also asked for ideas on how to deal with "overuse of park areas"—one goal of the program was to relocate visitor facilities away from prime scenic spots, such as the edge of Yellowstone's Grand Canyon.[9]

Mission 66 fit neatly within President Eisenhower's recession-fighting program of building interstate highways and developing the West's rivers. But it was more than a public works program; Wirth's intention was to secure a lasting place for the National Park Service in American life. It would also generate controversy as architecturally modern visitor centers replaced old but beloved rustic structures that could no longer accommodate heavy use. Conservation groups objected to the program's emphasis on road building, despite Wirth's and Vint's assurances that the parks' backcountry would be preserved. David Brower, whose Sierra Club was embroiled in a fight over building a scenic parkway over Tioga Pass in Yosemite National Park, observed that "little roads led to bigger roads" and that smooth asphalt highways ruined the experience of driving on a narrow dirt road, where one could smell the pine trees and see the roadside flowers.[10] Wirth, Brower believed, was too closely allied with the American Automobile Association and other highway interests. Indeed, some of the program's publicity materials were sponsored by oil companies such as Phillips 66.

Despite the criticism, Mission 66 came just in time for park administrators who were trying to cope with ever-mounting visitation and overused facilities and infrastructure. Zion and Bryce Canyon National Parks each gained new visitor centers, augmented their interpretation facilities, and built new roads to alleviate traffic congestion. Zion superintendent Paul Franke also sought to expand the park to incorporate the Kolob Canyons, which had been designated as Zion National Monument in 1938. This was accomplished in record time with the help of Utah senator Wallace Bennett and congressman Aldous Dixon. President Eisenhower signed the necessary legislation on July 11, 1956, increasing the size of the park to 147,000 acres. The Kolob section would not gain a paved road or visitor facilities for another two decades, however.

Hoping to reduce pressure on the main Zion Canyon, Franke decided to convert the campground at the Grotto to a picnic area and expand the South Campground near the entrance station. The centerpiece of Zion's Mission 66 improvements was a new visitor center at Oak Creek, which opened in 1960. It featured a spacious, well-lit lobby as well as offices and an auditorium. The modern, glass-walled structure stood in sharp contrast to the historic Zion Lodge and the former museum building at the Grotto, both of which featured native stone and were intended to blend with the canyon environment.

By the mid-1950s, Bryce Canyon had grown popular enough to warrant its administrative detachment from Zion and its own superintendent and ranger staff. Conrad Wirth paid a visit to Bryce Canyon in the summer of 1956, during which he approved plans for a new visitor center, employee housing, and a bypass road around the lodge area. The park's campgrounds were also modernized and doubled in capacity. These improvements spelled trouble for the Utah Parks Company, which saw its bus tours increasingly supplanted by auto tourists.[11]

Capitol Reef National Monument and the bucolic village of Fruita remained off the main tourist track, a place many visitors simply chanced upon during their travels. In 1946 two California investors began building a tourist lodge in the heart of Fruita on land they purchased from A. L. Inglesby. Intended to be a replica of Zion Lodge, the venture grew by fits and starts, hampered by lack of capital.[12] In 1954 local resident Dewey Gifford built a motel nearby, while a small store and gas station owned by Cass Mulford, another local, rounded out the tourist facilities within the monument.[13] These businesses and the privately owned orchards and farmland in and around Fruita presented a dilemma for monument superintendent Charles Kelly and his successors. They understood the desire of local residents to hold on to their property but feared the inevitable expansion of tourist facilities in this highly scenic locale. Kelly used Mission 66 funds to begin acquiring some private lands as their owners died or decided to sell, a process that was mostly completed by 1964 under superintendent William Krueger. The lodgings at Fruita continued to operate into the 1970s. Farther south, along Pleasant Creek, a property once belonging to pioneer Ephraim Hanks was acquired in 1939 by Lurt Knee, who with his wife, Alice, operated it as the Sleeping Rainbow Guest Ranch. Following Lurt's death in 1995, Alice deeded the property to the National Park Service. In 2008 Utah State University opened an educational field station on the site.[14]

Capitol Reef retained its out-of-the-way flavor owing in large part to the lack of highway access. As late as the 1950s no paved road led through the Waterpocket Fold. In 1957 the state of Utah paved the monument's western access road along a new alignment leading from Torrey to Fruita, which induced the Park Service to seek a northward expansion of the monument to take in the new road. After some discussion and a public hearing, President Eisenhower approved the 3,030-acre expansion in July 1958.[15] Further extension of the road eastward presented difficulties, however. The state wanted to route the highway through Pleasant Creek, which would have involved a long jog to the south. It ultimately opted for a more direct route along the Fremont River, which required blasting through cliffs and rerouting the river itself. Once the highway was completed in 1962, Superintendent Krueger closed Capitol Wash to through traffic. This angered local residents who enjoyed using the historic route.[16] But with new hiking trails, a campground, and a visitor center that opened in 1965, all constructed with Mission 66 funds, tourists could more easily access the Fold and its attractions.

At Arches National Monument, bids were opened in May 1957 for construction of a new, nine-mile-long entrance road leading from monument headquarters to Balanced Rock. Construction got underway in late August, following heavy late-summer rains that flooded Courthouse Wash and stranded motorists on the existing Willow Springs access road. Formally dedicated on August 24, 1958, the road opened the monument to thousands more motorists.[17] By summer 1962 a spur road to the Windows area was open for travel, and the following summer crews were extending the main road another nine miles to Devils Garden, where a sixty-unit campground was being built. The completed road was opened to travel on October 29, 1963, a year that saw 107,000 visitors taking in the monument's sights.[18] A new visitor center along Highway 160 north of Moab was completed in January 1960, and the following year Senator Bennett introduced legislation to designate Arches as a national park. Once an out-of-the-way collection of sandstone curiosities, Arches was destined to become one of Utah's most popular tourist attractions. The Mission 66 projects in the monument "prove without a shadow of a doubt that development is the key to area travel," exulted the *Moab Times-Independent*.[19]

For more than a decade, Natural Bridges National Monument had remained in essentially the same condition that Zeke Johnson left it when he retired in 1941. Getting to the monument was no longer as difficult, thanks to the completion of Utah Highway 95 from Blanding to Hanksville, and in 1953 the eastern approach to the monument was relocated from atop Elk Ridge to a lower-elevation route over the northern edge of Comb Ridge. Visitors arriving at the monument found only a picnic area, two pit toilets (one of them facing the Owachomo Bridge), an interpretive kiosk, and a self-guiding nature trail that wound down into White Canyon.

J. Wiley Redd, a part-time uranium prospector and rancher from Blanding, served as custodian at Natural Bridges during the summer months. It was still a three-mile walk from the entrance road to the Sipapu Bridge, which the Park Service believed was beyond the reach of the average tourist. Bates Wilson, using more than $750,000 in Mission 66 funds (an amount

The beginning of a new entrance road to Arches National Monument in the mid-1950s.
The monoliths in the center-right of the photograph are known, anthropomorphically,
as the "Three Gossips." *Lloyd Pierson/National Park Service, Southeast Utah Group
Archives.*

that Zeke Johnson, who lived in an army tent and paid for many of his supplies himself, could hardly have dreamed of), set about modernizing its facilities. A new access road was constructed from the southeast that afforded
a closer rim-side approach to the Kachina and Sipapu Bridges. A new visitor center, a campground, and employee housing were built, leading visitation to mushroom from 2,700 in 1954 to more than 10,000 in 1962. Natural
Bridges, like Arches, had entered the tourist age. No longer would Zeke Johnson's rough-and-ready approach, which demanded more effort and interest
on the part of the visitor, suffice.[20]

Mission 66 permitted park administrators to deal with the extensive back-log of repairs and make significant improvements to roads, buildings, and other services, but some agency staff in the Southwest were concerned that opening parks and monuments to new development would mean the loss of their wild character. Several incidents of vandalism occurred in Arches after the new entrance road was opened, prompting Bates Wilson to close it to nighttime travel for a time in 1962.[21] Easier public access also meant more opportunities for pothunters and vandals to damage archaeological sites, according to Erik Reed, chief of interpretation services for the Park Service's Southwest Region. He witnessed a large increase in what he termed "deliberate vandalism" of priceless cultural sites, as well as inadvertent losses from construction projects. He asked Director Wirth, perhaps facetiously, if it would not be better to entrust places such as New Mexico's Gila Cliff Dwellings to the Forest Service, which could protect them as designated wilderness areas.[22]

Reed also brought up an idea that had been circulating among the Park Service's interpretive staff: setting aside "reserve monuments" to be protected primarily for ecological and scientific research. "I wish that the Service could and would be concerned with preservation of biotic areas and archaeological sites, undeveloped for visitation," he told Wirth. This was a variant on the research reserves that had gained only a slim foothold in the National Park System in the 1930s. Such designations, Reed wrote, would aid in protecting areas such as the Yampa River that were threatened by inappropriate development. He noted that the Park Service's traditional emphasis on recreation made it harder to protect lands of high ecological or cultural value that received little public use.

Conrad Wirth maintained that Mission 66 was not a wilderness-busting roads program; he insisted that if new roads and facilities were located in less sensitive locations, overuse of scenic viewpoints and the backcountry itself would be alleviated. But there was no denying that Mission 66 brought an end to the long isolation of the national monuments of southeastern Utah. As late as 1957, as Bates Wilson noted, Arches National Monument was a destination for "the hardy and adventuresome [who] could see the natural wonders of the area only on feet, horseback or by jeep, and then only with a guide. Camping facilities were nil, trails were mostly those made by sheep and cattle, interpretation was almost nonexistent and protection was no problem."[23]

This was the situation that greeted a twenty-nine-year-old novelist named Edward Abbey when he showed up at Arches National Monument in April 1956 to begin the first of two seasons as a field ranger. Taking residence in a Park Service trailer near Balanced Rock, he set to work patrolling Devils Garden, the Windows, and Delicate Arch, all the while trying to hone his craft as a writer and interpreter of the southwestern desert. *Desert Solitaire*, his partly fictionalized account of those seasons, became a sensation among hikers, conservationists, and desert lovers when it was published in 1968.

Like John Muir in the Sierra Nevada and Bob Marshall in the Alaskan Arctic, Abbey viewed the Colorado Plateau as a place where humans could come under the influence of an intimidating yet lovely landscape. The key was direct contact with the Earth, mediated by as few modern conveniences as possible, especially the automobile. In a chapter of *Desert Solitaire* titled "Polemic: Industrial Tourism and the National Parks," Abbey recounted his horror at learning that the Willow Springs entrance road was to be replaced by a paved road coming up from the southern end of the monument. This meant a radical change for the visitor's experience: "Where once a few adventurous people came on weekends to camp for a night or two and enjoy a taste of the primitive and remote," he wrote, "you will now find serpentine streams of baroque automobiles pouring in and out, all through the spring and summer, in numbers that would have seemed fantastic when I worked there: from 3,000 to 30,000 to 300,000 per year."[24]

Many of the Mission 66 road projects in Utah's and Arizona's national parks and monuments drew Abbey's ire. Natural Bridges, where Abbey's brother John worked as a ranger during the 1957 season, had been a "small gem in the park system," but the new loop road now made it a simple matter to see its largest spans. The new highway along the Fremont River through Capitol Reef National Monument, although not a Mission 66 project, sliced through what Abbey called "the most beautiful portion of the park." The Kolob Canyons adjacent to Zion National Park were almost a wilderness, he wrote, until a "broad highway, with banked curves, deep cuts and heavy fills" was built through them.[25]

The National Park Service, according to Abbey, could not be relied on to protect the wild lands under its jurisdiction. "All they can think of is more asphalt paving, more picnic tables, more garbage cans, more shithouses, more electric lights, more Kleenex dispensers."[26] In *Desert Solitaire* he wondered why the Park Service was so eager to accommodate "the indolent millions born on wheels and suckled on gasoline" who desired access to the parks. It was partly a matter of business, he said, with everyone from restaurant owners to road contractors cheering the increase in tourism.

The conclusion to Abbey's polemic pleased some readers and appalled others. He described how he walked the flag line left by the road surveyors in Arches and pulled up their stakes—doing his job, as he saw it, to safeguard this small remnant of the American wilderness. It seems unlikely that he actually risked his job in this manner—he was always coy about his "monkey-wrenching" activities—but he undoubtedly wished that the offending road would somehow disappear. As the decade-long Mission 66 program unfolded, other Park Service rangers in the Southwest must have noticed how their lonely domains were being catapulted into the age of mass tourism.

Edward Abbey's voice carried far beyond Utah, helping to spark serious opposition to the assumption that more tourists could be brought into the wilderness without diminishing its essence. The overwhelming sense of remoteness and isolation that had greeted visitors to Arches, Natural Bridges, and Capitol Reef during the first half of the twentieth century was giving way to a more standardized park experience—one that was more familiar to visitors to Zion, Bryce Canyon, or any of the larger western parks. It had become, as Joseph Sax noted in his classic work *Mountains without Handrails*, "little more than an extension of the city and its life-style transposed onto a scenic background."[27]

Whatever its shortcomings in terms of architectural design and its impact on wilderness solitude, Mission 66 succeeded in keeping the national parks abreast of the ravenous demand for scenic vacations among Americans of the 1950s and 1960s. That the growth in tourism benefited local and regional businesses only added to the program's appeal. Conrad Wirth, like Stephen Mather and Horace Albright before him, understood that tourism could be an engine of economic growth in rural regions, making "a real contribution to the American standard of living," as he put it in a speech to his fellow Park Service staff in 1955.[28]

Although civic leaders in southern Utah willingly embraced tourism, many of them remained skeptical of the overall aims of the National Park Service. Parks might bring economic benefits to their communities, but they also wanted no diminishment of livestock grazing and mineral development.

This question was about to be debated once again as proposals took shape for a new national park in the Utah canyon lands. The Park Service superintendent at the heart of this controversy was the same one who had just overseen construction of the new paved road into Arches—an improvement that only his misanthropic ranger out at Balanced Rock seemed to oppose.

HIDDEN CANYON

The Sierra Club cut its political teeth a half century before Echo Park in a battle over a dam on the Tuolumne River in the remote northern corner of Yosemite National Park. The granite-walled valley called Hetch Hetchy pitted San Francisco's municipal water interests against the preservationism championed by John Muir, the club's president and cofounder. Muir lost that fight and was said to have been heartbroken over the flooding of this magnificent river canyon. The same sense of impending loss would grip many of those who floated Utah's Glen Canyon in the years after 1956, when Congress approved the Colorado River Storage Project (CRSP) and consigned 186 miles of tapestried cliffs and shadowy side canyons to the same fate.

Through the CRSP and the dams it authorized, Utah and Colorado hoped to reserve their share of the Colorado River's flow against demand from downstream users in California and Arizona. The tremendous storage capacity of the reservoirs behind Glen Canyon and Flaming Gorge Dams assured the lower-basin states a continued supply of water during drought years. Lake Powell, the centerpiece of the CRSP, would be a multipurpose reservoir, generating electric power, keeping silt out of Lake Mead, and offering recreation for thousands upon its still waters. In the eyes of Congress and probably most Americans, the benefits of river-basin development far outweighed the loss of a remote canyon that few had seen.

The problem conservationists faced was that Glen Canyon, like most of the Colorado River canyon lands, lay out of sight of towns and highways. Following the war, most Americans wanted to see the Southwest from a car window or perhaps a cabin cruiser on a lake, not by taking an expensive float trip down a muddy desert river. Tourists who drove from the Grand Canyon through the Painted Desert to Mesa Verde—perhaps detouring

Glen Canyon on the Colorado River. *Al Watkins Morton/Used by permission, Utah State Historical Society.*

north to see Zion or Bryce Canyon—got only a hint of what lay concealed beneath the rims and mesas.

A handful of writers were beginning to celebrate this unusual topography during the postwar years. Roderick Peattie's 1948 book The Inverted Mountains focused on northern Arizona sights and made only passing reference to the Utah canyon lands.[1] Even the book's title suggested that canyon scenery could best be understood in terms of more conventional, mountainous places. Randall Henderson's California-based *Desert Magazine* dug deeper into the wilderness of southeastern Utah, including an article on a float trip he made in Glen Canyon with Jim Rigg and Frank Wright in July 1952, but this reached a limited audience.[2] Of the East Coast literati, probably only Wallace Stegner knew the Utah backcountry. He had floated Glen Canyon in 1947 with Norm Nevills while researching a book on John Wesley Powell, finding the canyon "unimaginably beautiful." He sang its praises in an article titled "Backroads River" in *Atlantic* magazine the following year, but he did not mention its impending inundation. As Stegner recalled years later, "at the moment Dinosaur was threatened; Glen Canyon wasn't."[3]

Photographers, too, would do a great deal to publicize southern Utah's canyon lands, just as the pioneers in that field had made Yellowstone and Yosemite known to the nation in the previous century. In 1938 Joseph Muench, a German immigrant who settled in California, sold a photograph of Rainbow Bridge to *Arizona Highways* magazine, launching an illustrious career of photographing the Desert Southwest. His images of Monument Valley helped to popularize the area as a travel destination, but he also photographed scenes in Capitol Reef, where he was a frequent guest at Lurt Knee's Sleeping Rainbow Guest Ranch, as well as Natural Bridges and other national monuments.

In 1944 *Life* magazine featured a twelve-page photo spread depicting the Colorado River canyons and nearby scenic features such as Arches, the Land of Standing Rocks, and Glen Canyon, as well as scenes from a Nevills boat trip down Cataract Canyon. "The strength which makes the Colorado dangerous is what makes it useful," read the accompanying text. "The deep canyons it has cut are probably the best natural dam sites in the world."[4] The Utah canyons made for a picturesque subject, but it was assumed that they would soon be brought into the modern world. *National Geographic* ran several articles on southern Utah during the 1940s that stressed the remoteness and unexplored grandeur of canyon country. Jack Breed, a landscape photographer from Massachusetts who had relocated to Tucson, Arizona, wrote and illustrated these articles, the first two of which covered Monument Valley and Arches National Monument.[5] Breed returned to Utah in the spring of 1948 to explore the upper Paria River basin and locate the Crossing of the Fathers in lower Glen Canyon. Traveling by automobile, truck, and jeep, the party traversed the benchlands east of Cannonville, naming Kodachrome Flat (local ranchers called it "Thorny Pasture") and Grosvenor Arch, the latter honoring Gilbert Grosvenor, president of the National Geographic Society.

The authors of these and other articles took a paradoxical view of canyon country, presenting it as a wild, romantic region of mysterious rock formations, hardy cowboys, and stoic Indians, while at the same time touting its potential for economic and industrial development. Progress was coming to the Colorado River and its canyons, so one needed to see them before it was too late. Few gave any hint that substantial parts of this region might be designated as national parks or monuments, despite the Park Service's Escalante proposals of the previous decade.

For those who had witnessed Glen Canyon before the reservoir, it was not always a question of balancing aesthetics with water supply and hydropower. There was something magical about Glen's intimate, shadowy side canyons, its sweeping cliff walls, and its long history of human use. One visitor who felt this connection most strongly was Katie Lee, a folk singer and actress from Tucson, Arizona, who first floated the canyon in 1953. Often traveling with river guide Frank Wright and photographer Tad Nichols, she grew to love the grottoes and labyrinthine stream courses that highlighted their leisurely explorations. On her first trip with Wright and Nichols in 1955, she recorded in her journal the question that had risen in many canyon explorers' minds: "*What's* here that triggers an emotion so overwhelming it brings tears? . . . This is rock—inert—water, air, aromas, silence, light, and shadowplay. Words would mock this scene. . . . We've just been handed a spectacular gift—rare, flawless, stunning to the senses—and the privilege has touched our hearts in a wash [of] humility and reverence."[6]

Lee entertained guests on commercial trips with her singing and guitar playing, but she preferred to voyage with Wright and Nichols, taking time to explore side canyons, lounge by the moonlit river, and breathe in Glen's sensuous ambience. Like Dave Rust, who had taken a small number of guests down this stretch of river three decades earlier, they would climb up to the rim wherever possible for views over the slickrock. Above Wildhorse Bar, Lee and her friends found "no prints but animal's and our own; no sound save a whistle of wind and an occasional cranky raven riding thermals."[7]

Lee's evocation of the wonder and mystery of Glen's side canyons joined similar paeans by Edward Abbey, her kindred spirit in desert exploration.

Abbey's description of his 1959 voyage down the canyon with his buddy Ralph Newcomb, which formed a chapter of his book *Desert Solitaire*, started a small industry of rapturous writing about Glen. Describing his trip as "a kind of waking dream," Abbey helped to elevate the canyon into an icon of the disappearing Utah wilderness.[8] But he also put these canyon scenes into the framework of contemporary southwestern culture. After Abbey, canyon country could no longer be viewed in the detached Romantic language of sublimity and awesomeness; his gritty prose depicted not only the harsh desert landscape, but also the boomers and politicians who always seemed ready to trade the old ways for modern industry.

Few river runners who knew Glen Canyon in the 1950s and early 1960s dared hope that its inundation could be avoided. One who did was Ken Sleight, a high school teacher from Bountiful, Utah, who contracted what he called "river fever" in the early 1950s while rafting Lodore Canyon on the Green River with a group of friends. Sleight began taking guests down Glen Canyon in 1955, using eighteen-foot war-surplus rafts. "A 'big booking' was a family of four," his friend and fellow guide Richard Quist recalled. The operation lost money during its first few years, notwithstanding Sleight's spartan camp fare, in which dinner might consist of tinned ham and lima beans.[9]

Sleight's clients, though, came not for camp luxuries but "to take in the beauty of the river, always in wonder of what lay around the next bend," he recalled in 1993. "Entertainment was spontaneous and self-provided. The customers would sing and play harmonicas and guitars back in the grottoes." Floating Glen touched something in his soul. "It was heaven on earth. . . . The deep canyons, the meanderings, the quiet of the water, the great beaches."[10]

Sleight was active in the Western River Guides Association, which mounted a last-ditch petition drive to forestall the reservoir by calling for Glen Canyon to become a national park. Working with Malcolm "Moki Mac" Ellingson, a Salt Lake City scout leader, and William R. Halliday, a physician and avid spelunker, Sleight spread word about Glen Canyon, but the campaign came too late. Halliday pleaded in a letter to the Sierra Club's Dave Brower to take a stand against the dam, but Brower replied that this was hardly possible, given how difficult it had been to stop the dams in Dinosaur. Glen Canyon, moreover, held no official status—only Rainbow Bridge National Monument stood to be affected, and a provision in the CRSP authorization bill seemed to afford this tiny monument the protection it needed.[11]

Most of the leaders of the nation's principal conservation groups knew little about the Utah canyon lands. Even after Wallace Stegner told Brower that Glen's scenery surpassed Dinosaur's, he held to his position, noting that one of their key arguments against the Echo Park dam in Dinosaur National Monument had been that a high dam at Glen Canyon would accomplish BuRec's water-storage objectives with lower cost and less overall loss of water. He recalled in an interview in the late 1970s that "since they were going to build that dam anyway as the big money-maker . . . they might as well make it a little higher while they were at it. But I was giving away Glen Canyon without knowing one cotton-picking thing about what was there."[12]

Indeed, when Brower finally saw Glen Canyon on a float trip in 1960, he was stunned by the canyon's beauty. However, as early as 1954 he had asked the directors of the Sierra Club to oppose the entire CRSP package, based in part on its high cost. He was overruled and was forced to withdraw the club's opposition.[13] A personal plea to Interior Secretary Stewart Udall to halt the filling of the reservoir brought no response. In later years Brower would often express deep regret that he had not been able to preserve Glen Canyon along with Echo Park. "That was one of the bitterest lessons I ever had," he told an interviewer.[14]

If Glen Canyon represented the spiritual center of canyon country, Rainbow Bridge lay at its apex. To Brower, Sleight, and others it was anathema to replace the hike up Forbidding and Bridge Canyons with a ride in a motorboat, concentrating tourists at a site they believed should be approached with respect and in solitude. At its planned "full pool" level of 3,700 feet, Lake Powell would back up underneath the bridge itself, well within the boundary of Rainbow Bridge National Monument. This was in direct violation of the CRSP's requirement that the Bureau of Reclamation take "adequate measures" to protect Rainbow Bridge from impairment.

Since 1956 BuRec engineers had been working on an engineering solution that involved placing one or more retaining dams in either Bridge Canyon or Forbidding Canyon, along with a nearly mile-long diversion tunnel and a pumping station to handle the flows coming down to the bridge. The cost would be enormous—a minimum of $15 million, according to the bureau—and accessing the site would involve building fifty miles or more of new road. Floyd Dominy, who was appointed commissioner of reclamation in 1959, thought the idea preposterous. "To perform this kind of construction would be so goddamn much more horrendous than to let a little water back in under that bridge," he recalled in a 1994 interview.[15]

The *Salt Lake Tribune* called the barrier dams "silly . . . a costly boondoggle that could do irreparable harm to the whole wilderness philosophy." Dr. Angus M. Woodbury, a biologist at the University of Utah, believed that the cost and environmental disruption of building the dams outweighed the benefit. In an article written for *Science* magazine in 1960, he asked whether it made sense to "permanently [mar] the natural scenic beauties of the region, including both approaches to the bridge" simply to prevent the reservoir's waters from filling the narrow canyon underneath it. "This is a case which calls for conservationists to do a little soul searching," he wrote.[16] Nonetheless, the Park Service and some conservationists, including Brower, favored such an approach, insisting that flooding a unit of the National Park System would open many more to such violations.

In 1960 Stewart Udall, then an Arizona congressman, floated down the Colorado River in Glen Canyon, stopping on the way to visit Rainbow Bridge and examine BuRec's check-dam sites. He called the bridge "unquestionably the most awe-inspiring work of natural sculpture anywhere in the United States" but conceded that letting the reservoir rise was the "lesser evil" compared to the massive earthworks and tunnel needed to keep out the rising waters.[17] To attempt to settle the question, Udall organized an on-site tour of the bridge in April 1961, featuring most of the principals in the case, including Utah senator Frank Moss, David Brower, Anthony Wayne Smith of the National Parks Association, and an entourage of other congressmen, journalists, and BuRec officials and engineers. Floyd Dominy arrived in his official airplane, bemused at Udall's elaborate show-me tour that featured a fleet of giant air force helicopters to shuttle the entourage from Page, Arizona, to a mesa near the monument. Transferring to smaller helicopters, the party landed in Bridge Canyon for a closer look at Rainbow Bridge. Udall pointed out paint marks on the canyon wall representing the high-water mark, which extended beneath the bridge itself.[18]

Udall understood the conservationists' concern about allowing intrusions into the National Park System. The law was also clear: the monument must be protected, and the Bureau of Reclamation had agreed it was possible to do so. But the argument that the barrier dams would cause much more damage was, to Udall, persuasive. He thought there might be a legislative solution to the impasse. At a meeting with Dominy and other administration officials earlier that year, he proposed that Rainbow Bridge become the centerpiece of a new national park that would take in much of the terrain around Navajo Mountain and the Rainbow Plateau. The reservoir would extend underneath the bridge, but this would offer convenient access for tourists. In compensation, a much larger landscape would be recognized and protected. "It seems to me," Udall suggested to Dominy, "that the real park is not the square box-like 160 acres. It is the whole area."[19]

Following their visit to the bridge, the party of dignitaries assembled in Page over dinner. Udall was noncommittal about the various engineering methods for protecting the bridge, hoping instead to win converts for expanding the tiny national monument into a new national park of some 350,000 acres. This idea dated to the 1930s and the Bernheimer proposal for a Navajo national park, and it met with general approval that evening. One person who was not persuaded was Navajo tribal chair Paul Jones, who had also come on the tour. He believed that such a park would benefit the Navajo Nation only if it were run by the Navajos themselves. In fact, the tribal council had recently established a tribal park on reservation lands in Monument Valley.[20]

Udall offered to find suitable lands in trade for the new park, but this did not satisfy Jones, and the proposal went no further. It was a sign, though, of how Udall was beginning to look at the larger landscape of the Colorado Plateau. In contrast to conservationists such as David Brower, who was more concerned about the precedent that would be set if Lake Powell were to rise beneath the bridge, Udall was looking beyond the confines of Bridge Canyon. Probably without knowing it, he was starting down the same course that led Roger Toll in the 1930s to envision larger possibilities in the Utah canyon lands. Toll's 1931 trip to the Navajo Reservation with M. R. Tillotson had opened his eyes to the mysterious beauty of sculpted sandstone landscapes, and now a new interior secretary was seeing a more expansive horizon as well. Principle was important, but the conservationists' tunnel vision at Rainbow Bridge seems to have blinded them to what might have been accomplished in the way of a larger national park. It would be Udall, in fact, who very shortly would open their eyes.

Unable to gain support for barrier dams to protect Rainbow Bridge, Brower, Smith, and their conservationist allies floated the possibility of keeping Lake Powell at a lower level of 3,600 feet. If the reservoir were held at an even storage capacity of forty million acre-feet, its waters would not back into the monument, and there would be less of a fluctuating "dead zone" around the reservoir. Brower pointed out that Lake Mead could hold much of the lost storage capacity and that evaporation rates would be lessened as a result.[21] But neither Udall nor Dominy would countenance such a plan.

Despite these setbacks, conservation groups deemed the principle at stake in flooding Rainbow Bridge National Monument important enough to carry on the struggle. In 1962 the National Parks Association, Sierra Club, and other conservation organizations sued the Interior Department to prevent Lake Powell from filling until protective measures were in place at Rainbow Bridge. The case was dismissed owing to the plaintiff's lack of standing, or personal loss, in the matter. The gates closed on Glen Canyon Dam the following March, and with the reservoir on the rise, Senators Frank Moss and Wallace Bennett introduced bills to strip the CRSP legislation of the requirement to protect Rainbow Bridge. These did not pass, but Congress simply mooted the issue by not appropriating money for the check dams. Lake Powell would fill to its planned 3,700-foot level, with Rainbow Bridge becoming the most popular single destination for boaters on the reservoir.[22]

The generation of environmentalists who came of age after Lake Powell believed, as did Edward Abbey, that Glen Canyon represented the very heart of canyon country. The submerged canyon would serve as a symbol of loss and a rallying point for action on other fronts such as BLM wilderness, the Burr Trail, and coal mining on the Kaiparowits. Those localities were sometimes difficult for environmental leaders to depict in ways that stirred people to write letters or call their congressional representatives— but there was always Glen Canyon to remind them of what had been lost. Dave Brower and his fellow environmental activists had experienced Utah's canyon country largely by floating its rivers, and to a great degree their perspective was from water level. Within a few years they would oppose Stewart Udall and Arizona's congressional delegation over the issue of placing dams in the Grand Canyon. Before that battle was joined, though, Udall would help direct their attention upward and outward, to a great canyon landscape farther north in Utah.

A PARK IN THE CANYON LANDS

Following their inspection tour of Rainbow Bridge National Monument in late April 1961, Stewart Udall, Frank Moss, and Conrad Wirth needed to return to Denver, where their flights to Washington awaited. Floyd Dominy happened to be flying that way in his agency's airplane (a perk that came with being commissioner of reclamation), so he offered them a ride. For Dominy, it was a chance to show off the site of the next great dam he planned to build on the Colorado River. Udall, for his part, wanted to get a closer look at the area surrounding the confluence of the Green and Colorado Rivers, which was under consideration as a potential national park.

Dominy's pilot took off from the airstrip in Page and set a course to the northeast, flying above the serpentine walls of Glen Canyon. Reaching the lower end of Cataract Canyon, Dominy pointed out the Dark Canyon dam site, behind which another huge artificial lake would tame the flow of the Green and Colorado.[1] Udall's attention, however, was riveted on the surrounding landscape. As they flew up the canyon, a spectacular tableau opened before them. To the north the land rose in massive stair steps to culminate in the high promontory called Grand View Point. To the west lay the Orange Cliffs, overlooking a network of remote canyons. Off to the east, a series of strange grabens ran parallel to the Colorado, beyond which stood the labyrinth of sandstone spires known as the Needles. Through it all the two mountain-born rivers sliced through the land to meet almost head-on at the Confluence.

Udall was well versed in western resource issues, but he knew little about this intricately eroded basin. At a conference of park superintendents he had just attended at Grand Canyon, Bates Wilson told him about the Park Service's ongoing studies of the scenic lands surrounding the confluence of the two rivers.[2] Peering out the plane window, Udall could see possibilities that had nothing to do with placing concrete and steel in a rocky riverbed. This entire erosional basin possessed a grandeur unlike any other part of the Southwest. "I thought, God Almighty, if that isn't a national park then I've never seen one," he recalled years later.[3]

Udall chose not to disclose these musings to his reclamation commissioner, who wanted no interference with the bureau's projected hydropower and water-storage dams in the Colorado River system. Frank Moss's and Conrad Wirth's thoughts during their May 2 overflight are not known, but they would be key players in any move to create a new national park in the Utah canyon lands. Moss was receptive to the idea; in March he and Utah congressmen David King and M. Blaine Peterson, who were fellow Democrats, had written to Udall requesting that he expedite a park proposal in the Confluence–Grand View Point area. Their interest came in response to a 1959 Park Service study that called for a relatively small national park centering on the Needles.[4] The study was the culmination of years of Park Service investigations dating to Ben Thompson's 1944 Grand View national park proposal.

That Udall, a native Arizonan, would be unacquainted with a million-acre expanse of high desert mesas and canyons in his neighboring state suggests that at the dawn of the Space Age, there were still parts of America's public domain that were segregated from mainstream life. The Mormon pioneers who settled the arid valleys of southern Utah and northern Arizona (Udall's ancestors among them) rarely shrank from a challenge, but they never attempted a permanent presence within the basin surrounding the confluence of the Green and Colorado Rivers. For nearly a century they let their cattle and horses wander beneath the Orange Cliffs in search of sparse forage; they cheered as oil companies in the 1920s drilled exploratory wells on the banks of the Colorado downstream from Moab; some of them joined the manic quest for uranium in the 1950s; but they could not find an answer to the near absence of water, the contorted topography, and the unyielding obstacles posed by the river canyons themselves.

All this would change, of course, given America's century-long push to conquer the West. Great forces were converging on Utah in the opening years of the 1960s, reaching in from Washington, Denver, San Francisco, and other centers of economic and political power for the prize these canyons might contain. It could be a new dam and reservoir, a tourism boom

made possible by a transcanyon highway, renewed mineral development—
or it might be something very different, as Stewart Udall imagined. A new
generation of outdoor lovers was discovering that the complex topography of southeastern Utah offered amazing opportunities for adventure,
whether by jeep, on foot, or by water. To them, making a new national
park out of this landscape made perfect sense, even if it meant forgoing
another mining boom.

Park Service staff, too, were taking another look at the region surrounding the Green and Colorado and, anxious to avoid the mistakes their
predecessors made with the Escalante national monument proposal, were
floating a wide range of ideas for a new national park. They found a strong
ally in Udall, but with Utah state officials keenly interested in developing
the area's resources, it was clear that any new park proposal would face a difficult time in Congress.

Stewart Udall came to the Kennedy administration with ambitious goals
for the National Park System. Intending to end the laissez-faire approach to
public lands that had prevailed during the Eisenhower years, he promised
to add fifteen to twenty million acres to the National Park System, including areas close to urban centers that involved costly land purchases. Utah's
canyon lands region quickly rose to the top of his list, however, owing to the
prominence of its landforms and the sense that it was not receiving proper
care under the Bureau of Land Management. Indeed, a month before Udall
took office, the BLM floated a proposal for a "National Cooperative Recreation Area" around Dead Horse Point, to be jointly administered by the BLM
and the state of Utah.[5] This did not happen, but roads, jeep tracks, and adits
from the recent uranium boom were everywhere to be seen, and Park Service officials worried that renewed exploration would further riddle the area.

Even the U.S. military got into the act, firing Athena and Pershing rockets over the area from a joint army–air force launch site near Green River.
The booster stages jettisoned from these rockets crashed into the red rocks,
requiring whole areas to be closed to travel during launches. All this led
Udall to believe the time had come to move a park proposal before more
of the landscape's essential character was lost. But despite his commitment
to a new park in southeastern Utah, Udall would not have gotten very far

Arches National Monument superintendent Bates Wilson (center) holds forth in front of a campfire during a 1962 trip into the Maze for the filming of the Charles Eggert movie *The Sculptured Earth*. Other support personnel present include (left to right) NPS photographer Norm Herkenham, Hanksville rancher Art Ekker, Wilson, Moab physician Paul Mayberry, and NPS Advisory Board chair Frank Masland. *Lloyd Pierson/National Park Service, Southeast Utah Group Archives.*

without the help of a Park Service official who knew both the physical and cultural landscapes of southeastern Utah.

Bates Wilson was probably the ideal person to introduce a canyon country park to the world. A native of Silver City, New Mexico, Wilson had transferred to Moab in 1949 from a custodian position at Organ Pipe Cactus National Monument to take charge of Arches and Natural Bridges National Monuments.[6] Here he became a Park Service "homesteader"—someone who passes up further transfers and promotions in order to stay with one assignment. He assimilated easily into life in Moab, serving in the Rotary Club, leading Boy Scout expeditions, and patiently explaining the Park Service's role to business and civic leaders who yearned for a major "billboard" park like Zion or Bryce Canyon.

Wilson knew deserts and liked the people who lived in them. As the Canyonlands issue blossomed—due in no small part to his efforts—the principals in the debate often found themselves out in the boonies with this friendly man with the weather-beaten smile. Not one to stand on formality or bureaucratic procedures, Wilson often appeared in jeans instead of his Park Service uniform. After eating his sumptuous Dutch-oven meals and sharing a few drinks, if inclined, his guests found it easier to accept the view that this was a landscape unlike any other—and one that was worth protecting.

Wilson grew interested in the area around the Confluence during his long drives between Arches and Natural Bridges. The view from the highway gave only a hint of the mysterious canyon landscape to the west, but that was enough to arouse his curiosity. In March 1951 he made an exploratory trip into the Needles with his son Tug and his cousin Robert Dechert of Philadelphia, with Ross Musselman of Monticello as guide. Bad weather and mishaps plagued the trip, but the men were impressed with the country. Dechert called the Needles and its surroundings "one of the most fascinating wilderness areas in the world" and said the area ought to be a national park. Tug Wilson recalled the native silence of this landscape: "There was not a sound except for a bird or deer in the canyon. When you went to a ruin or an arch or a viewpoint, it often felt like the first time anyone had been there since the Anasazi left."[7]

Wilson returned to the Needles and the surrounding area many times over the years, often with veteran guide Kent Frost, also of Monticello. He introduced many writers, photographers, and Park Service personnel to these remarkable geological features, some of whom would become key players in the effort to obtain a new national park in the Canyonlands region.

Mission 66 brought great changes to the national parks of the western states, but there was little expansion of the park system itself. After the creation of Grand Teton National Park in 1950 (by combining the smaller national park established in 1929 with Jackson Hole National Monument), there had been no new national parks or monuments of appreciable size created west of the Mississippi.[8] The Glen Canyon National Recreation Area, established in 1958 through an administrative agreement between the National Park Service and the Bureau of Reclamation, was the only large land unit in the Southwest to come under NPS management, but many in the agency regarded recreation areas as not properly part of their jurisdiction.[9]

The conservatism of the Eisenhower years did not seem to extend to the Park Service's Southwest regional office in Santa Fe, which on its own initiative was taking a close look at possible new park acquisitions. In 1957 the office set up a planning branch under Les Arnberger, a botanist who had served as a ranger-naturalist at Grand Canyon National Park and Casa Grande Ruins National Monument in Arizona. Arnberger directed park and monument superintendents within the region to undertake field studies of potential new acquisitions.[10] The Canyonlands area offered some of the best candidates. Eager to take on this task, Bates Wilson organized a joint Park Service–BLM exploring trip in May 1959 to the Needles, Chesler Park, and the Confluence area, with Kent Frost as guide. Photographer Frank Jensen of the *Salt Lake Tribune* accompanied the group, filing an article that August titled "Jeep Jaunt to Purgatory." It featured a prominent photo of Druid Arch, one of several the group visited.[11] The weeklong excursion impressed the NPS officials with the potential for a new park in the Needles area, which they described in their report as "scenically and geologically of national significance." At seventy-five thousand acres, it would take in Chesler Park, Squaw Flat, Bobbys Hole Canyon, and upper Salt Creek, including the stunning Druid and Angel Arches. The Confluence area itself would remain within the Glen Canyon National Recreation Area, which at the time extended past Cataract Canyon.[12]

Thus far Wilson and his associates had been considering one or more smaller tracts such as Grand View Point or the Needles, which were scenic highlights within an immense region of stone sculpture. The impetus for a larger park in the Canyonlands region appears to have come from the agency's planning staff in Washington. In the fall of 1960 Leo Diederich, who headed the agency's planning branch, joined Les Arnberger and Bates Wilson on an examination of areas north and west of the Needles. After seeing the Land of Standing Rocks—one of several areas they were considering as separate park units—they visited Grand View Point, where the entire sweep of the Canyonlands basin was on display. Here Diederich, much as Roger Toll did on the Aquarius Plateau thirty years earlier, put the whole picture together. Gesturing to the vast stretch of dissected land reaching from the Orange Cliffs in the west to the Hatch Point cliffs in the east, he told his companions, "There's the park—the entire erosional basin, from the top of the Wingate cliffs to the level of the rivers."[13]

Back in Washington, Diederich drew a boundary around this million-acre expanse and sent it to Conrad Wirth. But regional director Thomas Allen was concerned about the reaction that such a park would receive in

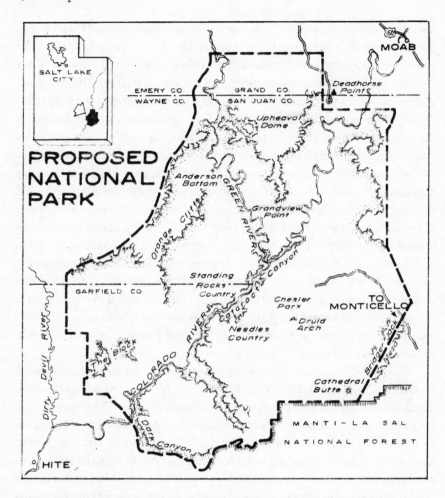

Map of Leo Diederich's proposal for a rim-to-rim park in Canyonlands, 1961.
National Park Service, Southeast Utah Group Archives.

Utah. He proposed a hybrid designation that would give national park status to the Needles, Standing Rocks, Grand View Point, and several other scenic areas, with the remainder of the basin held in "reserve" status until mineral claims and grazing rights could be retired. Less than fifty thousand acres would have been protected within the park units, but once oil drilling or mining had run its course, designation of the remainder of the area could follow.[14]

The concept of a two-tier park was unprecedented and perhaps unworkable, but Allen, who had served as superintendent of Zion National Park during the Escalante national monument fiasco, clearly wanted to avoid another overambitious proposal that would arouse opposition from Utah's miners and stockmen. Stewart Udall evidently toyed with the idea during the first part of 1961, but before firming up a proposal he wanted to see the area up close. Summer was coming on—hardly an ideal time to tramp around the Utah canyons—but he felt a sense of urgency to proceed with a park proposal. Oil exploration was encroaching on the backcountry and jeep parties were making increasing use of old uranium mining tracks. Stockmen had bulldozed a road over Elephant Hill into the Chesler Park area to build a series of stock reservoirs, and the increased accessibility placed its cultural resources at risk, according to Arches ranger Lloyd Pierson, who was trained as an archaeologist.[15] With the Bureau of Land Management exercising little oversight of these uses, Udall realized it was time to act.

It fell to Bates Wilson, master of backcountry outings, to organize Udall's July 1961 visit to the Utah canyon lands. The most complex field trip he had yet overseen, it brought together many well-connected individuals, including Agriculture Secretary Orville Freeman, assistant Park Service director George Hartzog, Senator Moss, Congressmen King and Peterson, and various state and local county officials. Thirteen journalists and writers were handpicked to cover the trip, representing *Life, American Heritage, National Geographic*, and other newspapers and periodicals.[16] Fifty participants in all were ferried around the area in air force helicopters, setting down at Grand View Point, Upheaval Dome, and Chesler Park, where members of the Moab Jeep Posse escorted them to nearby attractions.

The visit culminated in a long boat ride down the Colorado River to the Confluence and up the Green River to Anderson Bottom, where Udall held a press conference to announce his plans. Around an evening campfire beneath the darkening cliffs, with the softly flowing river to one side, Udall spoke of how Canyonlands National Park would anchor a "golden circle" of national parks and monuments in the Four Corners states. Connected by highway, these would take in major tourist attractions such as Bryce Canyon, Zion, Grand Canyon, Petrified Forest, and Mesa Verde as well as lesser-known sites such as Cedar Breaks, Natural Bridges, Hovenweep, and Colorado National Monument near Grand Junction. Udall called it "the greatest concentration of scenic wonders to be found in the country, if not in the world."[17] This was the latest formulation of the grand circle concept that had obsessed Utah tourism boosters since the 1920s. Canyonlands would be at the center of this wonderland, presumably to become as popular—and as easily accessible—as the others.

If a new park were to be created here, these were the men who could make it happen. Frank Masland, who participated in the trip as chair of the Park Service's Advisory Board on National Parks, wrote afterward that "all agreed that as a National Park it would rank second to none." Udall noted that "while no firm boundaries were established on the trip, the proposed national park would in all probability embrace more than 1,000 square miles." This was a nod to the rim-to-rim park conceived by Leo Diederich the previous fall.[18]

There were real obstacles to such a proposal, however. Utah governor George Clyde, who joined the party for a visit to the towering spires of the Needles, told a *Los Angeles Times* reporter that "Utah is a mining state, and we might need these as building stone." His statement, though probably facetious, was widely derided by park proponents. An engineer by profession, Clyde may simply have grown tired of hearing his companions wax eloquent about these sun-blasted pinnacles. He would go on to organize opposition to Udall's proposal among Utah's mining and petroleum industries. Equally significant was the opposition of Senator Wallace Bennett, who had declined to take part in Udall's trip, calling it a "publicity stunt." Bennett signaled from the outset of the Canyonlands issue that he would oppose any attempt to limit access to the region's natural resources. He termed Udall's proposal for an expansive park a "grandiose pie-in-the-sky scheme" and vowed to retain so-called multiple-use provisions in any new designation for the area.[19]

Udall and the Park Service knew that any new park in the Canyonlands region would have to deal with ongoing "hostile uses" such as livestock grazing and mining. The question was whether allowing for such uses was an acceptable price for obtaining a new park. Masland, who had come to appreciate this region on trips with Kent Frost and Norm Nevills, believed that when it came to a landscape such as Canyonlands, as much land as possible should be set aside in the hope that conflicting resource uses could eventually be dealt with. In a letter to the members of the National Parks Advisory Board, he noted that oil prospecting, livestock grazing, and hunting had left their marks throughout the Canyonlands area, "but against that we must balance what else we have—a land unique, a tremendous mass of land, an area so great, so difficult, so varied, so overwhelming in its geological treasures that it can absorb carefully regulated hostile uses to a degree less possible with land of lesser stature."

Masland appeared to favor the hybrid park advocated by certain Park Service planners as an expedient necessary to set aside a unique landscape in its entirety. Human imprints on the land were still scattered and insignificant in the Canyonlands basin, but Masland knew that could change if they did not act soon. In his letter to the National Parks Advisory Board, he stated the case for a large park in poetic terms:

> We must look ahead, not fifty years, not less than a hundred years. We must look at the needs of the future. I prefer to stand upon a mountain top and, slowly turning a full circle, behold nothing except the work of the Master Architect, but I know that those who come after me will be better men if by some act of mine I have helped to secure for them the opportunity to view but a quarter of the compass than if to protect a principle I have entirely lost a heritage.[20]

The "principle" Masland was referring to was the insistence on the highest standard of park quality, a concept that dated at least to Stephen Mather's time. National parks had long been held to represent only the most scenic and pristine landscapes, but Masland was arguing for a more pragmatic approach that recognized the many human uses that had altered the face of the Utah desert over the past century. Whether incompatible uses such as uranium mining and oil drilling, the scars of which were already so visible in this region, would be permitted to continue lay at the center of the debate in Congress over creating Canyonlands National Park. Three years of intense controversy would follow Udall's 1961 visit, pitting him, Frank Moss, and the Park Service against Governor Clyde, Senator Bennett, and business and ranching interests in San Juan County. Utah would get a magnificent new park—but as Frank Masland intuited, it would represent only a fraction of the strange and brilliant landscape between the Orange Cliffs.

²4

THE ROAD TO A NEW PARK

The first legislative proposals for Canyonlands National Park reflected widely divergent views of the meaning of "natural resources." The state's mining and petroleum industry looked underground to what they believed were potential oil and gas fields in the Canyonlands basin, while proponents of a large national park believed the land's truest values lay at the surface, in its amazingly sculpted erosional forms. With neither side willing to relinquish its vision of southeastern Utah's future, both Interior Secretary Stewart Udall and Utah senator Frank Moss would thread a difficult path down a legislative road as full of twists and turns as an incised canyon stream.

In March 1961, four months before Udall's headline-making field trip, Utah senator Wallace Bennett introduced a bill to create a seventy-five-thousand-acre national recreation area in the Needles, taking in Salt Creek Canyon, Horse Canyon, Chesler Park, and surrounding features. Bennett also introduced bills to give national park status to Arches, Capitol Reef, Cedar Breaks, and Rainbow Bridge National Monuments, as well as a third measure to authorize construction of a transcanyon parkway to link together most of these park units. Bennett presented his recreation area bill as a means of implementing the 1959 Park Service study of the Needles area, but to park proponents it looked like a way to preempt legislation that the rest of Utah's congressional delegation, all Democrats, were preparing. Had his measures passed, they would have frozen these small national monuments at their then-current size and sidetracked the entire Canyonlands proposal.[1]

On August 8, 1961, shortly after Udall's trip, Congressmen David King and Blaine Peterson each introduced bills to establish a Canyonlands National Park of no more than 300,000 acres, taking in the Needles and Island in the Sky areas as well as parts of the Maze, Doll House, and Land of Standing Rocks west of the Green River. Senator Frank Moss introduced a bill for a 330,000-acre park, largely along lines that the National Park Service was now favoring. It included provisions allowing mining, livestock grazing, and hunting—the so-called hostile uses—to continue. None of these bills contemplated a basin-wide park as Leo Diederich had suggested in 1960, nor did they contain the usual prohibitions against resource uses in national parks.[2] The three legislators emphasized that they were introducing their bills "to lay to rest the rumor that the park under discussion will encompass a million acres."[3]

Frank Moss was known for his advocacy of national parks, and it was primarily through his efforts that the ensuing legislative campaign would have a successful outcome. A conservationist of the old school, he understood the concerns of Utahns who did not want to "lock up" minerals and other resources for the sake of preserving landscapes, and he also favored making many of southern Utah's scenic wonders accessible by automobile. His Canyonlands bill, the first of several he would introduce, attempted to assuage Governor Clyde's concerns over resource uses by permitting continued mineral development in the new park, with the proviso that this would occur only under Park Service supervision to protect scenic and other values. It also allowed livestock grazing to continue within the new park for a twenty-five-year period, or for the lives of the existing permit holders. The Park Service strongly objected to this provision, but it would prove difficult to dislodge from the pending legislation. Livestock grazing was a long-established use of desert lands in the West, despite its slim returns. Only some 680 cattle grazed within the proposed park, chiefly on lands east of the Needles where the historic Dugout Ranch had operated since 1917.[4]

On August 30, Senator Bennett returned fire with a much more limited park bill, based on discussions he was having with Governor Clyde. It consisted of three small parcels around Grand View Point, Upheaval Dome, and the Needles and covered about eleven thousand acres in all.[5] Bennett's bill, like Moss's, contained provisions to allow grazing, mining, and hunting within the new park units, as well hydropower development on the Green and Colorado Rivers. These tiny park enclaves would form a "string of pearls" across the landscape, Bennett said, but Lloyd Pierson, Bates Wilson's chief ranger at Arches, dismissed them as "little cow pies stuck out there."[6]

In September 1962 Bennett expanded his proposal to include a national park of up to 102,000 acres centering on the Needles and Confluence areas, with an adjoining 208,000-acre recreation area in which hunting and limited resource extraction would be allowed. Based on the recommendations of a state committee appointed by Governor Clyde, the bill reflected the growing public demand for a significant park in the Canyonlands region. Frank Moss, however, dismissed the measure as "meaningless," since the Senate Interior Committee had already reported favorably on his own park bill. Bennett clearly wished to be a player as Canyonlands legislation took shape, but with Congress in Democratic hands, his role was limited.

Each of these legislative proposals met with a guarded reaction among editorial page writers in Utah, with most favoring some compromise between Bennett's and the Democrats' bills. Sam Taylor's *Moab Times-Independent* reminded readers in Grand County that "Utahns cannot allow vast, potentially-rich tracts of land to be 'locked' into reserves that would prohibit any future use," although he believed that the "10-12 thousand acre park advocated by Utah Republicans is not anywhere near adequate."[7] As editor of Grand County's only newspaper, Taylor steered a course between the pro-park factions and representatives of resource interests. He ran numerous articles extolling the scenic values of Canyonlands and its many recreational possibilities, from jeeping to river running, yet he was reluctant to bid goodbye to the area's potential mineral wealth.

Moab's days as the nation's uranium capital were waning, and while the presence of numerous seismic exploration crews in town raised hopes for oil development, significant amounts had yet to be produced. The greatest hope lay in developing the large deposits of potash that lay deep underground in the Paradox Formation. In 1960 Texas Gulf Sulphur sank a test well at Cane Creek near the Colorado River downstream from Moab and began clearing land the following year for a potash processing mill. By mid-1962 a thousand construction workers were being housed in town and their children were crowding the elementary school.[8] By the end of the year, however, work on the potash mill was winding down and the town's population declined again, with unemployment claims on the increase.[9]

Taylor and his friends in Moab's business community hoped that designating a new park in the vast red-rock basin southwest of town could substantially increase tourism revenues, which (as he wrote in an editorial in March 1962) were already contributing an estimated half million dollars annually to the local economy.[10] This would diversify the economy and partially make up for the lost revenues from mineral activity. Yet Moab's business community remained hopeful for a renewed mining boom and was reluctant to see any constraints placed on resource development in the area. Wanting to have it both ways—more tourism along with continued min-ing and grazing—led Grand County officials to favor Senator Bennett's and Governor Clyde's approach of designating a small park or cluster of park units, taking in only the area's most scenic features. The Needles, Grand View Point, the Doll House, and their environs fit the conventional notion of what a national park should be, but by limiting a park to these places, county officials turned their backs on the concept of an expansive, rim-to-rim park that excited certain Park Service personnel—and for a short time had caught the eye of Interior Secretary Stewart Udall.

Udall briefly considered asking President Kennedy to declare a substantial national monument in the Canyonlands area as a holding action until Con-gress could act, as had been done numerous times in the past, including at Zion and Bryce Canyon. Udall rejected this option as too controversial; as a former congressman, he understood the political headwinds such a move would generate for his ambitious parks agenda.[11] Yet he was also getting pressure from conservation organizations, which believed that the loop-holes in Moss's and Bennett's bills would set a bad precedent for other new parks. The National Audubon Society called the Moss proposal "a national park in name only . . . little different from a national forest or from the pres-ent public-domain status of the lands involved."[12] But Moss's support was essential if a Canyonlands bill was to advance in Congress—and for this the conservationists needed support from within Utah, where they had his-torically been a minor presence.

To make the Canyonlands proposal more palatable to county and state officials, the Park Service promised to build a network of roads in the new park, reaching such destinations as Grand View Point, Chesler Park, and the Confluence. Visitor centers and one-hundred-unit campgrounds would be located in both the Needles and Island in the Sky districts.[13] This proposal sowed the seeds for ongoing controversy once the park was established, after the Park Service, under pressure from conservationists, backed away from its Mission 66–style development program for Canyonlands.

It was in this conflicted arena that Stewart Udall exerted strong influence. Knowing that the best way to sell a new park was to show off its stunning scenery, he commissioned New York filmmaker Charles Eggert to make a 16-millimeter motion picture of the proposed park lands. Produced with considerable help from Bates Wilson, Eggert's *The Sculptured Earth* drew a large audience at its October 16, 1962, premiere in Salt Lake City. Both Udall and Wilson attended the showing, which was originally to be held at Kingsbury Hall on the University of Utah campus but had to be moved after university president Ray Olpin objected to its "political" nature. The controversy over the film helped to crystallize support for the new park in Utah's largest urban center.[14]

Another of Udall's initiatives was a study of the park's economic impact conducted by the University of Utah's School of Business. Its authors projected that visitation to the park would reach half a million in ten years and surpass one million in twenty-five years. Tourist expenditures and monies spent by the Park Service in developing the park would bring $3.2 million in personal income to Grand and San Juan Counties during the first five years of the park's existence, according to the study.[15] These projections were based on the assumption that the Park Service would extensively develop Canyonlands with roads and visitor facilities; in the absence of such development, visitation never met these optimistic projections. As a result, county and state leaders blamed the Park Service for failing to deliver on its promises.[16]

The competing Moss and Bennett bills were heard before the Senate Interior Committee in March 1962, just as controversy over the Canyonlands proposals was reaching a peak. Stewart Udall recommended a substitute measure covering 332,292 acres, with boundaries drawn in part by Bates Wilson and Frank Masland. It allowed existing livestock use to continue but closed off new mineral claims and disallowed hunting. He also promised that the park would come with a $17 million development program, to be carried out over a period of years.[17]

Bennett called the Udall proposal "an unqualified disaster to the state of Utah, to our school children, and indeed to our entire economy." He continued to favor limiting the park to the most scenic areas, with most of the canyon lands landscape devoted to resource extraction. Udall's frustration with this approach came out in his testimony before the Senate Interior Committee. "I have taken seven steps in the direction of compromise, and I asked the people on the other side to take three," he stated. The Park Service would spend "millions of dollars" to develop Canyonlands, just as it had in Grand Canyon and other national parks. Udall contrasted the prospect of a tourism boom with the paltry grazing fees that the federal government realized from the area, which amounted to "the magnificent sum of $2,700."[18] Livestock users, however, were not the main obstacle to the park—in fact, some cattlemen such as Art Ekker of Hanksville, who ran cows in the remote "Under the Cliffs" area west of the Green River, felt they had little to lose by relinquishing this poor range.[19]

The restrictions on resource development that came with national park designation stood in the way of something many Americans, including the Mormons of Utah, had long believed in: that the West could be made into a land of plenty. To forgo the opportunity for another mineral boom such as had vaulted the Colorado Plateau into national prominence in the 1950s seemed almost sacrilegious. It would deny what writer and historian Bernard DeVoto called "the West's great dream, the dream of economic liberation, of local ownership and control." This was the sentiment expressed by Blanding resident Robert S. Shriver, an independent miner, who spoke at a congressional hearing held on the proposed Canyonlands legislation in Monticello in 1962. Speaking of the park's "tremendous value as a potential producer of minerals, especially oil, gas, and potash," he went on to state that "we as a country or a nation must not stifle the incentive of those who would be productive; we must encourage those who would risk a loss in hope of attaining a gain."[20] To many Utahns, the land that had thus far yielded mostly hardship and disappointment still held great potential to produce wealth.

Yet there were those in southeastern Utah who kept an open mind about Senator Moss's proposal, hoping that a national park could generate a new kind of wealth through tourism. Some of these individuals stressed that they appreciated the magnificent Canyonlands landscape. For Moab mayor Norman G. Boyd, this was "a place of mystery and intrigue," a "sandstone kingdom" that was "the symbolic heritage of the American public. . . . If the people of southeastern Utah are willing to fulfill this one obligation to the people of America, then we cannot keep our land locked apart and in a state of detachment."[21] His hope, and that of a significant number of other local residents, was that mineral development and livestock grazing would be allowed to continue within the park under controlled conditions. But the issue of allowing hostile uses within a national park would remain a conundrum as Senator Moss's legislation moved forward.

The 1962 congressional midterm elections did not bode well for Moss's Canyonlands bill, with Representative David King losing his effort to unseat Wallace Bennett and Republican Lawrence Burton replacing Blaine Peterson. Sherman Lloyd, also a Republican, took King's House seat. Moss, now the only Democrat in the Utah delegation, was forced to compromise on his park legislation. In January 1963 he introduced a new bill for a 258,000-acre park, omitting the Maze area as well as BLM lands south of the Needles in Beef Basin, which was heavily used for livestock grazing. His measure no longer permitted hunting, and prospecting for new minerals would be limited to a twenty-five-year period. Development of existing mining claims and leases, however, would be permitted indefinitely—a provision that continued to draw opposition from conservationists.[22]

Even this greatly diminished bill faced opposition in Utah, so in April Moss sat down with Governor Clyde, Senator Bennett, and Representative Burton at a breakfast meeting in the governor's mansion in Salt Lake City to work out an agreement. He omitted an 18,000-acre parcel in the northeastern corner of the proposed park that contained potash deposits, adding in exchange 19,500 acres along the southern boundary. The grazing and mineral provisions were retained, and in a statement before the Senate Public Lands Subcommittee that April, Moss acknowledged that "we must hold in multiple use readiness the veritable storehouse of industrial raw materials" believed to exist on Utah's public lands. Yet he continued to insist that national park status was the best use for these canyon lands.[23]

Moss's compromise drew the expected criticism from those who wanted a larger park that was free from hostile uses. At congressional field hearings held in Utah that same month, Charles Eggert expressed dismay that places such as the Maze had been left out of the legislation. "To cut out the area west of the Green River to satisfy a requirement of size would be like tearing down a section of the Smithsonian and exposing everything in it for the scavengers to carry away." Instead, he asked that those responsible for its future "go into the land itself and let it speak its boundary lines."[24]

Despite having reached an agreement in principle with his colleagues for a park open to limited resource uses, Moss still was not able to obtain Bennett's support when he brought his bill before the Senate Subcommittee on Public Lands in April 1963. Dissatisfied that Moss had not omitted more

Druid Arch in upper Elephant Canyon, taken during a National Park Service reconnaissance of the Needles area in 1959. *National Park Service/Frank Moss Photograph
Collection, Special Collections, J. Willard Marriott Library, University of Utah.*

mineral lands from his bill, Bennett continued to offer weakening amendments. When it became clear that the Senate was going to pass the measure
anyway, he finally relented and gave it his reluctant support.[25]

Moss's Canyonlands park legislation then went to the House of Representatives, where its mining and grazing concessions came under fire from
an unlikely source: Wayne Aspinall, chair of the House Interior Committee
from neighboring western Colorado. Aspinall, who normally sided with the
mining industry, insisted that the multiple-use provisions be struck, calling
them "incompatible with national park status." Livestock grazing permits
would be renewed for one term and would then expire, mining would be
allowed only on valid existing claims, and the hydropower withdrawal for
the Green and Colorado Rivers would be rescinded, eliminating the possibility of a dam near the Confluence.[26] Once a House-Senate conference

committee reconciled differences between the two versions, the way was clear for passage. President Johnson signed the measure into law on September 12, 1964.

The new Canyonlands National Park, Utah's largest at 257,640 acres, did not include many areas that Bates Wilson and other Park Service officials believed worthy of inclusion. As historian Samuel Schmieding pointed out, "the Maze, Fins, Buttes of the Cross, Millard Canyon, Panorama Point, Lavender Canyon, Upper Salt Creek, Beef Basin, Ruin Park, and Lockhart Basin all were deleted because of partisanship and economic fears." The park's jagged borders, set along township and section lines, were "an injustice to the geographic basin framed by the Wingate Sandstone cliffs and everything in between."[27]

The new park amounted to one-fourth of the million-acre erosional basin that Leo Diederich had identified in 1959—almost exactly the "quarter of the compass" that Frank Masland had anticipated in 1961. Back then, park proponents appeared willing to accept mines and oil rigs in Canyonlands; fortunately, the new park would remain free from such uses. It would instead feature expansive mesas, two great rivers, intricate winding canyons, an infinity of pinnacles, fins, and hoodoos, and perhaps most important, the abiding quiet of what was still a little-known and lightly used region.

All this was likely to change, however, once a full slate of roads, visitor centers, and other tourist facilities were built. As initially envisioned, Canyonlands was to be developed like other national parks in the Southwest, taking full advantage of the economic opportunities apparent in its magnificent scenery. Bates Wilson and Stewart Udall had obtained the support of many residents in Grand and San Juan Counties with the promise of tourism development, and these people awaited the federal dollars that would make the new park accessible to the millions who were sure to come.

MASTER PLAN

Canyonlands National Park opened for visitors in the spring of 1965, with its headquarters in the modern Uranium Building in downtown Moab. Bates Wilson, who had done so much to make the park a reality, was the obvious choice for the job of superintendent. Fittingly, he learned of his new assignment over a field radio while in the park's backcountry. He began work with a small staff and essentially no facilities; out in the park's Needles district, rangers initially worked out of a field camp at Cave Spring.[1] The soot-stained ceiling of this historic cowboy line camp would have reminded them of the transition from the cattle frontier to the modern tourist age.

Much of the park's initial $2 million budget was allocated to basic infrastructure, including road construction, water wells, and temporary trailer housing for field employees. Primitive campgrounds and visitor contact stations were hastily built at Squaw Flat in the Needles district and in what was being called Island in the Sky in the northernmost part of the park. Five hundred people arrived at Squaw Flat on Memorial Day weekend in 1965, overwhelming the small campground. Despite these limitations, the park drew more than seventeen thousand visitors during its first year of operation.[2]

Wilson's new territory demanded much of his attention. Mining claims were said to be stacked three deep throughout the park, and oil and gas leases and grazing allotments needed to be examined and either retired or allowed to expire. With the uranium market at a standstill and no producing oil wells within the park's boundaries, Wilson did not face serious mineral development issues. Previous land claimants had to be dealt with, though, including Karl Tangren, who occupied a ramshackle homestead on leased state land at Anderson Bottom on the Green River.[3] Tangren operated a boat dock and supplied boaters with the only fresh water on that stretch of river, but the

Chesler Park in the Needles, 1959. *National Park Service/Frank Moss Photograph Collection, Special Collections, J. Willard Marriott Library, University of Utah.*

Park Service felt it needed to evict him in order to restore the bottom to a semblance of naturalness. Fortunately, such cases were few.

Bates Wilson loved being in the field and sometimes pitched in to help his scattered staff and construction crews. Throughout 1965, though, he would spend considerable time in agency offices in Washington and Denver, helping to devise a master plan that would guide development throughout the park. Adopted in 1966, the plan advanced a program of road and infrastructure development that had more in common with Yellowstone and Yosemite than with the conditions found in this arid, rugged landscape. Canyonlands would become a drive-through park, its scenery made accessible to a million or more visitors arriving each year in their automobiles.

Up to this point, anyone who wanted to view the pinnacles of Chesler Park, travel through the Grabens, or take in the scene from Grand View Point needed a horse, a jeep, or a tough pair of legs. The new master plan would change that by developing an extensive system of paved roads throughout the park. Island in the Sky would be served by a road branching off the existing road to Dead Horse Point, continuing over the narrow passage called The Neck to reach Grand View Point. At this stunning overlook, visitors would find an observation deck and amphitheater, while a campground, store, and lodging would be located farther back at Willow Flat. Another paved road would extend westward from Grays Pasture to Mineral Bottom on the Green River and then head downstream to service a new marina and lodge at Upheaval Bottom. Visitors could then drive east up scenic Taylor Canyon, past Upheaval Dome, and rejoin the Grand View Point road at Willow Flat, creating an eighty-mile loop drive suitable for the family sedan. The jeep trail that meandered along the plateau below Island in the Sky, known as the White Rim, was also scheduled to be paved.[4]

The Needles area would be rendered accessible by paving the road that led down Indian Creek past Dugout Ranch, ending—for the time being—at Squaw Flat at the edge of the Needles. A visitor center would be built here, along with a campground, store, and possibly a lodge for overnight stays.[5] But the master plan envisioned extending this road clear around the Needles and south to Beef Basin, with spur roads leading to Chesler Park, a scenic opening ringed by colorful sandstone pinnacles, as well as to a spectacular overlook of the confluence of the Green and Colorado Rivers. South of Beef Basin, this "Needles parkway" would tie in with a projected road connecting Monticello to Natural Bridges National Monument, known as the Kigalia highway.[6]

The Park Service's planning team believed that the vast majority of visitors to Canyonlands would be "city folk" who would need easy vehicle access to the new park, since much of the backcountry was too difficult to traverse on foot. Loop roads, in particular, were "vital to the visitors' enjoyment," the master plan stated—a distant echo of principles elucidated by Good Roads advocates half a century ago. For those seeking greater adventure, jeep roads would be available west of the Green and Colorado Rivers, and there would be trails for hikers and horse users as well. The 1966 master plan, however, discouraged "indiscriminate exploring by visitors," since cross-country travel would often necessitate search and rescue operations.[7]

Initial development costs under the master plan would run to nearly $6 million over its first five years.[8] Work on improving the road to Squaw Flat in the Needles district began in the fall of 1966. Meanwhile, a crew from the Bureau of Public Roads flagged road locations for the Needles parkway, following an old cattle trail that led over the rugged sandstone formation known as Elephant Hill. Two decades earlier, a bulldozer operator working for cattleman Al Scorup had bladed this route to permit construction of stock reservoirs and to maintain watering tanks. By the 1960s it was growing in popularity as a recreational jeep route.[9]

Work on the Island in the Sky road was to begin in 1972, with pavement reaching Grand View Point by 1975.[10] The intent was to use the nearly blank slate represented by Canyonlands for major tourist development. Bates Wilson loved jeep roads, but his agency had promised local boosters that it would develop the park with paved scenic drives and in-park accommodations. Whatever his reservations, he went along with the program for now.

Many residents of Moab, Monticello, and Blanding eagerly awaited the promised development of Canyonlands. Funds were limited, however, and Wilson had his hands full providing basic needs such as housing for park rangers and a reliable water supply. The delays did not sit well with local tourism boosters, as Moab writer (and Park Service employee) Maxine Newell noted in a 1966 article in the *Moab Times-Independent*. "Where are the roads, the museums, and the camping facilities which traditionally go with the national parks?" she asked rhetorically, referring to the many queries she and other park employees were fielding. The Park Service was approaching development carefully, she answered, with an eye to making new roads and facilities blend with the landscape. Landscape architect Paul Fritz had been brought in to help design paved roads to "tempting overlooks" where visitors could explore further on foot, horseback, or by jeep. The roads would be "teasers" leading visitors farther into the landscape, Fritz said.[11]

Newell's article hinted that the ultimate development of Canyonlands might fall short of the 1966 master plan. Paul Fritz brought strong conservationist leanings to his work, and his comment suggested that not every scenic attraction in the park would have pavement leading to it. Bates Wilson admitted privately that he had concerns about paving and extending the Needles access road, since this would bring an influx of visitors he did not feel prepared to handle.[12] Yet he was under considerable pressure to do so from Senators Frank Moss and Wallace Bennett, as well as from his superiors in the Park Service, who were acutely aware of where their funding came

from. Moss, having sponsored the original Canyonlands legislation, particularly wanted to see a paved road built to the Confluence.

Although Moss was the most conservation-minded member of Utah's
congressional delegation and was known as "Mr. National Parks" for his
support of expanding the National Park System,[13] he took pains to distance
himself from preservationism. In a widely publicized speech he gave on the
floor of the Senate in 1968, titled "Parks Are for People," he emphasized that
automobile-based tourism should be given priority over wilderness within
the National Park System. The nation's flagship parks were overcrowded,
he said, with traffic jamming their roads and campers "crowded together
almost tent peg to tent peg." Road construction had not kept pace with the
postwar increase in use, which meant that nearly all visitors were wedged
into a small fraction of the parks' land area. The answer, he insisted, was
more roads—enough to open up one-fourth to one-third of the parks to
those who want to see "our magnificent scenery from the window seats of
their automobiles."[14]

The Confluence road was one project Moss thought the Park Service
ought to begin at once. The agency's environmental analysis for the road
claimed it would have limited impact on local flora and fauna,[15] but there
was no getting around the fact that it would open up one of the least developed sections of the park to what Bates Wilson termed "Sunday drivers."
Once it was built, moreover, the call was certain to go out for extending it
southward past the Needles and Beef Basin toward Natural Bridges, as San
Juan County officials hoped. All of these projected roads drew opposition
from conservationists who were concerned about retaining the park's wild
character. Jeffrey Ingram, the Sierra Club's southwestern staff representative, told Wilson that there was no need for further road development in
Arches, Natural Bridges, or Canyonlands. "One of the saddest things I have
seen in the Southwest is the loop road in Natural Bridges . . . the whole loop
is dominated by asphalt & posts & concrete walks. . . . Somehow I feel that
not only are the Bridges diminished by such an approach, but so are we."[16]

Wilson, too, was rethinking plans for extensive parkway development
in the Canyonlands region. Not only would paved roads open up backcountry areas he preferred to see by jeep, but they were fiscally unrealistic
in a time of tightening Park Service budgets. In the spring of 1968 he circulated several memos to his staff proposing revisions to the existing master
plan, which was only two years old but reflected ideas of park development

that belonged to the 1950s. Canyonlands, Wilson believed, should be set apart from other national parks to promote "close contact between man and nature, undistracted by crowds, traffic, alteration of landscape, or provision of facilities and services. The visitor should be aware of nature, not of works or numbers of his fellow men." In general, visitor services, including lodging, should be located outside the park, as should through roads or parkways. Canyonlands' major scenic features should be accessible only by foot, jeep, or horseback.[17]

Wilson believed that only the main access roads to Island in the Sky and the Needles should be paved. Beyond these roads, visitors could enjoy the park by jeep or on foot, while some sensitive locales should not even have trails to them. Most of Canyonlands would qualify for wilderness designation, he noted, and those areas should be delineated before further improvements were made. Wilson specifically recommended scrapping the loop road to Upheaval Bottom and up Taylor Canyon, along with the planned marina on the Green River. The White Rim jeep road would be left unpaved, with most of the park's backcountry remaining essentially wild.

In the Needles district, Wilson opposed extending the Squaw Flat road past Elephant Hill, which would require extensive blasting through sandstone fins and possibly several tunnels.[18] Instead he wanted the road to end a short distance east of Big Spring Canyon, at the edge of Squaw Flat, where a campground and picnic area would be located. Wilson likewise objected to a road entering Chesler Park, which was already showing signs of damage from excessive jeep use. He assented, however, to a road from Squaw Flat to the Confluence, as well as a revised Needles parkway leading from the Confluence to Beef Basin, forming a new southern entrance to the park and connecting to the proposed Kigalia highway.[19]

Wilson underscored that Canyonlands was a special place that called for a different approach than in other national parks. Emphasizing a more primitive backcountry experience would be an asset, not a liability, he believed, and he advised park personnel that "no apologies should or need be made for lack of development." Sufficient tourist facilities existed outside the park, including scenic overlooks such as Dead Horse Point. Canyonlands, he maintained, "should be retained as the natural, undeveloped core" of this magnificent region.

The Confluence overlook road would prove to be the issue that swung Canyonlands National Park toward preservation. Although Wilson and his superiors wanted to see it built, the cost was prohibitive. Federal expenditures for the war in Vietnam had drastically shrunk the Park Service's budget for capital improvements, leaving little for new roads. By 1975 the Park Service had completed only the road's first segment from Squaw Flat campground to Big Spring Canyon. Bridging the canyon would require a seven-hundred-foot span costing $5.3 million, with the total cost of completing the road approaching $9 million.[20] In June 1977, citing environmental as well as fiscal concerns, Park Service director Gary Everhart put a hold on the project. By then superintendents Robert Kerr and Pete Parry, who had succeeded Bates Wilson, had little interest in completing the road. As a result, the road still ends abruptly at Big Spring Canyon, where in place of a massive bridge, a narrow, rocky hiking trail threads across the canyon and leads west to the Confluence overlook.

For most of its half century of existence, the National Park Service had been in the business of developing roads and tourist facilities within the parks. Its leadership culture, according to former Park Service historian Richard Sellars, was "defined largely by the demands of recreational tourism management and the desire for the public to enjoy the scenic parks." State politicians and local business interests wanted national parks to be tourist magnets, and the agency was generally happy to comply. By the late 1960s, however, some Park Service staff were arguing that development under Mission 66 had amply provided for such uses, and the wilder portions of the western parks ought to remain that way. In May 1968 Park Service director George Hartzog Jr. approved Bates Wilson's recommendations for a less-developed Canyonlands National Park. A paved road to Chesler Park—an offshoot of the planned Needles parkway—"would violate the beauty and serenity of the Canyonlands country and would be a contradiction of national park purposes," he stated in a press release.[21]

This sudden about-face angered Grand and San Juan County officials as well as the prodevelopment *Moab Times-Independent*. Defending his new plan before a meeting of the Moab Chamber of Commerce, Wilson observed that the trend in the Park Service was to encourage visitors to engage with the landscape, not merely drive through it. Dirt roads and trails amounted to "physical and psychological filters" that would screen out those who did not have a genuine interest in seeing the land. "Do we have to get everyone into every nook and cranny of the park?" Wilson asked. "We need to give people a chance to get away from the mobs."[22]

Wilson's retreat from his earlier prodevelopment stance arose out of the same concerns that had animated Edward Abbey a decade earlier. But the projected roads in Canyonlands, and especially the Confluence over- look segment, still appealed to Chamber members and to *Times-Indepen- dent* publisher Sam Taylor, who said that if the Park Service could engineer a new access road up the cliff behind the Arches visitor center, it could eas- ily build a parkway through a little-used section of Canyonlands.[23]

The Confluence road issue, like the struggle over the Mineral King resort in Kings Canyon National Park and the paving of the Wonder Lake road in Mount McKinley National Park, symbolized the gulf between tourism backers and preservation advocates. Calvin Black, the outspoken chair of the San Juan County Commission, led the chorus of "betrayal" that greeted Wilson's revised master plan. "We all remember the promises of develop- ment at Canyonlands during the debate on its creation," he wrote to Sam Taylor in 1971. Projections made at the time envisioned millions of tourists flocking to the area, but with further road construction delayed or shelved, "it becomes apparent that these areas will be 'preserved' for only those who have the time, money, and physical stamina to charter airplanes, jeeps, and horses, or to do extensive hiking."[24]

Black was one of southeastern Utah's most active businessmen and entre- preneurs, and a leading force in developing roads and highways through- out San Juan County. An unapologetic proponent of all forms of economic development, Black had staked numerous uranium claims throughout the county and often bulldozed roads to them himself. His vision of parks as economic drivers was an old one, and he had at least a nominal ally in Frank Moss, although Black distrusted the senator's park initiatives. But the notion that the national parks were designed principally for automobile tourism conflicted with the newer vision advanced by environmentalists such as Edward Abbey, which held that the remoteness of these unpopulated des- ert places was one of their most significant values.

Black and Abbey clashed repeatedly over this question, especially regard- ing the paving of Utah Highway 95 from Hanksville to Blanding (a sub- ject of Abbey's ire in his 1975 comic novel *The Monkey Wrench Gang*). Black also promoted the construction of Utah Highway 276, which led to Halls

Crossing on Lake Powell.[25] What Black viewed as the bare minimum of highway infrastructure struck Abbey and his allies as a desecration of an unpeopled landscape—perhaps the last real wilderness left in the Lower 48 states.

Although by 1968 Bates Wilson had disavowed the grandiose development plans envisioned in the 1966 Canyonlands master plan, he was willing to see limited road development in the Needles region and a paved parkway coursing along Canyonlands' western edge. Pressed hard by both the development and preservation factions, he would waver between keeping his park as a kind of frontier museum piece and turning it into a top-drawer tourist attraction. Even Wilson's winning personality could not smooth over the underlying tensions that resulted from these differing conceptions of what a national park should be.

26

JEWEL OF THE COLORADO

While Bates Wilson was pondering how best to develop Canyonlands National Park, an even greater change was taking place miles downstream on the Colorado River, where the waters of Lake Powell were backing up behind Glen Canyon Dam. The National Park Service, which managed recreation at Glen Canyon under an agreement with the Bureau of Reclamation, was laying a concrete boat ramp at Wahweap Creek, hundreds of feet above the filling reservoir, with others planned at Hite and Bullfrog Basin. The latter would be accessed by paved roads branching off Utah Highway 95, which was still under construction. Completing the development of the upper reservoir area were three shiny new bridges where U-95 crossed White Canyon and the canyons of the Dirty Devil and Colorado Rivers.

All this work was part of a master plan for the Glen Canyon National Recreation Area that would guide development along the reservoir. Heavily oriented toward mass recreation, it called for another marina to be built near Hole-in-the-Rock, which would be served by a paved road leading south from the town of Escalante. Additional marinas or smaller docks and facilities would be built at Warm Springs Basin, Gunsight Bench, Oil Seep Bar, Halls Crossing, and Castle Butte. Roads would connect to scenic overlooks over the San Juan and Colorado Rivers at Nokai Dome, Ocean Point, Navajo Point, the Rincon, and Dark Canyon.[1] It was a blueprint for the full development of the reservoir's recreational potential, with little thought given to the nature of the surrounding wild landscape.

Lake Powell was geoengineering on a huge scale, creating a new surface for recreation that was not limited by Earth's usual irregularities. As water skiers and houseboaters fanned out onto the new reservoir, they discovered a world of red rock and blue water stretching to the horizon. Flat water opened side canyons to easy access, bypassing the quicksand and pouroffs

Aerial view of Lake Powell. *Carol M. Highsmith/Library of Congress Prints and Photographs Division, Washington, D.C.*

that had turned back earlier parties. The reservoir quickly grew in popularity, attracting adventurous boaters who wanted to explore what appeared to be a pristine landscape.

To the Bureau of Reclamation, Lake Powell was the "Jewel of the Colorado." In a color brochure of that title, published in 1965, the bureau announced that "the wild red outlaw river" had been tamed and was now "flowing clean and blue, unmaimed." A poetic epigraph assured readers that "multitudes hunger for a lake in the sun."[2]

Multitudes did come to Lake Powell's shores—nearly two hundred thousand visitors in 1964, with half again as many arriving the following year. At last Utah had a scenic attraction to compete with the Grand Canyon—even, eventually, with Yellowstone and Yosemite—if enough new roads could be brought to its shores.

Yet there were those who held on to memories of the former canyon. One who felt the loss acutely was Ken Sleight, who took hundreds of guests down Glen in the years before the dam. In 1964, no longer able to float the canyon, he moved to the town of Escalante, where he outfitted horse packing trips in the Escalante River canyons. He began taking guests down

Cataract Canyon and the Grand Canyon and ventured out on the reservoir a few times to access side canyons, but he found it too painful to watch his old haunts disappear. He recalled in 1999 how the reservoir "would rise a foot overnight, and you saw things you loved go under. First it was Music Temple. Then it was Gregory Natural Bridge. Then Cathedral in the Desert. I'd think of those fools that said this was a good thing, that we needed this dam. Then I'd see Hidden Passage or some other lovely spot with no name go under . . . it was unbearable."[3]

Katie Lee, who discovered the canyon in the 1950s and revisited it many times with her friends Tad Nichols and Frank Wright, expressed outrage at its transformation into a huge storage vessel. Viewing the rising waters of Lake Powell for the first time at Halls Crossing in November 1963, she recalled falling to her knees in anger and astonishment. "Spinach water lay in a silent trench between amputated cliffs. . . . A white drawdown scar rose thirty feet above the waterline, as if someone had pulled the plug in a dirty bathtub, then stuck it in again. Without their talus buttresses, the great walls leaned in, unsupported and menacing. . . . No more borders of lush green that had danced on the tawny river—everything out of balance, the harmony gone."[4]

To Lee, the reservoir without its side canyons—"those silent, sequestered, perfect places"—was no longer Glen Canyon. She returned several times to witness her favorite places going under but found it increasingly hard to watch. In 1967, while stopping at what remained of Music Temple, she listened to the ricochet of gunshots hitting the walls above her as several men sped by in a motorboat.[5] The canyon remained only as a burning memory for her.

The reservoir was also drawing nearer to Rainbow Bridge National Monument. Charles "Butch" Farabee, one of the early Park Service rangers to serve at Glen Canyon, patrolled this section of the reservoir from a small houseboat anchored in Forbidding Canyon. He recalled hiking the mile and a half up to the famous bridge, seeing beavers at work in the streambed but no human visitors.[6] A Park Service sign at the bridge asked visitors to respect this sacred Navajo site. "The next week," he said, "the lake came up and buried the sign and the trail."[7]

As the reservoir rose, conservation groups once again brought up the stipulations in the Colorado River Storage Act that forbade inundation of any unit of the National Park System, including Rainbow Bridge. In 1970, with the reservoir nearing the monument boundary, David Brower brought suit against the Interior Department to prevent it from flooding Rainbow Bridge. He did so in his new capacity as director of Friends of the Earth, having been fired the previous year as head of the Sierra Club. Ken Sleight and the Wasatch Mountain Club joined the case, which was heard before Judge Willis Ritter in Salt Lake City. To the surprise of many, Ritter found in their favor, and for several months in the spring of 1973 BuRec was forced to draw down the reservoir. Interior won its appeal of the case, however, based on the contention that Congress's overall goals in passing the CRSP effectively invalidated the requirement to protect the monument.[8]

Conservationists had thrown everything they had against the Bureau of Reclamation, but unlike in the Dinosaur battle two decades earlier, it was to no avail. Did slipping water within sight of Rainbow Bridge constitute "significant impairment?" It depended. For those who boated up the reservoir to the Park Service dock just below the bridge, ease of access trumped all consideration of remoteness, mystery, or the living biota of a river. But for Ken Sleight, who watched the still water cover landmarks he had known for a decade, it was a time of painful mourning. "Motoring up the reservoir to the Cathedral in the Desert, I found the sacred amphitheater drowned out, and I had to weep," he recalled. "At the end of the canyons, lizards clung to sticks or branches, waiting to die. At the end of other canyons, I found dead carcasses of beaver, no longer able to harvest their cottonwood supply. . . . The massive Gregory Natural Bridge was devastated and covered over."[9] This along with the loss of countless prehistoric sites, including major ruins and rock art panels, makes his desire to somehow thwart BuRec from rendering Rainbow Bridge accessible to the masses seem more understandable.

The inundation of Glen Canyon also meant the displacement of members of the Southern Paiute Tribe from lands they farmed along the lower San Juan River.[10] The new visitation at Rainbow Bridge was also of concern to members of the Navajo Nation, who regarded the bridge and the land around it as sacred. In their eyes, the commotion and trash that tourism brought to the bridge desecrated the site, interfering with ceremonies they wished to perform and lessening its rain-bringing and healing powers. Attempts by the Park Service to encourage more respectful behavior by visitors, including not climbing or standing under the bridge, had limited success.[11] The bridge, it turned out, had been protected more by its isolation than by its status as a national monument. That story would be played out in a hundred other locales in southern Utah as the modern age of motor-propelled tourism clashed with older ways of experiencing the red-rock landscape.

Lake Powell was a godsend for Utah tourism boosters, accomplishing what Canyonlands National Park had thus far failed to do: draw large numbers of vacationers to what had been a blank place on the map. The problem was that the reservoir was separated from Utah's flagship parks by miles of empty desert. The solution was simple: connect Arches and Canyonlands to Lake Powell via a parkway that would extend from Highway 160 near Moab to the new Wahweap Marina on Lake Powell. Known variously as the golden circle highway or canyon country parkway, the route would be a desert version of the Blue Ridge Parkway in Virginia's Shenandoah Mountains. Once it was in place, tourists could drive from Moab to Kanab on one direct route, putting Zion and Bryce Canyon within easy reach.

Much of the impetus for the canyon country parkway came from county commissions and chambers of commerce in Grand, San Juan, and Garfield Counties, which hoped to benefit from increasing tourism at Lake Powell. The parkway would "'open the gate' for the three million tourists coming to the Grand Canyon to head into Utah instead of east to Colorado," according to San Juan County commissioner Cal Black, who supported the concept even though it would not run through his county. It would be "the most beautiful sightseeing road in the world," he claimed, giving motorists "a reasonable 'taste' of this great country that they can see and enjoy from their car."[12]

The parkway received strong support from the Utah State Highway Department, whose director, Henry Helland, believed that southern Utah's "treasure house of scenic and recreational attractions should be made available for the masses."[13] The only question was how close his road engineers could get to the scenery. The most ambitious plan called for extending the Squaw Flat road westward to bridge the Colorado River somewhere near Spanish Bottom and then continuing south and west along benches north of Lake Powell. Another concept routed the parkway west of the Green and Colorado Rivers beneath the Orange Cliffs, traversing the remote, arid benchlands that local cowboys called "Under the Rim." Still another route had the highway crossing the Green River at Anderson Bottom.

The proposed parkway would traverse some of southern Utah's most spectacular terrain, including the cliffs rising above Lake Powell at Wahweap Creek, Fortymile Ridge, and Stevens Canyon in the lower Escalante River drainage, and a cross section of the Dirty Devil River canyons. Motorists would get a close look at Stevens Arch, a 220-foot-wide span that rose directly above the Escalante River near the mouth of Coyote Gulch. Canyonlands superintendent Bates Wilson initially supported the parkway, calling it "one way of letting the visitor get off the transcontinental highway to see some spectacular country." He preferred to see the road cross the Green River north of Canyonlands National Park near Mineral Bottom, continuing west of the Orange Cliffs. To run "a black strip of asphalt down on those benches" beneath the rim would "wreck the whole setting," he said in a 1967 interview.[14] Park Service leaders hoped to work with state and congressional leaders to ensure the best alignment.

Utah senator Frank Moss offered bills in 1967 and 1969 to study the proposed parkway alignments, stating that "we can't improve on what Nature has provided, but we can show it off to millions of visitors in the future."[15] His colleagues in Utah's congressional delegation agreed. Senator Wallace Bennett released a statement in support of the parkway that said that "the lack of adequate roads to the many scenic attractions in the state has been one of the major factors blocking a great potential tourist industry."[16]

The parkway idea persisted among Utah travel boosters for more than two decades, taking different alignments depending on who was proposing it, but the concept remained the same: tourists would be able to glide from Arches to Lake Powell in a single day, presumably to lavish their money at either end—although why they would spend more by traveling faster was never made clear. Larry Davis, who ran the small Anasazi State Park in Boulder, Utah, far off the parkway route, cautioned that the road would "funnel visitors through our state via an area with little or no population, leaving little possibility for tourist trade."[17]

The goal of parkway proponents was to make southern Utah's scenery accessible to more people. Tourists did not like dead-end roads, state highway officials insisted, and preferred scenic drives with ever-changing vistas. In a country as rugged as southern Utah, this meant building highways against the grain of the land—crossing canyons, blasting through hogbacks, and bridging rivers. Given sufficient money, the engineering obstacles could be overcome. The wilderness would not be destroyed, Utah's leaders assured conservationists, just made more accessible to the millions who wanted to see it.

Frustrated by the unwavering support for the canyon parkway among Utah Highway Department officials, members of the Sierra Club and Wasatch Mountain Club in Salt Lake City formed the Escalante Wilderness Committee, led by June Viavant, a longtime member of both organizations. With fellow Salt Lake City environmentalists Jack McLellan and Ruth Frear, Viavant reached out to a small mailing list of canyoneering fans inside and outside Utah. The three spent years attending hearings, cranking out flyers, and writing news releases opposing the parkway, working with a budget that seldom exceeded a few hundred dollars. The committee's mimeographed newsletters and action alerts highlighted the beauty of the Escalante canyons as seen on foot or horseback, as opposed to highway speeds. Driving through this landscape at sixty miles per hour would, Viavant said, "reduce the subtleties of that beautiful country and its own peculiar twists and turns to a blur of slick rock with an arch or two. This road would only enable more and more people to see less and less."[18]

By 1970 national conservation groups such as the Sierra Club were becoming aware of the crisis in Utah's canyon country and were mobilizing their members. Frank Moss received dozens of letters each month urging him to drop the parkway proposal, although most came from outside Utah. Few of his correspondents were familiar with the lands involved, although one Californian who had explored the Escalante canyons, an accomplished rock climber named Royal Robbins, described a trip he had made there as "one of the most moving experiences of my life.... I was overwhelmed by the form of the canyons, the delicate, clearly-delineated ecology, the sharp contrasts between sky and rock, the combination of warmth and coolness." Robbins felt that the "quiet beauty of this land" would "perish under the impact of numbers of people."[19]

Such comments reflected the deep antipathy some Americans felt toward mass tourism, which brought large numbers of people into landscapes they believed were better suited to reverence and quiet contemplation. It was also an indication of the growing nationwide interest in southern Utah's red-rock canyons, which would become the basis of a nationwide campaign by preservation groups to sequester these areas from all forms of commercial and industrial development. This campaign gained further publicity in 1971 with the Sierra Club's publication of *Slickrock*, a full-color, coffee-table book featuring Philip Hyde's photographs of the Escalante River and text by Edward Abbey. Building on the exposure given Glen Canyon in the club's 1963 book *The Place No One Knew*, this large-format book was for many readers their first exposure to the Escalante region. Abbey's trenchant essays extolled the mysterious light and superb rock forms found within the canyons' recesses, all the while excoriating developers who were bent on transforming the entire Southwest into a smoke-filled, highway-riddled, and thoroughly tamed landscape.

The Escalante Wilderness Committee proposed an alternative to the parkway that would link existing roads and highways farther north from Lake Powell. If the dirt road leading from Boulder over the Aquarius Plateau to Torrey were upgraded, tourists could continue on the newly completed U-24 through Capitol Reef to Hanksville and the soon-to-be-completed U-95 to Natural Bridges and Blanding. They believed these routes would create a more logical connection between Bryce Canyon and the Canyonlands–Natural Bridges area, funneling tourists through existing towns instead of sending them into the uninhabited region along the north side of Lake Powell.

The parkway issue brought out the sharp divisions between urban and rural Utah regarding tourism and economic development. A two-lane road could hardly spoil the wilderness, one Kane County official stated at a field hearing on Senator Moss's parkway proposal in the town of Kanab in May 1972. "This is a vast, beautiful, and undeveloped region—so vast and so beautiful that we feel that every man, woman, and child in the United States should have the opportunity and privilege of seeing it."[20]

The NPS took no official position on the parkway but agreed to study it if Congress passed enabling legislation. Canyonlands superintendent Bates Wilson, however, was becoming disenchanted with the whole concept of a transcanyon throughway. In a meeting held at the Utah State Capitol in February 1970 with Governor Calvin Rampton and members of the Escalante Wilderness Committee, he favored the conservationists' alternative route that utilized existing highways. "I firmly believe the system should tie in with the communities," Wilson said. "The state is trying to promote tourists staying in Utah an extra day. This won't be accomplished with a route that shunts travelers on a Colorado to Arizona diagonal."[21]

Wilson and many of his colleagues in the Park Service were coming to believe that the wilder parts of the Colorado Plateau held intrinsic values that could easily be lost through indiscriminate road building. This was a watershed in Park Service thinking, and it came at a cost to bureaucrats such as Wilson who lived and worked in southeastern Utah. Local sentiment in places such as Moab, Monticello, Kanab, and Escalante favored roads—the more the better, and preferably paved. Their vision for the region included parkways, marinas, and hotels that would draw millions of tourists each year to a new Zion in the desert. It was a vision that also included massive industrial development of the region's mineral resources, as would become clear in the years ahead. These attitudes meant that as Wilson and his colleagues began to espouse a stronger environmental ethic, they would raise the ire of local authorities on whose support they had long depended.

27

PRESERVATION AND EXPANSION

On September 3, 1964, the same day that Congress passed Senator Frank Moss's Canyonlands National Park legislation, President Lyndon Johnson was occupied in a Rose Garden ceremony that had lasting importance for the nation's public lands. Before a large group of dignitaries that included Interior Secretary Stewart Udall, Vice President Hubert Humphrey, and Wyoming conservationist Mardy Murie, Johnson put his pen to the Wilderness Act, a measure that had reached the White House on a wave of conservation sentiment. First introduced in 1956, the bill gave immediate protection to 9.1 million acres of wilderness in the national forests and required studies of potential wilderness areas within national parks, national monuments, and national wildlife refuges. Congress retained the final say over which areas would become part of the National Wilderness Preservation System—and in the case of Utah's national parks, that process is still far from complete.

Park Service director Conrad Wirth was reluctant to embrace the Wilderness Act's study requirements, believing that backcountry areas in the larger national parks were already adequately protected. As he put it in a letter to the Wilderness Society's Howard Zahniser, "primeval areas of national parks and monuments are, in fact, already wilderness areas with adequate protection against future nonconforming use."[1] Park administrators sometimes saw the act's strictures as complicating their job of providing public access to scenic areas. The result was that the first round of NPS wilderness studies in 1967 yielded fairly conservative recommendations, typically involving the most remote sections of each park and excluding all human-made features—even fence lines and water wells. At Bryce Canyon, the agency limited its wilderness recommendation to the steep, dissected terrain below the rim, comprising 17,900 acres, while a preliminary wilderness recommendation for Canyonlands National Park left out roadless lands west of the Green River and in the Island in the Sky, corresponding to one possible route for the proposed canyon country parkway.

Conservationists affiliated with the Sierra Club, Wilderness Society, and National Parks Association criticized these proposals for fragmenting roadless lands and leaving large buffer zones around nonconforming uses. The conservation groups urged the agency to include roadless lands that had relatively minor nonconforming features such as fences, stock tanks, and irrigation ditches. The National Parks Association went so far as to propose that *all* roadless and undeveloped lands in Utah's national parks and monuments be brought under the umbrella of the Wilderness Act, with access roads confined to narrow corridors between wilderness units. The group wanted most visitor facilities to be located outside the parks, with mass transit systems to provide access to trailheads and interpretative sites.[2] This proposal had much in common with Edward Abbey's controversial essay "Polemic: Industrial Tourism and the National Parks," which appeared in his book *Desert Solitaire* one month after the group issued its statement.

This proposal was not given serious consideration within the Park Service, although the agency revisited its wilderness recommendations in 1974, enlarging them for the most part and proposing fewer exclusions and nonconforming corridors. It took until 2009, however, for Congress to enact the first Park Service wilderness in Utah, covering roadless lands within Zion National Park and adjacent Bureau of Land Management lands.[3]

Desert lands administered by the BLM were not addressed in the 1964 Wilderness Act; this agency instead came up with its own "primitive area" designation, which called for management similar to that of wilderness areas but did not have the force of law. Beginning in 1969, the agency established three of these in Utah: the 57,200-acre Dark Canyon Primitive Area south of Canyonlands National Park, the 24,000-acre Grand Gulch Primitive Area in the heart of Cedar Mesa, and the 27,500-acre Paria Canyon Primitive Area on the Utah-Arizona border.[4] Each covered outstanding wild country, but beyond their borders the agency continued to promote resource development projects such as oil and gas drilling. This left most of southern Utah's roadless lands without permanent forms of protection—an issue that would be hotly contested in the years ahead.

It took Congress eight years of legislative wrangling to pass the Wilderness Act, but less controversy attended a number of important environmental laws enacted later in the 1960s, including the Wild and Scenic Rivers Act and the National Trails System Act, both of which President Johnson signed into law in 1968. The latter established two national scenic trails, the Appalachian and Pacific Crest, and called for a study of various other recreational and historic routes such as the Continental Divide Trail, the Oregon Trail, and the Mormon Pioneer Trail. The bill was an outgrowth of a request by Interior Secretary Stewart Udall for a study of America's trail system, including long-distance trails of recreational and historical interest, as well as shorter trails near urbanized areas.[5]

A set of amendments to the National Trails System Act in 1978 established a category of national historic trails, three of which pass through Utah—California (designated in 1992), Pony Express (1992), and Old Spanish (2002). The Mormon Pioneer National Historic Trail, established in 1978, terminates in Salt Lake City. These trails commemorate the Euro-American exploration and colonization of the Southwest, as does Utah's only national historic park, Golden Spike, which was established in 2002. Golden Spike includes the final fifteen miles of the nation's first transcontinental railway, as well as the site of the historic meeting of the Central Pacific and Union Pacific tracks. It is managed by the National Park Service, which since Horace Albright's time has taken a strong role in preserving evidence of America's past. The Park Service also serves as administrator of the California, Pony Express, and Mormon Pioneer Trails and shares this duty with the BLM for the Old Spanish Trail.

None of these trails pass through Utah's national parks, although a segment of the Old Spanish Trail crosses the Glen Canyon National Recreation Area, following the route used by the Domínguez-Escalante exploration party of 1776–77. The "Crossing of the Fathers," where the party forded a shallow point in the Colorado River on November 7, 1776, is now underneath Lake Powell. The crossing was long used by Native Americans and was also known as the Ute Ford; the Spanish padres were fortunate to find it. The steps they chiseled into sandstone ledges to let their remaining horses down to the ford were a favorite stop for Glen Canyon river guide Dave Rust. Many years later, an inscription believed to have been made by the padres (*Paso por Aqui,* or "passed by here") was located above Lake Powell. Heavily vandalized, it is now protected by a steel cage.[6]

Each of these historic routes impinged heavily on Native American peoples by promoting settlement, commerce, and ecological change; the

A small part of the Maze, an area added to Canyonlands National Park in 1971.
National Park Service, Harpers Ferry Center, VA.

transcontinental railroads aided the extirpation of the Great Plains bison, a major food source for many Indian tribes. No comparable historic sites commemorate the long human use of the Colorado Plateau and Great Basin between the Puebloan era and the Spanish *entradas,* yet as geologist Charles B. Hunt observed, Utah's canyon country was once laced with "Indian trails"—shorter routes that often led to water, which fellow geologists such as G. K. Gilbert made good use of in their explorations. Largely obliterated by livestock, these lost trails marked a continuous habitation of a landscape that later settlers saw as harsh and unforgiving.[7]

As President Johnson prepared to leave office in early 1969 under the cloud of the Vietnam War, Stewart Udall saw an opportunity to add to the administration's already substantial conservation legacy by further expanding the National Park System. Utah would once again be the beneficiary—some would say victim—of Johnson's actions in the waning hours of his presidency. Once again Bates Wilson would play a major role in this expansion, thanks to his close relationship with Secretary Udall.

The 1964 law that established Canyonlands National Park left out many scenic sections west of the Colorado River, including the Maze, the Land of Standing Rocks, Ernie's Country (a remote section of sandstone fins, towers, and hidden arches south of the Maze), and the wondrous Desert Archaic pictographs in Horseshoe (or Barrier) Canyon, known as the "Great Gallery." Bates Wilson had been taking various Park Service planners into these remote sections for years and had wanted to include them in the park all along. In November 1964, just two months after Canyonlands' creation, the acting director of the Park Service's southwestern regional office identified the Maze area to be "as fully deserving of National Park status as anything in the authorized Canyonlands boundaries."[8]

Lands still farther west, including the Orange Cliffs, Millard Canyon, and upper French Spring Canyon, were equally scenic, but Wilson and Udall proposed that they be added to the Glen Canyon National Recreation Area. East of the Green River, Wilson sought to include more of Taylor Canyon and the White Rim north of the existing park boundary. He also advocated a modest expansion to the southeast to take in portions of Davis and Lavender Canyons, known for their prehistoric rock art and stone structures. There was even talk of annexing Dead Horse Point State Park, the superb promontory that was ceded to the state of Utah in 1958.

Frank Moss introduced legislation to expand Canyonlands in 1966, largely along lines recommended by Wilson and the NPS. Intended to complete the vision that had been so badly compromised during the legislative wrangling of 1962–64, the bill came too late for action in the Eighty-Ninth Congress. Reintroduced the following year, it gained endorsements from the National Parks Advisory Board and the *Moab Times-Independent*.[9] The measure would have added 102,000 acres to the park, taking in the Maze and a detached parcel within Horseshoe Canyon that included the Great Gallery.

In testimony before Congress on Moss's bill in 1970, Wilson again brought up the need for more road access in the Needles district. These were not to be major parkways—he said he had little desire to cater to what he called "the man in the pink Cadillac"—but he saw a need for additional routes that led to jumping-off points into the backcountry.[10] Wilson seemed to have no firm position on the roads issue, to the consternation of both the conservation community and local county commissioners. His job as a park superintendent placed him under great pressure from business interests in Grand and San Juan Counties, yet he was also widely praised by conservationists as the father of Canyonlands National Park. He was no longer the overseer of a minor national monument in the desert hinterlands, and his relationship with Stewart Udall and his folksy, quotable presence before the news media gave him a chance not only to complete his Canyonlands vision, but also to expand Arches into a full-fledged national park, taking in a wide expanse of terrain leading clear to the Colorado River.

Disagreement over the routing of the canyon country parkway delayed action on Moss's Canyonlands expansion bill until 1971, when the Senate held field hearings on this and his other park bills, including one that would redesignate Arches and Capitol Reef as national parks. But with little progress being made on the legislative front in the last year of Lyndon Johnson's administration, Stewart Udall turned to executive action for quicker results. Once again he relied on Bates Wilson for guidance on how far he could reach—which turned out to be a long way indeed.

Wilson especially wanted to enlarge Arches, then a thirty-four-thousand-acre enclave taking in little more than Devils Garden, the Windows–Balanced Rock area, and Delicate Arch. By including Salt Valley, Herdina Park west of Devils Garden, and the Klondike Bluffs, the monument would represent more of the geologic and topographic setting for its iconic arches. Wilson also wanted to expand the monument southeastward to the Colorado River, where prospectors were filing mineral claims.

At Capitol Reef, it had long been realized that the 1937 monument proclamation omitted some of the most scenic portions of the Waterpocket Fold, including the remarkable sandstone spires of Cathedral Valley. In October 1961 Udall dispatched Wallace Stegner to investigate the area, but action was deferred in favor of efforts to create Canyonlands National Park.[11] In 1968 Udall turned to Bates Wilson for suggestions, although the monument was not under his jurisdiction. After consulting with Lurt Knee of the Sleeping Rainbow Guest Ranch on Pleasant Creek, Wilson proposed an expansion to take in Cathedral Valley to the north, along with a separate unit in the portion of the Waterpocket Fold lying between Oak Creek and the Burr Trail.[12]

When this idea came to the attention of Capitol Reef superintendent Robert Heyder that September, he had a ready response: Why not include the *entire* length of the Fold, from Thousand Lake Mountain to the Glen

Canyon National Recreation Area?[13] Heyder also proposed including the Henry Mountains, most of the Circle Cliffs east of the village of Boulder, and a long stretch of the Escalante River below Calf Creek. This daring concept would have exceeded Canyonlands in size and practically reincarnated the old Escalante national monument proposal. Heyder ultimately limited his proposal to the Waterpocket Fold and Cathedral Valley, still a significant expansion.

Back in Washington, the expansion proposals for Arches and Capitol Reef were handled in secret as part of a major package of new national monuments that Udall prepared for President Johnson to sign. It included huge acquisitions in Alaska as well as in Arizona's Marble Canyon and Sonoran Desert. Johnson, after consulting with his advisers and House Interior Committee chair Wayne Aspinall, agreed to the expansion of Arches and Capitol Reef, along with additions to Katmai National Monument in Alaska and a new monument in Marble Canyon, which adjoined Grand Canyon National Park. The Utah proposals were seen as relatively noncontroversial, although that would prove far from true.

On January 20, 1969, only hours before he left office, President Lyndon Johnson signed proclamations expanding or creating four national monuments using his authority under the 1906 Antiquities Act. Arches was more than doubled in size to 77,863 acres, while a 215,056-acre addition to Capitol Reef made it nearly four times larger. When residents of Wayne and Garfield Counties learned of this move, they exploded in anger and disbelief. Unsure of where the new boundaries lay, the town council of Boulder passed a resolution renaming their tiny village "Johnson's Folly." Superintendent Heyder had to quell rumors of a vast new park domain extending as far west as Bicknell.[14]

Many Utahns objected to the suddenness and secrecy behind both monument proclamations—a theme that would surface years later when President Clinton designated the Grand Staircase–Escalante National Monument. The expansion of Park Service authority replaced the comfortable relationship they had long enjoyed with the Bureau of Land Management, an agency that permitted livestock grazing and most forms of mineral development. Following Johnson's proclamations, Garfield County commissioner Dale Marsh chaired a meeting of angry constituents in Escalante, who protested the transfer of so much land from BLM "multiple-use" management. Wayne County commissioner Don Pace said that the monument expansion would mean the loss of winter range for 1,100 cows, sacrificing $40,000 in annual calf production. Cal Black, in San Juan County, stated that "we are not despoilers of the land" and decried "selfish people" who "want our lands for the single use of sightseeing."[15]

Perhaps the most telling comment to emerge from the 1969 Capitol Reef controversy came from Leland Haws of the Garfield County Research and Development Office, who insisted that park designations such as Capitol Reef "be confined to certain spectacular spots, and the greater area left for development of oil and uranium and the continued use as grazing lands."[16] This summarized Utah officialdom's approach to national parks. Lyndon Johnson's Capitol Reef proclamation broke with this tradition, building on the long history of Park Service interest in substantial new park designations in the Utah canyon lands. His eleventh-hour action in January 1969 served notice that the idea behind the old Escalante national monument was not dead, and that preservation advocates would continue to seek official protection for a large part of this unique, though highly contested, region.

Despite the controversy over the expansion of Capitol Reef National Monument, Frank Moss was still able to move his park-related legislation through Congress during the early 1970s. The winds were favorable for conservation measures in the post–Earth Day years, and even with a new Republican administration in Washington, Moss could count on support from his Democratic colleagues in Congress. He was able to not only expand Canyonlands but also reclassify Capitol Reef and Arches National Monuments as national parks and formally designate the Glen Canyon National Recreation Area.

With little in the way of good grazing land involved in the Canyonlands expansion or the Glen Canyon area, attention focused instead on how thoroughly these park units would be developed for tourism. Senator Wallace Bennett sought amendments to Moss's bills that would allow the state of Utah to construct new roads within Glen Canyon and Canyonlands, including the controversial Confluence overlook road, but these were defeated in votes that fell almost exactly along party lines.[17] Instead, the final bills called only for the Park Service to conduct studies of roads that would be needed in both park units.

The election of Democrat Gunn McKay in 1970, replacing Lawrence Burton, helped smooth the path for Moss's Capitol Reef and Arches bills in the House. The latter was bundled with his Canyonlands expansion measure, which passed Congress and gained President Nixon's signature on November 12, 1971. Utah's largest national park now took in 337,258 acres, while Arches National Park stood at 73,379 acres, a net reduction of 4,500 acres from the former national monument. Moss's measure to create a 241,671-acre Capitol Reef National Park was signed into law on December 18.

The Glen Canyon National Recreation Area, which had been administratively established in 1958 when Glen Canyon Dam was under construction, became an official Park Service unit on October 27, 1972, also through legislation sponsored by Senator Moss. National park lands now took in almost two million acres in southern Utah, and while this was less than half the size of the original Escalante proposal of the 1930s, it was enough to place the National Park Service in charge of most of the scenic lands on either side of Colorado River in Utah. Millions of visitors would seek adventure, scenery, and relaxation in these places during the coming years, giving the Beehive State the tourist draw it had long wanted. But the transcanyon parkway issue remained unresolved, and meanwhile a major industrial complex was being proposed for the Kaiparowits Plateau—leaving conservationists worried for the wild character of the entire region.

SMOKESTACKS ON THE PLATEAU

Senator Frank Moss promoted his canyon country parkway as a way to lure more tourists to Utah's national parks, but a less-advertised rationale was to open the remote landscape north of Lake Powell to industrial development. During the 1960s Interior Department officials were quietly talking with several California and Arizona utility companies that wished to build a giant coal-fired power-generating plant on the Kaiparowits Plateau north of Warm Creek. The plant would obtain coal from nearby strip or underground mines, creating an industrial complex that would benefit from having close highway access.[1]

Herbert Gregory and Robert Moore had assessed the coal reserves of the Kaiparowits Plateau for the U.S. Geological Survey in 1922, but forty years would pass before a consortium of utility companies applied for and received federal coal prospecting permits on the plateau. In the fall of 1963, a contractor for the Arizona Public Service Company began test drilling on a remote site atop the plateau. Word soon got out that three regional utilities—Southern California Edison, San Diego Gas & Electric, and Arizona Public Service—along with Arizona's Salt River Project, intended to build a three-thousand-megawatt generating complex on Nipple Bench, an arid upland north of Wahweap Bay.[2] The power project, according to utility officials, would help meet the "critical need" for electricity in the fast-growing Southwest, according to the utility consortium. The plant's emission control equipment would keep it within state and federal air pollution standards, making it "one of the cleanest coal-fired plants in the world," a utility fact sheet promised.[3] The project would bring three thousand construction workers and a $95 million payroll to Kane County, as well as a new town beneath

Artist's rendering of the proposed Kaiparowits power generating station. *Used by permission, Utah State Historical Society.*

the cliffs at New Clark Bench. All this drew the enthusiastic approval of county commissioners and elected officials in southern Utah.

Development of the Kaiparowits Power Project was initially held up over concern from the state of Utah over the large water diversion it would require from Lake Powell. Governor Calvin Rampton approved the diversion in 1965, but Interior Secretary Stewart Udall withheld federal approval until September 1968. Numerous regulatory hurdles remained, however, with more than 220 permits and authorizations needed from various federal, state, and local agencies before the project could get underway.[4] Utah senator Wallace Bennett, along with Representatives Lawrence Burton and Sherman Lloyd, urged the Interior Department to expedite the project, saying that "the economic boon to our State as a whole would be tremendous."[5] In October 1969 Walter Hickel, Udall's replacement, issued a preliminary contract for "mutual assistance" in the project, which allowed the utility consortium to proceed with planning and permitting.

These rosy economic predictions could not hide the transformative nature of the Kaiparowits project. Beside the generating plant itself, ancillary facilities would include a slurry pond nearly a mile square, which would impound forty-three million cubic yards of waste material. The coal mines and power generation facilities would require 870 miles of permanent roads, along with 1,457 miles of new transmission lines to carry power to Southern California and Arizona. A limestone quarry sixteen miles northeast of Bryce Canyon National Park would deliver crushed rock for use in the plant's emission scrubbers, with thirty trucks per day making the trip over the road from Cannonville to the plant site. The plant at full operation would release eight tons of particulate matter and twenty-one tons of sulfur dioxide daily to the atmosphere.[6]

Environmental groups across the nation raised alarms about the loss of clean air in a region that hosted dozens of national park units. Already the huge Four Corners power plant near Farmington, New Mexico, was emitting pollution visible for hundreds of miles downwind, and a brown plume from the first generating unit at the Navajo station near Page could be seen spreading over Lake Powell. Two new coal-fired plants were under consideration in southern Nevada, which would obtain coal from strip and underground mines near Alton, Utah, southwest of Bryce Canyon National Park, while a third plant was proposed near Escalante, Utah. These projects were only part of what the Department of the Interior projected to be a nearly fivefold increase in power-generating capacity within the region by 1980.[7] The Sierra Club, Friends of the Earth, and other allied organizations were taking out advertisements in national newspapers calling the Four Corners region a "national sacrifice area."

The newly formed Environmental Protection Agency issued a stark assessment of the effect of these plants on regional air quality. Southwestern skies would be "increasingly and significantly degraded," with pollutants such as sulfur dioxide causing "threats to human health, terrestrial biota, and surface water quality."[8] In June 1973 Rogers Morton, Walter Hickel's replacement as Interior Secretary, denied federal permits for the project, citing the proximity of the planned Nipple Bench site to the Navajo power station and the Glen Canyon National Recreation Area. The power companies responded with a new proposed site on Fourmile Bench, farther from Glen Canyon and the Navajo plant, which they believed would lessen the impact on regional air quality. The environmental studies continued, culminating in a nine-volume, 2,700-page environmental impact statement that the Bureau of Land Management released in 1976.

The National Park Service raised concerns about what it termed the "progressive deterioration of air quality in the Four Corners region" from the existing power plants at Page and Farmington. It believed that mining and power plant operations would impinge on the view from Rainbow and Inspiration Points in Bryce Canyon, and that visible air pollution would create "a significant aesthetic intrusion" at Grand Canyon and Capitol Reef National Parks. Visitors would notice the odor of nitrogen oxides in the air, while fish in Lake Powell could become contaminated with mercury from the soot fall.[9] The agency noted that Congress was considering adopting more stringent air quality standards for national parks under the Clean Air Act—the so-called prevention of significant deterioration rule—which the new plant would not meet.

In the end, it was economics as much as environmental concerns that pulled the plug on Kaiparowits. By 1975 the cost of the project had ballooned to more than $2.5 billion, $600 million of which was for emission control equipment.[10] On December 30, 1975, the power company consortium announced a one-year delay in the project owing to "objections by environmental groups and lengthy approval processes."[11] The following April, shortly before Interior Secretary Thomas Kleppe was to issue his final decision on the project, the consortium announced that it was withdrawing the proposal. It cited the cost of meeting more stringent pollution standards, but an additional reason was slower-than-anticipated growth in the demand for electricity in its service areas. Arizona's Salt River Project had dropped out of the consortium the previous year, and Southern California Edison saw its "load base," or demand for electricity, actually decrease as a result of conservation efforts and an economic recession. By March 1976 the company was predicting low growth rates for another ten years. In August the project's sponsors met with representatives of twenty-four other utilities to solicit additional contracts. According to a spokesperson for Utah Power & Light, "the power went begging to the last."[12]

The vagaries of the power market were probably not on the minds of several hundred local citizens who gathered at the Kane County Courthouse following the announcement of the project's cancellation. Environmentalists were to blame, and the crowd watched as four effigies representing actor Robert Redford (a vocal opponent of the project), Environmental Protection Agency director Russell Train, former interior secretary Rogers Morton, and the Sierra Club were burned.[13]

Environmental groups cheered the news of the project's demise, but the threat to the region's air quality—and to the vistas from its national parks—was not over. Another utility group comprising thirty utilities and rural cooperatives in Utah, eastern Nevada, and southern Wyoming had been looking at sites in Wayne and Garfield Counties for a three-thousand-megawatt power plant, utilizing coal from underground mines in Utah's Carbon and Emery Counties. The Intermountain Power Project, or IPP, quickly dubbed "son of Kaiparowits," would include a coal-haul railroad to the plant site, a reservoir, a new town, and deep wells to tap the Navajo Sandstone aquifer. After rejecting a site near the town of Escalante in Garfield County, participants settled on a location fifteen miles east of Capitol Reef National Park, between the prominent features of Factory Butte and North Caineville Mesa.

Environmental reviews disclosed that the plant would severely impact air quality in both Capitol Reef and Canyonlands National Parks, with particulate pollution easily exceeding the new, tougher Class I ambient air quality standards. A gray haze would spread over the long-distance vistas from high points in the northern part of Capitol Reef.[14] This time the controversy was resolved relatively quickly, with Interior Secretary Cecil Andrus favoring an alternative site in Utah's west desert north of the town of Delta. This site received final approval in 1979, sparing the airshed of two of Utah's most pristine national parks.

The demise of the Kaiparowits Power Project and the relocation of the IPP disappointed many southern Utah residents who wanted few or no restrictions on oil, gas, uranium, and other mineral development. Hoping for a reprise of the boom times of the 1950s, they eagerly greeted news of any potential industrial project in the region. The recently opened Upper Valley oil field west of Escalante hinted at the industrial development that might be possible in Garfield and Kane Counties. Sometimes this sentiment amounted to outright boomerism, as when Kanab mayor Claude Glazier, lamenting the demise of Kaiparowits, told a reporter, "That power plant would have made Kanab. We would have had money like we never, never dreamed."[15]

An even greater prize was tar sands, the oil-laden sandstones found deep underground in the Circle Cliffs and western Canyonlands areas. Senator Frank Moss went so far as to amend his Canyonlands park expansion bill to omit areas of tar sand deposits within a wedge of land between the Dirty Devil and Colorado Rivers, known as the Tar Sand Triangle. The Park Service, which managed part of the area within the Glen Canyon NRA, cooperated with the BLM on a study of potential tar sand extraction, which, like the Kaiparowits study a decade earlier, painted a nightmarish picture of full-scale hydrocarbon development in one of the most remote parts of Utah. Active field development would involve drilling nearly a thousand steam injection wells, with an equal number of production wells to draw off the hydrocarbon product. Water would be pumped from the Dirty Devil River a dozen or more miles to a power plant utilizing fluidized-bed combustion to produce the electricity required for hydrocarbon extraction. Its emissions would violate Class I air quality standards in both Canyonlands National Park and the Glen Canyon NRA. The entire facility would be relocated laterally up to five times as tar sand beds were depleted, ultimately disturbing thirty thousand acres over its anticipated 160-year lifetime.[16]

During the oil-embargo years of the 1970s, when the Ford administration launched Project Independence and the Carter administration subsidized the development of oil shale in the West, it appeared that such a project might be feasible. Various oil shale demonstration projects were undertaken in western Colorado's Piceance Basin and elsewhere, but the collapse of the synthetic fuels market in the early 1980s meant that tar sands, which were equally difficult to utilize, would remain on the back burner for some time.

Although declining oil prices helped to forestall massive energy development at the edges of southern Utah's national parks, the Kaiparowits, IPP, and Tar Sand Triangle projects left their mark on a seemingly unrelated issue: the Bureau of Land Management's review of potential wilderness lands in southern Utah. This was a massive, nationwide undertaking required under the 1976 Federal Land Policy and Management Act, the law that updated the archaic patchwork of laws and policies governing public domain lands in the West. Beginning in 1979, BLM district offices made a broad-brush inventory of roadless tracts ranging from the Mojave Desert in far southwestern Utah to the culturally rich Grand Gulch plateau in southeastern Utah. Mining and stockmen's groups worried that resource lands would be placed off limits, but the BLM's study procedures virtually guaranteed that such lands would be excluded from the wilderness inventory, to the dismay of conservationists in Utah. The remote desert lands east of Capitol Reef National Park, where the IPP project was under review, were also left out of the BLM's initial wilderness inventory. Most of the coal lands on the Kaiparowits Plateau were removed, as were the badlands surrounding the Henry Mountains, including the striking South Caineville Mesa. All of these areas had once been considered as part of the Park Service's Escalante national monument proposal.[17]

Utah's environmental groups countered with their own proposals for BLM wilderness. The most sweeping proposal came from an ad hoc group called the Utah Wilderness Coalition (UWC), made up of fifteen established organizations such as the Sierra Club, Wilderness Society, and National Parks and Conservation Association (the former National Parks Association). In 1985 the coalition unveiled an ambitious proposal for BLM wilderness in Utah, consisting of 5.1 million acres in 141 units scattered throughout southern Utah's canyon lands and its western desert region. The proposal signaled that environmental organizations would take a more regional approach to landscape preservation in the Colorado Plateau instead of simply opposing development projects as they arose.

Many of the UWC's proposed wilderness reserves adjoined national parks and monuments, as in upper White Canyon, where some twenty thousand acres of undeveloped BLM land adjoined Natural Bridges National Monument. Coalition members believed that large, contiguous expanses of roadless land that crossed federal administrative boundaries should be protected as single entities.[18] But the BLM had a half-century-long history of catering to livestock and mining interests and was not about to embark on a crash program of land preservation in Utah's canyon country. Standing behind the agency was Congress, the final arbiter of what would be designated wilderness. With the exception of Wayne Owens, Utah's lone Democrat in the House during the mid-1980s, the state's congressional delegation remained solidly prodevelopment and antiwilderness. Senator Orrin Hatch stated in 1991 that "turning an excess of 5 million acres, which is approximately the size of the state of New Jersey, into an economic desert with no place for people would be an imprudent commitment of our resources and could well seal the fate of many rural Utah communities."[19]

Utah's growing community of wilderness activists, on the other hand, viewed the state's national parks as anchors for much larger roadless reserves. According to Terri Martin of the National Parks and Conservation Association, park boundaries "were all too often the result of political compromise, timid vision, and speculation about potential resource conflicts. . . . Wild lands under Park Service and BLM management alike should be brought under the management principles of the Wilderness Act."[20]

By the late 1980s the issue of BLM wilderness overshadowed all other land-use conflicts in southern Utah. Spurred on by new grassroots groups such as the Southern Utah Wilderness Alliance, the issue soon reached nationwide prominence. Unlike in the 1930s, when significant resource development within this region seemed a distant possibility, active proposals for new mines, power plants, and tourist highways were now surfacing almost monthly. Once again, a road would become the focal point for what was, in fact, a struggle for control of the wild landscape of the Colorado Plateau.

29

THAT RIBBON OF DIRT

Set picturesquely among the white sandstone cliffs and mesas of the upper Escalante River drainage, the little village of Boulder stood apart from mainstream American life until well into the twentieth century. Not until 1940 was the town connected to the outside world via an all-season road, laboriously constructed through the slickrock canyons and hogbacks leading east from Escalante.[1] In the early 1950s, the Atomic Energy Commission funded improvements to the Burr Trail, a rugged backcountry route that led east from Boulder over the Waterpocket Fold to Halls Creek. Originally a stock driveway, the route was named for nineteenth-century cattleman John Atlantic Burr, who used the route to access the Halls Crossing area on the Colorado River.

The improved road served uranium miners working in the Circle Cliffs area, but rain and flash floods often made it impassable to vehicles. Still, it was a way to avoid the winter snows up on the Aquarius Plateau, where another dirt road led north to the village of Torrey. That road would not be paved until 1985, when it joined up with the historic "lower road" coming from Escalante to complete Utah Highway 12. With the expansion of Capitol Reef National Monument in 1969, the Burr Trail accessed scenic park lands as well, suggesting to county leaders that it might one day become a significant tourist route. What took place, however, was yet another battle over building a highway through wild, undeveloped country.

Garfield County's efforts to further improve the Burr Trail began in 1965, when it requested $500,000 in state funds to make the route serviceable for passenger cars. The request was overshadowed by Frank Moss's canyon country parkway proposal, which stalled out amid controversy over its impact on the Escalante River canyons.[2] Mineral development also figured in the county's plans for the road. In 1978 Garfield County commissioners approved plans for a new town of eight hundred residents at Ticaboo, south of the Henry Mountains, in anticipation of a uranium mill opening in Shootaring Canyon. The mill operated for only a brief time, but hopes for a renewed mineral boom persisted, leading the commissioners to call for paving the Burr Trail in order to serve this isolated outpost. They also sought to have the boundary of Capitol Reef National Park (which was established in 1971) retracted so there would be no conflict with heavy truck traffic across the Waterpocket Fold.[3]

In the mid-1980s, with the transcanyon parkway no longer on the table and uranium mining again in decline, Garfield County resurrected the idea of an all-weather tourist highway that would connect Boulder to the marina at Bullfrog on Lake Powell. The project presented considerable engineering difficulties, especially where the route descended a series of steep switchbacks at the eastern edge of the Waterpocket Fold, but once completed it would offer tourists a much shorter route from Bryce Canyon National Park to the middle section of Lake Powell.

This time, Garfield commissioners found their ambitions thwarted by three newcomers who had purchased homesites in the eastern part of the county. Word of the county's road plans reached Grant Johnson, who homesteaded land on Deer Creek, a bucolic cottonwood-lined drainage that crossed the Burr Trail six miles southeast of Boulder. Johnson disliked seeing the dirt road below his property widened and paved, so along with Gordon Anderson and Lucy Wallingford, two environmental activists from Moab, he formed the Save the Burr Trail Committee. He was joined in this quixotic campaign by his neighbor, Clive Kincaid, who was building a cabin alongside Deer Creek, and Robert Weed, another newcomer to the area who had built a home next to the Escalante River at Calf Creek.[4] The three men were concerned about not only the increased traffic that paving would bring, but the possibility that it could open the Circle Cliffs and nearby areas to renewed mining and industrial development.

Their opposition did not sit well with Garfield County commissioners, who had already been stung by environmentalist opposition to the canyon country parkway and the Kaiparowits power plant. They reasoned that since the county had been blocked from pursuing its dream of heavy industry, it should be free to pursue the alternative presented by tourism.[5] The county sought an appropriation for road improvements from the state legislature during its 1983 and 1984 sessions, but Weed and Kincaid also made the rounds

The Burr Trail as it descends from the eastern escarpment of the Waterpocket Fold in Capitol Reef National Park. The National Park Service opposed Garfield County's plan to widen and pave the part of the Burr Trail running through the park. *Photo by author.*

in the Utah State Capitol, preaching fiscal responsibility and environmental awareness. The road was fine as it was, they told legislators, a mildly challenging backcountry route that offered a different experience than zooming along a paved highway. But their opposition to the Burr Trail project, as well as their support of extensive wilderness designations in southern Utah, made the three men anathema in Garfield County. Weed suffered vandalism to his Escalante River homestead, and all three men were identified by name on an effigy hanged in the town of Escalante. Environmental causes remained deeply unpopular in southern Utah's rural regions, whose longtime residents believed they had as much right to pursue economic development in their communities as people living along the Wasatch Front.

During the earlier battle over the canyon parkway system, some environmentalists had proposed that the Burr Trail might provide an alternative to routing a highway through the lower Escalante canyons. The scheduled completion of Utah Highway 12 over the shoulder of the Aquarius Plateau was also held out as better for local business than a parkway deep in the canyons. But the principals in the parkway fight, chiefly the Wasatch Mountain Club and the Uintah Chapter of the Sierra Club, now feared that paving the Burr Trail could bring calls for further development in the southern part of Capitol Reef National Park. The park's 1982 general management plan envisioned just such a possibility by calling for a ranger station, campground, employee housing, and a short spur road to the Strike Valley Overlook trail.[6] By 1985, however, the Park Service opposed paving the road, largely because Garfield County was asserting its own right-of-way across the park. If granted, this and many other old uranium tracks in the park and in nearby Canyonlands National Park would become subject to county control—a clear shot at Park Service authority over the lands it managed.

The battle over the Burr Trail replayed previous fights over roads in canyon country such as the Confluence road in Canyonlands. The magnitude of the project became clear after Garfield County commissioned an engineering report that called for widening and straightening the roadway to accommodate large recreational vehicles. The steep switchback section in Capitol Reef would be replaced with a long, built-up embankment, transforming this slow, winding, dust-on-the-windshield route into a blacktop cruise.

Outgoing governor Scott Matheson and his replacement, Norm Bangerter, joined Senators Jake Garn and Orrin Hatch in supporting Garfield County in its search for road funds. In early 1983 Garn and Hatch introduced a bill for a $600,000 road feasibility study, which passed the Senate but was defeated in conference committee after vigorous lobbying by conservation groups, including the Southern Utah Wilderness Alliance (SUWA), which Kincaid, Johnson, and Weed founded in 1984 in part to fight improvements to the Burr Trail. In 1985 Congress directed the Park Service to conduct an environmental review of the project, which brought Park Service director William Penn Mott to Utah to take a look at the roadway and consult with local authorities. Afterward he proposed a compromise in which the road would be given an all-weather gravel surface but retain the switchback section and most of the existing road alignment.

Some environmentalists supported this compromise, but when a bill authorizing $8 million in federal funds to create a "Burr Trail National Scenic Road" failed to pass, Garfield County took matters into its own hands, obtaining $2 million in state funds to proceed with initial roadwork east of Boulder. An environmentalist lawsuit held up the project for two years, but the county prevailed in federal district court in 1987 after Judge Aldon Anderson found that the county held a valid right-of-way to the road. Appeals led to further delays, but in 1991 the county got the go-ahead for a scaled-back, asphalt roadway that closely conformed to the land. An episode of vandalism to road equipment failed to delay the project for long,[7] although the project remained controversial for years as county road engineers continued to seek a wider, straighter roadway, while SUWA and its supporters attempted to keep the project within narrow confines.

By the mid-1990s the western part of this once neglected road had been transformed into an indisputably scenic, low-speed parkway, a far cry from the major realignments and widening that Garfield County had initially sought. The Park Service refused to allow the road to be paved within Capitol Reef National Park, although gravel was applied and wash crossings were hardened with concrete. The switchback section still remains a deterrent to large recreational vehicles.[8]

The battle over the Burr Trail began and ended as a clash of entrenched interests, each finding little reason to compromise. It became an "ideological contest," as historian Jedediah Rogers observed, leading to an "erosion of goodwill and possible future alliances with locals in a larger fight over wilderness that has yet to conclude." Rogers cited a Boulder rancher, Dell LeFevre, who said that the increased traffic on the road interfered with his cattle drives through the Waterpocket Fold.[9] No longer an emblem of the nineteenth-century cattle frontier, the Burr Trail became a conduit for modernity to reach the Circle Cliffs region. Today "Boulder Town," as it is still known, sports an upscale lodge and restaurant while land values in the community have soared, in part because of the attention focused on it from the lengthy road controversy.

The road itself, however, still lies lightly on the land, offering a modicum of economic value to eastern Garfield County while giving hikers access to the canyons along the Circle Cliffs. Thus far the industrialization that environmentalists feared has not materialized. Far from having become the major tourism route its boosters originally envisioned, the Burr Trail provides reasonable access to some marvelous backcountry without doing significant harm to the surroundings. It was an outcome that neither side desired, but perhaps all can live with.

The court decision in the Burr Trail case set a legal precedent that had a far wider effect than the paving of the road itself. By affirming the county's right-of-way to the road under a Civil War–era statute known as R.S. 2477, the federal court served up another three decades' worth of conflict over Utah's desert lands. Henceforth county governments throughout southern Utah, aided by state taxpayer dollars, would file claims to thousands of miles of old, often disused and eroded tracks through sage flats and blackbrush in an attempt to forestall any further wilderness or other protective designations. Attorneys for SUWA and other environmental groups contested the road claims at every step, and as of 2019 a few had been settled, but the right-of-way issue raised a cloud over their efforts to achieve significant wilderness designations in the region.

The clash over the Burr Trail came about because the principals could not agree on what constituted the best use of national parks and the wild lands surrounding them. No longer was there a shared vision for managing the Colorado Plateau's federally owned lands. In fact, by the end of the 1970s, adherents of the Sagebrush Rebellion would question the very legitimacy of the federal presence in southern Utah. Nor would environmentalists back down from their campaign to secure additional protective designations for these lands, whether wilderness areas or new national monuments.

The role of tourism in the rural economy of southern Utah was itself contested. As late as 1965, as historian Art Gómez points out, tourism was seen as an "inexhaustible resource" that could buffer the ups and downs of the extractive industries that had for so long defined the economies of western states. Speaking at the Rocky Mountain Governors Conference in Salt Lake City, Utah governor Calvin Rampton urged the leaders of his neighboring states to "take advantage of your state's natural resources for vacation travel to the fullest extent possible. . . . Open the doors of the Great American West's playground to all people of the nation."[10] Conservationist leaders in Utah essentially agreed with this viewpoint when they suggested alternative routings for the canyon country parkway, using existing paved routes such as Utah Highways 12 and 24.

Two decades later, however, Utah's environmental groups had successfully challenged not only the transcanyon parkway and the Confluence road in Canyonlands, but also Garfield County's plans for a considerably widened and smoothed Burr Trail. National parks, including Capitol Reef, were no longer seen as blank canvases for highway engineers. Touristic development would be located primarily within existing towns, with those offering the most services (notably Moab and Springdale) reaping a disproportionate share of the benefits (or problems, depending on the perspective taken). And away from towns and major roads, the conflict over individual industrial projects would go on endlessly, one brushfire battle succeeding another, as environmental advocates sought to hold on to what remained of the solitude and spaciousness of Utah's canyon country. By the 1980s the next struggle was already taking shape on the verge of Canyonlands National Park, and in many respects it was the scariest of all.

30

WASTED:
CANYONLANDS AT RISK

For centuries if not millennia, arid lands have been the refuge of mystics, the dispossessed, the seekers of truth and beauty. In more recent times, the deserts of the American Southwest have served as a place for stashing the unwanted refuse of our industrial civilization—urban trash, junk cars, even the military's unneeded airplanes. Anything obsolete or unusable could be hauled out to a dry wash or playa and left to slowly rust. Beginning in the 1970s, the federal government looked to these same lands as a place to dispose of another type of unwanted material: high-level nuclear waste, the strange brew of fission products and transuranic elements left over from nuclear reactions in commercial nuclear power plants. These substances decay over long periods to form yet other atomic by-products, emitting dangerous radiation for hundreds of thousands of years. With nearly nine thousand tons of the material held in temporary aboveground storage, and more being produced by the nation's seventy-eight nuclear reactors, some way needed to be found to sequester the dangerous waste.

Salt domes, geologically stable over long periods, offered one possible means for permanent storage of radioactive waste. In 1965 the Atomic Energy Commission initiated a study of a salt dome site in Kansas but later eliminated it owing to the possibility of groundwater infiltration. By 1979 the AEC's successor agency, the Department of Energy (DOE), widened the search to include salt structures in the Gulf Coast region, the Permian Basin of Texas, and the Paradox Basin within Utah. Nine potential sites were identified, including four in Utah. Two of these closely adjoined national parks: the Salt Valley site lay at the northern border of Arches, while Gibson Dome lay just east of Canyonlands in the lower drainages of Davis and Lavender Canyons. Other sites considered were the Lisbon Valley south of

Moab, and Elk Ridge, high in the Abajo Mountains near Natural Bridges National Monument.

Why were sites chosen that lay so close to national parks? The answer could be found deep underground in the massive salt deposits of the Paradox Formation, which underlay both the Salt Valley and Gibson Dome sites. Deeply buried salt flows under pressure, lifting overlying strata and forming shallow domes or anticlines. Exposed and fractured along myriad joint lines, these sandstone layers erode into ranks of sandstone fins, forming much of the scenery in Arches and Canyonlands. (A similar process can also form sunken valleys, or grabens, such as those on the western edge of the Needles.) Deep beneath the surface, however, salt domes (and especially the lenses of less-soluble gypsum within them) appeared to be stable enough for long-term waste disposal.[1]

After the Salt Valley, Lisbon, and Elk Ridge sites were dropped owing to geologic problems and other issues, attention focused on Davis Canyon, a place that until then had attracted only a few hardy exploring parties in jeeps or on horseback. (Nearby Lavender Canyon was retained as a possible site for a second waste repository.) The headwaters of Davis Canyon had been added to Canyonlands National Park in 1971, its walls sheltering ancient habitation sites and fascinating rock art. Closer to its juncture with Lavender Canyon and Indian Creek, the canyon widened into a nearly level plain. Only the line of cliffs to the west, above which rose the remarkable pinnacle of South Sixshooter Peak, separated the proposed site from Canyonlands National Park.

Both the Salt Valley and Davis Canyon sites could appear rather bleak in the harsh light of summer, which may be why DOE's engineers did not realize how attached people were to such landscapes. But the sites' proximity to two of Utah's national parks guaranteed a chilly reception for the waste repository—especially outside San Juan and Grand Counties. As with the creation of Canyonlands National Park, conservationists and local business and political leaders would square off over the disposition of lands that each saw with very different eyes.

The scale of the proposed Davis Canyon waste repository was staggering. The planned aboveground facility would cover nearly three-quarters of a square mile, serving underground storage caverns that would extend beneath the park boundary. Crowning the facility would be a 265-foot-tall headframe used to lower waste casks and workers down separate shafts. Nine square miles of BLM land adjacent to the park would be placed off limits to

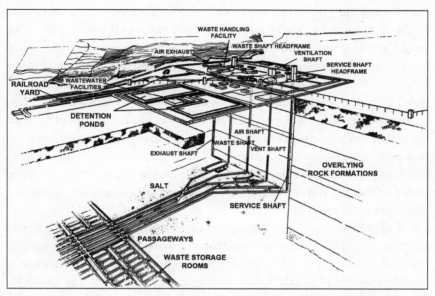

The Department of Energy's "Facility Concept" for the proposed nuclear waste repository in Davis Canyon gives an idea of its scale and complexity. Adapted from U.S. Department of Energy, Office of Civilian Radioactive Waste Management, *Environmental Assessment, Davis Canyon Site, Utah.*

public use and monitored with infrared sensors—all to provide, in DOE's words, "protection from radionuclide release."[2]

A fifty-three-mile-long rail line would run from the site to Potash on the Colorado River, one route traveling beneath the scenic Hatch Point and Harts Point cliffs, with an alternative route following higher ground to the east of Harts Draw. Railcars would deliver twenty-four shipments of radioactive fuel rods, encased in protective casks, to the repository site each week. These would return loaded with salt excavated from the underground burial caverns—some fourteen million tons in all, destined for disposal in distant underground salt mines. Trains on either route would be visible and audible for miles around. The facility would consume large quantities of natural gas for on-site power generation as well as huge amounts of water, which was one reason that Utah state officials, who almost without exception supported any new industrial project, grew concerned about the proposal.

The first sign that the waste dump could become a reality came on March 11, 1980, when DOE's contractor began drilling a 6,400-foot-deep borehole next to Indian Creek, beneath the cliffs of Harts Point. The test hole signaled the government's intention to proceed with detailed site characterization studies at the nearby Davis Canyon site, three miles to the southwest. This would have involved drilling nearly two hundred boreholes for stratigraphic and hydrologic sampling, not only in Davis Canyon but also along Indian Creek and below North Sixshooter Peak. Each drilling site (some with multiple boreholes) would require clearing up to a dozen acres of land, erecting a 130-foot-high drilling rig, and digging a waste pit. A network of seismic monitoring stations would be placed in the canyon, and workers would sink a 2,800-foot-deep exploratory shaft at the main repository site. Several hundred personnel would be working in the area at any one time, with the sound of drilling and the thumps from seismic testing echoing across the cliffs above Indian Creek.[3]

And this was merely the exploratory phase; if selected as the final repository site, some two thousand construction workers and their equipment would descend on lower Davis Canyon. Twelve hundred permanent staff would be needed to run the facility during its fifty-year operating life. DOE downplayed potential impacts on the park, claiming that air quality would not be affected over the long term, and noise or visual disturbance would be insignificant.[4] Cliffs would screen the dump from most park visitors, it noted, except for a brief view while driving down Indian Creek.

Canyonlands superintendent Pete Parry disagreed with DOE's assessment, saying that the repository "would change the whole experience for the southern end of the park [with] a railroad, a highway, and trains rattling around twenty-four hours a day." He told a reporter that "we've had a very difficult time getting DOE to acknowledge that there is a park there."[5] But DOE had a congressional mandate to find a suitable site, and it enjoyed the support of Interior Secretary James Watt, who allowed the agency to proceed without preparing a full environmental impact statement on the project. Taking to heart Watt's statement that "a nuclear waste dump will always be next to something," DOE insisted that geologic and technical considerations trumped such niceties as scenery or quiet.

Many business and political leaders in southeastern Utah welcomed the proposed waste repository, hoping it signaled a renewed industrial boom. The omnipresent Cal Black, who famously carried a lump of uranium ore in his shirt pocket, viewed the waste dump as nothing more than the back side of the uranium processing cycle. "There are risks in everything we do," he told one reporter. "I say there would be less people killed and injured if they put the repository here than in any other activity, including recreation and tourism."[6] Blanding mayor D. L. Gibbons agreed, saying that local citizens "do not share the irrational fears of atomic energy many uninformed people of the county shout about." Farther north, in Moab, bank president Irving Nightingale, chair of the Grand County Economic Development Commission, pointed to the county's 20 percent unemployment rate as reason to invite the massive new facility. Moab's Atlas uranium processing mill had closed in 1984, but Nightingale fondly recalled the boom days of the 1950s. "It was great back then," he said. "Without that waste repository, the town has got to go downhill."[7]

Some Moab tour operators and river running outfitters feared that the dump would transform the recreation-friendly image they were trying to build in Grand County. Bill Hedden and Bob Phillips formed a group called Utahns Against the Dump to defend what they saw as an attack on Canyonlands National Park. "The Canyonlands are as beautiful and wild in a way that is totally unique," Phillips said. "You can have all the logical information and all the studies you want. But unless you have the sensitivity of James Watt, this area will impress you."[8]

Choosing a site for a national nuclear waste repository was as much a political exercise as an environmental matter, and the governors of each of the involved states weighed in with their concerns. In March 1980, shortly after DOE began drilling its first borehole near Davis Canyon, Utah governor Scott Matheson announced the formation of a state Nuclear Waste Repository Task Force to keep tabs on the department's activities. Matheson stopped short of opposing the dump, insisting only that DOE conduct a thorough environmental study and that the state of Utah be given a voice in the matter. The governor's stance did not reassure waste dump opponents, nor were they satisfied with DOE's assurances, made at informational meetings held that September in Moab and Blanding, that it would take all necessary safety precautions at the Davis Canyon site. Particularly worrisome was how the siting study addressed only the direct effects on land, water, and air quality. Aesthetic factors such as noise, visual disturbance, and the presence of a massive industrial facility next to a national park were not germane to the discussion, DOE representatives said.

It took a concerted effort by park personnel and outside advocates to focus attention on the risk to Canyonlands itself. Moab activist Terri Martin, who worked as a field representative for the National Parks and Conservation Association, launched the "Don't Waste Utah" campaign, which brought attention to the issues posed by the waste repository. Martin organized letter-writing efforts and distributed postcards featuring a beautiful image of South Sixshooter Peak for supporters to mail to their political representatives. She took reporters to the waste dump site, noting their surprise when they learned that the area was not already part of Canyonlands. Leading one group farther up Davis Canyon to view thousand-year-old archaeological sites, Martin pointed out that the simple stone granaries of the ancient Puebloans represented state-of-the-art storage for that era. She suggested that people in the distant future would view our waste containment technology with similar incredulity.[9]

Martin's efforts drew support from national environmental organizations such as the Sierra Club and Friends of the Earth, helping to raise the profile of Canyonlands National Park in the public's eye. The opposition to the waste dump emboldened Governor Matheson to get off the fence. At a press conference in May 1984, he declared that the Davis Canyon site was "inherently unsuitable" and reminded listeners of the heavy price that Utah residents paid for nuclear weapons testing in Nevada during the 1950s.[10] Other Utah political figures were less adamant; Senator Jake Garn said that he would accept the Canyonlands site so long as the selection process gave equal scrutiny to candidate sites in other states, such as Nevada's Yucca Mountain.[11]

Scott Matheson decided not to run for a third term in 1984, but the issue remained in play during the gubernatorial campaign, with Democratic candidate Wayne Owens stating he was "flatly opposed" to siting a waste dump in Utah. Norm Bangerter, his Republican opponent, straddled the issue during the campaign, but after winning the election he took a stronger stance against the waste dump. "Parks are precious to everybody," he told the Salt Lake City Deseret News.[12]

Perhaps as a result of this relatively united opposition, DOE in late 1984 issued an environmental analysis that placed Davis Canyon in a second tier of possible repository locations, ranked below sites at Yucca Mountain, Nevada; Hanford, Washington; and Deaf Smith County, Texas. Neither the Yucca Mountain nor the Hanford site was a salt dome, however, which led critics to question their long-term safety.[13] Then, in September 1985, DOE announced that it was considering a revision of its selection criteria that would give greater emphasis to geologic stability—a move that could once again place Davis Canyon under consideration. Even the conservative *Deseret News* editorialized against the move, calling it a "travesty" that could damage tourism in southeastern Utah.[14]

After the state of Utah filed a lawsuit challenging the selection process, DOE slowly backed away from the Canyonlands site. In May 1986 it settled on the Nevada, Texas, and Washington sites for site characterization studies, to the relief of park advocates.[15] The following year Congress short-circuited the lengthy selection process by directing DOE to adopt Yucca Mountain as the repository site. By the end of 1987, the Park Service and its supporters could breathe a little easier about the fate of Davis Canyon and Canyonlands National Park. Nonetheless, Terri Martin and other advocates continued to put pressure on public officials to keep Davis Canyon out of DOE's crosshairs.

The nuclear waste issue—which has yet to be resolved satisfactorily, despite the selection of Yucca Mountain—demonstrated once more the need for a comprehensive, region-wide approach to federal planning in the Colorado Plateau. National parks continued to face challenges from outside their borders, though perhaps nothing as egregious as a nuclear waste dump. The National Park Service would continue to be a junior voice in the federal bureaucracy, outgunned by agencies such as the BLM that represented powerful client industries with clear designs on the nation's arid lands. Individual threats to park integrity from oil and gas leases, new coal mines, and other forms of resource extraction would continue to arise during the 1980s and 1990s, each bringing an alarmed response from the Park Service and its environmentalist allies. What was lacking was a comprehensive framework within the federal government for considering such actions in the context of a superb natural region such as the Colorado Plateau's canyon lands.

31

OUT OF THE BLUE:
A MONUMENT FOR THE BLM

Paving the western part of the Burr Trail brought the Circle Cliffs and southern Waterpocket Fold closer to civilization, yet the road resulted in only a modest increase in tourism in eastern Garfield County. With the Park Service refusing to allow more than minimal improvements within Capitol Reef National Park, and BLM lands on either side of the park still under wilderness study, the road remained a narrow passageway through a mostly wild landscape. The same was true of the country that stretched far to the west and south, across the intricate canyons of the Escalante River and the broad expanse of the Kaiparowits Plateau, clear to the Paria River drainage. It was here that the next major protective designation for Utah's canyon country would take place—thanks to the same law that set up the first national monuments in the Colorado Plateau.

President Bill Clinton's 1996 designation of the 1.7-million-acre Grand Staircase–Escalante National Monument further dampened hopes of major industrial development in eastern Garfield and Kane Counties. Those who still dreamed of a renewed mining boom in southern Utah refused to accept this sweeping land reserve—and in 2017, they succeeded in substantially reducing the size of the monument and splitting it into three units. Grand Staircase–Escalante is a prime case of the disparate visions of landscape protection and utilization in the Colorado Plateau.

President Clinton signed the proclamation creating Grand Staircase–Escalante on September 18, 1996, at a ceremony at the edge of the Grand Canyon, in neighboring Arizona. The location, miles distant from the lands in question, did not go unnoticed among Utah officials, who condemned both the "lockup" of resources within the new monument and the secrecy with which it was established. Governor Mike Leavitt said that the president acted "with almost unilateral power" in a breach of public trust. Senator Orrin Hatch called it "the mother of all land grabs. . . . There has been no consultation; no hearings; no town meetings; no TV or radio discussion shows; no input from federal land managers." In Kanab, townspeople held a rally at which many wore black armbands and released black balloons. Clinton "never walk[ed] on one square inch of the land he's designating," said state House speaker Mel Brown. But Salt Lake City legislator Mary Carlson compared the controversy to those who objected to the creation of Canyonlands National Park. "Many of those people now would admit they're better off because of the park," she said.[1]

Like the controversy that greeted Lyndon Johnson's monument proclamations of January 1969 and Franklin Roosevelt's designation of Jackson Hole National Monument in 1943, the creation of the Grand Staircase–Escalante monument was seen as an excessive widening of the Antiquities Act's scope. Utah congressman James Hansen introduced legislation to strip the president of the authority to designate national monuments greater than five thousand acres, while Senator Bob Bennett offered a bill that would require monument lands to be managed for "multiple use," including timber, minerals, and oil and gas development.[2] Neither bill passed, but neither did the resentment over Clinton's action abate.

Some environmental leaders and scholars asked whether in the interest of simple fairness, local interests ought to have been consulted before taking such a drastic step.[3] This remains a valid question. Until 1964, Utah's national parks and monuments were created under a largely consensual view of what these federal reservations ought to accomplish. By protecting unusual geologic features of great scenic beauty, they would encourage the building of roads—at Uncle Sam's expense—that would draw tourists to Utah and connect its isolated desert communities. (Cultural resources figured more prominently in designating national monuments in Arizona and New Mexico.) This consensus began to unravel in the 1930s with the Escalante national monument proposal and was further eroded by the designation of Canyonlands National Park in 1964 and President Johnson's expansion of Arches and Capitol Reef National Monuments in 1969. Grand Staircase–Escalante resurrected all of the old animosities that had simmered in Utah for more than half a century, but in a way that caught the state's political leaders (and many environmentalists) completely off guard.

Lower Calf Creek Falls, a popular destination for day hikers in Grand Staircase–Escalante National Monument. *Bob Wick/Bureau of Land Management.*

It was an underground resource, not a spectacular natural bridge or canyon, that gave impetus to the largest federal land withdrawal to date in the Colorado Plateau. In the early 1990s Andalex Resources, a company based in Delaware but owned by Scottish investors, filed applications to develop an underground coal mine in a remote location called Smoky Hollow on the Kaiparowits Plateau. Although the mine was projected to have a surface footprint of only forty acres, its proximity to five BLM wilderness study areas alarmed wilderness proponents in Utah. The coal would be hauled by truck to railheads at Cedar City, Utah, and Moapa, Nevada, raising concerns about traffic on U.S. Highway 89 and in small towns along the route. Environmentalists viewed Andalex's Smoky Hollow mine as a door opener for more industrial development on the Kaiparowits, bringing roads and infrastructure that would likely spur development of other coal leases on the plateau. Ken Rait of the Southern Utah Wilderness Alliance (SUWA) called it "the biggest single threat to southern Utah wilderness. We are watching the transformation of a spectacular wilderness to a zone of industrialization."[4]

The Andalex project appealed strongly to civic leaders in Kane and Garfield Counties, some of whom recalled the demise of the Kaiparowits

Power Project and had always hoped that a significant industrial project might appear on their horizon. They pointed out that the mine and associated facilities would employ up to six hundred people and bring $20 million into the state's school fund during its twenty-five-year lifetime. Utah State Land Board member Doug Bates said the project was "very carefully designed [and] would create minimal and temporary destruction in a very localized area, which would then be reclaimed."[5]

By 1995 the Andalex mine was on track for approval, despite SUWA intervening in the permitting process. Coal mines were overseen by state regulators, not the BLM, and Utah had always been friendly toward the industry. Nor were wilderness study areas likely to stop mines from dotting the Kaiparowits; the BLM had not recommended designation for any of the wilderness inventory units surrounding the Andalex site. These were, however, included in H.R. 1500, a massive BLM wilderness bill introduced in 1989 by Utah congressman Wayne Owens at the request of Utah conservationists. After Owens left office in 1993, the bill's sponsorship passed to New York congressman Maurice Hinchey, but its enactment continued to be a long shot—especially after the 1994 elections placed the Republican Party in control of both houses of Congress. Wilderness advocates looked to other means of forestalling the Andalex mine, including presidential action under the Antiquities Act. As in 1969, when Lyndon Johnson dramatically expanded Capitol Reef National Monument, the result would be total surprise, leading to furious antagonism.

In 1994 Utah environmental leaders toured the Andalex mine site and surrounding area with Kathleen McGinty, director of the president's Council on Environmental Quality (CEQ). It appears that at some point they discussed possible monument designation as a means of halting the project, although SUWA executive director Mike Matz told the *Salt Lake Tribune* that he was not consulted on the actual proposal and first learned of it when the *Washington Post* broke the story on September 7, 1996.[6]

Top Interior Department officials, including Secretary Bruce Babbitt, were closely involved in crafting the Grand Staircase proposal. Babbitt wanted the BLM to retain control of the new monument in order to give the agency a mandate to manage land for more than livestock and minerals. Strangely, Utah BLM officials were not consulted, unlike with most Park

Service designations, which either originated with or were carefully vetted by the agency. Instead, Babbitt assigned department solicitor John Leshy to craft a proposal for the Escalante-Kaiparowits region. Leshy recruited University of Colorado law professor Charles Wilkinson, who was familiar with the lands involved and had a particular interest in the Antiquities Act.[7]

Wilkinson drew up a monument proposal encompassing lands reaching from Capitol Reef National Park on the east to Johnson Canyon on the west, sharing a southern boundary with the Glen Canyon National Recreation Area. It spanned three distinct geologic and physiographic sections, the best known of which was the middle stretch of the Escalante River north of the Glen Canyon NRA. Anchoring the monument was the broad, heavily dissected upland of the Kaiparowits Plateau, while the western portion took in the stair-stepped cliffs and mesas of the upper Paria River—part of the larger geologic feature known as the Grand Staircase. The entire area was a showcase of exposed geology, revealed in such unusual formations as the Straight Cliffs, the Cockscomb, the White Cliffs, and the Burning Hills, where buried coal seams smoldered from long-ago lightning strikes.

Although the area contained well-known scenic features such as Grosvenor Arch, and the Escalante canyons were prime backpacking territory, vast parts of the monument lacked water and received little recreational use. The monument's purpose went well beyond recreation, as Wilkinson made clear in his draft of the proclamation. The first national monument to fall under BLM jurisdiction, Grand Staircase–Escalante was intended to preserve "exemplary opportunities for geologists, paleontologists, archeologists, historians, and biologists" as well as protect outstanding biotic and cultural features.[8] Scattered throughout the area were prehistoric sites that, while nowhere as spectacular as in Mesa Verde or Cedar Mesa, represented a significant record of early humans' adaptation to a harsh environment. The range of life zones in the new monument, coupled with its aridity and highly varied microclimates, gave rise to relict species that had persisted since the last ice age. Hidden within the area's Cretaceous strata were an unusual variety of fossils, including the bones of yet-unknown dinosaurs.

Wilkinson enumerated these features in order to demonstrate that the monument contained "objects of historic or scientific interest," as required by the Antiquities Act. (The 1906 act did not specifically include scenic and conservation purposes, even though previous national monuments such as Grand Canyon and Jackson Hole were established exactly for those reasons—and had stood up to legal challenges.)[9] Knowing there would be an outcry over the size of the monument, he also tried to show how it represented "the smallest area compatible with the proper care and management of the objects to be protected," as the act specified. His argument did not sway opponents, who insisted that the Antiquities Act should be limited to much smaller areas enclosing specific natural or archaeological features.

The Grand Staircase–Escalante proclamation honored existing grazing privileges and mineral rights, which left difficult issues for BLM managers to resolve. With support from the Clinton administration, the agency was able to exchange coal leases for others in less sensitive areas, forestalling the Andalex mine and others that might have been developed. But the monument also included eighty-five oil and gas leases covering 136,000 acres, as well as many sections of Utah state land that were not subject to the same protective measures. Oil companies wasted no time in asserting their rights to explore within the monument. Shortly after President Clinton established the monument, Conoco received approval from Utah regulators to drill an exploratory well on a lease it had recently acquired in a section of state land between Reese and Rogers Canyons, in a remote part of the Kaiparowits Plateau. The company owned fifty-eight federal mineral leases within the monument, and a spokesperson claimed the area could harbor "up to fifty giant exploration projects."[10] To environmentalists, the sudden interest in drilling looked like an attempt to obtain lucrative buyouts of otherwise marginal leases.[11] When Conoco's first well failed to find oil, the company abandoned further testing, making it possible to negotiate an exchange agreement that was ratified by law in October 1998.[12] Conoco worked for several years to reclaim the drill site—a tricky process in this arid region. It remains today as a partly revegetated clearing in the pinyon-juniper forest.

Ranchers in Kane and Garfield Counties also asserted their rights, pressing the BLM to increase livestock numbers in the monument. Efforts by the Grand Canyon Trust to buy livestock grazing rights in the Escalante River drainage on a willing-seller basis have met with resistance. Conservationists point out that monument designation did not lead to a decrease in permitted livestock grazing levels, but actual use by cattle has decreased. Whether this stems from onerous management restrictions (as the ranchers claim) or drought and the poor condition of the rangelands (as environmentalists argue) remains open to debate.[13]

At public ceremonies held in scenic places in the Desert Southwest, representatives of Indian nations are sometimes invited to offer an introductory prayer. Before Bill Clinton addressed the waiting crowd at the edge of the Grand Canyon in September 1996, several Hopi elders offered a blessing, saying "This is a time of healing. The healing must begin."[14] It may not have been clear to those listening whether this referred to healing the scars of overgrazing, strip-mining, and other marks of Euro-Americans' century-long occupancy of the southwestern landscape, or to bridging the equally deep divisions that existed between Native peoples and whites, or between southern Utah's ranchers and environmentalist backpackers. Perhaps the Hopi elders meant to include all of these in their prayer, but Clinton's bold declaration brought no appeasement of political and cultural differences among rural and urban Utahns.

Somewhat less controversy greeted Clinton's next proclamations in the region, the 1,048,325-acre Grand Canyon–Parashant National Monument and the 294,000-acre Vermilion Cliffs National Monument, both in northern Arizona. Designated in 2000, Grand Canyon–Parashant is jointly managed by the BLM and the National Park Service, while Vermilion Cliffs, designated the same year, is under BLM administration. Both monuments take in spectacular landforms, including long sections of cliff and plateau that bound vast, mostly arid uplands. Vermilion Cliffs includes the extremely popular photography destination called the Wave, and it is the site of a successful introduction of California condors. Objections were raised by Arizona state officials to both monuments, chiefly over what was termed a lack of consultation by the Interior Department, but there was nothing like the firestorm that greeted Grand Staircase–Escalante.[15]

Twenty years later, anger over President Clinton's lightning-bolt action still simmers in southern Utah. Garfield County officials blame the monument for limiting economic opportunity and in 2015 declared a "state of emergency" over declining school enrollments. Yet new businesses catering to outdoor adventurers and tourists on Highway 12 have found opportunity in towns such as Escalante and Boulder. Garfield and Kane Counties experienced continued population growth in the first twelve years of the monument's existence, according to Headwaters Economics, a proconservation consulting firm. Service jobs and personal income showed significant

increases, the latter reflecting the influence of nonlabor income from retir-
ees and newcomers who were drawn to the area's natural amenities, and who
brought investment income with them.[16] Mining jobs in the two counties held
steady from 1996 to 2008 at 0.6 percent of total employment, while agriculture maintained its 5 percent share. This did not suit the conservative leadership of either county, who maintained that service-sector jobs could not
support families—at least not the sizable ones that traditionally lived there.

All of these issues—the lost mining jobs, perceived restrictions on
grazing, resentment over the timing and secrecy of the monument proclamation—culminated in Grand Staircase–Escalante becoming one of two
national monuments targeted under President Donald Trump's 2016 order to
review all such monuments created since 1996. On December 4, 2017, acting
on the recommendation of Interior Secretary Ryan Zinke, Trump issued a
proclamation modifying the monument's original boundary to include three
separate and smaller units: Grand Staircase (209,993 acres), Kaiparowits
(551,034 acres), and Escalante Canyon (242,836 acres). The reduction in size
amounted to about 42 percent of the original 1.7-million-acre monument.

In 2018 the Bureau of Land Management began drafting a new management plan for the "Kanab-Escalante Planning Area," which includes all of
the original monument lands. When adopted, it will likely open at least some
of the former monument lands to mineral development and increased livestock grazing. While many political leaders in Utah applauded the changes,
environmental groups saw it as a major retreat from the region-wide protected landscape they had sought for decades. Some paleontologists feared
that resource development could mean the loss of irreplaceable fossils for
scientific study—a field for which the original national monument had
become renowned.[17]

For more than a century after Mormon ranchers turned their livestock
out onto the pinyon-covered benchlands of the Kaiparowits Plateau, this
isolated remnant of the western frontier has seesawed between differing
visions of what a frontier represented. To Clyde Kluckhohn, the Kaiparowits
was the pole of remoteness, the stuff of high adventure; to today's Earth scientists it serves up exciting evidence of a distant, prehuman past. To many
local residents this plateau, as well as the more conventionally scenic lands
in the Paria and Escalante River drainages, offers hope of well-paying jobs
in mining industries as well as limitless places to ride ATVs. There never
was much consensus as to what could be made of these lands, and political

actions from 1996 onward have vaporized what little agreement there was. In a state that treasures its national parks, it remains unclear whether large, landscape-scale designations such as the one President Clinton put in place in 1996 have a future.

32

MANAGING PARKS IN A
CROWDED WORLD

From the Great White Throne to Delicate Arch, from Timpanogos Cave to Rainbow Bridge, Utah's geologic wonders stand as emblems of all that its national parks offer. By the mid-1970s they had become popular vacation destinations: annual visitation to Zion National Park topped the million mark in 1975, with Arches and Capitol Reef drawing about one-fourth that number. Bryce Canyon logged a respectable 579,200 visitors during the 1975 season, while Canyonlands still lagged considerably at 71,700 visitors. The Glen Canyon National Recreation Area would prove as popular as Zion, drawing 1,108,800 visitors that year, principally as boaters on Lake Powell.[1] These were numbers that tourism promoters could bank on. Utah's national parks were showing they were equal to its ski industry in their ability to draw paying guests from out of state.

Park managers faced serious challenges in accommodating these visitors while at the same time protecting the parks' fragile cultural and geologic features. In an attempt to better manage auto traffic and visitor impact, the National Park Service proposed removing overnight visitor facilities from Zion and Bryce Canyon following the 1972 season. This opportunity arose when the Union Pacific Railroad, which had built the first guest facilities in these parks, donated its lodges and ancillary buildings to the Park Service at the end of the 1971 season. By then the age of railroad-based tourism to the national parks was nearly over, and the UP no longer wished to incur the heavy annual expenditures needed to keep these structures in good repair—especially the aging, 1920s-era Bryce Lodge. (The original Zion Lodge burned down in 1966 and had been replaced with a more modern building.)

TWA Services, a subsidiary of Trans World Airlines, successfully bid to operate the lodges in the interim, with their eventual closure written into the terms of the contract. The Park Service wanted Zion and Bryce Canyon to adopt the model in use at Arches and Canyonlands, where lodging and most other tourist facilities were in nearby towns. This would help to "reverse the trend toward urbanization of these parks," according to Phillip Iversen, director of the Park Service's information office in Salt Lake City.[2] NPS officials feared that Zion could become another Yosemite, with too many people crowding into a narrow canyon and business interests refusing to let go of obsolete facilities.

Removing accommodations from the parks would likely have increased economic opportunities in gateway towns such as Springdale, Cedar City, and Tropic, but many local residents had a sentimental attachment to the lodges, which had served visitors since the mid-1920s and offered summertime employment for young people. Opposition to their removal also came from Utah's congressional delegation, the state legislature, and the Utah Travel Council. Ultimately the Park Service allowed the lodges at Zion and Bryce Canyon to remain. The Union Pacific lodge at Cedar Breaks, the oldest in the state, closed in 1972 under the contract agreement.

Despite steadily increasing auto traffic to the parks, the Park Service did not contemplate any serious measures to limit the influx of tourists. A master plan devised for Zion National Park in 1976 called for using shuttle buses in the main canyon to alleviate summertime traffic congestion, but these did not come into use until 1997, after park use had more than doubled. The Zion shuttle, which was mandatory for all visitors except lodge guests, proved highly popular and dramatically reduced auto traffic on the upper canyon road. It was an expensive solution, however, consuming as much as three-fourths of the park's entrance fees.[3] The buses also had the paradoxical effect of increasing use on popular trails such as to Angels Landing, where parking formerly was limited.

Arches also experienced increasing traffic congestion during the 1970s and 1980s, but a shuttle bus system was considered too expensive to implement in the park, whose scenic features were more widely spread than in Zion Canyon. Instead the Park Service turned to structural solutions, including expanded parking lots at popular sites such as Delicate Arch and the Windows. Bryce Canyon inaugurated shuttle buses in 2000, but their use was not mandatory, and congestion at popular overlooks such as Inspiration Point continued to worsen.[4] Each round of improvements seemed only to encourage more use, leaving park administrators running an endless treadmill of further improvements to accommodate traffic. Rangers in the field had to deal with mounting traffic problems, congestion at popular sites, and millions of feet pounding trails into dust each season. In spite of the growing environmental consciousness in the nation, the national parks were simply too attractive to permit meaningful limits on use.

Zion, Bryce Canyon, and Arches lacked extensive backcountry road systems, but Utah's two wildest parks—Capitol Reef and Canyonlands—had hundreds of miles of dirt roads and former uranium mining tracks lacing through their remotest sections. In the early 1980s Capitol Reef considered paving the Notom Road, which followed the eastern escarpment of the Waterpocket Fold for dozens of miles, as well as creating a paved loop drive through the remote Cathedral Valley. The plan was dropped, to the relief of backcountry enthusiasts; funding for extensive road improvements was unlikely, and park administrators had more pressing priorities, such as building a new visitor center and enlarging the campground at Fruita.[5]

Paved parkways had been an option in Canyonlands ever since its first master plan was issued in 1966, but with the adoption of a new general management plan in 1978, only the Confluence road remained under consideration. Even this route faced stiff opposition from conservationists.[6] Nor were paved roads a high priority for devotees of mechanized recreation; for them, the harder the terrain, the better. In Salt Creek Canyon, jeep users had long enjoyed a twenty-four-mile long drive through a riparian area that led to numerous prehistoric rock art panels and habitation sites. The highlight of the route was Angel Arch, one of the park's most outstanding geologic features. Fully three-fourths of off-highway vehicle travel in the Needles district—an average of five hundred vehicles per month during the peak spring season—took place in this canyon.[7]

Environmental groups turned their attention to this route, pointing out the need to protect Salt Creek from erosion and contamination by vehicle fluids. This led the Park Service in 1995 to limit vehicle use in the canyon to twenty per day—well within the average monthly use. The Southern Utah Wilderness Alliance and National Parks and Conservation Association

Angel Arch in Salt Creek Canyon of the Needles district, Canyonlands National
Park. *National Park Service/Frank Moss Photograph Collection, Special Collections,
J. Willard Marriott Library, University of Utah.*

continued to litigate the issue, and after many years and court appearances
they succeeded in getting the upper part of the canyon permanently closed
to vehicles. Today it is a popular destination for backpackers.

In most of Canyonlands and Arches, though, the NPS hewed to a preservationist stance. Hiking and backpacking enjoyed wide popularity, and Canyonlands offered some of the most outstanding backcountry travel options
of any park in the Southwest. By 1973 the park would need to draft a plan
simply to manage backcountry use. It limited the number of river runners,
required backpackers and river runners to use designated campsites, and
otherwise regulated visitors in ways that would have seemed inconceivable
when the park was created. Driving off of established jeep roads was prohib-
ited, and Chesler Park was closed to vehicles. Private and commercial float
trips through Cataract Canyon were regulated by setting passenger limits
and implementing a permit reservation system.[8]

By 1984, with backcountry use increasing further, Canyonlands adopted a new plan that set limits on numbers of backpackers and required "leave no trace" practices for all parties, whether traveling by foot, jeep, or boat. Backpackers visiting heavily used areas of the park such as the Needles must now stay in designated campsites, although in more remote areas (primarily within the Maze and parts of Island in the Sky) they are free to camp where they wish—limited, of course by water availability. Reserving campsites spreads out use and preserves a measure of solitude, but even within open-camping zones, few backcountry users experience the exhilarating freedom that Kent Frost, Ed Abbey, and Bates Wilson enjoyed in previous decades. Rules now govern the wilderness; a degree of regimentation is the trade-off for preserving the resource.

Despite occasional conflicts between jeep users and backpackers, Canyonlands offered an alternative to windshield tourism, preserving a more adventurous, close-to-the-land experience. Utah's least visited national park would not become a drive-through experience for restless Americans on their way to the next park. Its roads would dead-end at the edge of a wilder landscape, where primitive tracks and trails would entice tourists to lock their car doors and let the real adventure begin.

Concern for limiting roads and infrastructure development in the national parks also reflected a growing awareness that their ecological health was as important as their touristic value. Ecological research had lost its early foothold within the Park Service in 1940, when George M. Wright's biological division was transferred out of the agency. Park managers were left largely on their own to deal with wildlife issues, whether managing bears in Yellowstone or controlling feral burros in Grand Canyon. Then, in 1963, a commission chaired by the noted zoologist A. Starker Leopold issued a report calling for a renewed emphasis on biological research and ecological management within the agency, arguing specifically against predator control and hunting within the parks. These concerns were amplified in the 1980s when new research in the field of island biogeography led to the realization that many parks and monuments were too small to ensure the survival of their historical fauna. It had long been known that Yellowstone's great elk herds depended on winter habitat outside the park, but a 1987 study by ecologist

William Newmark indicated that the problem was much more widespread. After studying forty-two cases of mammals that had been extirpated from fourteen North American national parks, Newmark concluded that "all but the largest western North American national parks are too small to retain an intact mammalian fauna."[9] He noted that Bryce Canyon was no longer home to red fox, pronghorn, and beaver, among other species. The chief culprit was alteration of habitats on adjoining public lands, which were open to hunting, livestock grazing, logging, and road construction. The Newmark study provided yet another demonstration of how Utah's national parks and monuments could not be managed in isolation from their surrounding lands.

In some cases park managers have attempted to reintroduce species missing since the early 1900s, notably desert bighorn sheep, which were reintroduced to Zion National Park in 1973. Additional sheep were translocated from herds in the Island in the Sky district of Canyonlands to the Maze district in 1985, as well as to Arches National Park. Capitol Reef received similar translocations in the mid-1980s and again in the mid-1990s.[10] Herds in the Glen Canyon National Recreation Area, which had long been in decline, were also supplemented. The project was successful by and large, especially in Zion, where the animals now number about five hundred. Bighorns in the Needles district of Canyonlands have suffered ongoing losses from disease, however. These elusive wild sheep can thrive only where they are isolated from domestic sheep, which carry a respiratory disease fatal to the bighorn.

Visitors who arrive at Zion's eastern tunnel portal can often spy these nimble animals on the surrounding slopes. Less often do they see the park's top predator, the cougar, which numbers around two dozen or fewer. Cougars prey chiefly on deer, and their absence from the heavily used main canyon has allowed deer herds to increase. Deer abundance, in turn, has meant fewer young cottonwoods growing along the North Fork of the Virgin River, leading to higher rates of stream-bank erosion and a decline in native fish populations. In contrast, researchers found that the wild, unroaded drainage of North Creek supports stable populations of both deer and cougars, leading to a much more diverse flora and fauna.[11]

Concern for wildlife in our national parks must also take into account the changing climate, which is shifting suitable habitats to higher and cooler locations. In Zion National Park, for example, the number of days experiencing temperatures of one hundred degrees or higher nearly doubled during the period 2001–2010, when compared to the previous eighty years.[12] This could affect species that may not be able to adapt to hotter summers, such as the pika, a lagomorph that lives in higher-elevation talus fields. This species has not been seen in Zion National Park in the last nine years.

At the same time, however, protected federal lands may provide critical migration corridors for species that are able to follow shifting conditions. The "connectivity" of protected landscapes is crucial to climate resilience; researchers have identified the complex of protected park lands reaching from Canyonlands and Capitol Reef National Parks south through the Glen Canyon National Recreation Area and Grand Staircase–Escalante National Monument as being of high importance for migrating species.[13] Attempts to introduce heavy industry and motorized recreation into these landscapes, as proposed for Grand Staircase–Escalante and surrounding BLM lands, will be problematic for maintaining this connectivity.

Ensuring natural conditions in the parks requires a constant balancing of visitor needs with ecological requirements. The National Park Service has taken the lead among federal agencies in promoting the maintenance of natural values, from restoring a full complement of predators in some parks (as with the reintroduction of wolves to Yellowstone), to calling attention to less glamorous values such as natural quiet and dark skies. Here, too, as with wildlife habitat, size matters: small parks such as Arches and Zion are influenced by lighting from nearby towns such as Moab and Springdale, and noise from oil and gas operations on adjacent BLM lands can be intrusive in Hovenweep National Monument. Even Bryce Canyon, which has some of the darkest skies in the country and hosts a popular astronomy festival each June, is experiencing increased nighttime glow from the burgeoning urban centers of Utah's Dixie region. Park officials also fear that the planned expansion of a small coal strip mine near Alton, twelve miles southwest of the park, could further compromise its dark skies and natural quiet.

Today, as the federal government offers up BLM lands in the Colorado Plateau for wholesale mineral development, and off-road vehicle users make wide use of these lands for mechanized recreation, national parks and monuments will assume increasing importance as refuges for humans seeking a quieter and closer experience of nature. Yet with popularity come new challenges for the National Park Service, which faces severe budgetary constraints even as use of the parks continues to grow. Reconciling human uses with the capabilities of the land will require a broader view than our customary focus on individual parks—or on the individual human desire to recreate as we please.

33

PROMOTING USE—AND
UNDERSTANDING

When Reuben and Minnie Syrett opened their rustic "Tourists' Rest" lodge at the edge of what was then called Bryce's Canyon, their guests had to navigate poor roads and risk frequent breakdowns just to reach the little-known wonderland on the Paunsaugunt Plateau. By the end of the twentieth century, tourists arriving by car at Bryce Canyon National Park faced a different challenge: finding a place to park. With one parking space available for every four cars entering Bryce on a typical summer day, it was no easy task to get to the visitor center or enjoy the view at Inspiration Point. A park news release in June 2000 stated that "much of the magic of Bryce Canyon is lost as visitors spend time waiting in lines to enter parking lots or fighting traffic in congested areas."[1]

More than a million visitors came to Bryce Canyon that year—a number the Syretts could not have imagined in the 1920s. Many arrived on one of the five thousand tour buses that wheeled into the park, disgorging passengers at overlooks and onto trails that were not designed to handle large numbers of people.[2] Officials hoped that those arriving by car would take advantage of the park's new shuttle bus system, which served Ruby's Inn as well as most of the popular viewpoints along the rim. Its use was not mandatory, however, and most visitors continued to prefer the flexibility of their own vehicles. By 2014, with visitation to the park reaching 1.4 million, administrators were considering a variety of options for reducing congestion, including an expanded shuttle system, bicycle and walking trails leading into the park, and traffic alerts to encourage visitation at off-peak times.[3]

All of the great landscape parks of the West experience heavy use during peak seasons, but southern Utah's mild spring and fall weather bring crowds to gateway towns such as Moab and Springdale from February through

Visitors to Arches National Park enjoy a sunset at Delicate Arch. Popular sites such as this are rarely without a crowd during spring, summer, and fall. *Neal Herbert/ National Park Service.*

November. Utah's four-day school holiday in October is especially popular; in 2015 the Park Service advised visitors to Arches National Park to expect "heavy traffic, crowded trails, and limited parking." Even Canyonlands National Park, usually a quiet place, saw long lines at the Island in the Sky entrance station as many tourists bypassed the crowds at Arches.[4]

Zion National Park, with its milder climate, receives heavy use nearly all year long. Its facilities were designed to serve perhaps a million visitors annually, not the four million it receives today. The long season of use makes it difficult to meet personnel needs with seasonal park staff, which are limited to six-month appointments. Yearlong congestion allows little opportunity to repair roads and maintain facilities. The park's vaunted shuttle bus system is also strained beyond capacity. In 2016, a record year for park attendance, superintendent Jeff Bradybaugh noted that "we are beginning to lose some of the values people are often seeking in the park . . . including quiet, solitude, and an escape from crowding."[5]

Well-known attractions such as the Emerald Pools in Zion, Mesa Arch in Canyonlands, and Delicate Arch and Double O Arch in Arches routinely find dozens of people packed into limited spaces. The concentration of visitors leads to shortcutting and social trails, which damage vegetation and erode desert soils. At many sites human waste and toilet paper are concealed behind rocks and bushes; at Angels Landing in Zion National Park, the Park Service uses helicopters to service a portable toilet. Rangers assigned to traffic control have less time to patrol trails and educate visitors about low-impact practices. Wildlife, too, suffers stress from constant human presence or becomes habituated to proffered snacks.

Burgeoning use also affects the quality of the visitor's experience. Beginning in the 1990s, Arches National Park attempted to quantify social crowding under the rubric of "carrying capacity," a concept long used by ecologists to describe the ability of ecosystems to provide useful habitat under conditions of population increase. Utilizing a research tool called Visitor Experience and Resource Protection (VERP), park managers identified zones of heavier or lighter human use in Arches according to social and physical measures, including the number of social trails, how many people one might encounter on a trail, the number of vehicles on backcountry roads, and the level of damage to soil and vegetation. Researchers took photographs of Delicate Arch with various numbers of visitors present and then showed them to hikers returning from the arch. Their responses suggested that most visitors would tolerate from twelve to thirty people at one time sharing their view of the arch. Some, of course, preferred to be alone, but that is rarely possible today.[6]

Arches was the first national park to employ the VERP program, but it proved to be difficult to implement. One outcome was a 2006 proposal for a shuttle bus system—something that had been considered as far back as 1989 in the park's general management plan—but this was rejected due to its cost.[7] Parking lots were expanded and roadside pulloffs were marked with striping and boulders, but these were stopgap measures in the face of steadily increasing visitation. The VERP program was also explored in other national parks, notably Yosemite, with similar results.[8]

By 2015, park managers were considering a timed-entry system for Arches in which visitors would be allotted a three-hour window to get into the park. This approach would allow visitors to "have a better experience where they didn't have to fight to drive in and fight to find a place to park," according to park superintendent Kate Cannon. She expected that the new system, if adopted, would permit the park to accommodate an additional 40 percent more visitors.[9] The reaction among some Moab business owners to such a system has been decidedly negative. One motel owner told a *High Country News* reporter that tourists "are just going to have to accept that it's not going to be a pristine experience. People need to drive in, take their pictures, leave some money, and drive away." But Cannon says her primary concern is for the quality of the visitor's experience. "How many people can be here and still enjoy the values that the park was established to provide?" she asks.[10]

Zion National Park is also considering a timed-entry system or even a lottery to limit the number of people within Zion Canyon at any one time. Limits on the number of people making the popular hike to Angels Landing or descending the Narrows of the Virgin River are also under consideration. These approaches are major departures for an agency that for the past century has emphasized getting people into the parks and providing them with things to do once they are there. The Park Service has long maintained that it could accommodate large numbers of visitors in "hardened" front-country sites served by paved roads, leaving backcountry areas in the larger parks undeveloped. Without visitor facilities, a park would be "merely a wilderness," agency leaders noted in 1922, "not serving the purpose for which it was set aside, not benefitting the general public."[11] What was true for the park visitor then now appears to have reversed, with solitude the rare, sought-after quality.

While the Park Service has long recognized that crowds detract from most visitors' experience, it also recognizes that demographics are changing and that national parks must develop a constituency among younger people, urban dwellers, people of color, and the less economically advantaged. Visitors among these diverse populations may have different expectations of what is an appropriate "park experience." Seeing nature in the company of others can add to visitors' social experience, according to former Park Service director Jonathan Jarvis, who observed that people still enjoy Zion's River Walk trail despite its heavy use. "The next century of the National Park Service is going to be about [how] we engage the next generation in taking care of the parks," he said in 2016, the service's centennial year.[12]

Writer Lauren McCrady, a member of the millennial generation, observes that her first experience of Arches National Park came "on a group hike to

Delicate Arch, not on a lone ramble." She "slept in a chain motel, ate breakfast at a trendy café, watched a short film on cryptobiotic soil at the visitor's center, and bought a bright orange Moab sweatshirt.... [I] do not feel that my experience or affection are somehow diminished by these dubious beginnings."[13]

If the Park Service hoped that its visitor studies would help it get a handle on crowding in the parks, it saw the goal recede further after the Utah Office of Tourism launched a major advertising campaign in 2014 featuring the state's national parks. Dubbed the "Mighty 5," Utah's parks were offered up "as a single, bucket list entity . . . on par with life adventures like the Inca Trail, the Amazon, the Pyramids and the Grand Canyon," according to the advertising firm engaged for the campaign.[14] The program was wildly successful, with visitation to Utah's national parks and monuments growing by 17.5 percent in the campaign's first year and 12.7 percent in 2015. (Bryce Canyon saw a jump in use of more than 20 percent.)[15] With additional publicity from the Park Service's centennial in 2016, visitation set new records, with more than four million people entering Zion National Park that year.

Utah's advertising campaign accomplished what tourism promoters had been trying for a century to achieve: to turn the national parks of the Four Corners states into a "golden circle" of popular vacation destinations. This dream originated with Fisher S. Harris's See America First campaign, but he could not have imagined the modern-day "branding" of Utah's national parks as lifetime adventure destinations. This is profitable territory for what is now the state's largest export industry. Visitors to Utah's national parks and monuments spent more than $1.1 billion in 2016 for lodging, gasoline, meals, guide services, and other expenses, according to the National Park Service, supporting nearly eighteen thousand jobs and $547 million in labor income within the state. The impact was even greater in southern Utah, where one-third to one-half of all private-sector jobs in Kane, Garfield, and Wayne Counties depend on tourism.[16] The yearlong stream of visitors brought significant income and tax revenues to gateway towns, with Moab receiving a million dollars in tax revenue from hotel stays in 2017.[17] But park traffic added to the congestion in this already booming adventure-sports destination. Residents of Springdale likewise see their small town virtually taken over by tourists from February through October. Traffic entering Zion National Park sometimes backs up into town, making it a challenge to cross its main street, and town residents must compete with tourists for parking spaces.

In 2016 the Utah Office of Tourism revised its marketing strategy to emphasize attractions found along the travel routes to the state's five national parks, but most out-of-state visitors still wind up in Arches, Bryce Canyon, or Zion. Photogenic beyond compare, Utah's flagship parks will continue to hold an irresistible mystique, stoked by tourist bureaus, chambers of commerce, and guidebook writers. Adventure blogs and social media will spread word of "secret" places to compete with Delicate Arch, Inspiration Point, and the Great White Throne. Park administrators and harried rangers will struggle to keep up with the crush, finding what time they can to educate visitors on how to behave once they're there. Somewhere away from these throngs may be found the remnants of solitude and unpeopled vistas for which Utah's national parks were once known.

Stephen Mather understood the need for an informed constituency for the national parks if they were to withstand continual pressure to develop them for commercial purposes. Today, with the parks' integrity at stake from development outside their borders as well as from the sheer number of visitors, the need for such a constituency is even greater. The Park Service's interpretive programs, which range from visitor center displays to campfire talks and guided trail hikes, are essential to help visitors understand these issues and the value of the parks themselves. Interpretation has historically received less funding than the agency's infrastructure and recreation programs, and administrators are sometimes reluctant to allow rangers to venture into controversial topics such as power plant haze and climate change. But as Freeman Tilden observed in his influential 1957 book *Interpreting Our Heritage,* such programs should provoke visitors as well as educate and entertain them.[18] In his day, that meant a lecture on not leaving litter or dropping lighted cigarettes, whereas today's interpretive rangers point out how hikers' footsteps can destroy unseen microfilaments in cryptobiotic soil, how mountain lions regulate whole ecosystems through predation, or how light pollution can affect the behavior of migrating birds. All are important facets of the park experience today.

Bringing up these issues in park literature and at campfire talks challenges visitors to move beyond conventional notions of scenic beauty and try to comprehend their place as humans in a dynamic but threatened ecosphere. As William Tweed, a thirty-year Park Service veteran from California, observed in 2010, "In a culture that accepts accelerating human consumption of the earth as a necessity and where the natural world means less and less to each succeeding generation, national parks remain the best place to share the knowledge that will allow us to sustain biodiversity on this planet."[19] They can serve this role only if they protect a full complement of native flora and fauna, including endangered and declining species whose existence may not carry obvious benefits for humans. As Utah author and legal scholar Robert Keiter notes, national parks are "vital cores of much larger ecosystems" and should anchor "landscape-level planning efforts."[20]

Wider public understanding of the ecological importance of desert environments will be critical if land managers are to confront abuses such as unrestrained off-road vehicle use, coal-fired power plant haze, blowing dust from heavily grazed rangelands, and diversions of water from oversubscribed rivers. Fostering such awareness will be a top challenge for administrators and field personnel in the Park Service's next century, for only a concerned and informed public can keep our parks whole.

34

SACRED LAND, DIVIDED NATIONS

Eighty years after the Interior Department unveiled the Escalante national monument proposal to skeptical Utah officials, another major land designation in southeastern Utah would prove just as controversial. On December 28, 2016, President Barack Obama set aside 1.35 million acres of federal public domain in San Juan County as Bears Ears National Monument, covering a huge swath of plateau and canyon lands stretching from the San Juan River to the Hatch Point cliffs near Moab.[1] Although not as sweeping as the Escalante proposal of 1936, Bears Ears completed an important piece of the land protection network that conservationists had long sought in southern Utah.

It was also to be the shortest-lived national monument in the nation's history, at least in its original form. On December 4, 2017, President Donald Trump signed a proclamation reducing the size of Bears Ears National Monument by 1,150,860 acres, leaving the remaining 201,876 acres split between two units: one along Indian Creek east of Canyonlands National Park, and another on the eastern edge of Cedar Mesa. He also split up the twenty-one-year-old Grand Staircase–Escalante National Monument, leaving three smaller units centering on the Escalante canyons, the Kaiparowits Plateau, and the upper Paria River.[2]

The president's actions, which were immediately contested in court by Native American and environmental groups, followed a six-month Interior Department review of all national monuments designated since 1996. Despite the more than 1.4 million responses that flooded Interior's online comment page—the vast majority of which opposed any shrinkage of existing monuments—Interior Secretary Ryan Zinke chose the two Utah monuments as the first—and so far, the only—units to be dismantled. He told

Puebloan habitation or storage structure in a part of the original Bears Ears National Monument. *Photo by author.*

the *Salt Lake Tribune* that the rescission "really is about multiple use and multiple use is grazing, timber management, recreation, being able to use in some places four-wheel drives."[3] Opening lands to potential uranium and coal mining also appears to have played a strong role in reducing the size of the two monuments.[4]

The old animosities that derailed the Escalante proposal in the 1930s and limited the size of Canyonlands National Park in 1964 surfaced once again in this latest Utah land protection effort. Shortly after President Obama issued his Bears Ears proclamation, Utah senators Orrin Hatch and Mike Lee reintroduced legislation to strip the president of the power to declare national monuments without the approval of Congress and the affected states. Hatch said the Antiquities Act was intended to give presidents only "limited authority to designate special landmarks, such as a unique natural arch or the site of old cliff dwellings."[5] Several members of Utah's congressional delegation introduced legislation to ratify the new monument boundaries and have vowed to limit funding for them.[6] The result could be thousands of new visitors coming to see national monuments that lack the staff to protect the very resources they were meant to safeguard.

Unlike the Park Service–initiated Escalante and Canyonlands proposals, Bears Ears was advanced by a grassroots coalition of Native American tribes—Navajo, Hopi, Uintah and Ouray Ute, Ute Mountain Ute, and Zuni—some of whose members had long made use of Cedar Mesa and surrounding lands for subsistence and ceremonial purposes. "Our ancestors variously inhabited, crossed, hunted, gathered, prayed, and built civilizations on these lands," according to the Bears Ears Inter-Tribal Coalition, which submitted its proposal for a 1.9-million-acre national monument to President Obama in October 2015. "Their presence is manifested in migration routes, ancient roads, great houses, villages, granaries, hogans, wikiups, sweat lodges, corrals, petroglyphs and pictographs, tipi rings, and shade houses."[7]

It was in this region that some of the final armed conflicts of the Anglo occupation of Native American lands occurred, including the so-called Posey War of 1923, in which a posse of Blanding residents rounded up and imprisoned forty Utes, including women and children, in retaliation for two tribal members raiding a sheep camp. Days of sporadic fighting led to the death of Posey, a Paiute who had married into a Ute family and was believed to have instigated the raids.[8] This was the culmination of decades of conflict between Anglo settlers and Native people in southeastern Utah, who by the late 1880s were mostly forced off the lands they had used for centuries and onto their respective reservations. Cedar Mesa, however, remained for them a strong memory and a place of pilgrimage.

The Bears Ears Inter-Tribal Coalition was organized in 2015 following five years of unsuccessful attempts by the Navajo Nation to negotiate with federal, county, and state officials over land protection goals in and around Cedar Mesa. Discussions centered on Representative Rob Bishop's Public Lands Initiative (PLI), an attempt to forge an agreement between county officials and user groups over wilderness designations and other land uses in six eastern Utah counties. The PLI called for a mix of resource uses and wilderness designations, but conservationists opposed provisions that would have given the counties a virtual veto over federal resource decisions as well as granting legal rights-of-way to numerous backcountry routes and emphasizing grazing and energy production in many areas.

Dissatisfied with Bishop's approach, tribal coalition members met with representatives of Utah environmental groups, including the Friends of Cedar

Mesa, Southern Utah Wilderness Alliance, and Grand Canyon Trust, to come up with a joint proposal for a 1.9-million-acre national monument.[9] It included lands of long-standing interest to conservationists, such as Lockhart Basin adjoining Canyonlands National Park, the White Canyon drainage below Natural Bridges National Monument, and Mancos Mesa next to the Glen Canyon National Recreation Area.

Unique to the Bears Ears monument was a provision that promised Native Americans a significant role in its management. A standing commission consisting of representatives of the five tribes was to make recommendations to the Interior and Agriculture Departments, which in turn were required to "carefully and fully consider integrating the traditional and historical knowledge and special expertise of the Commission," according to the monument proclamation. President Trump's December 2017 proclamation placed a representative of the San Juan County Commission on the Bears Ears Commission, renaming it "Shash Jáa" after the Navajo name for the Bears Ears.[10] Tribal coalition members objected, saying the name broke with the spirit of intertribal unity they sought to promote.

The original Bears Ears proposal received a boost in July 2016 when Interior Secretary Sally Jewell toured the area and met with supporters and opponents of the proposal. Afterward she recommended that its boundaries be pared from 1.9 to 1.35 million acres, leaving out lands on the periphery thought to be suitable for oil, gas, and uranium development, or where livestock grazing predominated. This became the basis for President Obama's proclamation of December 2016. It specified that traditional, noncommercial uses of the area by members of the five tribes, including plant and herb collecting and firewood gathering, would continue. Valid rights for grazing, minerals, water and other uses would be respected, but new mineral claims and energy leases would not be allowed. Vehicles would be limited to designated roads and trails, and protection of cultural and archaeological resources would take precedence over other uses, including recreation. State and private lands within the monument's perimeter, which amounted to 8 percent of its total area, were specifically excluded from the monument.[11] It was a bold application of the Antiquities Act and was certain to antagonize many residents of San Juan County who feared it would bring additional regulation of resource uses and vehicle access.

In establishing Utah's first national parks and monuments, the National Park Service looked almost exclusively at recreational and scenic values. The Bears Ears Inter-Tribal Coalition advanced its proposal for much broader reasons. Even "antiquities," as commonly understood, do not capture the essential meaning of this landscape for many Native Americans. To them, the monument's cultural resources comprise not just interesting "ruins" and rock art, but living sites carrying sacred meanings for their daily lives. According to Jim Enote, director of the A:shiwi A:wan Museum and Heritage Center in Zuni, New Mexico, the Cedar Mesa area "is a place many Native peoples in the Four Corners area continue to define as home, soul, and the setting for the cultivation of cultures."[12]

Presiding over these lands are the twin buttes known as the Bears Ears, so named by Navajos who used the area beginning in the seventeenth century (calling them Shash Jaa') and by Spanish explorers who arrived not long after (Las Orejas del Oso).[13] Other tribes gave these summits the same name in their own languages, so striking is their resemblance to a bear's rounded ears. The animal has spiritual significance to Native Americans who use the area, including the Ute Mountain Utes, who hold their Bear Dance each spring on their nearby reservation. To the Navajos, the Bears Ears stand as guardians of their ancestral homeland.[14]

Mormon settlers arriving in southeastern Utah in the 1880s attached their own meanings to these lands, which provided them with forage and water for their livestock and wood for their fences and homes. Their persistence in the face of floods, drought, and competition from Texas and Colorado cattle interests is among the remarkable sagas of the western frontier. No individual better exemplified these traits than J. A. Scorup, who with his brother James set up a small cattle operation in White Canyon in 1891. The Scorups, as historian Gary Topping observed, learned that the way to succeed was to "push your cattle into country so rough that nobody else can handle it, live with the cattle in the canyons and become as tough as they are, and wait for the competition to go broke."[15]

This history of moving into and establishing cattle ranches, farms, and homesteads in San Juan County, dating to the Hole-in-the-Rock expedition of 1879–80, informs the views of many of its residents today. As Bruce Adams, a rancher and San Juan County commissioner, observed at a Senate field hearing on the proposed monument, "When you are raised in a family that depends on cattle grazing, it becomes part of your soul and fiber. You live and breathe the cattle business. You raise your children to love the land and take care of it so that it will take care of you."[16]

Adams and his fellow county commissioners firmly rejected the national monument proposal. With the support of Governor Gary Herbert and the Utah congressional delegation, they lobbied the president-elect to undo the monument once he was in office. According to the *Deseret News*, Senator Orrin Hatch met with President Trump five days after the inauguration and obtained his promise to return the monument lands to state control, although they were in federal ownership. Trump announced his monument review three months later.[17]

The BLM acted quickly to revise its management plans for both Bears Ears and Grand Staircase–Escalante, despite the ongoing legal challenge to the monument rescissions. It has offered oil and gas leases on lands released from the Bears Ears National Monument, including Alkali Ridge east of Blanding, an area rich in prehistoric cultural artifacts that was first studied by Byron Cummings of the University of Utah in 1908. The sale was protested by the group Friends of Cedar Mesa, whose director, Josh Ewing, fears that wellheads, pipelines, and access roads could destroy many smaller, less visible cultural sites that are important to understanding the context of prehistoric life in the area. Ewing stated that such sites "might be subtle above the ground," but they "could be destroyed by a bulldozer on the way to a drill pad."[18]

The BLM has also proposed opening nearly all the lands removed from Grand Staircase–Escalante to mining claim location and mineral leasing. It did not take long for mining companies to respond: in June 2018 Glacier Lake Resources, a Canadian firm, acquired a group of mining claims underneath Colt Mesa in the Circle Cliffs area, touting its potential for cobalt, copper, and other minerals.[19] The lands involved were part of a massive $50 million exchange of state school trust lands that was ratified by Congress in 1998 for the express purpose of preventing such disturbance within the national monument.

The tribal leaders supporting the Bears Ears National Monument saw it as a way to not only protect their traditional uses but also address long-standing rifts between Anglo and Native communities. "Healing forms the inner core of our Bears Ears movement," said Regina Lopez-Whiteskunk, a Ute Mountain Ute council member who served on the Bears Ears Inter-Tribal Coalition. Mary Benally of Utah Diné Bikéyah said that "all we're asking is respect our culture, respect nature, and be sensitive to it. It's not just for the Native Americans, it's not just for the Navajo, it's for everybody to enjoy the beauty that's there."[20]

Willie Grayeyes, chair of Utah Diné Bikéyah at the time of the proposal and since elected to the San Juan County Commission, also stressed the theme of healing. "What we are seeking to do with the Bears Ears National Monument is to stabilize our community and to bring the youth back to the reality of the natural world. We want to teach them how to utilize these resources in a way that not only benefits them in their pockets, but spiritually." Hopi anthropologist Lyle Balenquah stressed that national monument designation is not only for the "protection of archaeological sites from wanton vandalism or . . . for solely scientific purposes. It's about the protection of indigenous cultures so that we retain our ability to pass on our traditional knowledge to future generations."[21]

A divergent view of the monument was expressed by Rebecca Benally, a Navajo tribal member who served on the San Juan County Commission, in a 2016 commentary in the Monticello *San Juan Record.* She feared that monument lands "will ultimately be controlled by bureaucrats unfamiliar with our history and traditional ways." She cited a record of "repeated broken promises of trust responsibilities and broken treaties, again and again and again for the last 200 years." Benally pointed specifically to Wupatki National Monument, which was designated in 1924. "After generations of herding sheep in the area, Navajo were told by NPS that environmental group concerns took priority over their access to lands their families had managed since the 1870s," she said.[22] Bears Ears would not be managed by the National Park Service, but her concern that tribal members' historical uses would be usurped mirrors similar distrust of federal management by many Euro-American residents of San Juan County.

Jim Stiles, a newspaper publisher formerly from Moab, pointed out that monument designation would draw many more visitors to Cedar Mesa, making it harder to protect antiquities. He feared a repeat of the "tourism nightmare" he had witnessed in Moab, in which thousands of recreationists crowded into the town during nine months of the year, and that the monument's antiquities could become one more commodity to be "packaged and sold" to a public eager for adventure.[23] This is a serious concern, for even appreciative visitors to ancient habitation sites can unknowingly trample middens and damage masonry walls. As in most national parks, increasing human use will require more visitor regulation and monitoring, which itself can change the mysterious attraction of these sites. Funding for ranger patrols is often the first to go during budget crunches, but close monitoring of visitors will be crucial to the success of any new national monument in the Cedar Mesa region.

These disparate views indicate how difficult it will be to reconcile conflicting uses of public lands in southeastern Utah, whether for mass tourism, oil and gas development, livestock grazing, wildland protection, or off-road vehicle use—not to mention the preservation of antiquities, which may be the most problematic of all. It also illustrates a limitation of the Antiquities Act itself, which sets a high standard of protection but does not specify the means by which it is to be obtained. Granting the president authority to designate monuments also means that subsequent officeholders can undo such actions, as President Trump did in 2017.

One possible avenue toward settling land-use conflicts rests with the Wilderness Act, which prohibits many forms of resource development on public lands. In March 2019 President Trump signed major new legislation that, among other things, established 661,000 acres of new BLM wilderness in Emery County, Utah, including the western part of Desolation and Labyrinth Canyons on the Green River and significant parts of the San Rafael Swell. This legislation grew out of decades-long efforts by conservationists and Emery County officials to negotiate land uses across this broad region, a process that until very recently appeared not to be leading anywhere. It is by far the largest congressional land designation in the Utah canyon lands to date, dwarfing even Canyonlands National Park, and it secures a high level of protection for many landscapes of long interest to hikers, river runners, archaeologists, and botanists. Livestock grazing is a permitted use in wilderness areas, while off-road vehicle enthusiasts will continue to have access to the newly designated 217,000-acre San Rafael Swell Recreation Area.[24]

This legislation, which was constrained to the boundaries of Emery County, fell short of a comprehensive, regional approach to planning and management of federal lands in southeastern Utah. Another instance of negotiation between so-called stakeholders in the region was the BLM's recent initiative to develop a master mineral leasing plan for the public lands surrounding Arches and Canyonlands National Parks. This plan, which was finalized in December 2016, arose out of the ongoing conflicts over oil and gas development on the outskirts of these parks. Spearheaded by the National Parks Conservation Association (NPCA), the process brought together conservationists and Moab-area business interests to help identify areas containing important scenic, recreational, and cultural resources that should remain off limits to mineral leasing. The plan would have permitted mineral leasing on hundreds of thousands of acres in Grand and San Juan Counties under stipulations designed to protect these resources, but the Interior Department under Ryan Zinke, responding to concerns from the oil and gas industry over what it termed redundant planning, moved quickly to rescind it. Similar plans in the works elsewhere in Utah and Colorado were also halted. This will likely mean a return to land-use decisions made in isolation and can only spell further conflict in the years ahead.

The original Bears Ears and Grand Staircase National Monuments represented an opportunity to restore damaged landscapes, enforce the preservation of antiquities, and educate visitors about the meaning of these lands to science, history, and present-day cultures. The diminished monuments of today continue the past approach of fragmented and spotty protection of important public resources. A different approach would examine the canyon country region on a broad scale, looking for common purposes that might help to heal old divisions. This would require all parties to take a hard look at how we have historically treated the land and its longtime inhabitants, and then chart new directions that encompass the entire range of values we seek in our public lands. Such a process, though largely untried, offers perhaps the best hope that Utah's national parks and monuments will remain as living examples of the magnificence of Earth's creation.

CODA: A LAND OF WONDER

It's a perfect evening in early May at Natural Bridges National Monument, 6,500 feet high on southeastern Utah's Cedar Mesa. As the day's warmth fades under a cloudless sky, a park ranger wheels a large reflecting telescope onto the patio of the visitor center, where I've joined a dozen other tourists. Before uncapping the telescope, he invites us to imagine how the indigenous peoples of Cedar Mesa might have regarded the night sky a thousand years ago. In this arid climate, scanning the heavens would have been an almost nightly affair, and evidence from their rock art and ceremonial sites indicates the importance they placed on celestial events.

As the sky darkens and the Milky Way rises over the Bears Ears, an even fainter illumination appears above the western horizon. It is the zodiacal light, the result of sunlight reflecting off small particles in the inner orbits of the planets. We are seeing the glow of extraterrestrial dust left over from the original cloud that coalesced into Mercury, Venus, and Earth. The former inhabitants of Cedar Mesa certainly witnessed this sight, although they would have interpreted it differently. Even though no telescope is needed to see this subtle display, few people are able to today. We tourists could enjoy it only because the light of our cities has not encroached into this part of the Colorado Plateau.

Today a splendid night sky is considered an amenity—something to enjoy when visiting a national park or national forest. But the absence of human-generated light generally signifies other important values as well, including pristine air and deep quiet (the ubiquitous jet airliners passing overhead being an exception). That night in camp, I listened to an owl call from across the canyon, and toward dawn a coyote chorus came from somewhere farther off. These creatures pursue livelihoods that evolved among natural sounds and the diurnal cycle of light and dark. The products of industry and our well-lit consumer lifestyle are increasingly disruptive of such ancient patterns.

A recent study by the group Conservation Science Partners indicates that the lands that surround Natural Bridges, including the original Bears Ears National Monument, represent some of the most diverse and ecologically connected landscapes in the Lower 48 states.[1] Such values cannot be contained in reservations the size of Natural Bridges. Its 7,600 acres may safeguard the sandstone spans for which it is named, but not the clean air, the dark night sky, or the encompassing silence that entranced Henry Culmer and Byron Cummings when they first set eyes on the White Canyon bridges in the early 1900s. Such qualities make a visit to these places memorable today—especially when one ventures out after dark.

Few people today question the importance of large national parks such as Yellowstone and Grand Canyon, yet much more recent landscape reservations such as Bears Ears and Grand Staircase–Escalante have been and will continue to be strongly contested. The value of such landscapes may not be apparent to those who expect spectacular geologic wonders such as those found in most national parks. But if one takes a walk through any of the canyons, forests, or shrublands that make up these areas, one can observe ancient lithic scatters, pockets of relatively intact native vegetation, and the burrows, nests, and tracks of an astonishing variety of small mammals, birds, and insects. Away from machines and road noise, traveling at the speed that humans have for millennia, one hears lizards skittering in the leaves and canyon wrens calling from beneath the cliffs. Then, as night falls, come the sounds of other creatures that live under an arching canopy of stars and stardust.

To designate a national park or monument is far from the end of the story, as I have tried to show in these pages. With record numbers of visitors coming to southern Utah's park lands, the management of these areas assumes critical importance—and we are no closer today to solving the conundrum of recreational use in natural landscapes than in Horace Albright's time, when rangers welcomed a few hundred visitors into Zion and Bryce Canyon on a busy day. Today no part of canyon country remains an undiscovered hinterland; Ed Abbey's "back of beyond" has been transformed into

Gateway to Adventure, a quasi theme park whose red cliffs and rushing rivers are marketed worldwide and appear in countless social media. What this means for the remaining landscapes where solitude and stillness prevail will be worked out during the next few decades—either by vanquishing the last quiet places with our noise and our numbers, or by finding some way to hold on to such qualities.

The one factor that most easily compromises solitude, antiquities, and biotic integrity is vehicle access. The simplest way to reduce human impact in sensitive areas, whether from illegal pothunting or simply too many pounding feet, is to close off more of the hundreds of miles of old uranium and oil exploration tracks that lace through much of Grand Staircase, Bears Ears, and Canyonlands. This never sits well with those who assume that "access" requires a motor vehicle, but in the prewar era people managed to make good use of these lands for ranching and recreation without ATVs, dirt bikes, and jeeps. I see nothing sacred in pistons and tires, and for those who cannot face the rigors of the desert there are wonderful front-country trails, many of them suitable for the aged and infirm, as well as numerous drive-in campsites in and near our national parks and monuments.

Rules and regulations are a necessary feature of park management in the modern age. Yet we cannot rely on the Park Service to protect Utah's national parks and monuments in the absence of commonsense visitor behavior. With budgets starved by Congress and personnel rosters shrunk through executive fiat, park rangers and staff in the Southwest are overwhelmed by the ever-growing influx of tourists, many of whom visit for a day and move on. Rangers understandably despair of educating visitors who are always in a hurry. Nor is today's emphasis on high-adrenaline adventure conducive to learning about the natural environment.

Over the years, the National Park Service has addressed these issues in various studies and reports, but its recommendations tend to be undercut by more pressing budget needs. Does anyone remember the Vail Agenda of 1992, which called for a renewed commitment to ecological management, scientific research, and visitor education?[2] No statement of principles, however worthy, is going to solve our parks' problems unless their administrators, informed by scientific inquiry and cultural awareness, are given a free hand and enough money to do their job. They must be guided by a landscape-wide vision that places ecological health above immediate human desires and that pays close attention to what is happening on public and private lands outside the region's national parks and monuments. Finally, national parks and monuments should be dedicated to learning and discovery, not to pushing up numbers. Let visitors to Zion, Arches, Hovenweep, Cedar Breaks, or Capitol Reef be intellectually stimulated—let them find their sense of wonder aroused, their thoughts provoked—and new park advocates may emerge.

Visitors who take the time to learn about their national parks and monuments are more likely to demand that they be managed professionally, without undue deference to concessionaires, advertisers, tour promoters, or anyone else who stands to benefit from increased visitation. Education must take place on an individual level, encouraging each of us to develop what Utah writer Julia Corbett calls "the humility, knowledge, and understanding to really know the land."[3] Utah's park lands offer far more than scenery and adventure. They can enrich our knowledge of the Earth's biota and geology, connect us to our past, and help us discern a way into an uncertain future.

In 1912, four years before the National Park Service was created, a prescient visitor to the United States warned that setting aside a few choice reservations among the West's scenic landscapes was not going to be enough—not at the rate that America was growing. James Bryce, the British ambassador to the United States, traveled widely in the American West and visited many of its national parks. In a speech to the American Planning and Civic Association, he noted that "the world is circumscribed and we feel the narrowness of it more and more as all its corners are explored and surveyed." America's supply of natural beauty was vast, he said, but it was nonetheless limited. When it came to "the beauties of nature," Bryce warned, "you have not any more than you need."[4]

Our need for wild nature has not diminished since Lord Bryce's day. To experience the Colorado Plateau on its own terms is what brought adventurers such as Henry Culmer, Byron Cummings, T. Mitchell Prudden, and Clyde Kluckhohn to the Utah desert when most of it was still unknown. It's what drew soulful, poetic explorers like Dave Rust, Ward Roylance, Katie Lee, and Ken Sleight to return again and again to the great overlooks and winding rivers of the Plateau Province. It was devotion to the land that spurred June Viavant, Ruth Frear, and Jack McLellan to devote years of effort to safeguarding the Escalante wilderness from an intrusive tourist highway, and Terri Martin and Bill Lockhart to work just as hard to forestall a nuclear waste dump from sprawling across the eastern edge of Canyonlands. The wild, sweeping vistas of canyon country also drew far-seeing government officials like Roger Toll, Jesse Nusbaum, and Stewart Udall to Utah, where they attempted to cast a wide net of official protection around the most amazing landscape they had ever witnessed.

These women and men understood the intrinsic value of national parks and monuments. In Lord Bryce's day, this was often expressed as a sense of wonder, a term we might do well to employ once again. To see the deeper beauty surrounding Utah's geological marvels requires that we cultivate an awareness of what Ward Roylance, a longtime exponent of this region, called "the ineffable ... beyond expression, even comprehension."[5] This sense may be difficult to account for in the hard-nosed world of land politics, but I would wager that many visitors to Utah's national park lands are looking for it.

In the end, our obligation is to care for these lands in ways that will lead those who follow us to praise our foresightedness. The national parks that sufficed a century ago are now stretched beyond their limits. Somehow as a society we will have to come to grips with the dominant philosophy of limitless growth, unrestrained power, and easy access. To fail to do so will abandon the highest purposes of our national parks and monuments. If we do not halt the transformation of southern Utah's canyons and plateaus into an industrialized and overtouristed landscape, their quietude, expansiveness, and mystery will vanish. We will see a steady diminishment of the land's biotic richness, of which we still know so little. Saddest of all, there will remain no part of the land that we do not control and supervise, where to walk quietly is to know humility.

We can instead embrace the values inherent in the wild lands of the Colorado Plateau. As many before us have shown, our national parks, national monuments, and adjacent public lands show us the innermost workings of the Earth and its myriad life-forms. As refuges from our noise, lights, and eternal hurry, these lands can be monuments to our foresight, not our folly. We owe this to ourselves as well as to those who follow us. Our efforts will be repaid in knowledge, beauty, mystery, and wonder.

NOTES

PREFACE

1. C. Gregory Crampton, *Standing Up Country: The Canyon Lands of Utah and Arizona* (Kaysville, UT: Gibbs Smith, 1983), 12.
2. For a list of the National Park Service units within the Colorado Plateau Province, see "Colorado Plateaus Province," National Park Service, https://www.nps.gov/articles/coloradoplateaus.htm. The Utah canyon lands, or "canyon country" as it is often called, is a subset of the Colorado Plateau Province and is generally thought to begin at the Book Cliffs and extend south and west to Lees Ferry, taking in a broad swath of terrain surrounding the Green, Colorado, and San Juan Rivers. Zion and Bryce Canyon NPs lie in the High Plateaus section of the Colorado Plateau Province, while Dinosaur NM is at the edge of the Uinta Basin section. Timpanogos Cave NM lies in the Wasatch Range and is not part of the Colorado Plateau Province.

INTRODUCTION

1. The 1916 law that created the National Park Service laid out its duty: "To conserve the scenery and the natural and historic objects and the wild life therein and to provide for the enjoyment of the same in such manner and by such means as will leave them unimpaired for the enjoyment of future generations." What this means for management of the national parks has been vigorously debated over the years; see, for example, Robin W. Winks, "The National Park Service Act of 1916: 'A Contradictory Mandate?,'" *George Wright Forum* 24 (2007): 6–21, www.npshistory.com/publications/winks.htm.
2. John Ise, *Our National Park Policy: A Critical History* (Baltimore: Johns Hopkins Press, for Resources for the Future, Inc., 1961), 1.
3. See Alfred Runte, *National Parks: The American Experience*, 4th ed. (New York: Taylor Trade, 2010).
4. The Kolob section of Zion National Park was first designated as a national monument in 1937 by Franklin Roosevelt. It was merged with Zion in 1956. For details of the national monuments created in Utah, see "Antiquities Act, 1906–2006," Archeology Program, National Park Service, https://www.nps.gov/archeology/sites/antiquities/monumentslist.htm.

CHAPTER 1

1. "Diary of Charles H. Dimmock," in Steven K. Madsen, *Exploring Desert Stone: John N. Macomb's 1859 Expedition to the Canyonlands of the Colorado* (Logan: Utah State University Press, 2010), 159.
2. Madsen, *Exploring Desert Stone.* Their camp on August 21 was in the tributary of present-day Hatch Wash.
3. Madsen, 150. According to F. A. Barnes, a Moab author who retraced the route of the Macomb expedition, Dimmock's party descended today's Harts Draw into the basin of Indian Creek, following the latter onward toward the Colorado River. F. A. Barnes, *The 1859 Macomb Expedition into Utah Territory* (Moab, UT: Canyon Country Publications, 2003), 85.
4. "Topographic Memoir of Charles H. Dimmock," in Madsen, *Exploring Desert Stone*, 203.
5. Had Dimmock and his companions been able to descend Indian Creek Canyon to the Colorado River, they would have found themselves some eight miles (as the raven soars) from the river's confluence with the Green. At the time, the Colorado above its confluence with the Green was known as the Grand River. At the state of Colorado's behest, Congress in 1921 changed it to the name we know today. Although the Grand was the shorter of the two tributaries, it contributed the larger flow.
6. "Diary of Charles H. Dimmock," in Madsen, *Exploring Desert Stone*, 160–61.
7. "Journal of J. S. Newberry," in Madsen, *Exploring Desert Stone*, 75.
8. Madsen, *Exploring Desert Stone*, xvi.
9. Madsen, 75.
10. Paul T. Nelson, *Wrecks of Human Ambition: A History of Utah's Canyon Country to 1936* (Salt Lake City: University of Utah Press, 2014), 2–3.
11. Nelson, *Wrecks of Human Ambition*, 91.
12. Madsen, *Exploring Desert Stone*, 65.
13. Robert S. McPherson, *Comb Ridge and Its People: The Ethnohistory of a Rock* (Logan: Utah State University Press, 2009), 87.
14. J. W. Powell, *Exploration of the Colorado River of the West and Its Tributaries: Explored in 1869, 1870, 1871, and 1872 under the Direction of the Secretary of the Smithsonian Institution* (Washington, D.C.: Government Printing Office, 1875), 57–59.
15. Wallace Stegner, *Beyond the Hundredth Meridian: John Wesley Powell and the Second Opening of the West* (Lincoln: University of Nebraska Press, 1953), 146.
16. Stegner, *Beyond the Hundredth Meridian*, 56–58. Smithsonian Butte and the West Temple (as it is known today) stand out to travelers passing through the towns of Virgin and Rockville on their way to Zion National Park. For many years local residents called the latter the Steamboat.
17. Stephen J. Pyne, *How the Canyon Became Grand: A Short History* (New York: Viking, 1998), 53.

18. Martha C. Knack, "From the Beginning," in Nathan N. Waite and Reid L. Neilson, eds., *A Zion Canyon Reader* (Salt Lake City: University of Utah Press, 2014), 46–47.

CHAPTER 2

1. James H. Knipmeyer, *Cass Hite: The Life of an Old Prospector* (Salt Lake City: University of Utah Press, 2016), 79–86. The 1883 party continued on to prospect in the Henry Mountains, but Hite, who preferred placer mining, soon returned to the warmer banks of the Colorado.
2. Crampton, *Standing Up Country,* 152. Other accounts of the discovery place Hite in the company of two fellow prospectors or a Paiute Indian guide. Historian Gary Topping believes that Hite and Hoskaninni encountered the bridges during their initial visit in the fall of 1883. Gary Topping, *Glen Canyon and the San Juan County* (Moscow: University of Idaho Press, 1997), 121.
3. Crampton, *Standing Up Country,* 138.
4. J. Wiley Redd, "History of the Natural Bridges," folder 48, series 2631, Natural Bridges National Monument files.
5. W. W. Dyar, "The Colossal Bridges of Utah: A Recent Discovery of Natural Wonders," *Century Illustrated* 68 (August 1904): 505–11. Dyar's article included drawings of the arches taken from Long's photographs.
6. "Will Spy Out the New Land," *Salt Lake Tribune,* March 30, 1905.
7. "Exploration of the Wilds of Southeastern Utah," *Deseret News* (Salt Lake City, UT), April 1, 1905.
8. H. L. A. Culmer, "Country of Natural Bridges," *Technical World Magazine,* September 1908, 52.
9. Excerpts from Culmer's journal are from Charlie R. Steen, "The Natural Bridges of White Canyon: A Diary of H. L. A. Culmer, 1905," *Utah Historical Quarterly* 40 (Winter 1972): 55–87.
10. "Wonders of San Juan County," *Ogden* (UT) *Standard,* May 3, 1905.
11. Edwin F. Holmes, "The Great Natural Bridges of Utah," *National Geographic* 18 (March 1907): 204.
12. Culmer's paintings of the Augusta and Caroline bridges are reproduced in Donna L. Poulton and Vern G. Swanson, *Painters of Utah's Canyons and Deserts* (Kaysville, UT: Gibbs Smith, 2009), 168–71.
13. Crampton, *Standing Up Country,* 153.

CHAPTER 3

1. Burl Armstrong, "Variety of Scenic Wonders in Southeastern Utah," *Inter-Mountain Republican* (Salt Lake City, UT), August 4, 1907. The Geological Survey published topographic maps of the lower San Juan region in 1884, but these were "of little practical use" to travelers, according to USGS geologist Herbert E. Gregory. Herbert E. Gregory, *The San Juan Country: A Geographic and Geologic Reconnaissance of Southeastern Utah.* U.S. Geological

Survey Professional Paper 188 (Washington, D.C.: Government Printing Office, 1938), 5.

2. Byron Cummings, "Describes Famous Region of the Cliff Dwellers," *Salt Lake Herald*, August 4, 1907. In 2006 Natural Bridges National Monument was designated an International Dark Sky Park in recognition of its superb night-sky conditions.

3. Cummings called for protecting the White Canyon bridges even before visiting them in the summer of 1907 ("National Park Southern Utah," *Salt Lake Tribune*, January 17, 1907). Newspaper reports at the time often did not distinguish between national parks (which require an act of Congress) and national monuments (which are designated by presidential proclamation under the Antiquities Act of 1906).

4. The names were suggested by Walter Hough, curator of ethnology at the Smithsonian Institution in Washington, D.C. Don D. Fowler, *Glen Canyon Country: A Personal Memoir* (Salt Lake City: University of Utah Press, 2011), 121.

5. "Natural Bridge Takes Attention," *Inter-Mountain Republican*, April 1, 1909, 8.

6. Francis P. McManamon, "The Antiquities Act and How Theodore Roosevelt Shaped It," *George Wright Forum* 31 (2014): 329.

7. Marietta Wetherill, *Life with the Navajos in Chaco Canyon* (Albuquerque: University of New Mexico Press, 1992), 41–42.

8. Fred M. Blackburn, *The Wetherills: Friends of Mesa Verde* (Durango, CO: Durango Herald Small Press, 2006), 38.

9. Duane A. Smith, *Mesa Verde National Park: Shadows of the Centuries* (Boulder: University Press of Colorado, 2002), chap. 3, https://www.nps.gov /parkhistory/online_books/smith/index.htm.

10. "Cummings Describes Natural Wonders and Scientific Treasures of San Juan Region," *Salt Lake Herald*, November 1, 1908.

11. Hal K. Rothman, "Ruins, Reputations, and Regulation: Byron Cummings, William B. Douglass, John Wetherill, and the Summer of 1909," *Journal of the Southwest* 35 (1993): 318–40. See also "The Cedar Mesa Project: Historical Expeditions into Southeastern Utah," Boulder Community Network, http:// bcn.boulder.co.us/environment/cacv/cacvexpd.htm.

12. David Harmon, Francis P. McManamon, and Dwight T. Pitcaithley, "The Antiquities Act: The First Hundred Years of a Landmark Law," *George Wright Forum* 23 (2006): 12.

13. See "American Antiquities Act of 1906," National Park Service, U.S. Department of the Interior, https://www.nps.gov/history/local-law/anti1906.htm.

14. Montezuma Castle and El Morro National Monuments in Arizona and Gila Cliff Dwellings National Monument in New Mexico were each 160 acres in size, although Petrified Forest National Monument, also in Arizona, included 25,625 acres.

CHAPTER 4

1. Archaeologists have located prehistoric occupation sites dating as old as seven thousand years within a dozen miles of Rainbow Bridge. In 1994 a stone hearth beneath the bridge was tentatively dated to 540 ad. David Kent Sproul, *A Bridge between Cultures: An Administrative History of Rainbow Bridge National Monument,* Cultural Resources Selections No. 18 (Denver: National Park Service, Intermountain Region, 2001), chap. 2, https://www.nps.gov/rabr/learn/historyculture/upload/RABR_adhi.pdf.
2. Sproul, *Bridge between Cultures,* chap. 4.
3. Harold Carey Jr. "Rainbow Bridge—Tsé'naa Na'ní'áhí," Navajo People Culture and History, January 21, 2013, http://navajopeople.org/blog/rainbow-bridge-utah-tsenaa-naniahi/.
4. Kevin Luckert, *Navajo Mountain and Rainbow Bridge Religion* (Flagstaff: Museum of Northern Arizona, 1977), 5; Sproul, *Bridge between Cultures,* chap. 1.
5. J. Donald Hughes and Jim Swan, "How Much of the Earth Is Sacred Space?," *Environmental Review* 10 (Winter 1986): 248.
6. Robert S. McPherson, *Navajo Land, Navajo Culture: The Utah Experience in the Twentieth Century* (Norman: University of Oklahoma Press, 2001), 135.
7. Crampton, *Standing Up Country,* 121–24.
8. Stephen C. Jett, "The Great 'Race' to 'Discover' Rainbow Natural Bridge in 1909," *Kiva* 58 (1992), https://www.nps.gov/rabr/learn/historyculture/upload/Stephen%20Jett%20Article.pdf. McPherson *(Navajo Land, Navajo Culture,* 124*)* terms "credible" the claim of a miner named W. F. Williams to have seen the bridge in 1884. See also Sproul, *Bridge between Cultures,* chap. 2.
9. According to Stephen Jett ("Great 'Race'"), Louisa Wetherill may have heard about Rainbow Bridge as early as 1907 from a Navajo named Sharkie. Jett also conjectures that John Wetherill made it to the bridge in 1908, but with an eye to his guiding business, he told no one. See also Cummings Publication Council, *The Discovery of Rainbow Bridge, the Natural Bridges of Utah, and the Discovery of Betatakin,* Bulletin No. 1 (Tucson, AZ: The Council, [1959]).
10. Rothman, "Ruins, Reputations, and Regulation." Three years later, following a better survey of the area, the monument was reduced to 160 acres.
11. Cummings Publication Council, *Discovery of Rainbow Bridge.*
12. Jett, "Great 'Race.'"
13. Byron Cummings, "The Great Natural Bridges of Utah," *National Geographic* 21 (February 1910). William Douglass may have been the first to apply the name Nonnezoshi to the bridge, believing it to be Nasja Begay's term, but on his map of the bridge he labeled it "barahoine," a Paiute word he presumably got from Mike's Boy (Sproul, *Bridge between Cultures,* chap. 3).
14. Rainbow Bridge is currently held to be the fifth largest natural bridge in the world, with Fairy Bridge in China's Guangxi region the largest. David Brandt-Erichsen and Jay Wilbur, "A Tour of the Big 19," The Natural Arch and Bridge Society, http://www.naturalarches.org/big9.htm.

15. "Rainbow Bridge to Be Preserved," *Salt Lake Herald*, June 3, 1910.

16. Theodore Roosevelt, *A Book Lover's Holiday in the Open* (New York: Charles Scribner's Sons, 1916), 31–32.

17. Zane Grey, *The Rainbow Trail: A Romance* (New York: Grosset and Dunlap, 1915), 335.

18. Charles L. Bernheimer, *Rainbow Bridge: Circling Navajo Mountain and Explorations in the "Bad Lands" of Southern Utah and Northern Arizona* (Garden City, NY: Doubleday, Page, 1924), 109–10.

CHAPTER 5

1. Thomas J. Harvey, *Rainbow Bridge to Monument Valley: Making the Modern Old West* (Norman: University of Oklahoma Press, 2011), 59–60.

2. T. Mitchell Prudden, *On the Great American Plateau: Wanderings among Canyons and Buttes, in the Land of the Cliff-Dweller, and the Indian of To-day* (New York: G. P. Putnam's, 1907), 3.

3. Samuel Joseph Schmieding, "Visions of a Sculptured Paradise: The Colorado Plateau as American Sacred Space" (PhD diss., Arizona State University, 2002), 407–8.

4. Prudden, *On the Great American Plateau*, 3.

5. Prudden, 54.

6. Jedediah S. Rogers, *Roads in the Wilderness: Conflict in Canyon Country* (Salt Lake City: University of Utah Press, 2013), 17.

7. Topping, *Glen Canyon*, 231.

8. Beatrice Scheer Smith, "The 1872 Diary and Plant Collections of Ellen Powell Thompson," *Utah Historical Quarterly* 62 (Spring 1994): 104–31.

9. Alice Eastwood, "General Notes of a Trip through Southeastern Utah," *Zoe 3 (1892)*. See also James M. Aton and Robert S. McPherson, *River Flowing from the Sunrise: An Environmental History of the Lower San Juan* (Logan: Utah State University Press, 2000), 51–53.

10. Eastwood, "General Notes," 358. Interestingly, Alice Eastwood became a good friend of geologist G. K. Gilbert, whom she married in 1918. They were looking forward to returning to Utah when Gilbert died suddenly. Stephen J. Pyne, *Grove Karl Gilbert: A Great Engine of Research* (Austin: University of Texas Press, 1980), 262–63.

11. Eastwood, "General Notes," 356.

12. For more on these researchers' ecological studies in the Utah canyon lands, see chapter 17. Ecological issues were mostly absent from the debate over creating Utah's national parks, even Canyonlands in the 1960s. Concern for preserving natural habitats in national parks was focused on other regions such as Alaska, Yellowstone, and the High Sierra, where Park Service botanists and biologists raised ecology to the level of policy. See James A. Pritchard, "The Meaning of Nature: Wilderness, Wildlife, and Ecological Values in the National Parks," *George Wright Forum* 19 (2002).

13. Topping, *Glen Canyon*, 209–26.

14. Herbert E. Gregory and Robert C. Moore, *The Kaiparowits Region: A Geographic and Geologic Reconnaissance of Parts of Utah and Arizona,* U.S. Geological Survey Professional Paper 164 (Washington, D.C.: Government Printing Office, 1931), 12.

15. Gregory and Moore, *Kaiparowits Region,* 4.

16. Ibid., 13.

17. Ibid., 30–32.

18. Ibid., 35.

19. Pyne, *How the Canyon Became Grand,* 53.

CHAPTER 6

1. Nancy C. Crawford and Merwin G. Fairbanks, *A Pioneer History of Zion Canyon to 1947* (Spanish Fork, UT: J-Mart Publishing, 1972), 3; A. M. Woodbury, "History of Zion" [1926], box 6, folder 6–8, Angus Woodbury Collection, MLSC.

2. Brigham Young's retort was recalled by O. D. Gifford, an early canyon resident, as related by Crawford and Fairbanks (*Pioneer History of Zion Canyon,* 3). The use of tobacco was not permitted among members of the Church of Jesus Christ of Latter-day Saints. Behunin, according to historian Angus Woodbury, had witnessed the Mormon exodus from Missouri and Illinois and regarded the canyon as a potential place of refuge should persecution of the Mormons resume. Angus M. Woodbury, *A History of Southern Utah and Its National Parks* (Salt Lake City: Utah Historical Society, 1950), 157.

3. See, for example, Henry Louis Dodge's 1926 article "All Aboard for Zion," which was reprinted in 1927 by the Union Pacific Railway as a promotional brochure. Dodge quoted an unnamed person as telling him, "Go there [to Zion NP] for the spiritual influence of it. If you are threatened with . . . atheism, go there."

4. Sara Black observes that "Zion went from a place both groups [Paiute Indians and Mormon settlers] interacted with on a subsistence level to one that was commoditized into an aesthetic spectacle." Sara Black, "Homeland, Homestead, and Haven: The Changing Perspectives of Zion National Park, 1700–1930" (PhD diss., University of Nevada, Las Vegas, 2016), 11.

5. Ronald L. Holt, *Beneath These Red Cliffs: An Ethnohistory of the Utah Paiutes* (Logan: Utah State University Press, 2006), 3.

6. Richard W. Stoffle et al., *Ethnographic Overview and Assessment: Zion National Park, Utah, and Pipe Spring National Monument, Arizona* (Denver, CO: National Park Service, 1997; revised 2013), 77–78. One Paiute informant for this study said that they did not fear the canyon, but rather the Mormon settlers who lived at its mouth. She noted that "we didn't go there (Zion Canyon) often, because the plants belong to the spirits."

7. Don D. Fowler and Catherine S. Fowler, "The Ethnography of the Canyon Country," in *John Wesley Powell and the Anthropology of the Canyon Country,* ed. Don D. Fowler, Robert C. Euler, and Catherine S. Fowler, U.S. Geological

Survey Professional Paper 670 (Washington, D.C.: Government Printing Office, 1969), 20–22.

8. According to Ronald Holt (*Beneath These Red Cliffs*, 26), some of the Southern Paiutes sold their children to Mormon settlers rather than see them starve. Brigham Young encouraged this practice, saying it would give the children a chance for a better (and more Christian) life.

9. J. W. Powell, *Exploration of the Colorado River*, 111. Powell, for unknown reasons, reported the year of this exploration as 1870.

10. John W. Van Cott, *Utah Place Names: A Comprehensive Guide* (Salt Lake City: University of Utah Press, 1990).

11. Gaell Lindstrom, "Thomas Moran in Utah," Sixty-Eighth Honor Lecture, Utah State University, November 29, 1983, 3–5, https://digitalcommons.usu.edu/honor_lectures/. Moran's quotation is from "Thos. Moran on Utah Scenery, *Salt Lake Tribune*, June 9, 1900.

12. "The Colorado Cañon," *New York Times*, September 4, 1873.

13. Lambourne's visits to Zion are recounted in the Mormon youth magazine *Improvement Era* ("The Mu-Kun-Tu-Weap," April 1911, 528–32) and the Salt Lake Herald ("On Scenery," December 25, 1889). Poulton and Swanson (*Painters of Utah's Canyons and Deserts*, 38) place Lambourne in Zion Canyon in 1870, again with Savage.

14. Deborah Reeder, "The Art of Zion: A Stunning Visual History," in *A Century of Sanctuary: The Art of Zion National Park*, ed. Lyman Hafen (Springdale, UT: Zion Natural History Association, 2008), 21–33.

15. Clarence E. Dutton, *Tertiary History of the Grand Cañon District, with Atlas*, Monographs of the U.S. Geological Survey (Washington, D.C.: Government Printing Office, 1882), 36.

16. Gilbert's 1875 account of his descent of the narrows is cited in Robert Sterling Yard, *The Book of the National Parks* (New York: Charles Scribner's Sons, 1919), 364.

17. Dellenbaugh's "Temple of the Virgin" refers to a tower northwest of the Zion Canyon Visitor Center.

18. Compare Dellenbaugh's 1903 painting *Zion Canyon* with the photograph "Up the Valley in Zion Canyon" taken the same year. Yale Collection of Western Americana, Beinecke Rare Book and Manuscript Library, 2025501, http://brbl-dl.library.yale.edu/vufind/Record/3439711.

19. Woodbury, *History of Southern Utah*, 187.

20. Woodbury, 187–88; Wayne K. Hinton, "Getting Along: The Significance of Cooperation in the Development of Zion National Park," *Utah Historical Quarterly* 68 (Fall 2000): 314.

21. Hinton, "Getting Along," 315.

CHAPTER 7

1. Dena Markoff Sabin, *The Dudes Are Always Right: The Utah Parks Company in Zion National Park, 1923–1972* (Springdale, UT: Zion Natural History Association, 1980), 19.

2. J. Philip Gruen, *Manifest Destinations: Cities and Tourists in the Nineteenth-Century American West* (Norman: University of Oklahoma Press, 2014), 44. Jared Farmer notes that around the turn of the century, the Great Salt Lake was drawing two hundred thousand tourists annually (*On Zion's Mount: Mormons, Indians and the American Landscape* [Cambridge, MA: Harvard University Press, 2008], 163). Zion National Park would not reach this visitation level until after World War II.

3. For one traveler's description of the trip from Lund to Zion Canyon and the North Rim, see George C. Fraser, *Journeys in the Canyon Lands of Utah and Arizona, 1914–1916*, ed. Frederick H. Swanson (Tucson: University of Arizona Press, 2005), 6–15.

4. Fisher S. Harris, "See Europe If You Must, But See America First," *Deseret News*, December 16, 1905. The Trossachs are a vacation area near Scotland's Loch Lomond.

5. Marguerite S. Shaffer, *See America First: Tourism and National Identity, 1880–1940* (Washington, D.C.: Smithsonian Institution, 2001), 26–30.

6. Marguerite S. Shaffer, "Seeing the Nature of America: The National Parks as National Assets, 1914–1929," in *Being Elsewhere: Tourism, Consumer Culture, and Identity in Modern Europe and North America*, ed. Shelley Baranowski and Ellen Furlough (Ann Arbor: University of Michigan Press, 2001), 155–84.

7. Wesley King, quoted in *Woodbury, History of Southern Utah*, 189.

8. Data on paved roads in Utah are from table 1 in Peter J. Hugill, "Good Roads and the Automobile in the United States 1880–1929," *Geographical Review* 72 (July 1982): 339.

9. Janet R. Balmforth, "'Good Roads Roberts' and the Fight for Utah's Highways," *Utah Historical Quarterly* 49 (Winter 1981): 56–65.

10. Virginia Rishel, *Wheels to Adventure: Bill Rishel's Western Routes* (Salt Lake City: Howe Brothers, 1983), 71–76.

11. Woodbury, *History of Southern Utah*, 195; H. H. Hays, "Salt Lake City Is Gateway Country, Systematic Exploitation Is All That Is Needed," *Salt Lake Tribune*, November 23, 1913.

12. "Return from Trip to Southern Utah," *Washington County News* (St. George, UT), August 24, 1916.

13. Woodbury, *History of Southern Utah*, 199; Michael F. Anderson, "Zion National Park Roads and Bridges," Historic American Engineering Record HAER UT-72 (Washington, D.C.: Department of the Interior, National Park Service, [1972?]), 29–30.

14. Hal Rothman, *Preserving Different Pasts: The American National Monuments* (Urbana: University of Chicago Press, 1989), 99.

15. Sabin, *Dudes Are Always Right*, 34.

16. *The Arrowhead* [San Pedro, Los Angeles and Salt Lake Railroad], July 1917, PAM 10408, USHS, 32; Jane Galloway Demaray, *Yellowstone Summers: Touring with the Wylie Camping Company in America's First National Park* (Pullman: Washington State University Press, 2015), 190–91.

17. Janet B. Seegmiller, "Selling the Scenery: Chauncey and Gronway Parry and the Birth of Southern Utah's Tourism and Movie Industries," *Utah Historical Quarterly* 80 (Summer 2012): 246; Sabin, *Dudes Are Always Right*, 38.

18. Kenneth Carpenter, "Rocky Start of Dinosaur National Monument (USA), the World's First Dinosaur Geoconservation Site," *Geoconservation Research* 1 (January–June 2018): 3. What Douglass termed a brontosaur was later determined to be an apatosaur. Brontosaurus has since been proposed as a separate genus.

19. *Vernal Express*, August 20, 1909.

20. Carpenter, "Rocky Start of Dinosaur National Monument," 6.

21. "Earl Douglass," Dinosaur National Monument, National Park Service, https://www.nps.gov/dino/learn/historyculture/douglass.htm.

22. U.S. Department of the Interior, National Park Service, *Quarry Visitor Center, Dinosaur National Monument, Utah/Colorado: Historic Structure Report* (Denver: NPS Denver Service Center, October 2003), 17.

CHAPTER 8

1. Horace M. Albright and Marian Albright Schenck, *Creating the National Park Service: The Missing Years* (Norman: University of Oklahoma Press, 1999), 129.

2. Thomas G. Alexander, "Red Rock and Gray Stone: Senator Reed Smoot, the Establishment of Zion and Bryce Canyon National Parks, and the Rebuilding of Downtown Washington, DC," *Pacific Historical Review* 72 (February 2003): 1–38; Hinton, "Getting Along," 316.

3. Jeff Crane, *The Environment in American History: Nature and the Formation of the United States* (London: Routledge, 2014), 230.

4. Albright and Schenk, *Creating the National Park Service*, 60. In 1916 Mesa Verde was the only national park in the Southwest. Utah had no entries in Yard's National Parks Portfolio.

5. Richard West Sellars, *Preserving Nature in the National Parks: A History* (New Haven, CT: Yale University Press, 1997), 37–38, https://www.nps.gov/parkhistory/online_books/sellars/contents.htm. For more on the legislative campaign for the Park Service organic act, see Horace M. Albright and Robert Cahn, *The Birth of the National Park Service: The Founding Years, 1913–33* (Salt Lake City: Howe Brothers, 1985), 35–41. Robin Winks gives a somewhat different account, suggesting that Congressman Kent opposed grazing in the parks as antithetical to their purpose. Robin W. Winks, "The National Park Service Act of 1916: A Contradictory Mandate?," *George Wright Forum* 24 (2007): 6–21, www.npshistory.com/publications/winks.htm.

6. R. Dixie Tourangeau, "Franklin Knight Lane, 1864–1921," in *The National Park Service: The First 75 Years*, ed. William H. Sontag (Fort Washington, PA: Eastern National Park and Monument Association, 1990), 20, https://www.nps.gov/parkhistory/online_books/sontag/lane.htm.

7. Albright and Cahn, *Birth of the National Park Service*, 63; Albright and Schenck, *Creating the National Park Service*, 241; "Director of Parks Lauds Zion Canyon," *Salt Lake Tribune*, September 9, 1917.

8. Albright and Cahn, *Birth of the National Park Service*, 63.

9. Rothman, *Preserving Different Pasts*, 98.

10. Sellars, *Preserving Nature in the National Parks*, 16–18, 21–22.

11. Statement of Thomas Cooper to 1912 National Parks Conference, cited in Dietmar Schneider-Hector, "Forging a National Park Service: 'The Necessity for Cooperation,'" *Journal of the Southwest* 56 (Winter 2014): 648.

12. Peter Blodgett, "Defining Uncle Sam's Playgrounds: Railroad Advertising and the National Parks, 1917–1941," *Historical Geography* 35 (2007): 86.

13. Roderick Frazier Nash, *Wilderness and the American Mind*, 4th ed. (New Haven, CT: Yale University Press, 2001), 143.

14. Mrs. John Dickinson Sherman, "Women's Part in National Park Development," address delivered at the National Parks Conference, January 2, 1917, Washington, D.C., http://lcweb2.loc.gov/service/gdc/scd0001/2000/200011o9005wo/20001109005wo.pdf.

15. John Muir, *Our National Parks* (New York: Houghton Mifflin, 1901), 1–2.

16. F. V. Fisher, "'The Canyon Sublime'; Mukuntuweap So Named," *Washington County News*, October 12, 1916.

17. Report of Horace Albright, in *Salt Lake Herald*, January 20, 1920; "Zion Canyon Is Now Ready to Receive Tourists," *Salt Lake Telegram*, June 14, 1918; Anderson, "Zion National Park," 40; Seegmiller, "Selling the Scenery," 250–53.

18. The Parrys accommodated North Rim tourists at a lodge in DeMotte Park run by Will Rust, Dave Rust's brother. For more on early North Rim tourism, see Michael F. Anderson, *Living at the Edge: Explorers, Exploiters, and Settlers of the Grand Canyon Region* (Grand Canyon, AZ: Grand Canyon Association, 1998), 154.

19. "Utah's Contribution to America's Curiosity Shop," *Goodwin's Weekly*, July 14, 1917.

20. Angus M. Woodbury, "Biotic Relationships of Zion Canyon, Utah with Special Reference to Succession," *Ecological Monographs* 3 (April 1933): 162.

21. Hinton, "Getting Along," 318. The Crawford family stayed at their homestead at Oak Creek until 1931, when the elder Crawford's sons accepted a Park Service offer to buy their 360-acre farm.

22. Hinton, "Getting Along," 316.

23. "Zion Monument Bill Is Favored," *Salt Lake Telegram*, June 19, 1919; Alexander, "Red Rock and Gray Stone," 13.

24. "Park Banquet to Be Gala Event," *Salt Lake Tribune*, November 23, 1919; "After We Celebrate," *Salt Lake Telegram*, November 20, 1919.

CHAPTER 9

1   This interpretation of the Paiute origin story of Bryce Canyon is from Herbert E. Gregory, *The Geology and Geography of the Paunsaugunt Region, Utah*, U.S. Geological Survey Professional Paper 226 (Washington, D.C.: Government Printing Office, 1951), 17.

2.   Gregory, *Geology and Geography*, 5.

3.   Gregory, 5, 6.

4.   Clarence E. Dutton, *Report on the Geology of the High Plateaus of Utah, with Atlas*, U.S. Department of the Interior, Geographical and Geological Survey of the Rocky Mountain Region (Washington, D.C.: Government Printing Office, 1880), 254, 204.

5.   Cited in C. C. Presnall, "Early Days in Bryce and Zion," *Utah: The State Magazine of National Interest* 2 (July 1936), 13.

6.   J. W. Crawford, "Bryce Canyon National Park—The Early Years, 1916–1946," Special Collections, Dixie State University Library, St. George, UT; Wendell A. Bryce, "Ebenezer Bryce," in Ebenezer Adam Bryce genealogical record, Geni. com, https://www.geni.com/people/Ebenezer-Bryce/6000000002542133845.

7.   U.S. Department of Agriculture, Forest Service, *The Dixie National Forest: Managing an Alpine Forest in an Arid Setting* (Ogden, UT: Intermountain Region, 1987), 78; Nicholas Scrattish, "Historic Resource Study Bryce Canyon National Park" (Denver: U.S. Department of the Interior, National Park Service, Rocky Mountain Regional Office, Branch of Historic Preservation, 1985), 16, http://digitalcommons.usu.edu/elusive_docs/46. The 1916 article in the Denver & Rio Grande's Red Book appeared under the name of J. J. Drew, a Union Pacific employee. Scrattish attributed it to forest supervisor Humphrey ("Historic Resource Study," 16). For more on the Forest Service–Park Service rivalry, see Hal Rothman, "Shaping the Nature of a Controversy: The Park Service, the Forest Service, and the Cedar Breaks Proposal," *Utah Historical Quarterly* 55 (Summer 1987): 213–35.

8.   Le Roy Jeffers, "The Temple of the Gods in Utah," *Scientific American* 119 (October 5, 1918): 267.

9.   O. J. Grimes, "Utah's New Wonderland," *Salt Lake Tribune*, August 25, 1918.

10. Scrattish, "Historic Resource Study," 32.

11. Alexander, "Red Rock and Gray Stone," 17; Finis Dunaway, *Natural Visions: The Power of Images in American Environmental Reform* (Chicago: University of Chicago Press, 2005), 3. Herbert Gleason saw Bryce Canyon the preceding October and dispatched an enthusiastic letter to Mather; his enthusiasm led Reed Smoot to introduce his park bill on November 3, 1919, ahead of Mather's visit. U.S. Department of the Interior, "Report of Director of the National Park Service," in Reports of the Department of the Interior for the Fiscal Year Ended June 30, 1920 (Washington, D.C.: Government Printing Office, 1920), 88.

12. "'Center of Scenic America' Slogan of Utahns," *Salt Lake Telegram*, November 25, 1919.

13. Stephen Mather, 1923 annual report to Congress, cited in Kathleen L. McKoy, *Cultures at a Crossroads: An Administrative History of Pipe Spring National Monument*, Cultural Resources Selections No. 15 (Denver: National Park Service, Intermountain Region, 2000), 88, https://www.nps.gov/parkhistory /online_books/pisp/adhi/.

14. Stephen T. Mather, *Progress in the Development of the National Parks* (Washington, D.C.: Government Printing Office), 1916.

15. Albright and Schenck, *Creating the National Park Service*, 244–45.

16. Hinton, "Getting Along," 321.

17. "Zion Park Opened by Utah's Governor," *Washington County News*, May 21, 1925; "Zion National Park to Have Good Road," *Washington County News*, June 4, 1925; "Indian Chiefs Help Open Zion National Park," *Davis County Clipper* (Ogden, UT), June 5, 1925.

18. Schneider-Hector, "Forging a National Park Service," 649.

19. U.S. Department of the Interior, National Park Service, *Proceedings of the National Park Conference Held at the Yellowstone National Park, Sept. 11–12, 1911* (Washington, D.C.: Government Printing Office, 1912), 30. David Louter discusses the successful efforts of automobile clubs to open the national parks to cars in *Windshield Wilderness: Cars, Roads, and Nature in Washington's National Parks* (Seattle: University of Washington Press, 2006), 24.

20. Chester C. Davis, "Motoring through Wonderland: A Tour with the Montana A. A.," *American Motorist* 7 (October 1915): 594.

21. Blodgett, "Defining Uncle Sam's Playgrounds," 91, fig. 3.

CHAPTER 10

1. "Making It Possible for Americans to See America," *American Motorist* 8 (September 1916): 36.

2. W. D. Rishel, "Highways Are Great Factor in Expansion," *Salt Lake Telegram*, May 25, 1924. See also Virginia Rishel, *Wheels to Adventure*, 80.

3. J. E. Broaddus, "Utah's New Wonderland" (pamphlet, Denver & Rio Grande Western Railroad, 1921, in author's possession).

4. U.S. Department of the Interior, National Park Service, *Annual Report of the Director of the National Park Service to the Secretary of the Interior for the Fiscal Year Ended June 30, 1922 [–1932] and the Travel Season, 1922 [–1932]* (Washington, D.C.: Government Printing Office, 1922 [–1932]), 153.

5. McPherson, *Comb Ridge and Its People*, 141–42.

6. Anderson, *Living at the Edge*, 154.

7. Hinton, "Getting Along," 328; Scrattish, "Historical Resource Study," 60–61.

8. Hinton, "Getting Along," 328; Sabin, *Dudes Are Always Right*, 87–89. The Utah Park Company's tour offerings were described in a Union Pacific booklet issued in 1925 titled *Zion National Park: Bryce Canyon, Cedar Breaks, Kaibab Forest, North Rim of Grand Canyon*.

9. Woodbury, *History of Southern Utah*, 24.

10. Cami Pulham, *Heart of the Mountain: The History of Timpanogos Cave National Monument* (Washington, D.C.: U.S. Department of the Interior, National Park Service, 2009), 14–15, https://catalog.hathitrust.org/Record/011327596.

11. Farmer, *On Zion's Mount*, 26. Farmer's book gives a fascinating account of how the name "Timpanogos" came to be associated with a mountain instead of with the Native Americans who oriented themselves toward Utah Lake and its environs.

12. For more background on Hovenweep NM, see "History and Culture," Hovenweep National Monument, National Park Service, https://www.nps.gov/hove/learn/historyculture/index.htm.

13. David Lavender, *The History of Arizona's Pipe Spring National Monument* (Springdale, UT: Zion Natural History Association, 1984), 35–37.

14. Hal Rothman discusses Stephen Mather's concept of a two-tiered system of national parks and monuments in *Devil's Bargains: Tourism in the Twentieth-Century American West* (Lawrence: University Press of Kansas, 1998), 151–53.

15. Rothman, *Devil's Bargains*.

16. Patti Bell, *Bryce Canyon National Park: The Early Years, 1916–1946* (Bryce Canyon, UT: Bryce Canyon Natural History Association, 2011), 27.

17. Kendall Hughes Williams, *The Syrett Family: From Buckinghamshire, England to Utah to Ruby's Inn, Utah, 1606–2006*, ed. Roderick K. Syrett and Kathern Syrett (Salt Lake City: Price & Associates, 2006), 207–8.

18. The Syretts' five-year sojourn at Sunset Point is described in Nicholas Scrattish, "The Modern Discovery, Popularization, and Early Development of Bryce Canyon, Utah," *Utah Historical Quarterly* 49 (Fall 1981): 348–62. Construction of Bryce Canyon Lodge is described in Scrattish, "Historic Resource Study," 82–84.

19. Scrattish, "Historic Resource Study," 95.

20. Sabin, *Dudes Are Always Right*, 87–89.

21. In his administrative history of Bryce Canyon National Park, Nicholas Scrattish ("Historic Resource Study," 33–34) documents how UP officials, beginning in 1921, undertook park improvements in Utah in order to lure tourists away from competing rail lines, including the Denver & Rio Grande Western in Utah and the Santa Fe in Arizona. Company officials even foresaw that Utah's national parks might compete with Yellowstone, Glacier, and Canadian national parks.

22. Robert Sterling Yard, *The New Zion National Park: Rainbow in the Desert* (Washington, D.C.: National Parks Association, 1919), 28.

CHAPTER 11

1. "Bryce Canyon Is Formally Opened by Utah's Chief Executive and Notables"; "Governor and Congressman Are Visitors Here," *Richfield* (UT) *Reaper*, June 4, 1925.

2. "Wayne County in the Lime Light," *Richfield Reaper*, September 24, 1924.

3. Cathy A. Gilbert and Kathleen L. McKoy, *Cultural Landscape Report: Fruita Rural Historic District, Capitol Reef National Park*, Cultural Resource Selections No. 8 (Denver: Intermountain Region, National Park Service, 1997), https://www.nps.gov/parkhistory/online_books/care/clr/clr.htm.

4. Charles Kelly, "The Fathers of Capitol Reef National Park," *Utah History to Go* (blog), *History Blazer*, September 1995, https://historytogo.utah.gov /capitol-reef-national-park/.

5. "Wayne Wonderland Booklet Issued," *Richfield Reaper*, June 25, 1925. The name "Capitol Reef" refers to the domes of Navajo Sandstone that suggest the nation's Capitol building, and to the jagged eastern edge of the Waterpocket Fold, which supposedly reminded early prospectors working in the area of coral reefs. See "Capitol Reef National Park Frequently Asked Questions," National Park Service, https://www.nps.gov/care/faqs.htm. G. K. Gilbert refers to "Capitol Canyon" (Capitol Wash) in his 1880 work *Report on the Geology of the Henry Mountains*, Department of the Interior, U.S. Geographical and Geological Survey of the Rocky Mountain Region (Washington, D.C.: Government Printing Office, 1887), 14.

6. "Capitol Reef Is Dedicated by State Officials," *Richfield Reaper*, July 23, 1925; Miriam B. Murphy, *A History of Wayne County* (Salt Lake City: Utah State Historical Society and Wayne County Commission, 1999), 348–50.

7. "Scenic Wonders to Be Exploited; More Glories in Southern Utah," *Salt Lake Telegram*, January 1, 1925.

8. "600 Attend Services for Joseph S. Hickman"; "Part of Wayne County Is Set Aside as a National Park," *Richfield Reaper*, July 30, 1925. The *Reaper's* report was based on a purported Interior Department telegram received by the *Salt Lake Tribune*.

9. Steen, "Natural Bridges of White Canyon," 63.

10. "Some of Nature's Handiwork near Moab," *Grand Valley Times* (Moab, UT), December 19, 1913. Marvin Turnbow acquired the hundred-acre ranch and its primitive cabin from homesteader John Wolfe and his son Fred. The cabin stands today near the start of the Delicate Arch trail.

11. Mozelle Gray Tonne, *From Ikevar to Devil's Garden: The Saga of Alexander Ringhoffer* (San Angelo, TX: Anchor Publishing, 1992), 98, 130. Ringhoffer spelled "Devil's Garden" with an apostrophe, which was the common usage until the 1970s, when the National Park Service adopted "Devils Garden."

12. "Wonderful Scenic Attractions at 'The Windows' to Be Set Aside as Monument," *Moab Times-Independent*, July 17, 1924. Wadleigh's letter to Stephen Mather, dated November 2, 1923, was excerpted in the *Moab Times-Independent*, September 9, 1955 ("The Arches, Top Lure for Tourists, Are Bringing More Here Each Year"). See also Tonne, *From Ikevar to Devil's Garden*, 144.

13. Richard A. Firmage, *History of Grand County* (Salt Lake City: Utah State Historical Society and Grand County, 1996), 269. See also S. W. Lohman, *The Geologic Story of Arches National Park*, U.S. Geological Survey Bulletin 1398 (Washington, D.C.: Government Printing Office, 1975), 1–2.

14. Frederick H. Swanson, *Dave Rust: A Life in the Canyons* (Salt Lake City: University of Utah Press, 2007), 186.

15. John H. McNeeley, "Utah Has Glorious Rival to Garden of the Gods," *New York Times*, May 9, 1926.

16. John F. Hoffman, *Arches National Park: An Illustrated Guide* (San Diego: Western Recreational Publications, 1985), 66.

17. Samuel J. Schmieding, *From Controversy to Compromise to Cooperation: An Administrative History of Canyonlands National Park* (Washington, D.C.: U.S. Department of the Interior, National Park Service, 2008), 50–51.

18. "J. M. Turnbow Named Monument Custodian," *Moab Times-Independent*, November 30, 1933.

19. "'The Arches,' New National Monument in Grand County, Granted by President Hoover," *Moab Times-Independent*, April 25, 1929.

20. "15 Men Start Work in Arches Monument," *Moab Times-Independent*, December 14, 1933; Frank A. Beckwith, Arches National Monument scrapbook, 1934, Delta City Library, Delta, UT, https://collections.lib.utah.edu/ark:/87278/s6b884bj; Frank Beckwith, "Officials of Park Service Visit Arches," *Moab Times-Independent*, March 15, 1934. For a detailed account of the 1933–34 NPS survey in Arches, see Hoffman, *Arches National Park*, 68–70.

21. "To Make National Park of Arches Monument," *Moab Times-Independent*, March 29, 1934.

22. "First Car Makes Trip to Arches Monument," *Moab Times-Independent*, June 18, 1936.

CHAPTER 12

1. Scrattish, "Historic Resource Study," 95–103. Bryce Canyon now covers 35,835 acres.

2. Scrattish, 68, 73, 97–98.

3. Park visitation statistics and breakdowns by mode of travel are given in the annual reports of the director of the National Park Service for the years indicated (e.g., U.S. Department of the Interior, National Park Service, *Annual Report of the Director of the National Park Service to the Secretary of the Interior for the Fiscal Year Ended June 30, 1925 [1929, 1930]*).

4. Wayne Hinton ("Getting Along," 328) observes that the Union Pacific "looked upon private motorists as pests" and refused to "accept the viewpoint that money spent by motorists was as good as that spent by rail passengers."

5. Robert Sterling Yard, "Making a Business of Scenery," in *The Nation's Business*, June 1916, quoted in Sellars, *Preserving Nature in the National Parks*, 28. According to Sellars, Yard's article "reflected the pervasive utilitarian tenor of the drive to establish the National Park Service."

6. Soulliére, *Historic Roads*, 41.

7. Jim Ohlman, "The 1919 Transcanyon Aerial Tramway Survey," in Michael F. Anderson, ed., *A Gathering of Grand Canyon Historians* (Grand Canyon, AZ: Grand Canyon Association, 2005), 7–14.

8. Fisher S. Harris, in *Los Angeles Arrowhead,* December 1905, quoted in Shaffer, *See America First: Tourism and National Identity,* 38–39.
9. Pyne, *How the Canyon Became Grand,* 116.
10. C. Frank Brockman, "Park Naturalists and the Evolution of National Park Service Interpretation through World War II," *Journal of Forest History* 22 (January 1978): 29.
11. *Intelligence Tours through Utah's Geologic Wonders* (Salt Lake City: Intelligence Tours, [1927?]). Pamphlet, MLSC.
12. Clyde Kluckhohn, *Beyond the Rainbow* (Boston: Christopher Publishing House, 1933), 13.
13. Neil Judd, "Beyond the Clay Hills," *National Geographic* 45 (March 1924): 275.
14. Kluckhohn's 1926–28 expeditions are detailed in *Beyond the Rainbow,* from which these excerpts are taken. See especially pp. 194, 203–8.
15. The Bernheimer-Wetherill proposal is discussed in chapter 13.
16. Kluckhohn, *Beyond the Rainbow,* 207–8.
17. Harvey, *Rainbow Bridge to Monument Valley,* 7, 9.
18. Harvey, 15.
19. Harvey, 10.

CHAPTER 13

1. Zion and Bryce Canyon National Parks did not gain a full-time superintendent until 1927, when E. T. Scoyen assumed management of both units, serving in this capacity until 1931.
2. Hal Rothman, "Second-Class Sites: National Monuments and the Growth of the National Park System," *Environmental Review* 10 (Spring 1986): 53.
3. Ezekiel Johnson's observations on Natural Bridges NM are found in the National Park Service's Southwestern Monument Reports, dated from July 1933 to August 1938 (historical files, Natural Bridges National Monument).
4. Helen Brewster Owens, "Zeke Johnson, a Biography," p. 308, MS 511, MLSC.
5. Frank Pinkley, "What Is a National Monument?," in *Guide to Southwestern National Monuments* (Coolidge, AZ: National Park Service, Southwestern Monuments Office, 1938).
6. "Opening Dates Set for National Parks," *Garfield County News* (Panguitch, UT), April 1, 1932. Visitation statistics are from "National Park Service Visitor Use Statistics," National Park Service, https://irma.nps.gov/STATS/.
7. Automobile use in Zion NP is from U.S. Department of the Interior, National Park Service, *Annual Report of the Director of the National Park Service, 1932,* tables 7 and 8, pp. 85–87. Of the 51,650 visitors arriving at Zion National Park in 1933, only 1,087 came on Utah Parks Company tour buses, down significantly from a few years earlier. Hotel fares are from "Reduced Rates for Summer Tourists in Park Hotels," *Garfield County News,* February 17, 1933.
8. "Utah Parks Enjoy Huge Patronage," *Garfield County News,* November 17, 1933; "Funds Cut for Park Roads," *Garfield County News,* May 20, 1932. The

road to Rainbow Point was completed in September 1934 and was asphalted the following year (Scrattish, "Historic Resource Study," 142).

9.   Scrattish, "Historic Resource Study," 158–59.

10. Jasper Louis Crawford, interview by Lyman Hafen, April 20 and 24, 2004, Pioneer Voices of Zion Canyon Oral History Collection, Special Collections, Dixie State University Library, St. George, UT.

11. Scrattish, "Historic Resource Study," 107–11. Scrattish observed that "in 1936, 6 years after the Park Service began imposing grazing restrictions, grass was still scarce along the Paunsaugunt rim."

12. Rothman, "Shaping the Nature of a Controversy," 223.

13. Rothman, 220.

14. Pulham, *Heart of the Mountain*, 40–42.

15. Pulham, 44–46.

16. "Utah May Be Given New National Park," *Salt Lake Telegram,* May 22, 1933; "New National Park Sure, Gammeter Says," *Moab Times-Independent,* August 10, 1933; "Representative Gammeter Praises San Juan," *San Juan Record* (Monticello, UT), March 7, 1935.

17. Sproul, *Bridge between Cultures,* chap. 4.

18. Harvey Leake, "The Early Fight for Glen Canyon and the Rainbow Plateau," *Canyon Country Zephyr* (Moab, UT), December 2, 2018, http://www .canyoncountryzephyr.com/2018/12/02/the-early-fight-for-glen-canyon-and -the-rainbow-plateau-by-harvey-leake/.

19. Roger A. Toll to director, National Park Service, April 28, 1931 (Records of Roger W. Toll 1928–1936, National Park Service, Record Group 79, National Archives, Washington, D.C.). I am indebted to Harvey Leake for supplying this letter.

20. Leake, "Early Fight for Glen Canyon."

21. Robert McPherson discusses the livestock reduction program on the Navajo Reservation in chapter 6 of *Navajo Land, Navajo Culture.*

CHAPTER 14

1.   For further discussion of Toll's activities in evaluating potential new national monuments, see Robert W. Righter, "National Monuments to National Parks: The Use of the Antiquities Act of 1906," *Western Historical Quarterly* 20 (August 1989): 281–301, http://npshistory.com/publications/righter/index .htm.

2.   Bradford J. Frye, *From Barrier to Crossroads: An Administrative History of Capitol Reef National Park, Utah,* Cultural Resources Selections No. 12 (Denver: Intermountain Region, National Park Service, 1998), 127–30, https://www .nps.gov/parkhistory/online_books/care/adhi/adhi.htm; Murphy, *History of Wayne County,* 354–55.

3.   Roger Toll to Horace Albright, November 8, 1932, folder 1, box 1, Capitol Reef National Park records, MLSC.

4.   Toll to Albright, November 8, 1932. Toll's discussion of the San Rafael area and the Colorado River canyon lands was part of an addendum titled "Eastern Utah."

5.   "'Wayne Wonderland' Trip Opens the Eyes of Visitors to Attractions So Close By," *Richfield Reaper,* August 13, 1931. Broaddus's original article appeared in the *Salt Lake City Municipal Record* in 1930.

6.   Roger Toll, report on proposed Wayne Wonderland area, April 13, 1934, folder 4, box 1, Roger Toll papers, DPL.

7.   Roger Toll, report on proposed Wayne Wonderland area. Subsequent quotations of Toll in this chapter are from this report.

8.   "Park Service Director Will Recommend Wayne Monument," *Richfield Reaper,* February 14, 1935.

9.   Frye, *From Barrier to Crossroads,* 142. The Capitol Reef Lodge opened at Fruita in 1946 but had limited success, while Dewey Gifford built a motel on his Fruita property in 1954. Neither was successful in the long run and the Park Service eventually acquired the properties (Frye, chap. 5).

10. Toll, memo to director [Arno Cammerer], August 19, 1935, re: "Proposed Capitol Reef National Monument," folder 2, box 1, Capitol Reef National Park records, MLSC. See also Frye, *From Barrier to Crossroads,* 139–40.

11. Harry A. Aurand to Roger Toll, March 19, 1934, folder 1, box 1, Capitol Reef National Park records, MLSC.

12. Toll to director [Cammerer], March 29, 1934, folder 1, box 1, Capitol Reef National Park records, MLSC.

13. A. E. Demaray to secretary [Harold Ickes], December 28, 1934, folder 1, box 1, Capitol Reef National Park records, MLSC.

14. In a 1937 report on the Escalante monument proposal, Park Service landscape architect Merel S. Sager remarked that "as a result of various recommendations by technical men of the Service the proposed National Monument area grew until it embodied about 6,000 square miles including the Capitol Reef area." Merel S. Sager to director [Cammerer], February 13, 1937, Escalante Monument files, series 2495, Glen Canyon National Recreation Area, Page, AZ.

15. Roger Toll, memo to director [Arno Cammerer], August 19, 1935, titled "Proposed Capitol Reef National Monument," folder 1, box 1, Escalante National Monument Proposal Collection, MLSC.

16. Many documents related to the origin of the Escalante national monument proposal, including M. R. Tillotson's 1935 report, were apparently not retained in Park Service files. This excerpt from Tillotson's report was attached to a 1942 memorandum that is cited in Schmieding, *From Controversy to Compromise,* 55–56.

17. Roger W. Toll to director [Cammerer], NPS, September 21, 1935, folder 1, box 1, Escalante National Monument Proposal Collection, MLSC.

18. M. R. Tillotson and Frank J. Taylor, *Grand Canyon Country* (Palo Alto, CA: Stanford University Press, 1929), 60–61.

CHAPTER 15

1. The Park, Parkway, and Recreational Area Study Act of 1936 was drafted by the Department of the Interior in 1934 to promote cooperation between the federal government and the states' various park agencies. State parks and recreation areas were its focus, but in Utah the study also assessed the potential for new national parks on federal lands in southern Utah, drawing in part on Roger Toll's field surveys during the early 1930s. The final report was not published until 1941.

2. Murdock to Blood, February 11, 1936, Henry H. Blood correspondence, folder 66, box 12, series 186, Utah State Archives, Salt Lake City, UT.

3. The Wayne Wonderland national park appears to have been suggested by Paul Arentz, a staff engineer for the Utah State Planning Board, after he visited the Waterpocket Fold country in the summer of 1934. He initially proposed a 570-square-mile park, but this was reduced to a still-impressive 360 square miles in a state recreation plan released by the planning board in April 1935 (Frye, *From Barrier to Crossroads*, chap. 8).

4. K. C. Wright to Ray West, March 18, 1936, folder 66, box 12, Blood correspondence. Wright was chief engineer of the Utah State Road Commission.

5. Ray West, "The Proposed Escalante National Monument," Utah State Planning Board files, series 22028, State Archives, Salt Lake City, UT.

6. Henry Blood to Abe Murdock, May 6, 1936, folder 14, box 13, Blood correspondence; Ray West to Elbert D. Thomas, May 6, 1936, State Planning Board files.

7. Madsen's remarks are part of a transcript of the June 9, 1936, meeting in Price, Utah, in the State Planning Board files.

8. Statements of J. M. MacFarland and Milton Twitchell, transcript of the June 9, 1936, meeting in Price, Utah, State Planning Board files.

9. "Huge Withdrawal of Monument Is Opposed," *Moab Times-Independent,* June 11, 1936.

10. Merel S. Sager to director, NPS, February 13, 1937, Escalante Monument files, series 2495, Glen Canyon National Recreation Area, Page, AZ.

11. Sager to director, NPS, February 13, 1937, 32. At the time that Sager wrote his report, the planned Glen Canyon dam site was four miles above Lees Ferry. It was later changed to a point fifteen miles above the historic river ford. Hank Hassell, *Rainbow Bridge: An Illustrated History* (Boulder: University Press of Colorado, 1999), 99.

12. Sager to director, NPS, February 13, 1937, 25.

CHAPTER 16

1. "Meeting Called to Take Action on Arches," *Moab Times-Independent,* January 1, 1937; "On Expansion," *Moab Times-Independent,* March 18, 1937. On November 25, 1938, President Franklin Roosevelt signed Proclamation 2312, expanding Arches National Monument by 29,160 acres. See "Presidential

Proclamation 2312," National Park Service, https://www.nps.gov/arch/learn/management/presidential-proclamation-2312.htm.

2. "Arches National Park Main Entrance Road," Historic American Engineering Record HAER No. UT-70, http://cdn.loc.gov/master/pnp/habshaer/ut/ut0300/ut0397/data/ut0397data.pdf.

3. "Beautiful Kolob Canyon Now a Nat'l. Monument," *Iron County Record* (Cedar City, UT), February 4, 1937.

4. Gregory is cited in Robert F. Biek, *Geologic Map of the Kolob Quadrangle,* Utah Geological Survey Map 217, 2007.

5. Ben H. Thompson, memo to "Mr. Moskey," February 19, 1937, folder 5, box 1, Capitol Reef National Park records, MLSC.

6. Mark W. T. Harvey, *Symbol of Wilderness: Echo Park and the American Wilderness Movement* (Albuquerque: University of New Mexico Press, 1994), 10–11.

7. "Dinosaur Area to Be Scenic Attraction," *Vernal Express,* July 28, 1938.

8. Jon M. Cosco, *Echo Park: Struggle for Preservation* (Boulder, CO: Johnson Books, 1995), 5–6; Harvey, *Symbol of Wilderness,* 12–14. The Bureau of Reclamation fielded survey teams for the Echo Park and Split Mountain dam sites less than a year after the monument was established (Cosco, 9). The prospect of losing a major dam turned most of the local populace against the Park Service.

9. Elmo R. Richardson, "The Escalante National Monument Controversy of 1935–1940," *Utah Historical Quarterly* 33 (April 1965): 114.

10. Sumner G. Margetts, "Proposal to Create the Escalante National Monument," April 29, 1938, folder 47, box 18, series 186, Henry H. Blood correspondence, Utah State Archives, Salt Lake City.

11. Sumner G. Margetts to director of grazing, Dept. of Interior, January 6, 1938, folder 47, box 18, series 186, Blood correspondence; "Further Reduction of Park Asked," *Moab Times-Independent,* November 25, 1937.

12. By showing that most of the Green and Colorado Rivers in Utah were historically navigable, the state won ownership of their riverbeds, where it hoped to lease minerals such as oil and gas. Only Cataract Canyon on the Colorado and the San Juan River were held to be unnavigable and hence remained under federal control. The case did not apply to the water in these rivers or to the surrounding lands. See John Weisheit, "The Colorado Riverbed Case, 1929–1931," On the Colorado, October 17, 2007, http://www.onthecolorado.com/articles.cfm?mode=detail&id=1194838609070.

13. Blood to Elbert Thomas, William King, and Will Robinson, February 2, 1938, folder 47, box 18, Blood correspondence.

14. Arno Cammerer to William H. King, February 11, 1938, State Planning Board files, series 22028, Utah State Archives; Cammerer to Blood, March 21, 1938, folder 47, box 18, Blood correspondence.

15. E. K. Burlew, telegram to Blood, October 14, 1938, folder 47, box 18, Blood correspondence.

16. Arthur Demaray to acting secretary, U.S. Department of the Interior, October 14, 1938, folder 1, box 1, Escalante National Monument Proposal Collection, MLSC.

17. Harold Ickes to Franklin Roosevelt, n.d. [but received at the White House "around October 19," 1938], folder 48, box 18, Blood correspondence. Ickes's mention of the scientific purposes of the monument anticipated the rationale for the Grand Staircase–Escalante National Monument nearly forty years later.

18. "Escalante Monument Soon to Be Created, Is Report," *Moab Times-Independent,* November 23, 1938.

19. Oscar L. Chapman to Blood, December 10, 1938, folder 48, box 18, Blood correspondence.

20. Richardson, "Escalante National Monument Controversy," 133.

21. Nelson, *Wrecks of Human Ambition,* 219.

CHAPTER 17

1. Robert Marshall, "The Universe of the Wilderness Is Vanishing," *Nature Magazine* 29 (April 1937): 235.

2. See Paul S. Sutter, *Driven Wild: How the Fight against Automobiles Launched the Modern Wilderness Movement* (Seattle: University of Washington Press, 2002).

3. Louter, *Windshield Wilderness,* 79. Development at Mount Rainier is from James J. Flink, *The Automobile Age* (Cambridge, MA: MIT Press, 1990), 174. Louter (72) points out that the availability of cheap labor during the Depression, through programs such as the Civilian Conservation Corps, aided the NPS's road construction effort.

4. P. P. Patraw, "Administration of the National Parks and Monuments," *Utah: The State Magazine of National Interest* 2 (July 1936): 37. *Utah* was a joint publication of the Utah State Highway Commission and the Associated Civic Clubs of Utah.

5. Robert Marshall to Harold Ickes, May 21, 1937, quoted in Douglas W. Scott, "National Parks and Their Wilderness: A Compilation of Historic Viewpoints," Pew Wilderness Center Briefing Paper (Washington, D.C., n.d.), author's possession.

6. William P. Wharton, "The National Primeval National Parks," *National Parks Bulletin* 13 (February 1937): 3.

7. Ickes was quoted in the *New York Times* for May 14, 1933, as cited in Donald C. Swain, "The National Park Service and the New Deal," *Pacific Historical Review* 41 (August 1972): 330.

8. Sutter, *Driven Wild,* 234.

9. Scott, "National Parks and Their Wilderness," 5; John C. Miles, *Wilderness in National Parks: Playground or Preserve* (Seattle: University of Washington Press, 2009), 86.

10. Robert Marshall and Althea Dobbins, "Largest Roadless Areas in the United States," *Living Wilderness* 2 (November 1936). Marshall's 1936 roadless area map was reprinted in Dave Foreman and Howie Wolke, *The Big Outside: A Descriptive Inventory of the Big Wilderness Areas of the U.S.* (Tucson, AZ: Ned Ludd Books, 1989), appendix C.

11. Correspondence on Hugh Calkin's Escalante wilderness proposal, folder 10, box 63, series 4, Wilderness Society Records, DPL.

12. Aldo Leopold, "The Last Stand of the Wilderness," *American Forests and Forest Life* 31 (October 1925): 600–601.

13. Adolph Murie, *Fauna of the National Parks of the United States: Ecology of the Coyote in the Yellowstone.* National Park Service, Fauna Series No. 4 (Washington, D.C.: Government Printing Office, 1940).

14. George M. Wright, Joseph S. Dixon, and Ben H. Thompson, *Fauna of the National Parks of the United States: A Preliminary Survey of Faunal Relations in National Parks.* National Park Service, Fauna Series No. 1 (Washington, D.C.: Government Printing Office, 1933).

15. Wright, Dixon, and Thompson, *Fauna of the National Parks,* chap. 4.

16. Sellars, *Preserving Nature,* 108–19.

17. Topping, *Glen Canyon,* 241–43; letter [undated] from Elzada Clover to Norman Nevills, folder 23, box 6, Norman and Joan Nevills papers, MLSC.

18. Elzada U. Clover and Lois Jotter, "Floristic Studies in the Canyon of the Colorado and Tributaries," *American Midland Naturalist* 32 (November 1944): 591–642.

19. Angus M. Woodbury, "Biotic Relationships of Zion Canyon."

20. Louter, *Windshield Wilderness,* 78.

CHAPTER 18

1. Herb Evison, "Jesse L. Nusbaum: Defender of American Antiquities," *Courier* 4 (January 1981), http://npshistory.com/persons-of-the-month/person-of-the-month-0614.htm.

2. Jesse L. Nusbaum, "Certain Aspects of the Proposed Escalante National Monument in Southeastern Utah," *Moab Times-Independent,* November 30, 1939.

3. Resolution of Moab Lions Club, February 14, 1938, folder 47, box 18, series 186, Henry H. Blood correspondence, State Archives, Salt Lake City, UT.

4. "Moab Entertains Associated Civic Clubs of Utah," *San Juan Record* (Monticello, UT), April 28, 1938; Jesse L. Nusbaum, "Certain Aspects of the Proposed Escalante National Monument."

5. "Park Visitors Enthused over Scenic Beauties of Moab Area," *Moab Times-Independent,* October 19, 1939.

6. "Creation of Escalante Area Nears Agreement," *Moab Times-Independent,* February 22, 1940.

7. "Creation of Escalante Area"; "Lions Favor Early Creation of Escalante Monument," *Moab Times-Independent,* January 12, 1940; "Utah Water Storage

Commission Opposed Escalante National Monument for Recreational Area," *Iron County Record*, June 27, 1940.

8. Harry J. Brown, "Ickes Presses for Utah Area Control," *Salt Lake Tribune*, August 11, 1940.

9. "Blood Offers Solution in Escalante Tilt," *Salt Lake Tribune*, August 17, 1940.

10. Jesse Nusbaum memo to unidentified NPS official [probably Asst. Chief Arthur Demaray], June 18, 1940, folder 1, box 1, Escalante National Monument Proposal Collection, MLSC.

11. Ronald F. Lee to director, Park Service, February 23, 1940, Escalante Monument files, series 2495, Glen Canyon National Recreation Area, Page, AZ.

12. Rolf Diamant, "Frederick Law Olmsted, Jr.," National Park Service: The First 75 Years, https://www.nps.gov/parkhistory/online_books/sontag/olmsted.htm.

13. U.S. Department of the Interior, National Park Service, *A Survey of the Recreational Resources of the Colorado River Basin* (Washington, D.C.: Government Printing Office, 1950), 20–21. This massive work, compiled in 1946 but not published until 1950, was based on field studies in the Colorado basin beginning in the 1930s.

14. D. Elden Beck to William H. King, December 12, 1938, folder 47, box 18, series 186, Blood correspondence.

CHAPTER 19

1. Sellars, *Preserving Nature*, 151.

2. "Uranium Still Spells Boom," *Deseret News*, December 14, 1955.

3. Charles Kelly, oral history interview by Lenard Brown, May 26, 1969, Capitol Reef National Park files. See also Frye, *From Barrier to Crossroads*, chap. 15.

4. Charles Kelly, "New Road into the Utah Wilderness," *Desert Magazine* 10 (February 1947): 10–14. "Arth" Chaffin, as he was known, married Della Taylor Hickman in 1948.

5. "Post-War Period in U.S. to Be an 'Age of Wonders,'" *Moab Times-Independent*, July 24, 1942.

6. Kent Frost, *My Canyonlands: I Had the Freedom of It* (New York: Abelard-Schuman, 1971), 122–23.

7. "Contemporary Daguerreotypes of Western Landscapes on Exhibit at Department of the Interior Museum," news release, U.S. Department of the Interior, January 8, 2003, https://www.doi.gov/sites/doi.gov/files/archive/news/archive/03_News_Releases/030108a.htm.

8. Charles Kelly, "Valley of the Cathedrals," *Desert Magazine* 13 (December 1949); Frye, *From Barrier to Crossroads*, chap. 9.

9. Ward J. Roylance, *The Enchanted Wilderness: A Red Rock Odyssey* (Torrey, UT: Four Corners West, 1986), 21–22.

10. Paul V. Brown to George Olcott, July 28, 1943, folder 3, box 1, Escalante National Monument Proposal Collection, MLSC.

11. Ben H. Thompson to Conrad Wirth, September 11, 1944, folder 3, box 1, Escalante National Monument Proposal Collection.

12. John C. Diggs, memo to regional architect, August 21, 1956, folder 656, series 36607, NPS-SEUG.

13. NPS correspondence regarding proposals for a national park or monument at Dead Horse Point is summarized in "The Dead Horse Point Story," an unattributed typescript in folder 124, series 36607, NPS-SEUG.

14. Conrad Wirth, memo to director, Bureau of Land Management, October 17, 1952, in "The Dead Horse Point Story."

15. "Dead Horse Point Is State Park after Friday Ceremonies," *Moab Times-Independent*, December 17, 1959.

CHAPTER 20

1. Cosco, *Echo Park*, 10–11.

2. Cosco, 16.

3. Carl P. Vetter, "Corralling the Colorado," *Reclamation Era* 9 (September 1946): 190. See also U.S. Department of the Interior, Bureau of Reclamation, *The Colorado River: "A Natural Menace Becomes a National Resource": A General Plan for the Development and Utilization of the Water Resources of the Colorado River Basin for Irrigation, Power Production, and Other Beneficial Uses in Arizona, California, Colorado, Nevada, New Mexico, Utah, and Wyoming* (Washington, D.C.: Government Printing Office, 1946).

4. U.S. Department of the Interior, National Park Service, *Survey of the Recreational Resources*, xxi, 133, 136. In 1932 President Hoover established Grand Canyon National Monument west of and contiguous to Grand Canyon National Park.

5. "Dark Canyon Power Site Meets with U.S. Favor," *Moab Times-Independent*, July 3, 1941; "Dark Canyon Location Favored," *Moab Times-Independent*, July 10, 1941. Alunite is a sulfate mineral sometimes used to produce alumina. Deposits occur within the Paradox Basin in southeastern Utah.

6. U.S. Department of the Interior, National Park Service, *Survey of the Recreational Resources*, xxi–xxii.

7. "Local Group Push River Power Site," *Vernal Express*, September 25, 1941.

8. "Krug Turns 'Thumbs Down' on Echo Park Project," *Vernal Express*, September 21, 1949.

9. "Chapman Approves Reservoirs for Echo Park, Split Mountain," *Roosevelt (UT) Standard*, June 29, 1950.

10. "Utahns Will Cheer Echo Park Decision," *Salt Lake Telegram*, June 28, 1950.

11. Bernard DeVoto, "The West against Itself," in *The Easy Chair*, 231–55 (Boston: Houghton Mifflin, 1955). DeVoto's article originally appeared in *Harper's Magazine* in January 1947.

12. Bernard DeVoto, "Shall We Let Them Ruin Our National Parks?," *Saturday Evening Post* 223 (July 22, 1950): 17.

13. Harvey, *Symbol of Wilderness*, 95–97.

14. "S. L. Official Tags Echo Foes 'Screwballs,'" *Salt Lake Telegram*, April 7, 1950.

15. Mark Harvey discusses Brower and the evaporation issue in chapter 7 of *Symbol of Wilderness*.

16. "The Dinosaur Dams Are Not Needed," *Living Wilderness* 15 (Autumn 1950): 24.

17. In April 1955 western Colorado congressman Wayne Aspinall offered a CRSP bill that did not include Echo Park dam, paving the way for its final adoption the following year (Cosco, Echo Park, 88).

CHAPTER 21

1. Henry G. Schmidt, monthly report, October 22, 1941, in U.S. Department of the Interior, National Park Service, *Arches National Park Main Entrance Road*, Historical American Engineering Record UT-70 (Washington, D.C.: The Service, 1993), 8, http://www.nps.gov/parkhistory/online_books/reports /arch/Arches%20Superintendent%20Report%201941.pdf.

2. Henry G. Schmidt, monthly reports for April and May 1942, http://www.nps .gov/parkhistory/online_books/reports/arch/Arches%20Superintendent %20Report%201942.pdf.

3. Extract from visitor log, Arches National Monument, October 3, 1945, folder A40, Arches NP files, series 8NS-079-93-291, Record Group 79-64F-307, NARA-DNV.

4. U.S. Department of the Interior, National Park Service, *Arches National Park Main Entrance Road*, 12–13; "About 400 People Attend Barbecue Celebrating Opening of Arches Road," *Moab Times-Independent*, May 13, 1948.

5. "$700,000 Road to Arches Planned by Park Service," *Moab Times-Independent*, May 20, 1948.

6. Bates E. Wilson, memorandum for regional director, region 3, Arches National Monument, October 29, 1949, http://www.nps.gov/parkhistory /online_books/reports/arch/Arches%20Superint.%20Report%3BJan%20 1949-Dec%201949.pdf.

7. Bernard DeVoto, "Let's Close the National Parks," *Harper's Magazine* 207 (October 1953): 50.

8. Arthur Gómez, "America's National Parks System: Sunset or New Dawn?," *Perspectives on History*, October 2007, https://www.historians.org /publications-and-directories/perspectives-on-history/october-2007 /americas-national-parks-system-sunset-or-new-dawn.

9. Conrad L. Wirth, memo to Washington Office and field staff, February 18, 1955, folder A9815, box 21, series 8NS-079-93-281, Record Group 79-64F-307, NARA-DNV.

10. Harold C. Bradley and David R. Brower, "Roads in the National Parks," *Sierra Club Bulletin* 34 (June 1949): 31–54.

11. Scrattish, "Historic Resource Study," 167–68.

12. Frye, *From Barrier to Crossroads,* chap. 14.

13. Gilbert and McKoy, *Cultural Landscape Report.*

14. Stephen Trimble, ed., *The Capitol Reef Reader* (Salt Lake City: University of Utah Press, 2019), 173–77; Frye, *From Barrier to Crossroads,* chap. 7.

15. Frye, *From Barrier to Crossroads,* chap. 9.

16. Frye, chap. 7.

17. "Major Rock Work Finished on New Arches Road," *Moab Times-Independent,* November 14, 1957; "Dedication Ceremony Opens New Paved Arches Highway," *Moab Times-Independent,* August 28, 1958.

18. "New Road into Devil's Garden Officially Opened on Tuesday," *Moab Times-Independent,* October 31, 1963.

19. "Arches Opens New Facilities for Overnight Campers," *Moab Times-Independent,* July 9, 1964.

20. Mission 66 prospectus, Natural Bridges National Monument, 1955; National Park Service, "Mission 66 for Natural Bridges National Monument," both in folder A9815, box 22, series 8NS-079-93-281, Record Group 79-64F-307, NARA-DNV.

21. "Vandalism in Arches Forces Action," *Moab Times-Independent,* May 3, 1962.

22. Erik K. Reed, memo to director, July 12, 1955, in "Mission 66 1955," folder A9815, box 22, series 8NS-079-93-281, Record Group 79-64F-307, NARA-DNV.

23. "Mission 66 Draft for Arches National Monument," January 30, 1957, folder A40, series 8NS-079-93-291, Record Group 79-64F-307, NARA-DNV.

24. Edward Abbey, *Desert Solitaire: A Season in the Wilderness* (Tucson: University of Arizona Press, 1988), 43. In fact, official visitation to Arches in 1956 was 28,500, down from 31,800 the previous year. Visitation did not top 300,000 until 1977.

25. Abbey, *Desert Solitaire,* 45. In 1967 the Park Service completed a five-mile-long oiled road from Utah Highway 91 (later Interstate I-15) to a viewpoint of the five "finger canyons" of the Kolob, with a shorter spur dead-ending in Taylor Creek canyon. Steven H. Heath, "Notes on the History of the Kolob Canyons," Washington County Historical Society, October 21, 2010, http://wchsutah.org/documents/kolob-canyons-heath.php.

26. Edward Abbey, journal entries for April 7, 1957, and June 15, 1956, in Abbey, *Confessions of a Barbarian: Selections from the Journals of Edward Abbey, 1951–1989,* ed. David Petersen (New York: Little, Brown, 1994), 140, 132.

27. Joseph L. Sax, *Mountains without Handrails: Reflections on the National Parks* (Ann Arbor: University of Michigan Press, 1980), 12.

28. Conrad Wirth, "'Mission 66': Statement by Conrad L. Wirth, Director of NPS," folder A9815, box 21, series 8NS-079-93-281, Record Group 79-64F-307, NARA-DNV. Wirth's talk was presented at the NPS Public Services Conference, Great Smoky Mountains NP, September 21, 1955.

CHAPTER 22

1. Roderick Peattie, *The Inverted Mountains: Canyons of the West* (New York: Vanguard Press, 1948), 211–52.

2. Randall Henderson, "Glen Canyon Voyage," *Desert Magazine* 15 (October 1952): 7–12. Rigg and Wright operated Mexican Hat Expeditions after the deaths of Norman and Doris Nevills in an aviation accident in 1949.

3. Wallace Stegner, "Backroads River," *Atlantic* 181 (January 1948): 56–64; Stegner, "The Artist as Environmental Advocate," oral history interview by Ann Lage, Sierra Club History Series, Regional Oral History Office, Bancroft Library, University of California, Berkeley, 1982, 23.

4. "The Colorado: A Wild and Beautiful River Is Put to Work for Man," *Life* 17 (October 23, 1944): 72–84.

5. Jack Breed, "Utah's Arches of Stone," *National Geographic* 92 (August 1947): 173–92; Breed, "Flaming Cliffs of Monument Valley," *National Geographic* 88 (October 1945): 452–61.

6. Katie Lee, *All My Rivers Are Gone: A Journey of Discovery through Glen Canyon* (Boulder, CO: Johnson Books, 1998), 161.

7. Lee, *All My Rivers Are Gone*, 197.

8. Photographers such as Philip Hyde (Edward Abbey and Philip Hyde, *Slickrock: The Canyon Country of Southeast Utah* [San Francisco: Sierra Club, 1971]) and Eliot Porter (*The Place No One Knew: Glen Canyon on the Colorado* [San Francisco: Sierra Club, 1963]) also played a significant role in placing Glen Canyon into the environmentalist pantheon. Tad Nichols, who made numerous voyages down Glen Canyon with Frank Wright and Katie Lee, presented his stunning black-and-white photos in *Glen Canyon: Images of a Lost World* (Santa Fe: Museum of New Mexico, 1999). Russell Martin discusses Hyde and Porter in *A Story That Stands like a Dam: Glen Canyon and the Struggle for the Soul of the West* (Salt Lake City: University of Utah Press, 1989), 176–84.

9. Quotations are from Richard Quist, "The River Gods Smiled," and Brad Dimock, "My First Sleight Trip," both in Martha Ham, ed., *Ken Sleight's Allies and Accomplices* (St. George, UT: privately published, 2014).

10. Vaughn Roche, "'Seldom Seen Smith' Mourns a Lost Canyon and Dead Foes," *High Country News*, October 18, 1993; Chris Ketcham, "The Original Monkey Wrencher," *Salon*, October 21, 2006, http://www.salon.com/2006/10/21/sleight/.

11. David R. Brower to William R. Halliday, January 16, 1954, folder 7, box 1, William R. Halliday papers, MLSC.

12. "David R. Brower: Environmental Activist, Publicist, and Prophet," oral history interview by Susan Schrepfer, Sierra Club History Series, Regional Oral History Office, Bancroft Library, University of California, Berkeley, 1980, 118.

13. "David R. Brower: Environmental Activist," 130. For a nuanced analysis of Brower's role in acceding to the Glen Canyon project, see Hassell, *Rainbow Bridge*, 109–12.

14. "David R. Brower: Environmental Activist," 138.
15. Floyd E. Dominy, oral history interviews by Brit Allan Storey, Boyce, VA, April 6, 1994, and April 8, 1996 (U.S. Bureau of Reclamation, 1996), 198, http://www.usbr.gov/history/CommissBios/DOMINYD3.pdf.
16. Angus M. Woodbury, "Protecting Rainbow Bridge," *Science* 132 (August 26, 1960): 1262; "Silly Wilderness Preservation Proposal," *Salt Lake Tribune*, March 8, 1960. David Sproul discusses the Rainbow Bridge issue at length in chapter 6 of *A Bridge between Cultures*.
17. Udall to Wayne Aspinall, August 27, 1960, folder 21, box 64, series 4, Wilderness Society Records, DPL.
18. John O'Reilly, "Udall at the Bridge." For another contemporaneous account of Udall's 1961 visit to Rainbow Bridge and the meeting in Page, see Weldon F. Heald, "Helicopters over Rainbow Bridge," *Westways*, September 1961.
19. Mark W. T. Harvey describes Udall's meeting with Floyd Dominy in "Defending the Park System: The Controversy over Rainbow Bridge," *New Mexico Historical Review* 73 (January 1998): 45–67.
20. Russell Martin describes Navajo tribal chair Paul Jones's reaction to Udall's national park proposal in *A Story That Stands like a Dam*, 234.
21. The Sierra Club's board of directors voted to support the low-reservoir proposal at a meeting in September 1960 (David R. Brower to Fred Seaton, September 15, 1960, folder 21, box 64, series 4, Wilderness Society Records, DPL). This proposal was resurrected years later by the Glen Canyon Institute, which advocates a "fill Lake Mead first" approach.
22. Floyd E. Dominy oral history interview, April 8, 1996, 200–201.

CHAPTER 23
1. In 1914 E. C. LaRue of the Bureau of Reclamation surveyed a potential dam site immediately below the confluence of the Green and Colorado Rivers; it was later superseded by the Dark Canyon site, only to reemerge during the debate over Canyonlands (Schmieding, *From Controversy to Compromise*, 67).
2. Bates Wilson recalled in 1967 that Secretary Udall first flew over the Confluence area while en route to the Grand Canyon conference. See Gaylord Staveley, "A Conversation with Bates Wilson," *Western Gateways*, Autumn 1967, https://www.nps.gov/cany/learn/historyculture/bateswilson.htm.
3. Schmieding, *From Controversy to Compromise*, 96.
4. Moss, King, and Peterson wrote a joint letter to Udall on March 4, 1961, advising him that the area between the Glen Canyon NRA and Dead Horse Point had "great potential as a National Park or Recreation Area" (folder 124, series 36607, NPS-SEUG).
5. Leslie P. Arnberger to Thomas J. Allen, June 27, 1961, folder 124, series 36607, NPS-SEUG.
6. For more on Bates Wilson, see Jen Jackson Quintano, *Blow Sand in His Soul: Bates Wilson, the Heart of Canyonlands* (Moab, UT: Friends of Arches and Canyonlands Parks, 2014).

7.   "Return from Pack Trip," *Moab Times-Independent*, April 5, 1951; Alan D. "Tug" Wilson, "Early Trips in the Needles: An Idea Takes Shape," *Canyon Legacy* 1 (Dan O'Laurie Museum, Moab, UT), Fall 1989.

8.   U.S. Department of the Interior, National Park Service, *The National Parks: Shaping the System*, 2005, 81, https://www.nps.gov/parkhistory/online_books/shaping/index.htm.

9.   Until 1970 recreation areas such as Glen Canyon were considered separate from the National Park System; Glen Canyon was not officially designated as a park unit until 1972. Arches ranger Lloyd Pierson recalled in 1985 that national recreation areas were "looked upon by most park field people then as nothing more than local play grounds and not fit to be in the National Park Service system." Pierson, "The New Park Studies at Canyonlands National Park, 1959 and 1960, and Events Leading Up to Them," typescript, 1985, folder 4, series 3-579, NPS-SEUG.

10. Memorandum 57-12, February 20, 1957, Region 3 National Park Service, cited in Pierson, "New Park Studies at Canyonlands."

11. Frank Jensen, "Jeep Jaunt to Purgatory," *Salt Lake Tribune*, August 30, 1959.

12. The "Needles Area Field Investigation Report" was compiled by Region 3 of the Park Service but was not formally published (copy in series 36607, folder 659, NPS-SEUG).

13. Bates Wilson recalled Diederich's comment at Grand View Point in Staveley, "Conversation with Bates Wilson."

14. Thomas J. Allen of the NPS's Santa Fe office proposed the hybrid designation for Canyonlands in a letter to Conrad Wirth, July 26, 1961 (folder 124, series 36607, NPS-SEUG). Diederich's memo outlining his million-acre proposal is unfortunately missing from this file.

15. Pierson, "New Park Studies at Canyonlands," 23, 32.

16. Udall's wife, Ermalee, and their two sons also came on the Canyonlands trip, as did members of other dignitaries' families. A full list of participants is in folder 124, series 36607, NPS-SEUG.

17. Udall news release, Region 3, National Park Service, July 12, 1961, folder 124, series 36607, NPS-SEUG.

18. F. E. Masland Jr. to members of National Parks Advisory Board, July 17, 1961, folder 124, series 36607, NPS-SEUG; Udall news release, July 12, 1961.

19. For more on Bennett's opposition to a national park in Canyonlands, see Thomas G. Smith, "The Canyonlands National Park Controversy," *Utah Historical Quarterly* 59 (Summer 1991): 216–42.

20. Masland to National Parks Advisory Board, July 17, 1961.

CHAPTER 24

1.   "Bennett Charges 'Distortion' of His Position on Parks," *Moab Times-Independent*, August 24, 1961.

2.   "Action Likely on Park Withdrawal Following Controversial Week," *Moab Times-Independent*, August 10, 1961. The bills were H.R. 8573 (King), H.R.

8574 (Peterson), and S. 2387 (Moss). The King and Peterson bills would not have permitted hunting within the park.

3.   "Democratic Lawmakers Set to Introduce National Park Bill," *Salt Lake Times,* August 18, 1961.

4.   Schmieding, *From Controversy to Compromise,* 123. Ranchers in the Canyonlands area also held permits for some 6,400 sheep.

5.   Smith, "Canyonlands National Park Controversy," 230; "Park Plot Thickens as New Bill Enters Hopper," *Moab Times-Independent,* September 21, 1961.

6.   Lloyd Pierson is quoted in Quintano, *Blow Sand in His Soul,* 101.

7.   "More Canyonlands Chatter," *Moab Times-Independent,* February 1, 1962.

8.   "Texas Gulf Test Proves Value of Potash Beds," *Moab Times-Independent,* June 1, 1960; "Excavation for Potash Mill Begins at Cane Creek Site," *Moab Times-Independent,* June 29, 1961.

9.   The *Moab Times-Independent* chronicled Moab's potash boomlet and subsequent bust through articles such as "Optimism Soars for Future in Moab after Announcement" (May 4, 1960); "Fifty-Six New Students Swell School Enrollment This Week" (January 12, 1961); "Crowded Schools" (August 23, 1962); "Claims Spiral Upward, Employment Office Says" (December 27, 1962); "Work Completion Seen Cause for Population Loss" (January 31, 1961).

10.   "What Is Value of Tourism?," *Moab Times-Independent,* March 3, 1962.

11.   Smith, "Canyonlands National Park Controversy," 222–23. Udall's reluctance to use the Antiquities Act in Canyonlands was undoubtedly astute, given the reaction that later presidents incurred with vast monument designations in Utah.

12.   Statement of Carl W. Buchheisteb, National Audubon Society, in U.S. Senate, Committee on Interior and Insular Affairs, *Proposed Canyonlands National Park in Utah: Part 2: Hearings, Eighty-Seventh Congress, Second Session, on S. 2387, Apr. 20, 21, 23, 1962* (Washington, D.C.: Government Printing Office, 1962), 206.

13.   National Park Service, "Canyon Lands National Park (Proposed)," n.d., folder 124, series 36601, NPS-SEUG.

14.   Schmieding, *From Controversy to Compromise,* 102–3. Eggert produced the film *Wilderness River Trail* during the Dinosaur National Monument controversy of the 1950s.

15.   Robert R. Edminster and Osmond L. Harline, *An Economic Study of the Proposed Canyonlands National Park and Related Recreation Resources* (Salt Lake City: Bureau of Economic and Business Research, University of Utah, March 1962), 15–16.

16.   Visitation at Canyonlands had reached only 33,400 by 1970 and 71,700 by 1975, the tenth year of the park's operation. Even by 1990, when the University of Utah study projected visitation to reach one million, it stood at 276,830, largely because the road system originally envisioned for the park had not been completed.

17.   Statement of Stewart Udall, in U.S. Senate, Committee on Interior and Insular Affairs, *Proposed Canyonlands National Park in Utah,* 49.

18. Statement of Stewart Udall, in U.S. Senate, Committee on Interior and Insular Affairs, *Proposed Canyonlands National Park in Utah*, 53–54.

19. Lloyd Pierson, "The New Park Studies at Canyonlands National Park, 1959 and 1960, and Events Leading Up to Them."

20. Bernard DeVoto, "West against Itself"; statement of Robert S. Shriver, in U.S. Senate, Committee on Interior and Insular Affairs, *Proposed Canyonlands National Park in Utah*, 268.

21. Statement of Norman G. Boyd, in U.S. Senate, Committee on Interior and Insular Affairs, *Proposed Canyonlands National Park in Utah*, 309, 268.

22. "New Canyonlands Bill Planned by Senator Moss," *Moab Times-Independent*, January 10, 1963; Smith, "Canyonlands National Park Controversy," 236.

23. Will Fehr, "Utah Lawmakers Unite on Canyonlands Plan," *Salt Lake Tribune*, April 7, 1963; statement of Frank Moss, in U.S. Senate, *Proposed Canyonlands National Park in Utah, Hearing Before the Subcommittee on Public Lands of the Committee on Interior and Insular Affairs, Eighty-Eighth Congress, First Session, on S. 27* (Washington, D.C.: Government Printing Office, 1963), 3.

24. Statement of Charles Eggert, in U.S. Senate, *Proposed Canyonlands National Park in Utah, Hearing Before the Subcommittee on Public Lands*, 53.

25. Smith, "Canyonlands National Park Controversy," 237–38.

26. Schmieding, *From Controversy to Compromise*, 105–6.

27. Schmieding, 106.

CHAPTER 25

1. S. W. Lohman, *The Geologic Story of Canyonlands National Park*, U.S. Geological Survey Bulletin 1327 (Washington, D.C.: Government Printing Office, 1974), 2.

2. "Canyonlands Travel Exceeds Expectations," *Moab Times-Independent*, June 3, 1965; "Improvement Continues in Canyonlands Park," *Moab Times-Independent*, June 30, 1966.

3. Schmieding, *From Controversy to Compromise*, 121.

4. Notes of planning meeting, November 18, 1964, folder 126, series 33607, NPS-SEUG.

5. "Master Plan Brief for Canyonlands National Park," 1965, folder 179, series 36607, NPS-SEUG. A map accompanying the plan identified an area northeast of Squaw Flat as the potential site of "Canyonlands Enterprises, Inc.," offering "lodging, meals, store, horse rental, swimming."

6. "General Development Map, Canyonlands National Park," fig. 52 in Schmieding, *From Controversy to Compromise*, 128.

7. "Master Plan Brief for Canyonlands National Park"; notes of planning meeting, November 18, 1964.

8. "What Are Costs of Developing Canyonlands?," *Moab Times-Independent*, August 27, 1964.

9. The Bureau of Public Roads' work on the Elephant Hill route is documented in notes of a staff meeting at Canyonlands National Park, December 20, 1966, folder 41, accession no. 339, NPS-SEUG.

10. "Program Schedules," NPS Southwest Region, folder 15, box 236, Frank Moss papers, MLSC.

11. Maxine Newell, "Canyonlands National Park Observes Second Anniversary," *Moab Times-Independent,* September 8, 1966.

12. Staveley, "Conversation with Bates Wilson."

13. Among Moss's proposals during this period was a bill to establish a Great Salt Lake national monument, which he introduced in January 1967. The bill passed the Senate but not the House of Representatives.

14. Frank E. Moss, "Parks Are for People," *Congressional Record—Senate,* August 1, 1968, 24616–19.

15. U.S. Department of the Interior, National Park Service, *Draft Environmental Statement, Proposed Squaw Flat–Confluence Overlook Road, July 26, 1972* (Washington, D.C.: Government Printing Office, 1972).

16. Jeffrey Ingram to Bates Wilson, November 22, 1967, folder 30, box 62, series 4, Wilderness Society Records, DPL.

17. Bates Wilson, memo to staff, April 9, 1968, file 339-003-181-1968-0409, NPS-SEUG.

18. Bates Wilson, "Canyonlands National Park Roads and Development" [mimeo], March 11, 1968, file 339-003-181-1968-0311, NPS-SEUG.

19. Clyde L. Denis, "Closing the Road to Chesler Park: Why Access to Canyonlands National Park Remains Limited," *Utah Historical Quarterly* 84 (Fall 2016): 329–46.

20. The cost of completing the Confluence road is outlined in an NPS briefing statement dated March 2, 1978 (folder 126, series 33607, NPS-SEUG). Clyde Denis shows how budgetary issues held up the Confluence overlook road and the Needles parkway in "Closing the Road to Chesler Park."

21. "Canyonlands Road Project Deferred," NPS news release, May 8, 1968, folder 17, box 236, Frank Moss papers, MLSC.

22. "Road Proposals Dominate Tuesday's Chamber of Commerce Meeting," *Moab Times-Independent,* November 5, 1968; Dick Wilson, "Superintendent Defends Policy of Limited Development of Canyonlands," *Moab Times-Independent,* September 12, 1968.

23. Dick Wilson, "Points of View on Park Planning Outlined," *Moab Times-Independent,* October 3, 1968.

24. Cal Black, letter to editor, *Moab Times-Independent,* December 23, 1971.

25. Rogers, *Roads in the Wilderness,* 46–47. Rogers notes that Abbey and Black developed a grudging respect for each other despite their profound disagreement over roads and wilderness.

CHAPTER 26

1. "Development Schedule, Proposed Development—Glen Canyon National Recreation Area (Proposed) Roads and Trails, Buildings, Utilities, and Miscellaneous," in U.S. Senate, *Canyonlands National Park and Glen Canyon National Recreation Area, Hearing, Ninety-First Congress, Second Session, on S. 26 and S. 27, 1970* (Washington, D.C.: Government Printing Office, 1970), 41–42. Planned boating facilities, many of which were never built, are shown on the 1969 U.S. Geological Survey map of the Glen Canyon National Recreation Area.

2. U.S. Department of the Interior, Bureau of Reclamation, *Lake Powell: Jewel of the Colorado* (Washington, D.C.: Government Printing Office, 1965), iv, epigraph credited to Gordon Michelle. Written and illustrated in the style of Dave Brower's Exhibit Format books, this brochure was intended to counter the Sierra Club's depictions of the lost glories of Glen Canyon.

3. Jim Stiles, "Ken Sleight," *Canyon Country Zephyr,* August–September 1999, https://www.canyoncountryzephyr.com/oldzephyr/archives/ken-sleight .html.

4. Lee, *All My Rivers Are Gone,* 236–37.

5. Lee, 241–42.

6. Butch Farabee, Lake Powell oral history, http://lakepowellhistory.com/ tourism/tourism.html.

7. Farabee, Lake Powell oral history.

8. Martin, *Story That Stands like a Dam,* 306–7.

9. "Ken Sleight Remembers: Rainbow Bridge," *Canyon Country Zephyr,* August 2, 2015, http://www.canyoncountryzephyr.com/2015/08/02/ken-sleight -remembers-rainbow-bridge/.

10. Angelita Bulletts, "Our Homeland: The Colorado Plateau Ecoregion," in Stoffle et al., *Ethnographic Overview and Assessment,* 66.

11. McPherson, *Navajo Land, Navajo Culture,* 137–39.

12. Black's comments on the canyon parkway were printed in a special issue of Ward Roylance's Enchanted Wilderness Association newsletter in 1971 (folder 8, box 1, Ward J. Roylance papers, MLSC).

13. Statement of Harry C. Helland during April 25–28, 1967, field trip to Waterpocket Fold, folder 17, box 62, series 4, Wilderness Society Records, DPL. Helland's predecessor, Clem Church, also advocated building a canyon parkway, and in early 1966 he made a field visit to the Glen Canyon area with Park Service and BLM officials to map out a route. "Big Shot's Road Tour Raises Hopes for New Highways," *Garfield County News,* January 20, 1966.

14. Staveley, "Conversation with Bates Wilson." In early 1966 NPS regional director George Miller told Henry Helland that his agency had no objection to studying an alignment between Bullfrog Basin and Hole-in-the-Rock and another west of Canyonlands National Park. Miller to Helland, January 25, 1966, folder 17, box 62, series 4, Wilderness Society Records, DPL.

15. "Canyonlands Plan Lists Priorities," *Moab Times-Independent*, December 9, 1966.

16. "Advocate Golden Parkway," *Garfield County News*, January 26, 1967.

17. Larry Davis noted that the village of Boulder saw a decrease in tourist traffic after Interstate 70 was opened well to the north of Garfield County. Ward Roylance, Enchanted Wilderness Association newsletter, August 1971, folder 8, box 1, Ward J. Roylance papers, MLSC.

18. Statement of June Viavant in U.S. House of Representatives, *Glen Canyon National Recreation Area: Hearings Before the Subcommittee on National Parks and Recreation, House of Representatives, Ninety-Second Congress, Second Session on H.R. 15073 and Related Bills: Hearing Held in Kanab, Utah, May 27, 1972, Washington, DC, June 8, 1972* (Washington, D.C.: Government Printing Office, 1972), 89.

19. Royal Robbins to Frank Moss, March 1970, folder 23, box 273, Moss papers, MLSC.

20. Statement of H. Burrell Lewis, U.S. House of Representatives, *Glen Canyon National Recreation Area*, 68.

21. "Supt. Wilson Comments on Proposal of Group to Switch Golden Circle System Plans," *Moab Times-Independent*, February 19, 1970.

CHAPTER 27

1. Conrad L. Wirth to Howard Zahniser, March 19, 1956, in Scott, "National Parks and Their Wilderness."

2. National Parks Association, "A Wilderness Plan for Arches National Monument and the Surrounding Region Including Canyonlands National Park," prepared by William J. Hart, Harold F. Wise/Robert Gladstone Associates, December 14, 1967, folder 3, box 2, Capitol Reef National Park records, MLSC.

3. Congress has designated considerably more wilderness in national parks outside Utah, notably in California, where nearly seven million acres hold this status. Robert B. Keiter, *To Conserve Unimpaired: The Evolution of the National Park Idea* (Washington, D.C.: Island Press, 2013), 23.

4. The Paria Canyon BLM Primitive Area was designated the Paria Canyon–Vermilion Cliffs Wilderness by Congress in 1984. Dark Canyon and Grand Gulch remain in primitive area status.

5. U.S. Department of the Interior, Bureau of Outdoor Recreation, *Trails for America: Report on the Nationwide Trail Study* (Washington, D.C.: Government Printing Office, 1966).

6. John Hollenhorst, "Steel Cage Erected to Protect Historic 1776 Lake Powell Inscription," *Deseret News*, March 11, 2016.

7. Charles B. Hunt, "Gilbert's Notebooks," in Trimble, *Capitol Reef Reader*, 90–93.

8. George W. Miller to director, Park Service, November 4, 1964, folder 126, box 3, series 36607, CANY.

9. "We Think It's Justified," *Moab Times-Independent,* May 11, 1967.
10. Statement of Bates Wilson, *in U.S. Senate, Canyonlands National Park and Glen Canyon National Recreation Area: Hearing Before the Subcommittee on Parks and Recreation of the Committee on Interior and Insular Affairs* (Washington, D.C.: Government Printing Office, 1968), 51–52.
11. Wallace Stegner, "The Artist as Environmental Advocate," oral history interview by Ann Lage, Regional Oral History Office, Bancroft Library, University of California, Berkeley, 1982, 17.
12. Lurt Knee recalled his involvement in the Capitol Reef boundary expansion in an interview with Stephen Trimble (Trimble, *Capitol Reef Reader,* 265–66).
13. Frye, *From Barrier to Crossroads,* chap. 10.
14. Udall presented the Capitol Reef proposal to Lyndon Johnson and his wife, Lady Bird, on December 11, 1968, but the president delayed action, fearing adverse reaction from Congress. Superintendent Heyder remained in the dark regarding the expansion until he heard about it on the radio while driving to Richfield. The events surrounding the January 20 proclamation are detailed in Frye, *From Barrier to Crossroads,* chapters 10 and 11. These make fascinating reading in light of later controversies over presidential use of the Antiquities Act.
15. Nethella Woolsey, "Congressman and Senator Attend Meeting as Many Protest Monuments 'Land Grab' in County," *Garfield County News,* February 20, 1969.
16. Woolsey, "Congressman and Senator Attend Meeting."
17. "Park Expansion," in *Congressional Quarterly Almanac 1970,* 26th ed., http://library.cqpress.com/cqalmanac/cqal70-1293842.

CHAPTER 28

1. "Moss Re-introduces Bill to Open Canyon Country," *Deseret News,* January 26, 1967.
2. M. Guy Bishop, "The Paper Power Plant: Utah's Kaiparowits Project and the Politics of Environmentalism," *Journal of the West* 35 (July 1996); Robert W. Bernick, "Utility Locates Coal in S. Utah Probing," *Salt Lake Tribune,* December 22, 1963; William R. Gould, "Kaiparowits Power Project," talk given to 11th Annual Engineering Symposium, Brigham Young University, Provo, UT, April 18, 1970, folder 8, box 40, William R. Gould papers, MLSC. Southern California Edison received its initial federal coal prospecting permits for the Kaiparowits Power Project on November 1, 1962, and the four partners in the project signed a Memorandum of Agreement on June 18, 1963. The consortium filed a water application from the Colorado River in Lake Powell on January 15, 1964 (folder 13, box 105, Gould papers, MLSC).
3. "The Kaiparowits Power Project," fact sheet distributed by Southern California Edison, April 1975, Kaiparowits Power Project Files, MLSC.

4. Ronald Jepperson, Eric Hemel, and Robert Hauptman, *The Kaiparowits Coal Project and the Environment: A Case Study* (Ann Arbor, MI: Ann Arbor Science Publishers, 1981).

5. "Interior Secretary Gives OK to Huge Kaiparowits Plan," *Iron County Record,* October 9, 1969.

6. Details of the Kaiparowits Power Project and its environmental effects are taken from U.S. Department of the Interior, Bureau of Land Management, *Kaiparowits: Environmental Impact Statement—Final,* vol. 1 (Washington, D.C.: Government Printing Office, 1976); and from Gould, "Kaiparowits Power Project."

7. J. W. Neuberger et al., *Southwest Energy Study: An Evaluation of Coal-Fired Electric Power Generation in the Southwest* (Washington, D.C.: U.S. Department of the Interior, 1972). The proposed 2,500-megawatt Allen-Warner Valley Energy System, consisting of power plants in Warner Valley, Utah, and Dry Lake, Nevada, was not completed, although a smaller coal-fired power plant was built near Moapa, Nevada, which operated until 2014. The first three generating units of the Four Corners station opened in 1963 and 1964, with two additional units opening in 1969 and 1970.

8. E. W. Kenworthy, "Southwest's Air Quality Held Periled," *New York Times,* April 27, 1972.

9. Comments of National Park Service, in U.S. Department of the Interior, Bureau of Land Management, *Kaiparowits: Environmental Impact Statement—Draft,* vol. 9 (Washington, D.C.: Government Printing Office, 1974), 202–3; "Utah Plant's Smog Would Drift into Parks, Federal Study Says," Arizona Republic (Phoenix), March 31, 1976.

10. William R. Gould, remarks to Utah State Bar, June 20, 1975, folder 11, box 42, Gould papers, MLSC.

11. "Kaiparowits Project History," folder 13, box 105, Gould papers, MLSC.

12. William R. Gould, "Energy and Growth in Southern California," March 5, 1976, folder 15, box 42, Gould papers, MLSC; Jack McLellan, "Kaiparowits Coal Power Plans Scuttled," *High Country News,* April 23, 1976.

13. McLellan, "Kaiparowits Coal Power Plans Scuttled."

14. U.S. Department of the Interior, Bureau of Land Management, *Intermountain Power Project: Draft Environmental Statement, 1979,* vol. 1, *Salt Wash Proposed Site* (Salt Lake City: Utah State Office, 1979), 1-1 to 1-3; table 3-5.

15. Larry Pryor, "Loss of Power Plant Evokes Hostility in Utah," *Los Angeles Times,* April 25, 1976.

16. U.S. Department of the Interior, Bureau of Land Management and National Park Service, *Tar Sand Triangle, Utah: Draft Environmental Impact Statement, Proposed Lease Conversions* (Washington, D.C.: Government Printing Office, 1984), iv.

17. Ray Wheeler, "The BLM Wilderness Inventory," in Utah Wilderness Coalition, *Wilderness at the Edge: A Citizen Proposal for Utah's Canyon's and Deserts* (Kaysville, UT: Gibbs Smith, 1991), 38.

18. Terri Martin, "Wilderness and Utah's Parks," in Utah Wilderness Coalition, *Wilderness at the Edge,* 32.
19. Lisa Jones, "Utah's Canyons Cut to the Bone," *High Country News,* June 17, 1991.
20. Martin, "Wilderness and Utah's Parks."

CHAPTER 29

1. Linda King Newell and Vivian Linford Talbot, *A History of Garfield County* (Salt Lake City: Utah State Historical Society, 1998), 305–6. In 1935 the Civilian Conservation Corps and the Forest Service completed a road from Escalante to Boulder via the rugged Hell's Backbone, and another route from Torrey to Boulder over Boulder Mountain, but both of these remained closed in winter.
2. "Golden Circle Highway Plans Call for Much Work in County," *Garfield County News,* December 9, 1965.
3. In a 1969 letter to Salt Lake City activist Jack McLellan, Nethella Griffin Woolsey of the Escalante Chamber of Commerce noted that "the Circle Cliffs area is on the verge of great oil production.... Development of this oil will mean much to this country" (folder 11, box 63, series 4, Wilderness Society Records, DPL). In 1981 Capitol Reef National Park superintendent Derek Hambly indicated he would oppose the use of the Burr Trail for commercial ore-hauling vehicles. "No Trucking on Burr Trail, Says Official," *Garfield County News,* May 7, 1981.
4. Grant Johnson, "A Personal Early SUWA History," *Canyon Country Zephyr,* August–September 2005.
5. Rogers, *Roads in the Wilderness,* 93–94.
6. Frye, *From Barrier to Crossroads,* chap. 18.
7. Grant Johnson was arrested and tried in connection with the sabotage incident but was not convicted. He maintained throughout the trial that he had been singled out for his opposition to the road and his unconventional lifestyle. Clive Kincaid became embroiled in a controversy over a stone cabin he was building on Deer Creek, which the BLM maintained sat partly on public land. Such were the hazards of high-profile environmentalism in Utah.
8. The Burr Trail switchbacks traversed a section of former state land that Garfield County had acquired, and only through great difficulty was the Park Service able to arrange a land swap that prevented this part of the road from being paved (Frye, *From Barrier to Crossroads,* chap. 18).
9. Rogers, *Roads in the Wilderness,* 110.
10. Arthur Gómez, *Quest for the Golden Circle: The Four Corners and the Metropolitan West, 1945–1970* (Albuquerque: University of New Mexico Press, 1994), 171–74.

CHAPTER 30

1. For a discussion of salt tectonic features in the Arches-Canyonlands area, see Annabelle Foos, "Geology of the Moab Region," https://www.yumpu.com

/en/document/read/7383854/geology-of-the-moab-region-introduction
. -national-park-.

2. This and the ensuing description of the waste facility are taken from chapter 5
    of U.S. Department of Energy, Office of Civilian Radioactive Waste Manage-
    ment, *Environmental Assessment, Davis Canyon Site*, Utah, DOE/RW0071, vol.
    1 (Washington, D.C.: Office of Civilian Radioactive Waste Assessment, May
    1986).

3. U.S. Department of Energy, Office of Civilian Radioactive Waste Manage-
    ment, *Environmental Assessment, Davis Canyon Site, Utah*, table 4-2 (p. 4-4), p.
    4-12.

4. Schmieding, *From Controversy to Compromise*, 202; U.S. Department of
    Energy, Office of Civilian Radioactive Waste Management, *Environmental
    Assessment, Davis Canyon Site, Utah*, table 5-47 (p. 5-191), p. 5-193.

5. Dan Whipple, "Feds Study Nuke Dump near Canyonlands," *High Country
    News*, February 5, 1982.

6. Iver Peterson, "Utah Towns Debate Nuclear Waste," *New York Times*, March
    5, 1984.

7. Whipple, "Feds Study Nuke Dump;" Karen M. Magnuson, "Utah Town
    Wants Everything: Nuke Waste Dump and Tourists," United Press Inter-
    national, August 28, 1983; Paul Perry, "The National Park and the Nuclear
    Dump," *Outside*, December 1983, 40–45, 83–88.

8. Perry, "National Park and the Nuclear Dump."

9. William Lockhart and Terri Martin, interview by Danielle Endres, Salt Lake
    City, Utah, May 22, 2009, for the Nuclear Technology in the American West
    Oral History Project, American West Center and Marriott Library, Univer-
    sity of Utah.

10. Christopher McLeod, "Utah Governor Declares War on a Canyonlands
    Nuclear Dump," *High Country News*, May 28, 1984.

11. "Sen. Garn Responds to DOE Proposal for Nuclear Waste," *Davis County
    Clipper* (Ogden, UT), January 9, 1985.

12. Joseph M. Bauman, "Canyonlands May Have Eluded Nuclear Waste Dump
    After All," *Deseret News*, December 21, 1984.

13. "Nuclear Dump Sites Narrowed to Three," *High Country News*, January 21, 1985.

14. "Feds May Again Eye a Canyonlands Dump," *High Country News*, September
    18, 1985.

15. "A Controversial Decision," *High Country News*, July 7, 1986.

CHAPTER 31

1. Paul Larmer, "'The Mother of All Land Grabs,'" *High Country News*, Septem-
    ber 30, 1996; Laurie Sullivan Maddox, "Taking Swipes at Clinton, Utahns Vow
    to Fight Back," *Salt Lake Tribune*, September 19, 1996; Dan Harrie, "Utah Law-
    makers Split over New Monument," *Salt Lake Tribune*, September 20, 1996.

2. The monument restriction bills included James Hansen's H.R. 4148 and Bob
    Bennett's S. 357 (105th Congress).

3. See James R. Rasband, "Antiquities Act Monuments: The Elgin Marbles of our Public Lands?," in *The Antiquities Act: A Century of American Archaeology, Historic Preservation, and Nature Conservation,* ed. David Harmon, Francis P. McManamon, and Dwight T. Pitcaithley (Tucson: University of Arizona Press, 2006), 158–70.

4. Katherine Bill, "Mega Coal Mine Proposed Again in Utah," *High Country News,* July 25, 1994.

5. Twila Van Leer, "Go-Ahead for Mining Could Enrich Schools," *Deseret News,* August 30, 1993.

6. Jim Woolf, "Making of a Monument: What Led to Clinton's Grand Staircase Decision?," *Salt Lake Tribune,* September 22, 1996.

7. Lee Davidson, "White House Secretly Worked on Grand Staircase for More Than a Year," *Salt Lake Tribune,* April 29, 1997. The article cites testimony on the development of the Grand Staircase–Escalante proclamation at a hearing of the House Resources Subcommittee, chaired by Utah representative Jim Hansen. Charles Wilkinson described his role in drafting the proclamation in his book *Fire on the Plateau: Conflict and Endurance in the American Southwest* (San Francisco: Island Press, 1999), 328–29. The absence of field studies of the Kaiparowits region prior to monument designation was unusual; in Alaska, for example, the National Park Service conducted extensive surveys of potential national park and monument lands before President Carter designated seventeen national monuments comprising fifty-six million acres in 1978.

8. "Proclamation 6920—Establishment of the Grand Staircase–Escalante National Monument," American Presidency Project, September 18, 1996, http://www.presidency.ucsb.edu/ws/?pid=51948.

9. See Ann E. Halden, "The Grand Staircase–Escalante National Monument and the Antiquities Act," *Fordham Environmental Law Journal* 8 (1997): 713–39.

10. Jim Woolf, "Monument Land Surveyed for Oil," *Salt Lake Tribune,* October 1, 1996.

11. Karl Cates, "Green Light for Conoco Oil Drilling Draws Fire," *Deseret News,* March 28, 1997.

12. Representative James Hansen and Senator Orrin Hatch each introduced bills to ratify the agreement between the BLM and the state of Utah to exchange school trust lands within the monument; these became law on October 31, 1998.

13. Permitted livestock use in the original Grand Staircase–Escalante NM remained at 76,457 animal-unit months (AUMs) after monument designation, although drought has resulted in significantly lower utilization of the range. See U.S. Department of the Interior, Bureau of Land Management and National Park Service, "Fact Sheet: Livestock Grazing," in *Grand Staircase–Escalante National Monument: Livestock Grazing Plan Amendment EIS* (Washington, D.C.: Government Printing Office, 2012); also Phil Taylor, "Grazing

in Clinton-Era Monuments—It's Complicated," *E&E News*, April 16, 2016, https://www.eenews.net/stories/1060035783; and John Hollenhorst, "BLM, Ranchers at Odds over Cattle Grazing in Escalante National Monument," KSL.com, April 29, 2015, https://www.ksl.com/article/34374555/blm-ranchers-at-odds-over-cattle-grazing-in-escalante-national-monument. For an analysis of the Grand Canyon Trust's actions regarding grazing allotments, see Raymond B. Wrabley Jr., "Managing the Monument: Cows and Conservation in Grand Staircase–Escalante National Monument," *Journal of Land, Resources, and Environmental Law* 29 (August 2009): 253–80.

14. Paul Larmer, "A Bold Stroke: Clinton Takes a 1.7 Million-Acre Stand in Utah," *High Country News*, September 30, 1996.

15. "Two New National Monuments Approved," *Phoenix Business Journal*, November 10, 2000.

16. "Grand Staircase–Escalante National Monument: A Summary of Economic Performance in the Surrounding Communities," Headwaters Economics, Spring 2011, https://headwaterseconomics.org/wp-content/uploads/Escalante.pdf.

17. April Reese, "Scientists Sue to Protect Utah Monument—and Fossils That Could Rewrite Earth's History," *Science*, January 17, 2019, doi:10.1126/science.aaw6866; "Paleontology: Discovery and History," Grand Staircase Escalante Partners, https://gsenm.org/paleontology-2/.

CHAPTER 32

1. Park visitation statistics are from "NPS Stats," National Park Service Visitor Use Statistics, https://irma.nps.gov/Stats/.

2. "Utah Park Visitor Facilities Subject of Heated Debate," *Moab Times-Independent*, June 12, 1973. Initially the Park Service wanted to close Zion Lodge at the end of 1972 and shutter Bryce Canyon Lodge by 1977.

3. Zion superintendent Jeff Bradybaugh, interview by David Nimkin, *National Parks Conservation Association Field Report*, Spring–Summer 2016, https://www.npca.org/resources/3094-southwest-regional-office-field-reports.

4. In 1994 a fee-based shuttle bus operated by a private firm debuted at Bryce Canyon, but it operated for only two summer seasons. "Shuttle Service Underway for Bryce Canyon Visitors," *Garfield County News*, May 12, 1994.

5. Frye, *From Barrier to Crossroads*, chap. 18.

6. Schmieding, *From Controversy to Compromise*, 177.

7. Schmieding, 243.

8. Schmieding, 174.

9. William D. Newmark, "A Land-Bridge Island Perspective on Mammalian Extinctions in Western North American Parks," *Nature* 29 (January 1987): table 1, 432.

10. Francis J. Singer and Michelle A. Gudorf, *Restoration of Bighorn Sheep Metapopulations in and near 15 National Parks: Conservation of a Severely*

Fragmented Species, vol. 1, U.S. Geological Survey Open File Report 99-102 (Reston, VA: The Survey, 1999).

11.   Betsie Blumberg, "Impact of a Cougar Decline on Zion Canyon, Zion National Park," *Park Science* 26 (Fall 2009), http://www.cesu.psu.edu /materials/parksci3-cougars.pdf.

12.   U.S. Department of the Interior, National Park Service, *State of the Park Report: Zion National Park, Utah, 2016,* 26, https://irma.nps.gov/DataStore /Reference /Profile/2227413.

13.   Carlos Carroll et al., "Climatic, Topographic, and Anthropogenic Factors Determine Connectivity between Current and Climate Analogs in North America," *Global Change Biology* 24 (November 2018): 5318–31.

CHAPTER 33

1.   "Bryce Canyon National Park to Begin New Shuttle System June 19," *Garfield County News,* May 5, 2000.

2.   U.S. Department of the Interior, National Park Service, "Transportation Planning Guidebook," [1999], 68; "New Shuttle Contract Announced," news release, Bryce Canyon National Park, April 2, 2010, https://www.nps.gov /brca/learn/news/shuttlenews.htm.

3.   U.S. Department of the Interior, National Park Service, *Environmental Assessment, Multimodal Transportation Plan, Bryce Canyon National Park, Utah* (Washington, D.C.: The Service, February 2014).

4.   "National Parks Expect Record Crowds This Weekend," *Moab Sun News,* October 20, 2016.

5.   U.S. Department of the Interior, National Park Service, *State of the Park Report, Zion National Park, Utah*; National Parks Conservation Association, *Southwest Region Field Report,* Spring/Summer 2016.

6.   Robert E. Manning et al., "The Visitor Experience and Resource Protection (VERP) Process: The Application of Carrying Capacity to Arches National Park," *George Wright Forum* 12 (1995): 41–55.

7.   Arches National Park, *Transportation Implementation Plan and Environmental Assessment,* September 2006, https://www.nps.gov/arch/learn/management /upload/ArchesTransportationImplementation.pdf.

8.   Keiter, *To Conserve Unimpaired,* 56–58.

9.   Brian Maffley, "Want to Go to Arches? You May Soon Need a Reservation," *Salt Lake Tribune,* November 2, 2017.

10.   Eric Trenbeath, "National Parks Scramble to Keep Up with the Crowds," *High Country News,* July 13, 2015.

11.   Sellars, *Preserving Nature,* 63.

12.   Brian Maffly, "National Park Service Faces Crowding Now, Apathy to Come in Its Second Century," *Salt Lake Tribune,* January 8, 2016.

13.   Lauren McCrady, "My Present Is Not Your Tombstone: Love and Loss in Utah's Canyon Country." *Terrain,* November 6, 2016, http://www.terrain .org/2016/nonfiction/my-present-is-not-your-tombstone/.

14. Ray Boone, "Selling Utah: How the Ad Agency behind the 'Mighty 5' Helped Boost Tourism," KSL.com, October 18, 2015, http://www.ksl.com/?sid=37004856&nid=148.

15. U.S. Department of the Interior, National Park Service, *Recreation Visitation by State and by Park*, 2014 and 2015 reports, https://irma.nps.gov/Stats/Reports/National.

16. U.S. Department of the Interior, National Park Service, *2018 National Park Visitor Spending Effects: Economic Contributions to Local Communities, States, and the Nation*, Natural Resource Report NPS/NRSS/EQD/NRR—2019/1922 (Fort Collins, CO: The Service, 2019), https://www.nps.gov/subjects/socialscience/vse.htm.

17. "The Economic Benefits of Tourism for Grand County," Moab Area Travel Council and Advisory Board, https://www.grandcountyutah.net/DocumentCenter/View/4046. In addition to Moab's city tax revenues, Grand County in 2016 received an estimated $4.6 million from hotel accommodation taxes.

18. Freeman Tilden, *Interpreting Our Heritage*, 3rd ed. (Chapel Hill: University of North Carolina Press, 1977), 39.

19. William C. Tweed, "An Idea in Trouble: Thoughts about the Future of Traditional National Parks in the United States," *George Wright Forum* 27 (2010): 12.

20. Robert B. Keiter, "Revisiting the Organic Act: Can It Meet the Next Century's Conservation Challenges?," *George Wright Forum* 28 (2011): 244–45. Keiter expands on the idea of national parks as cornerstones of protected landscapes in chapter 9 of *To Conserve Unimpaired*.

CHAPTER 34

1. "Presidential Proclamation—Establishment of the Bears Ears National Monument," Presidential Proclamation no. 9558, December 28, 2016, https://obamawhitehouse.archives.gov/the-press-office/2016/12/28/proclamation-establishment-bears-ears-national-monument.

2. The presidential proclamations modifying the Bears Ears and Grand Staircase–Escalante National Monuments are, respectively, nos. 9681 and 9682, both issued on December 4, 2017.

3. Brian Maffly, "Here's a Look at Key Lands Left Out of Trump's New Monuments," *Salt Lake Tribune*, December 5, 2017. One analysis of a sample of the public comments on Zinke's nationwide monument review found that 99 percent favored keeping them intact. Aaron Weiss, "New Analysis Shows National Monument Support Dominates Public Comment Period," *Westwise*, May 25, 2017, https://medium.com/westwise/new-analysis-shows-national—-monument-support-dominates-public-comment-period-7550888175e.

4. Jonathan Thompson, "At Bears Ears, Trump and Zinke Ignored Everyone but Industry," *High Country News*, March 13, 2018.

5. Courtney Tanner, "Utah Sens. Orrin Hatch, Mike Lee Push to Rein in Presidential Power in Wake of Bears Ears," *Salt Lake Tribune*, January 7, 2017. President Trump's 2017 proclamation asserts that antiquities in the declassified sections of the Bears Ears monument are adequately protected under federal law.

6. Amy Joi O'Donoghue, "Will Bears Ears National Monument Get Funded?," *Deseret News*, March 6, 2017; Josh Siegel, "Utah Republicans Introduce Bills to Enshrine Trump Monument Rollback into Law," *Washington Examiner*, December 5, 2017.

7. Bears Ears Inter-Tribal Coalition, "Proposal to President Barack Obama for the Creation of Bears Ears National Monument," Utah Diné Bikéyah, October 15, 2015, http://utahdinebikeyah.org/full-proposal/.

8. Robert McPherson discusses the Anglo displacement of Ute and Paiute people from traditional lands on and around Cedar Mesa in *Comb Ridge and Its People*, 106–26.

9. The tribal coalition's efforts were spearheaded by Utah Diné Bikéyah, a consulting group formed in 2010 to seek stronger Native American representation in the ongoing discussions over the Cedar Mesa area. After canvassing Navajo tribal members who used the area, the coalition developed a national monument proposal that tribal leaders presented to Interior Secretary Ken Salazar in 2011 (see "Origins of the Proposal," Utah Diné Bikéyah, http://utahdinebikeyah.org/history/). Terry Tempest Williams describes the meeting between the environmental and tribal groups that led to the Bears Ears proposal in *The Hour of Land: A Personal Topography of America's National Parks* (New York: Sarah Crichton Books, 2016), 290–95.

10. Placement of the intonation mark (') in the presidential proclamation differs from that in "Shash Jaa'," the spelling preferred by the Bears Ears Inter-Tribal Council.

11. "Presidential Proclamation—Establishment of the Bears Ears National Monument."

12. Jim Enote, "A Sacred Landscape," in "Bears Ears: A Native Perspective," Bears Ears Inter-Tribal Coalition, http://www.bearsearscoalition.org/wp-content/uploads/2016/03/Bears-Ears-bro.sm_.pdf.

13. Steve Allen, *Utah's Canyon Country Place Names* (Durango, CO: Canyon Country Press, 2012), 1:43. For differences in the spelling of Shash Jaa', see note 10.

14. "Native American Connections," in "Bears Ears: A Native Perspective."

15. Topping, *Glen Canyon*, 155.

16. Statement of Bruce Adams, in U.S. Senate, Committee on Energy and Natural Resources, *The Potential Impacts of Large-Scale Monument Designations: Field Hearing Before the Committee on Energy and Natural Resources, One Hundred Fourteenth Congress, Second Session, July 27, 2016* [Blanding, UT] (Washington, D.C.: Government Printing Office, 2017), 17.

17. Jesse Hyde, "Behind the Scenes: How Hatch's Loyalty Pushed Trump to Undo Bears Ears," *Deseret News*, May 5, 2017.

18. Brian Maffly, "In Utah Canyons Where an Ancient Civilization Once Flourished, the Feds Are Now Inviting Oil and Gas Drilling," *Salt Lake Tribune*, April 6, 2018.

19. "Acquisition of Colt Mesa Copper-Cobalt Property, Utah," press release, June 13, 2018, www.cnbc.com. The company has since announced it will not seek permission to develop the claims.

20. Regina Lopez-Whiteskunk, "It's Time to Heal Bears Ears," *Indian Country Today*, March 4, 2016; "Alberty: Seeing the Beauty: Bears Ears in the Eyes of Someone Who Calls It Home," *Salt Lake Tribune*, January 19, 2017.

21. "Interview with Willie Grayeyes," in Jacqueline Keeler, ed., *Edge of Morning: Native Voices Speak for the Bears Ears* (Salt Lake City: Torrey House Press, 2017), 39; Lyle Balenquah, "Spirit of Place: Preserving the Cultural Landscape of the Bears Ears," in Keeler, *Edge of Morning*, 79.

22. Rebecca M. Benally, "Bears Ears National Monument Designation Disastrous for Utah Grassroots Navajos," *San Juan Record*, April 12, 2016.

23. Jim Stiles, "How Environmentalists Could Do More for Bears Ears," *High Country News*, April 4, 2017.

24. The Emery County legislation was part of the John D. Dingell, Jr. Conservation, Management, and Recreation Act, which was signed into law on March 12, 2019. Bears Ears and Grand Staircase–Escalante National Monuments were larger designations but were made through the executive, not legislative, branch.

CODA

1. Brett G. Dickson, Meredith McClure, and Christine M. Albano, "A Landscape-Level Assessment of Conservation Values and Potential Threats in the Bears Ears National Monument," Conservation Science Partners, April 3, 2017, https://www.nationalparkstraveler.com/sites/default/files/attachments/csp-benm_landscape_assessment_032717_small.pdf.

2. U.S. Department of the Interior, National Park Service, *National Parks for the 21st Century: the Vail Agenda; Report and Recommendations to the Director of the National Park Service* (Washington, D.C.: The Service), 1992.

3. Julia Corbett, personal communication.

4. James Bryce, "National Parks: The Need of the Future," address delivered before the eighth annual convention of the American Planning and Civic Association, Baltimore, MD, November 20, 1912, reprinted in *University and Historical Addresses* (Freeport, NY: Books for Libraries Press, 1968).

5. Roylance, *Enchanted Wilderness*, 9.

BIBLIOGRAPHY

ABBREVIATIONS FOR MANUSCRIPT COLLECTIONS
DPL   Denver Public Library, Denver, CO
MLSC   Special Collections Division, J. Willard Marriott Library, University of
                Utah, Salt Lake City, UT
NARA-DNV   National Archives and Records Administration, Denver, CO
NPS-SEUG   National Park Service, Southeast Utah Group Archives, Moab, UT
USHS   Utah State Historical Society, Salt Lake City, UT

PRIMARY ONLINE SOURCES
Utah Digital Newspapers, https://digitalnewspapers.org/ (for historical Utah news
    articles)
National Park Service Administrative Histories, https://www.nps.gov/parkhistory/
    hisnps/NPSHistory/adminhistory.htm

BOOKS AND ARTICLES
Abbey, Edward. *Confessions of a Barbarian: Selections from the Journals of Edward Abbey,*
    1951–1989. Edited by David Petersen. New York: Little, Brown, 1994.
———. *Desert Solitaire: A Season in the Wilderness.* Tucson: University of Arizona Press,
    1988. First published 1968 by McGraw-Hill (New York).
———. *The Monkey Wrench Gang.* New York: J. P. Lippincott, 1975.
Abbey, Edward, and Philip Hyde. *Slickrock: The Canyon Country of Southeast Utah.* San
    Francisco: Sierra Club, 1971.
Albright, Horace M., and Robert Cahn. *The Birth of the National Park Service: The Founding*
    Years, 1913–1933. Salt Lake City: Howe Brothers, 1985.
Albright, Horace M., and Marian Albright Schenck. *Creating the National Park Service: The*
    Missing Years. Norman: University of Oklahoma Press, 1999.
Alexander, Thomas G. "Red Rock and Gray Stone: Senator Reed Smoot, the Establishment
    of Zion and Bryce Canyon National Parks, and the Rebuilding of Downtown
    Washington, DC." *Pacific Historical Review* 72 (February 2003): 1–38.
Allen, Steve. *Utah's Canyon Country Place Names.* Vol. 1. Durango, CO: Canyon Country
    Press, 2012.
Anderson, Michael F., ed. *A Gathering of Grand Canyon Historians.* Grand Canyon, AZ:
    Grand Canyon Association, 2005.

———. *Living at the Edge: Explorers, Exploiters, and Settlers of the Grand Canyon Region.* Grand Canyon, AZ: Grand Canyon Association, 1998.

———. "Zion National Park Roads and Bridges." Historic American Engineering Record HAER UT-72. Washington, DC: Department of the Interior, National Park Service, [1972?].

Aton, James M., and Robert S. McPherson. *River Flowing from the Sunrise: An Environmental History of the Lower San Juan.* Logan: Utah State University Press, 2000.

Balmforth, Janet R. "'Good Roads Roberts' and the Fight for Utah's Highways." *Utah Historical Quarterly* 49 (Winter 1981): 56–65.

Barnes, F. A. *The 1859 Macomb Expedition into Utah Territory.* Moab, UT: Canyon Country Publications, 2003.

Bell, Patti. *Bryce Canyon National Park: The Early Years, 1916–1946.* Bryce Canyon, UT: Bryce Canyon Natural History Association, 2011.

Bernheimer, Charles L. *Rainbow Bridge: Circling Navajo Mountain and Explorations in the "Bad Lands" of Southern Utah and Northern Arizona.* Garden City, NY: Doubleday, Page, 1924.

Bishop, M. Guy. "The Paper Power Plant: Utah's Kaiparowits Project and the Politics of Environmentalism." *Journal of the West* 35 (July 1996): 26–35.

Black, Sara. "Homeland, Homestead, and Haven: The Changing Perspectives of Zion National Park, 1700–1930." PhD diss., University of Nevada, Las Vegas, 2016.

Blackburn, Fred M. *The Wetherills: Friends of Mesa Verde.* Durango, CO: Durango Herald Small Press, 2006.

Blodgett, Peter. "Defining Uncle Sam's Playgrounds: Railroad Advertising and the National Parks, 1917–1941." *Historical Geography* 35 (2007): 80–113.

Blumberg, Betsie. "Impact of a Cougar Decline on Zion Canyon, Zion National Park." *Park Science* 26 (Fall 2009). http://www.cesu.psu.edu/materials/parksci3-cougars.pdf.

Bradley, Harold C., and David R. Brower. "Roads in the National Parks." *Sierra Club Bulletin* 34 (June 1949): 31–54.

Breed, Jack. "Flaming Cliffs of Monument Valley." *National Geographic* 88 (October 1945): 452–61.

———. "Utah's Arches of Stone." *National Geographic* 92 (August 1947): 173–92.

Brockman, C. Frank. "Park Naturalists and the Evolution of National Park Service Interpretation through World War II." *Journal of Forest History* 22 (January 1978): 24–43.

Carpenter, Kenneth. "Rocky Start of Dinosaur National Monument (USA), the World's First Dinosaur Geoconservation Site." *Geoconservation Research* 1 (January–June 2018): 1–20.

Carroll, Carlos, Sean A. Parks, Solomon Z. Dobrowski, and David R. Roberts. "Climatic, Topographic, and Anthropogenic Factors Determine Connectivity between Current and Climate Analogs in North America." *Global Change Biology* 24 (November 2018): 5318–31. https://doi.org/10.1111/gcb.14373.

Clover, Elzada U., and Lois Jotter. "Floristic Studies in the Canyon of the Colorado and Tributaries." *American Midland Naturalist* 32 (November 1944): 591–642.

Cosco, Jon M. *Echo Park: Struggle for Preservation*. Boulder, CO: Johnson Books, 1995.

Cottam, Walter P. "Is Utah Sahara Bound?" *Bulletin of the University of Utah* 37 (1947).

Crampton, C. Gregory. *Standing Up Country: The Canyon Lands of Utah and Arizona*. Kaysville, UT: Gibbs Smith, 1983. First published 1964 by A. A. Knopf (New York).

Crane, Jeff. *The Environment in American History: Nature and the Formation of the United States*. London: Routledge, 2014.

Crawford, J. L. *Zion Album: A Nostalgic History of Zion Canyon*. Springdale, UT: Zion Natural History Association, 1985.

Crawford, Nancy C., and Merwin G. Fairbanks. *A Pioneer History of Zion Canyon to 1947*. Spanish Fork, UT: J-Mart Publishing, 1972.

Culmer, H. L. A. "Country of Natural Bridges." *Technical World Magazine* 10 (September 1908): 49–55.

Cummings, Byron. "The Great Natural Bridges of Utah." *National Geographic* 21 (February 1910): 157–67.

Cummings Publication Council. *The Discovery of Rainbow Bridge, the Natural Bridges of Utah, and the Discovery of Betatakin*. Bulletin No. 1. Tucson, AZ: The Council, [1959].

Davis, Chester C. "Motoring through Wonderland: A Tour with the Montana A. A." *American Motorist* 7 (October 1915): 593–96.

Dellenbaugh, F. S. "A New Valley of Wonders." *Scribner's Magazine* 35 (January 1904): 1–18.

Demaray, Jane Galloway. *Yellowstone Summers: Touring with the Wylie Camping Company in America's First National Park*. Pullman: Washington State University Press, 2015.

Denis, Clyde L. "Closing the Road to Chesler Park: Why Access to Canyonlands National Park Remains Limited." *Utah Historical Quarterly* 84 (Fall 2016): 329–46.

DeVoto, Bernard. "Let's Close the National Parks." *Harper's Magazine* 207 (October 1953): 49–52.

———. "Shall We Let Them Ruin Our National Parks?" *Saturday Evening Post* 223 (July 22, 1950): 17–19ff.

———. "The West against Itself." In *The Easy Chair*, 231–55. Boston: Houghton Mifflin, 1955.

Diamant, Rolf. "Frederick Law Olmsted, Jr." National Park Service: The First 75 Years. https://www.nps.gov/parkhistory/online_books/sontag/olmsted.htm.

Dodge, Henry Louis. "All Aboard for Zion." *Elks Magazine* 4 (March 1926): 24–27, 65–70.

Dunaway, Finis. *Natural Visions: The Power of Images in American Environmental Reform*. Chicago: University of Chicago Press, 2005.

Dutton, Clarence E. *Report on the Geology of the High Plateaus of Utah, with Atlas*. U.S. Department of the Interior, Geographical and Geological Survey of the Rocky Mountain Region. Washington, D.C.: Government Printing Office, 1880.

———. *Tertiary History of the Grand Cañon District, with Atlas*. Monographs of the United States Geological Survey, vol. 2. Washington, D.C.: Government Printing Office, 1882.

Dyar, W. W. "The Colossal Bridges of Utah: A Recent Discovery of Natural Wonders." *Century Illustrated* 68 (August 1904): 505–11.

Eastwood, Alice. "General Notes of a Trip through Southeastern Utah." *Zoe* 3 (1892): 354–61.

Edminster, Robert R., and Osmond L. Harline. *An Economic Study of the Proposed Canyonlands National Park and Related Recreation Resources.* Salt Lake City: Bureau of Economic and Business Research, University of Utah, March 1962.

Evison, Herb. "Jesse L. Nusbaum: Defender of American Antiquities." *Courier* 4 (January 1981). http://npshistory.com/persons-of-the-month/person-of-the-month-0614.htm.

Farmer, Jared. *On Zion's Mount: Mormons, Indians, and the American Landscape.* Cambridge, MA: Harvard University Press, 2008.

Firmage, Richard A. *A History of Grand County.* Salt Lake City: Utah State Historical Society and Grand County, 1996.

Flink, James J. *The Automobile Age.* Cambridge, MA: MIT Press, 1990.

Foreman, Dave, and Howie Wolke. *The Big Outside: A Descriptive Inventory of the Big Wilderness Areas of the U.S.* Tucson, AZ: Ned Ludd Books, 1989.

Fowler, Don D. *Glen Canyon Country: A Personal Memoir.* Salt Lake City: University of Utah Press, 2011.

Fowler, Don D., and Catherine S. Fowler. "The Ethnography of the Canyon Country." In *John Wesley Powell and the Anthropology of the Canyon Country,* edited by Don D. Fowler, Robert C. Euler, and Catherine S. Fowler, 20–22. U.S. Geological Survey Professional Paper 670. Washington, D.C.: Government Printing Office, 1969. https://www.nps.gov/parkhistory/online_books/geology/publications/pp/670/sec3.htm.

Fraser, George C. *Journeys in the Canyon Lands of Utah and Arizona, 1914–1916.* Edited by Frederick H. Swanson. Tucson: University of Arizona Press, 2005.

Frost, Kent. *My Canyonlands: I Had the Freedom of It.* New York: Abelard-Schuman, 1971.

Frye, Bradford J. *From Barrier to Crossroads: An Administrative History of Capitol Reef National Park, Utah.* Cultural Resources Selections No. 12. Denver: Intermountain Region, National Park Service, 1998. https://www.nps.gov/parkhistory/online_books/care/adhi/adhi.htm.

Gilbert, Cathy A., and Kathleen L. McKoy. *Cultural Landscape Report: Fruita Rural Historic District, Capitol Reef National Park.* Cultural Resource Selections No. 8. Denver: Intermountain Region, National Park Service, 1997. https://www.nps.gov/parkhistory/online_books/care/clr/clr.htm.

Gilbert, G. K. *Report on the Geology of the Henry Mountains.* U.S. Department of the Interior, Geographical and Geological Survey of the Rocky Mountain Region. Washington, D.C.: Government Printing Office, 1887.

Gómez, Arthur. "America's National Parks System: Sunset or New Dawn?" *Perspectives on History,* October 2007. https://www.historians.org/publications-and-directories/perspectives-on-history/october-2007/americas-national-parks-system-sunset-or-new-dawn.

———. *Quest for the Golden Circle: The Four Corners and the Metropolitan West, 1945–1970.* Albuquerque: University of New Mexico Press, 1994.

Gregory, Herbert E. *The Geology and Geography of the Paunsaugunt Region, Utah.* U.S. Geological Survey Professional Paper 226. Washington, D.C.: Government Printing Office, 1951.

———. *Geology of the Navajo Country: A Reconnaissance of Parts of Arizona, New Mexico and Utah.* U.S. Geological Survey Professional Paper 93. Washington, D.C.: Government Printing Office, 1914.

———. *The San Juan Country: A Geographic and Geologic Reconnaissance of Southeastern Utah.* U.S. Geological Survey Professional Paper 188. Washington, D.C.: Government Printing Office, 1938.

Gregory, Herbert E., and Robert C. Moore. *The Kaiparowits Region: A Geographic and Geologic Reconnaissance of Parts of Utah and Arizona.* U.S. Geological Survey Professional Paper 164. Washington, D.C.: Government Printing Office, 1931.

Grey, Zane. *The Rainbow Trail: A Romance.* New York: Grosset and Dunlap, 1915.

Gruen, J. Philip. *Manifest Destinations: Cities and Tourists in the Nineteenth-Century American West.* Norman: University of Oklahoma Press, 2014.

Halden, Ann E. "The Grand Staircase–Escalante National Monument and the Antiquities Act." *Fordham Environmental Law Journal* 8 (1997): 713–39.

Ham, Martha, ed. *Ken Sleight's Allies and Accomplices.* St. George, UT: privately published, 2014.

Harmon, David, Francis P. McManamon, and Dwight T. Pitcaithley. "The Antiquities Act: The First Hundred Years of a Landmark Law." *George Wright Forum* 23 (2006): 5–27.

Harvey, Mark W. T. "Defending the Park System: The Controversy over Rainbow Bridge." *New Mexico Historical Review* 73 (January 1998): 45–67.

———. *Symbol of Wilderness: Echo Park and the American Wilderness Movement.* Albuquerque: University of New Mexico Press, 1994.

Harvey, Thomas J. *Rainbow Bridge to Monument Valley: Making the Modern Old West.* Norman: University of Oklahoma Press, 2011.

Hassell, Hank. *Rainbow Bridge: An Illustrated History.* Boulder: University Press of Colorado, 1999.

Heald, Weldon F. "Helicopters over Rainbow Bridge." *Westways,* September 1961.

Henderson, Randall. "Glen Canyon Voyage." *Desert Magazine* 15 (October 1952): 7–12.

Hinton, Wayne K. "Getting Along: The Significance of Cooperation in the Development of Zion National Park." *Utah Historical Quarterly* 68 (Fall 2000): 313–31.

Hoffman, John F. *Arches National Park: An Illustrated Guide.* San Diego: Western Recreational Publications, 1985.

Holmes, Edwin F. "The Great Natural Bridges of Utah." *National Geographic* 18 (March 1907): 199–204.

Holt, Ronald L. *Beneath These Red Cliffs: An Ethnohistory of the Utah Paiutes.* Logan: Utah State University Press, 2006.

Hughes, J. Donald, and Jim Swan. "How Much of the Earth Is Sacred Space?" *Environmental Review* 10 (Winter 1986): 247–59.

Hugill, Peter J. "Good Roads and the Automobile in the United States 1880–1929." *Geographical Review* 72 (July 1982): 327–49.

Ise, John. *Our National Park Policy: A Critical History.* New York: Resources for the Future Press, an imprint of Earthscan, 2011. First published 1961 by Johns Hopkins University Press (Baltimore).

Jeffers, Le Roy. "The Temple of the Gods in Utah." *Scientific American* 119 (October 5, 1918): 267.

Jepperson, Ronald, Eric Hemel, and Robert Hauptman. *The Kaiparowits Coal Project and the Environment: A Case Study.* Ann Arbor, MI: Ann Arbor Science Publishers, 1981.

Jett, Stephen. "The Great 'Race' to Discover Rainbow Natural Bridge in 1909." *Kiva* 58 (1992). https://www.nps.gov/rabr/learn/historyculture/upload/Stephen%20Jett%20Article.pdf.

Judd, Neil. "Beyond the Clay Hills." *National Geographic* 45 (March 1924): 275–302.

Keeler, Jacqueline, ed. *Edge of Morning: Native Voices Speak for the Bears Ears.* Salt Lake City: Torrey House Press, 2017.

Keiter, Robert B. "Revisiting the Organic Act: Can It Meet the Next Century's Conservation Challenges?" *George Wright Forum* 28 (2011): 240–53.

———. *To Conserve Unimpaired: The Evolution of the National Park Idea.* Washington, D.C.: Island Press, 2013.

Kelly, Charles. "New Road into the Utah Wilderness." *Desert Magazine* 10 (February 1947): 10–14.

———. "Valley of the Cathedrals." *Desert Magazine* 13 (December 1949): 4–7.

Kluckhohn, Clyde. *Beyond the Rainbow.* Boston: Christopher Publishing House, 1933.

———. *To the Foot of the Rainbow: A Tale of Twenty-Five Hundred Miles of Wandering on Horseback through the Southwest Enchanted Land.* Glorieta, NM: Rio Grande Press, 1967. First published 1927 by Century (New York).

Knipmeyer, James H. *Cass Hite: The Life of an Old Prospector.* Salt Lake City: University of Utah Press, 2016.

Lavender, David. *The History of Arizona's Pipe Spring National Monument.* Springdale, UT: Zion Natural History Association, 1984.

Lee, Katie. *All My Rivers Are Gone: A Journey of Discovery through Glen Canyon.* Boulder, CO: Johnson Books, 1998.

Leopold, Aldo. "The Last Stand of the Wilderness." *American Forests and Forest Life* 31 (October 1925): 599–604.

Lohman, S. W. *The Geologic Story of Arches National Park.* U.S. Geological Survey Bulletin 1398. Washington, D.C.: Government Printing Office, 1975.

———. *The Geologic Story of Canyonlands National Park.* U.S. Geological Survey Bulletin 1327. Washington, D.C.: Government Printing Office, 1974.

Louter, David. *Windshield Wilderness: Cars, Roads, and Nature in Washington's National Parks.* Seattle: University of Washington Press, 2006.

Madsen, Steven K. *Exploring Desert Stone: John N. Macomb's 1859 Expedition to the Canyonlands of the Colorado.* Logan: Utah State University Press, 2010.

Manning, Robert E., David W. Lime, Marilyn Hof, and Wayne A. Freimund. "The Visitor Experience and Resource Protection (VERP) Process: The Application of Carrying Capacity to Arches National Park." *George Wright Forum* 12 (1995): 41–55.

Marshall, Robert. "The Universe of the Wilderness Is Vanishing." *Nature Magazine* 29 (April 1937): 235–40.

Marshall, Robert, and Althea Dobbins. "Largest Roadless Areas in the United States." *Living Wilderness* 2 (November 1936): 11–13.

Martin, Russell. *A Story That Stands like a Dam: Glen Canyon and the Struggle for the Soul of the West.* Salt Lake City: University of Utah Press, 1989.

Mather, Stephen T. *Progress in the Development of the National Parks.* Washington, D.C.: Government Printing Office, 1916.

McKoy, Kathleen L. *Cultures at a Crossroads: An Administrative History of Pipe Spring National Monument.* Cultural Resources Selections No. 15. Denver: National Park Service, Intermountain Region, 2000. https://www.nps.gov/parkhistory/online_books/pisp/adhi/.

McManamon, Francis P. "The Antiquities Act and How Theodore Roosevelt Shaped It." *George Wright Forum* 31 (2014): 324–44.

McPherson, Robert S. *Comb Ridge and Its People: The Ethnohistory of a Rock.* Logan: Utah State University Press, 2009.

———. *Navajo Land, Navajo Culture: The Utah Experience in the Twentieth Century.* Norman: University of Oklahoma Press, 2001.

Miles, John C. *Wilderness in National Parks: Playground or Preserve.* Seattle: University of Washington Press, 2009.

Muir, John. *Our National Parks.* New York: Houghton Mifflin, 1901.

Murie, Adolph. *Fauna of the National Parks of the United States: Ecology of the Coyote in the Yellowstone.* National Park Service, Fauna Series No. 4. Washington, D.C.: Government Printing Office, 1940.

Murphy, Miriam B. *A History of Wayne County.* Salt Lake City: Utah State Historical Society and Wayne County Commission, 1999.

Nash, Roderick Frazier. *Wilderness and the American Mind.* 4th ed. New Haven, CT: Yale University Press, 2001.

Nelson, Paul T. *Wrecks of Human Ambition: A History of Utah's Canyon Country to 1936.* Salt Lake City: University of Utah Press, 2014.

Neuberger, J. W., R. L. McPhail, R. J. Shukle, C. H. Bell, and F. T. Carlson. *Southwest Energy Study: An Evaluation of Coal-Fired Electric Power Generation in the Southwest.* Washington, D.C.: U.S. Department of the Interior, 1972.

Newell, Linda King, and Vivian Linford Talbot. *A History of Garfield County.* Salt Lake City: Utah State Historical Society, 1998.

Newmark, William D. "A Land-Bridge Island Perspective on Mammalian Extinctions in Western North American Parks." *Nature* 29 (January 1987): 325, 430–32.

Nichols, Tad. *Glen Canyon: Images of a Lost World.* Santa Fe: Museum of New Mexico, 1999.

O'Reilly, John. "Udall at the Bridge." *Sports Illustrated* 14 (May 15, 1961): 26–27.

Patraw, P. P. "Administration of the National Parks and Monuments." *Utah: The State Magazine of National Interest* 2 (July 1936): 34–37, 62.

Peattie, Roderick. *The Inverted Mountains: Canyons of the West*. New York: Vanguard Press, 1948.

Perry, Paul. "The National Park and the Nuclear Dump." *Outside*, December 1983, 40–45, 83–84.

Pinkley, Frank. "What Is a National Monument?" In *Guide to Southwestern National Monuments*, edited by Dale S. King, 4–5. Coolidge, AZ: National Park Service, Southwestern Monuments Office, 1938.

Porter, Eliot. *The Place No One Knew: Glen Canyon on the Colorado*. San Francisco: Sierra Club, 1963.

Poulton, Donna L., and Vern G. Swanson. *Painters of Utah's Canyons and Deserts*. Kaysville, UT: Gibbs Smith, 2009.

Powell, J. W. *Exploration of the Colorado River of the West and Its Tributaries: Explored in 1869, 1870, 1871, and 1872 under the Direction of the Secretary of the Smithsonian Institution*. Washington, D.C.: Government Printing Office, 1875.

———. *Report on the Lands of the Arid Region of the United States, with a More Detailed Account of the Lands of Utah: With Maps*. Washington, D.C.: Government Printing Office, 1878.

Presnall, C. C. "Early Days in Bryce and Zion." *Utah: The State Magazine of National Interest* 2 (July 1936): 13–15, 55.

Pritchard, James A. "The Meaning of Nature: Wilderness, Wildlife, and Ecological Values in the National Parks." *George Wright Forum* 19 (2002): 40–56.

Prudden, T. Mitchell. "An Elder Brother to the Cliff-Dwellers." *Harper's New Monthly Magazine* 95 (June 1897): 56–62.

———. *On the Great American Plateau: Wanderings among Canyons and Buttes, in the Land of the Cliff-Dweller, and the Indian of To-day*. New York: G. P. Putnam's Sons, 1907.

Pulham, Cami. *Heart of the Mountain: The History of Timpanogos Cave National Monument*. Washington, D.C.: U.S. Department of the Interior, National Park Service, 2009. https://catalog.hathitrust.org/Record/011327596.

Pyne, Stephen J. *Grove Karl Gilbert: A Great Engine of Research*. Austin: University of Texas Press, 1980.

———. *How the Canyon Became Grand: A Short History*. New York: Viking, 1998.

Quintano, Jen Jackson. *Blow Sand in His Soul: Bates Wilson, the Heart of Canyonlands*. Moab, UT: Friends of Arches and Canyonlands Parks, 2014.

Rasband, James R. "Antiquities Act Monuments: The Elgin Marbles of our Public Lands?" In *The Antiquities Act: A Century of American Archaeology, Historic Preservation, and Nature Conservation*, edited by David Harmon, Francis P. McManamon, and Dwight T. Pitcaithley, 158–70. Tucson: University of Arizona Press, 2006.

Reeder, Deborah. "The Art of Zion: A Stunning Visual History." In *A Century of Sanctuary: The Art of Zion National Park*, edited by Lyman Hafen, 21–33. Springdale, UT: Zion Natural History Association, 2008.

Reese, April. "Scientists Sue to Protect Utah Monument—and Fossils That Could Rewrite Earth's History." *Science*, January 17, 2019. doi:10.1126/science.aaw6866.

Richardson, Elmo R. "The Escalante National Monument Controversy." *Utah Historical Quarterly* 33 (April 1965): 110–33.

Righter, Robert W. "National Monuments to National Parks: The Use of the Antiquities Act of 1906." *Western Historical Quarterly* 20 (August 1989): 281–301. http://npshistory.com
/publications/righter/index.htm.

Rishel, Virginia. *Wheels to Adventure: Bill Rishel's Western Routes.* Salt Lake City: Howe Brothers, 1983.

Rogers, Jedediah S. *Roads in the Wilderness: Conflict in Canyon Country.* Salt Lake City: University of Utah Press, 2013.

Roosevelt, Theodore. *A Book Lover's Holiday in the Open.* New York: Charles Scribner's Sons, 1916.

Rothman, Hal, ed. *The Culture of Tourism, the Tourism of Culture: Selling the Past to the Present in the American Southwest.* Albuquerque: University of New Mexico Press, 2003.

———. *Devil's Bargains: Tourism in the Twentieth-Century American West.* Lawrence: University Press of Kansas, 1998.

———. *Preserving Different Pasts: The American National Monuments.* Urbana: University of Chicago Press, 1989.

———. "Ruins, Reputations, and Regulation: Byron Cummings, William B. Douglass, John Wetherill, and the Summer of 1909." *Journal of the Southwest* 35 (1993): 318–40.

———. "Second-Class Sites: National Monuments and the Growth of the National Park System." *Environmental Review* 10 (Spring 1986): 44–56.

———. "Shaping the Nature of a Controversy: The Park Service, the Forest Service, and the Cedar Breaks Proposal," *Utah Historical Quarterly* 55 (Summer 1987): 213–35.

Roylance, Ward J. *The Enchanted Wilderness: A Red Rock Odyssey.* Torrey, UT: Four Corners West, 1986.

Runte, Alfred. *National Parks: The American Experience.* 4th ed. New York: Taylor Trade, 2010. First published 1979 by University of Nebraska Press (Lincoln).

Sabin, Dena Markoff. *The Dudes Are Always Right: The Utah Parks Company in Zion National Park, 1923–1972.* Springdale, UT: Zion Natural History Association, 1980.

Sax, Joseph L. *Mountains without Handrails: Reflections on the National Parks.* Ann Arbor: University of Michigan Press, 1980.

Schmieding, Samuel Joseph. *From Controversy to Compromise to Cooperation: The Administrative History of Canyonlands National Park.* Washington, D.C.: U.S. Department of the Interior, National Park Service, 2008.

———. "Visions of a Sculptured Paradise: The Colorado Plateau as American Sacred Space." PhD diss., Arizona State University, 2002.

Schneider-Hector, Dietmar. "Forging a National Park Service: 'The Necessity for Cooperation.'" *Journal of the Southwest* 56 (Winter 2014): 643–82.

Scott, Douglas W. "National Parks and Their Wilderness: A Compilation of Historic Viewpoints." Pew Wilderness Center Briefing Paper. Washington, D.C., n.d.

Scrattish, Nicholas. "Historic Resource Study: Bryce Canyon National Park." Denver, CO: US Department of the Interior, National Park Service, Rocky Mountain Regional Office, Branch of Historic Preservation, 1985. http://digitalcommons.usu.edu /elusive_docs/46.

———. "The Modern Discovery, Popularization, and Early Development of Bryce Canyon, Utah." *Utah Historical Quarterly* 49 (Fall 1981): 348–62.

Seegmiller, Janet B. "Selling the Scenery: Chauncey and Gronway Parry and the Birth of Southern Utah's Tourism and Movie Industries." *Utah Historical Quarterly* 80 (Summer 2012): 242–57.

Sellars, Richard West. *Preserving Nature in the National Parks: A History.* New Haven, CT: Yale University Press, 1997. https://www.nps.gov/parkhistory/online_books/sellars /contents.htm.

Shaffer, Marguerite S. "'See America First': Re-envisioning Nation and Region through Western Tourism." *Pacific Historical Review* 65 (November 1996): 559–81.

———. *See America First: Tourism and National Identity, 1880–1940.* Washington, D.C.: Smithsonian Institution, 2001.

———. "Seeing the Nature of America: The National Parks as National Assets, 1914–1929." In *Being Elsewhere: Tourism, Consumer Culture, and Identity in Modern Europe and North America,* edited by Shelley Baranowski and Ellen Furlough, 155–84. Ann Arbor: University of Michigan Press, 2001.

Sheire, James. *Cattle Raising in the Canyons: Historic Resource Study, Canyonlands National Park.* Denver: U.S. Department of the Interior, National Park Service, 1972.

Singer, Francis J., and Michelle A. Gudorf. *Restoration of Bighorn Sheep Metapopulations in and near 15 National Parks: Conservation of a Severely Fragmented Species.* Vol. 1. U.S. Geological Survey Open File Report 99-102. Reston, VA: The Survey, 1999.

Smith, Beatrice Scheer. "The 1872 Diary and Plant Collections of Ellen Powell Thompson." *Utah Historical Quarterly* 62 (Spring 1994): 104–31.

Smith, Duane A. *Mesa Verde National Park: Shadows of the Centuries.* Boulder: University Press of Colorado, 2002. https://www.nps.gov/parkhistory/online_books/smith /index.htm.

Smith, Thomas G. "The Canyonlands National Park Controversy." *Utah Historical Quarterly* 59 (Summer 1991): 216–42.

Soulliére, Laura E. *Historic Roads in the National Park System. Special History Study.* Denver: National Park Service, 1995. https://www.nps.gov/parkhistory/online_ books/roads/shst.htm.

Sproul, David Kent. *A Bridge between Cultures: An Administrative History of Rainbow Bridge National Monument.* Cultural Resources Selections No. 18. Denver: National Park Service, Intermountain Region, 2001. https://www.nps.gov/rabr/learn/ historyculture/upload/RABR_adhi.pdf.

Staveley, Gaylord. "A Conversation with Bates Wilson." *Western Gateways,* Autumn 1967. https://www.nps.gov/cany/learn/historyculture/bateswilson.htm.

Steen, Charlie R. "The Natural Bridges of White Canyon: A Diary of H. L. A. Culmer, 1905." *Utah Historical Quarterly* 40 (Winter 1972): 55–87.

Stegner, Wallace. "Backroads River." *Atlantic* 181 (January 1948): 56–64.

—. *Beyond the Hundredth Meridian: John Wesley Powell and the Second Opening of the West.* Lincoln: University of Nebraska Press, 1953.

—, ed. *This Is Dinosaur: Echo Park Country and Its Magic Rivers.* New York: Alfred A. Knopf, 1955.

Stoffle, Richard W., Diane E. Austin, David B. Halmo, and Arthur M. Phillips III. *Ethnographic Overview and Assessment: Zion National Park, Utah, and Pipe Spring National Monument, Arizona.* Denver, CO: National Park Service, 1997. Revised 2013.

Sutter, Paul S. *Driven Wild: How the Fight against Automobiles Launched the Modern Wilderness Movement.* Seattle: University of Washington Press, 2002.

Swain, Donald C. "The National Park Service and the New Deal." *Pacific Historical Review* 41 (August 1972): 312–32.

Swanson, Frederick H. *Dave Rust: A Life in the Canyons.* Salt Lake City: University of Utah Press, 2007.

Tilden, Freeman. *Interpreting Our Heritage.* 3rd ed. Chapel Hill: University of North Carolina Press, 1977. First published 1957.

Tillotson M. R., and Frank J. Taylor. *Grand Canyon Country.* Palo Alto, CA: Stanford University Press, 1929.

Tonne, Mozelle Gray. *From Ikevar to Devil's Garden: The Saga of Alexander Ringhoffer.* San Angelo, TX: Anchor Publishing, 1992.

Topping, Gary. *Glen Canyon and the San Juan Country.* Moscow: University of Idaho Press, 1997.

Tourangeau, R. Dixie. "Franklin Knight Lane, 1864–1921." In *The National Park Service: The First 75 Years,* edited by William H. Sontag, 20. Fort Washington, PA: Eastern National Park and Monument Association, 1990. https://www.nps.gov/parkhistory/online_books/sontag/lane.htm.

Trimble, Stephen, ed. *The Capitol Reef Reader.* Salt Lake City: University of Utah Press, 2019.

Tweed, William C. "An Idea in Trouble: Thoughts about the Future of Traditional National Parks in the United States." *George Wright Forum* 27 (2010): 6–13.

Udall, Stewart L. *The Quiet Crisis.* New York: Holt, Rinehart, and Winston, 1963.

Union Pacific Railroad. *Zion National Park, Bryce Canyon, Cedar Breaks, Kaibab Forest, North Rim of Grand Canyon.* Omaha: Union Pacific, [1925]. http://www.gutenberg.org/ebooks/47397.

U.S. Department of Agriculture, Forest Service. *The Dixie National Forest: Managing an Alpine Forest in an Arid Setting.* Ogden, UT: Intermountain Region, 1987.

U.S. Department of Energy, Office of Civilian Radioactive Waste Management. *Environmental Assessment, Davis Canyon Site, Utah.* DOE/RW0071. Vol. 1. Washington, D.C.: Office of Civilian Radioactive Waste Assessment, May 1986.

U.S. Department of the Interior. "Report of Director of the National Park Service." In *Reports of the Department of the Interior for the Fiscal Year Ended June 30, 1920.* Washington, D.C.: Government Printing Office, 1920.

U.S. Department of the Interior, Bureau of Land Management. *Intermountain Power Project: Draft Environmental Statement, 1979.* Vol. 1, *Salt Wash Proposed Site.* Salt Lake City: Utah State Office, 1979.

———. *Kaiparowits: Environmental Impact Statement—Draft.* 9 vols. [Washington, D.C.]: Government Printing Office, 1974.

———. *Kaiparowits: Environmental Impact Statement—Final.* Vol. 1. [Washington, D.C.]: Government Printing Office, 1976.

U.S. Department of the Interior, Bureau of Land Management, and National Park Service. *Grand Staircase–Escalante National Monument: Livestock Grazing Plan Amendment EIS.* Washington, D.C.: Government Printing Office, 2012.

———. *Tar Sand Triangle, Utah: Draft Environmental Impact Statement, Proposed Lease Conversions.* Washington, D.C.: Government Printing Office, 1984.

U.S. Department of the Interior, Bureau of Outdoor Recreation. *Trails for America: Report on the Nationwide Trail Study.* Washington, D.C.: Government Printing Office, 1966.

U.S. Department of the Interior, Bureau of Reclamation. *The Colorado River: "A Natural Menace Becomes a National Resource": A General Plan for the Development and Utilization of the Water Resources of the Colorado River Basin for Irrigation, Power Production, and Other Beneficial Uses in Arizona, California, Colorado, Nevada, New Mexico, Utah, and Wyoming.* Washington, D.C.: Government Printing Office, 1946.

———. *Lake Powell, Jewel of the Colorado.* Washington, D.C.: Government Printing Office, 1965.

U.S. Department of the Interior, National Park Service. *2018 National Park Visitor Spending Effects: Economic Contributions to Local Communities, States, and the Nation.* Natural Resource Report NPS/NRSS/EQD/NRR—2019/1922. Fort Collins, CO: The Service, 2019.

———. *Annual Report of the Director of the National Park Service to the Secretary of the Interior for the Fiscal Year Ended June 30, 1922 [–1932] and the Travel Season, 1922 [–1932].* Washington, D.C.: Government Printing Office, 1922 [–1932].

———. *Arches National Park Main Entrance Road. Historical American Engineering Record UT-70.* Washington, D.C.: The Service, 1993.

———. *Draft Environmental Statement, Proposed Squaw Flat–Confluence Overlook Road, July 26, 1972.* Washington, D.C.: Government Printing Office, 1972.

———. *Environmental Assessment, Multimodal Transportation Plan, Bryce Canyon National Park, Utah.* Washington, D.C.: The Service, February 2014.

———. *National Parks for the 21st Century: The Vail Agenda; Report and Recommendations to the Director of the National Park Service.* Washington, D.C.: The Service, 1992.

———. *The National Parks: Shaping the System.* 2005. https://www.nps.gov/parkhistory /online_books/shaping/index.htm.

———. *Proceedings of the National Park Conference Held at the Yellowstone National Park, Sept. 11–12, 1911.* Washington, D.C.: Government Printing Office, 1912.

———. *Quarry Visitor Center, Dinosaur National Monument, Utah/Colorado: Historic Structure Report.* Denver: NPS Denver Service Center, October 2003.

———. *State of the Park Report: Zion National Park, Utah.* 2016. https://irma.nps.gov /DataStore/Reference/Profile/2227413.

———. *A Survey of the Recreational Resources of the Colorado River Basin.* Compiled June 1946. Washington, D.C.: Government Printing Office, 1950.

U.S. House of Representatives. *Canyonlands National Park and Glen Canyon National Recreation Area: Hearing Before the Subcommittee on Parks and Recreation of the Committee on Interior and Insular Affairs, May 5, 1970.* Washington, D.C.: Government Printing Office, 1970.

———. *Glen Canyon National Recreation Area: Hearings Before the Subcommittee on National Parks and Recreation, House of Representatives, Ninety-Second Congress, Second Session on H.R. 15073 and Related Bills: Hearing Held in Kanab, Utah, May 27, 1972, Washington, D.C., June 8, 1972.* Washington, D.C.: Government Printing Office, 1972.

U.S. Senate. *Canyonlands National Park and Glen Canyon National Recreation Area: Hearing Before the Subcommittee on Parks and Recreation of the Committee on Interior and Insular Affairs.* Washington, D.C.: Government Printing Office, 1968.

———. *Canyonlands National Park and Glen Canyon National Recreation Area: Hearing, Ninety-First Congress, Second Session, on S. 26 and S. 27, May 5, 1970.* Washington, D.C.: Government Printing Office, 1970.

———. *Hearing Before the Subcommittee on Parks and Recreation of the Committee on Interior and Insular Affairs on S. 26, a Bill to Revise the Boundaries of the Canyonlands National Park.* Washington, D.C.: Government Printing Office, 1968.

———. *Proposed Canyonlands National Park in Utah: Hearing Before the Subcommittee on Public Lands of the Committee on Interior and Insular Affairs, Eighty-Eighth Congress, First Session, on S. 27.* Washington, D.C.: Government Printing Office, 1963.

U.S. Senate, Committee on Energy and Natural Resources. *The Potential Impacts of Large-Scale Monument Designations: Field Hearing Before the Committee on Energy and Natural Resources, One Hundred Fourteenth Congress, Second Session, July 27, 2016* [Blanding, UT]. Washington, D.C.: Government Printing Office, 2017.

U.S. Senate, Committee on Interior and Insular Affairs. *Proposed Canyonlands National Park in Utah: Part 2: Hearings, Eighty-Seventh Congress, Second Session, on S. 2387, Apr. 20, 21, 23, 1962.* Washington, D.C.: Government Printing Office, 1962.

Utah Wilderness Coalition. *Wilderness at the Edge: A Citizen Proposal for Utah's Canyons and Deserts.* Kaysville, UT: Gibbs Smith, 1991.

Van Cott, John W. *Utah Place Names: A Comprehensive Guide to the Origin of Geographic Names.* Salt Lake City: University of Utah Press, 1990.

Vetter, Carl P. "Corralling the Colorado." *Reclamation Era* 9 (September 1946): 190–92.

Waite, Nathan N., and Reid L. Neilson, eds. *A Zion Canyon Reader.* Salt Lake City: University of Utah Press, 2014.

Wetherill, Marietta. *Life with the Navajos in Chaco Canyon.* Albuquerque: University of New Mexico Press, 1992.

Wharton, William P. "The National Primeval National Parks." *National Parks Bulletin* 13 (February 1937): 3–5.

Wilkinson, Charles F. *Fire on the Plateau: Conflict and Endurance in the American Southwest.* San Francisco: Island Press, 1999.

Williams, Henry T., and Frederick E. Shearer. *The Pacific Tourist.* New York: H. T. Williams, 1876.

Williams, Kendall Hughes. *The Syrett Family: From Buckinghamshire, England to Utah to Ruby's Inn, Utah, 1606–2006.* Edited by Roderick K. Syrett and Kathern Syrett. Salt Lake City: Price & Associates, 2006.

Williams, Terry Tempest. *The Hour of Land: A Personal Topography of America's National Parks.* New York: Sarah Crichton Books, 2016.

Wilson, Alan D. "Tug". "Early Trips in the Needles: An Idea Takes Shape." *Canyon Legacy (Dan O'Laurie Museum, Moab, UT)* 3 (Fall 1989): 4–8.

Winks, Robin W. "The National Park Service Act of 1916: 'A Contradictory Mandate'?" *George Wright Forum* 24 (2007): 6–21. www.npshistory.com/publications/winks.htm.

Woodbury, Angus M. "Biotic Relationships of Zion Canyon, Utah with Special Reference to Succession." *Ecological Monographs* 3 (April 1933): 151–245.

———. *A History of Southern Utah and Its National Parks.* Salt Lake City: Utah Historical Society, 1950. First published 1944 by Utah State Historical Society (Salt Lake City).

———. "Protecting Rainbow Bridge," *Science* 132 (August 26, 1960): 519–28.

Wrabley, Raymond B., Jr. "Managing the Monument: Cows and Conservation in Grand Staircase–Escalante National Monument." *Journal of Land, Resources, and Environmental Law* 29 (August 2009): 253–80.

Wright, George M., Joseph S. Dixon, and Ben H. Thompson. *Fauna of the National Parks of the United States: A Preliminary Survey of Faunal Relations in National Parks.* National Park Service, Fauna Series No. 1. Washington, D.C.: Government Printing Office, 1933

Yard, Robert Sterling. *The Book of the National Parks.* New York: Charles Scribner's Sons, 1919.

———. *National Parks Portfolio.* New York: Charles Scribner's Sons, 1916.

———. *The New Zion National Park: Rainbow in the Desert.* Washington, D.C.: National Parks Association, 1919.

Zion Natural History Association. *A Century of Sanctuary: The Art of Zion National Park.* Springdale, UT: The Association, 2008.

INDEX

Page numbers in *italics* refer to figures or illustrations.